THE EDGE *of* ISLAM

THE EDGE *of* ISLAM

*Power, Personhood,
and Ethnoreligious Boundaries
on the Kenya Coast*

Janet McIntosh

DUKE UNIVERSITY PRESS
DURHAM AND LONDON
2009

© 2009 Duke University Press

All rights reserved.

Printed in the United States of America on
acid-free paper ∞

Designed by Heather Hensley

Typeset in Arno Pro by Keystone Typesetting, Inc.

Library of Congress Cataloging-in-Publication
Data appear on the last printed page of this book.

FOR TOBIAS, *who has brought great joy.*

CONTENTS

ACKNOWLEDGMENTS

It is a pleasure to thank the community of colleagues and informants whose assistance has been invaluable to this project and much of my other published work. For close and critical yet supportive readings of material related to the book, I thank Mark Auslander, Fred Cooper, Elizabeth Ferry, Marla Frederick, Larry Hirschfeld, Kai Kresse, Smita Lahiri, Sarah Lamb, Caitrin Lynch, Bruce Mannheim, Flagg Miller, Esra Özyürek, Penelope Papailias, Karen Strassler, Ann Marie Leshkowich, Rick Parmentier, Ajantha Subramanian, Chris Walley, and the anonymous readers for both Duke and Oxford University Press. I owe a debt of gratitude to all of these friends and colleagues; they have always treated me as though I have something interesting to say, and when that has not been true it has been a highly useful fiction. Special thanks to the members of the Cambridge Writers Circle, whose inspiration, friendship, food, tolerance of small squawking children, and deadlines have provided just the right crucible for writing. My colleagues at Brandeis University have provided an ideal environment of high expectations and support.

Most of the people who nourished my research in the field cannot be thanked by name because I have promised to keep their identity confidential; they include countless friends and acquaintances in Kenya who showed interest in my projects and, often, great kindness, patience, assistance, and hospitality. Those who can be named are Abdalla Ali Alaussy and his family, Attas Sharif Ali, Susan Beckerleg, Nyevu Chai, Emmanuel Safari Chai, Van and Kathy Davis, the late Kadzo Fondo, Ian Gordon and Lorna DePew, Doreen Hartley, Stanslous Kahindi Kiraga, Fatma and Muhalla Mansoor, Joseph Karisa Mwarandu, David Obura, Athman Lali Omar, the late Kahindi wa Ruwa and his son Salama, Ann and Ian

Robertson, the late Charo Shutu, Kaingu Kalume Tinga, Sally Gaye Thompson, Charo Thoya, Hilda Tucker, and Simiyu Wandibba. Special thanks to Maxwell Phares Kombe, a particularly ingenious research assistant who provided many adventures and much conversational companionship. The task of writing about such a diverse and subtle cultural milieu as the Kenya coast has not been straightforward, particularly in a context where one ethnic group feels subordinate to another that often has not intended to oppress. My apologies for the inevitable flaws in my understanding of the situation.

I am grateful for the solidarity of several other dear friends, some of whom provided crucial support during my dissertation-writing years and beyond: Rachel Heiman, Kelly Flynn, Antony Seely, Chris Demars, Adam Becker, Laura Kunreuther, Carla Daughtry, Emily McEwan-Fujita, Nira Pollock, Christine Rayner, Barbara Ehrenreich, Rosa Brooks, the incomparable Jim Herron and Rachel Meyer, our beloved Merrick Hoben and Diana Bermudez, and those shining bearers of cannoli, Jim Dawes and Baris Gumus-Dawes. Their kindness, laughter, and support have been so important along the way. Special thanks to Kate Long and Sanden Averett for providing Tom's and my son, Tobias, with superb child care while we work; they have really *listened* from the moment he could speak, and this is precisely what we all need, I think, as we figure out what we have to say.

Finally, I must thank my family. I could never have undertaken this career without the love, support, and example of my extraordinary parents. My sister and her family, my parents-in-law, and my extended family have also shown great generosity and wisdom along the way. Special thanks to Carey and Joanie for what has seemed like boundless encouragement. Most of this book was written in the company, physically or spiritually, of Tom and Tobias, and their love has made all the difference. (I'm so glad Tom's wit proved to be heritable.)

The research and writing for this project were carried out under a Fulbright-Hays Fellowship, the support of the University of Michigan's Rackham Graduate School and Anthropology Department, a Norman Award from Brandeis University, and a Kermit H. Perlmutter Award from Brandeis University. My research in Kenya was made possible through affiliation with the University of Nairobi's Institute of African Studies and Fort Jesus Museum in Mombasa.

Some material in chapter 4 previously appeared in "Baptismal Essentialisms: Giriama Code Choice and the Reification of Ethnoreligious Boundaries," *Journal of Linguistic Anthropology* 15, no. 2 (2005): 151–70. A version of the argument in chapter 3 appeared in "Reluctant Muslims: Embodied Hegemony and Moral Resistance in a Giriama Spirit Possession Complex," *Journal of the Royal Anthropological Institute* 10, no. 1 (2004): 91–112.

NOTE ON LANGUAGE

The material discussed in this book is drawn from three languages other than English: Kiswahili, Kigiriama, and Arabic. When I have included words and phrases from those languages, the reader can usually infer the language from the context; that is, in discussions of Swahili culture and quotations from Swahili individuals, the language in question is Kiswahili unless otherwise indicated; in discussions of Giriama culture and quotations from Giriama individuals, the language in question is Kigiriama unless otherwise indicated; and in discussions of Arabic cultures and pan-Islamic theology, the language in question is Arabic unless otherwise indicated. Some terms and phrases in these languages are bivalent, appearing routinely in two languages (Kiswahili and Kigiriama, or Arabic and Kiswahili). I draw attention to bivalent terms and phrases when their commonality might plausibly be relevant to the political dynamic between the groups (though this does not guarantee that it is). When I denote languages I do so as follows: Kiswahili is "Kisw.," Kigiriama is "Kigir.," and Arabic is "Ar."

In transcribed quotations, capital letters indicate the speaker's emphasis. I have applied an English speaker's pragmatic understanding of punctuation to translations and to transcripts in the original Kiswahili and Kigiriama for ease of understanding, even though such punctuation would be more sparingly deployed by native speakers.

The elderly diviner Haluwa seats me on a wooden stool low to the ground under an enormous baobab tree next to my research assistant, Maxwell. We're about five kilometers from the heart of Malindi, a Swahili town with vast, whitewashed mosques and tarmac roads bustling with commerce on the Kenya coast. Haluwa's homestead, though, is located in a quiet, outlying Giriama community where there are no mosques in sight. Just a few banana plants and goats flank three mud-and-wattle dwellings for Haluwa, her husband, and one of her grown children. The only sounds I can hear are the chatting of a few young men outside and the rattle of the wooden cart laden with secondhand clothes for sale that they trundle along the dirt road.

I turn my attention to Haluwa, who has placed Maxwell's ten-shilling payment on the ground before her and sprinkled it with the ashes of sacralized herbs. Maxwell tells her he has been having chronic headaches lately; he suspects that someone has bewitched him and wants to know who it might be and why. Haluwa holds a battered pamphlet in her lap. She refers to it as her Quran, though as I look at the rows of individual Arabic letters, oversized print, and sketches instructing children how to pray, I recognize it as a text used in the Quranic schools in town. She wraps her faded *kanga* cloth a little tighter around her waist, then picks up a calabash full of dried seeds and begins to rattle it close to her ear. She closes her eyes in concentration as she summons her helping spirit, Pepo Msikiti, the spirit of the mosque. After several minutes her toe begins to twitch and she exhales rapidly, indicating that the spirit has arrived. She puts down the calabash and picks up her "Quran," inadvertently holding it upside down and opening it to a seemingly arbitrary page. Her eyes are fixed on the paper as Pepo Msikiti begins to read in stuttering syllables that are unintelligible to my ear and Maxwell's. We hear sound fragments with a family resemblance to Kiswahili, and here and there the spirit seems to insert a glottal stop into the syllabic stream, a sound that marks the language as Arabic for Giriama listeners, most of whom are not Muslim.

In the end the spirit's prophesy has nothing to do with Islam per se; when Haluwa translates it into the Giriama tongue, it turns out that Maxwell's tormenter may be a Giriama neighbor of his, jealous that he may have prospered through the help of a white employer (myself). But the ethnoreligious identity of the spirit and the diviner's professed ability to wield Arabic when possessed by him speak volumes about Giriama life in Malindi. The use of Muslim spirits and Arabic in divination is so widespread in the Malindi area that Giriama frequently remark upon it. Indeed, when I first arrived in this community and began to ask people about the skills of local diviners, countless individuals regaled me with stories of the mystical link between diviners and the high-status language they speak: "When those diviners are doing their work, I'm telling you, they speak pure Arabic! The kind spoken by the original Arabs!" Evidently the powers of prophesy are bound up with a particular ethnoreligious group, and the Arabic language provides superior access to obscure knowledge inaccessible to ordinary Giriama.[1]

Closer to town, in the division known as Muyeye, which is dominated by Giriama, Maxwell and I seek out another well-known diviner and healer named Hawe Baya. Muyeye has become more and more crowded in recent years as Giriama flock to the fringes of Malindi in hopes of finding wage labor and other opportunities. Hawe Baya lives in a dilapidated mud dwelling cheek by jowl with the dwellings of other divorced or widowed Giriama women. We get to talking about the relationship between Giriama in this area and the Arabo-African Muslim group, the Swahili, who live in the center of town. Hawe Baya explains that the healers in the Swahili community have more power than Giriama healers "because the Swahili have the Quran." I glance with puzzlement at the Quran she holds in her hand, which she incorporates into her healing rituals by tearing talismanic strips from it or waving it in circles around an ailing client. "Giriama use the Quran too," I remark, "so why are the Swahili more powerful?" "Because," she says wistfully, "the Giriama doesn't have his OWN Quran."

Farther down the road in Muyeye, five young Giriama men, some of Maxwell's best friends, sit under a tree drinking palm wine, leaning back in their chairs. It is almost noon; tourism is low this month, and most of the young men are out of work, though a couple of them have been contracted to repair the steps of a Swahili home in the next week or so. I initiate a conversation about the small handful of Giriama who try to ingratiate themselves into the Swahili community in town by converting to Islam in hopes that they might marry a Swahili and assimilate into a Swahili family. The men nod in recognition. "Those types don't even speak Kigiriama [the Giriama mother tongue] when they come back into Muyeye. They pretend they never even heard the language." One of the men jokes about someone he knew who was just such a zealous convert: "He had one of those big calluses on his forehead from hitting the floor so hard as he prayed." He begins to rock his upper body forward and backward in mockery of violent supplication. The other men laugh at the image. Another one chips in, "They're trying to get to the Muslim side, but they'll never make it. They'll find themselves sweeping cake off the floor of the mosque at the end of the day."

The semiotic weight of Haluwa's use of Arabic, the riddle in Hawe Baya's claims about the Quran, and the cynicism of the young men, are all part of an array of complex attitudes toward Islam that circulate through the Giriama communities in and near Malindi town. As exemplified by these three stories, Islam is regarded as a repository of special spiritual and social potency. Indeed, although many Giriama in the Malindi area profess Christianity (perhaps as many as a third), Islam plays a distinct social and religious role in Giriama lives. Unlike Christianity, which has broad appeal across numerous ethnic groups in Kenya, Islam is closely associated with certain groups—most prominently, the several thousand coastal Arabs and the more sizable Arabo-African group, the Swahili, who populate the urban centers of the East African coast. Swahili have long been neighbors of the nine closely related ethnic groups known as Mijikenda, of whom Giriama are the largest. In the nineteenth century many Swahili patrons lived interdependently with their hinterland Giriama clients, often assimilating them into their religious, social, and kin networks (Cooper 1980; Willis 1993). Today, however, Giriama apprehensions of Islam are shaped by the shift from older patron-client relationships between Giriama and Swahili to an ethnically based class system, while assimilation into Swahili society, in Malindi anyway, has become much more difficult. More subtle divisions also inform Giriama attitudes toward religion in general, particularly Islam and the indigenous Giriama practices of ritual divination, healing, and ancestor propitiation that I term "Traditionalism" (Giriama themselves refer to it as *dini ya kienyeji*, literally, "indigenous religion," Kisw., Kigir.).[2] We can see from Hawe Baya's words, for instance, that the Quran itself, a material embodiment of the powers of Islam, is thought by at least some Giriama to be more deeply, intrinsically tied to Swahili than to themselves. Meanwhile, the gossip and mockery of the young men on the fringes of Malindi town indicate that although Swahili may encourage Giriama to convert, their full acceptance into the *umma* (Islamic community) may be hard to achieve. Islam is therefore formulated by many Giriama as a mystified power yoked to a privileged people, with a sheen of Otherness that both beguiles and frustrates.

Taken together, these vignettes provoke a series of questions that inform the rest of this study: If Giriama were once able to assimilate with relative ease into Swahili society, what has transpired to make the boundary between these ethnicities more rigid in Malindi? Why do some Giriama identify a supposedly universal religion, Islam, as belonging more deeply to certain ethnic groups than to others? Why do Giriama use Islam in their rituals despite the fact that so many do not consider it their own religion? And how might Giriama appropriations of Islam subtly reinforce a distance between themselves and Islam, from both Giriama and Swahili vantage points? To respond to these questions I consider both Giriama views of Swahili and Swahili views of Giriama in Malindi, exploring along the way broad historical and economic forces (such as colonialism and capitalism) and subtler matters of discourse and practice (in ritual and patterns of code choice, for instance) that have given hegemonic weight to the ethnoreligious separations I describe. Central to my investigation is the concept of the person in each group. I argue that Giriama and Swahili systematically valorize and enact different, often oppositional kinds of personhood, differences that make themselves known in economic practices and the moral discourses that surround them and that are especially dramatically expressed in the realms of conversion practices, spirit discourses and spirit possession, divination, ritual code switching, and other ritual forms. Ultimately, I suggest, these different forms of religious discourse and practice among Swahili and Giriama reinforce the widespread (albeit not unanimous) idea that Swahili and Giriama are essentially distinct categories and that Islam somehow belongs more to Swahili than to Giriama.

While the focus of this book is ethnoreligious tension and division, I am mindful that, from one perspective, the anecdotes I have already presented point to an interpretation of Giriama life that highlights both ethnic and religious fluidity. In fact, the ethnographer who arrives among Swahili and Giriama in Malindi seeking evidence of boundary crossing will find it. Not only do some Giriama still occasionally try to Swahilize by converting to Islam and shifting their ethnic affiliation, but the very parameters of Swahili ethnicity are continually redefined from without and within, often in response to political contingencies (Askew 1999; P. Caplan and Topan 2004; A. M. Mazrui and Shariff 1994; Salim 1973). Religious identity in the multiethnic coastal context might also be construed as permeable and fluid, as some Giriama shift affinities between Traditionalism, Islam, and Christianity over the course of a single life span, and sometimes within a single ritual. The Giriama use of the Quran and Arabic in rituals that also contain Traditionalist symbolism could be interpreted as a form of syncretic hybridity. In the linguistic domain the observer seeking boundary crossing can find it in several forms, including the fact that Giriama sometimes use several languages in a single ritual, while in the secular domain languages do not always map neatly onto ethnic groups in spoken practice. After all, Kiswahili, the mother tongue of the Swahili themselves, is spoken as a lingua franca across East Africa and is widely spoken by Giriama in the Malindi area.

Themes of boundary crossing, fluidity, permeability, and syncretic cultural blending have been prevalent in recent ethnographic literature, and for good reason. Over the past few decades, historians and anthropologists have come to question the idea that tribes and ethnic groups, in Africa and across the world, are as sharply divided as colonial rhetoric and traditional social science have construed them to be. Much scholarly effort has been devoted to debunking the notion that ethnicities are intrinsically stable, bounded social groupings (Barth 1969; Chabal 1996; Comaroff and Comaroff 1991; Fried 1966; Iliffe 1979; MacGaffey 1970;

Mafeje 1971; Ranger 1989; Thornton 1996; Vail 1989). Today, the notion of a timeless tribal entity, or of any "all purpose, unidimensional classification of sociocultural groups" (Southall 1997: 48), is typically rejected as a misconception unjustly applied to categories that are largely the products of political and economic influences and the modern imagination. Many scholars bring this point home by demonstrating the contingency and permeability of ethnic groups and other social categories that have been typically portrayed as rigid and static (cf. Barth 1969; Rosaldo 1989), an approach that has extended to scholarship on Swahili and Giriama identity. Indeed, earlier tussles over whether Swahili can be defined as a concrete ethnic group or whether they are "more Arab" or "more African" (concerns expressed both by scholars and the indigenous population) have been largely supplanted by a model that construes Swahili communities as paradigmatic embodiments of the incorporative, hybrid, and flexible qualities of ethnic groups more generally. Askew (1999: 73–74) explains the shift:

> Drawing on practice theory, discourse theory, and poststructuralism, scholars now emphasize the openness and permeability of coastal identity wherein oppositions constitute complementary elements, not conflicting essences (Amory 1994; Askew 1997; Fair 1996; Willis 1993). . . . The "elusiveness" of Swahili ethnicity (Salim 1985), then, boils down to a fundamental precept of ethnicity that is simply made obvious to a greater degree among coastal Swahili, namely, that "internal and external boundaries constantly shift, and ethnicity has to be constantly redefined and reinvented" (Yelvington 1991:165). The Swahili coast, therefore, presents an ideal case study for demonstrating the intangibility of cultural boundaries.

The present widespread scholarly interest in ethnic fluidity, permeability, and boundary crossing also informs the study of religions and languages in Africa and elsewhere. Rather than accepting the missionary model that frames Christianity as either purified of native elements or contaminated by them, some scholars have turned their attention to the ways religious practices creatively blur the boundaries between religious typologies (see, for example, Comaroff 1985; MacGaffey 1994; Shaw and Stewart 1994). Scholars of Islam have described it as an often fluidly imagined religion that continually incorporates local traditions (Asad

1986; Varisco 2005). Linguistic anthropologists, meanwhile, have debunked the colonialist and nationalist assumption that ethnic or other social groupings are or have always been rigidly linked to a single, stable language (Harries 1988, 1989: 85; Hymes 1984; Irvine and Gal 2000; J. Jackson 1974; Southall 1997: 46; Woolard 1998a). Instead, languages have been reconstrued as potentially protean entities whose borders have been enforced, with mixed success, by political policies and ideologies (Fardon and Furniss 1994: 10–13; Irvine and Gal 2000; Mignolo 2000). Yet speakers of a language identified with one ethnic group in many cases turn out to be polyglot code-switchers whose creative uses of language vex efforts to classify and strictly define the relationship between languages and ethnic communities. One could attempt to fit the Giriama case in Malindi into these rubrics and to see within the Giriama religious and linguistic improvisations I have described the hybrid qualities of their identity.

But the current anthropological fashion for valorizing boundary crossing can too easily lead to a fetishization of it that is misplaced, given that ethnic fluidity is not a universal experience. Indeed, some scholars have turned their attention to the paradoxical dynamic by which the globalizing forces of free markets and easy mobility have created displacement and competition that often trigger movements of exclusion, compartmentalization, and ethnoterritoriality (Chua 2003; Gupta and Ferguson 1997: 39; Meyer and Geschiere 1999). In Africa, furthermore, political liberalization has been met with anxiety regarding resource distribution, leading to "a general obsession with autochthony and ethnic citizenship" (Geschiere and Nyamnjoh 2001: 159). At the same time, the essentialisms that were so central to colonial taxonomies continue to echo in the ethnopolitics of postcolonial states and the cultural and linguistic revivals of many indigenous groups, despite, in the latter case, the irrefutable evidence of their cultural permeability (cf. Coulmas 1988: 11; Vail 1989; Van Binsbergen 1994; Woolard and Scheiffelin 1994: 60). It seems that for many, boundaries—however fictive, politically motivated, and pernicious they may be—are importantly and perhaps increasingly constitutive of social worlds and group identities and often become embedded in the social landscape as taken-for-granted premises about the way the world is.[3] Mindful of these patterns, Charles Stewart has detected a tension between popular scholarly approaches and the view from the ground: "Clashes of perspective are apparent when avant-garde cultural studies and literary theorists celebrate the fundamental cultural hybridity of postcolonial communities at the very moment when these communities are engaging in strategic, essentialist claims of cultural authenticity" (1999: 55; see also Asad 1993: 264).[4] In this book I insist that the theoretical notion of ethnoreligious and ethnolinguistic fluidity poorly accounts for what happens in Malindi as Giriama interact with Swahili, with Islam, and with languages other than their mother tongue. From a distance their behavior may appear to be an easy kind of cultural mixing or creolization, but careful scrutiny of the discourse, behavioral nuances, and reported experiences of individual Giriama produces a much more complex picture.

A central argument of this book is that Giriama communities in Malindi town and its outskirts cannot easily cross boundaries, but encounter obstacles, perceived and actual, at every turn. To be sure, the evidence clearly supports a history of connection between and interpenetration of Swahili and Giriama communities, yet in the current context of Malindi there is an equally clear insistence on their social differentiation, a differentiation that is laced with inequality. As the title *The Edge of Islam* suggests, Giriama find themselves on the margins of a spatial and metaphorical geography, peering in at a life of greater privilege and sometimes cognizant that they are on the brink of access but not quite able to break through. The distance that Giriama feel from Islam is expressed indexically through their recurrent references to what they term "the Muslim side" (*upande wa Kiislam*; Kisw., Kigir.) in contrast to "the Giriama side" (*upande wa Kigiriama*; Kisw., Kigir.), an orientational metaphor that suggests a virtual spatial separation between Islam and Giriama. The alienation expressed by this pervasive idiom can be found in many other domains of Giriama life. In their fluid pantheon of spirits, for instance, many Giriama distinguish between "high" (*wa hali ya tzulu*) or "big" (*bomu*) spirits located on the Muslim side and "low" (*wa hali ya tsini*) or "little" (*thithe*) spirits on the Giriama side. Ritual practitioners frequently appropriate Islamic powers from a metaphysical distance, without attempting to "become Muslim." And in healing rituals, most Giriama officiants address Muslim powers in the Swahili or Arabic language, further underscoring the notion that Islam is associated with ethnic groups other than their own.

The notion of an intrinsic and fundamental separation between ethnoreligious groups appears to provide a kind of premise or conceptual backdrop to a great deal of Giriama and Swahili discourse and practice. Yet in the complex social landscape I describe this ethnoreligious boundary work is not without its internal tensions. Giriama and Swahili identities are still entangled and contested, as are the various forms of Islamic practice on the coast. Two key theoretical concepts, *hegemony* and *personhood*, which I return to throughout the book, help to explain the dynamics of ethnoreligious separation in Malindi.

Boundary Work and Ambivalence:
Ethnic and Religious Identities on the Kenya Coast

Giriama life at the edge of Islam is not merely about feeling religiously excluded; it is simultaneously about feeling ethnically marginalized by Swahili. Although Swahili and Giriama (along with other Mijikenda) lived for many years in a relationship of interdependence and intermarriage, with Giriama converting to Islam, assimilating into Swahili kin networks, and "becoming Swahili" in the process (Willis 1993; see also Kusimba 1999; Parkin 1991a; Spear 1978), most Giriama in Malindi today do not see the category Swahili as so incorporative. This change in viewpoint can be explained by the enduring influence of colonial efforts at administrative control that also helped to shape aspects of African self-identity and the African economy. For instance, some of these efforts involved partitioning complex and often socially fluid populations into tightly bounded tribes, ranking them and stereotyping their characters along the way. Such modes of categorization guided the administrative and political allocation of resources and left their mark on African infrastructure and the narratives that many in Africa tell about themselves. These processes continue to inform Giriama politics and Kenyan ethnopolitical strife. In Malindi, furthermore, all sides feel anxiety over their access to resources. Swahili have been marginalized from national politics and increasingly reach out to their Middle Eastern connections for economic support and social identification. Giriama grumble bitterly about their impoverishment and alienation from the land they say was once their own. These historical and economic forces have given rise to ethnic divisions that have shifted Swahili and Giriama relations. Eastman (1994: 85, 94) writes that under recent pressures "participants in a Swahili pattern of culture" have increasingly distinguished between "insiders" and "outsiders" while enhancing the "boundary mechanisms" that reify the idea of their ethnic distinctiveness, which they attach in part to their Arab connections. Meanwhile Giriama living on the fringes of Malindi increasingly resent their structural role as petty wage laborers in a steep class hierarchy and sometimes politically agitate in ways that pit them directly and deliberately against Swahili.

In Malindi today ethnic divisiveness makes itself known in the emotional lives and the ontological claims of Swahili and Giriama alike. Middle-class Swahili women sometimes express revulsion at the prospect of marrying a Giriama, while many Giriama harbor moral antipathy toward Swahili, whom they tend to see as self-serving elites. They also mock or scorn those few Giriama who attempt to assimilate into Swahili communities. And although the possibility of ethnic upward mobility lives on in a residual (if rare) form for Giriama in Malindi, powerful prejudices and essentialisms circulate among Malindi's Swahili and Giriama communities, shaping their discourses about their own ethnic identity and the alterity of the other group. The term *essentialism* is defined by Gelman (2003: 3) as "the view that categories have an underlying reality or true nature that one cannot observe directly but that gives [category members their] identity." Social scientists often use the term to designate scholars' harmful and misguided homogenization or naturalization of a social group. But while ethnicity is always historically contingent and often contested, it is nevertheless the case that certain social and political formations, as well as certain religious and linguistic practices, encourage *folk* essentialisms that reinforce ethnic boundaries.[5]

Boundary work plays an important, if inconsistent role in the ethnoreligious hierarchy between Swahili and Giriama. As I explain in chapter 1, about half of Swahili and a strong majority of Giriama I spoke to in Malindi contend that it is not possible for a Giriama to "become Swahili." They sometimes adduce such intrinsic characteristics as "blood," "birth," or inborn, ethnically linked "temperament," and sometimes merely insist upon the ontological impossibility of such a change without offering a clear or consistent reason.[6] In Malindi, furthermore, Swahili and Giriama claims about natural ethnic boundaries, when they appear in discourse and practice, seem to be impervious to empirical counterclaims, including the widely known fact that Swahili and Giriama have a history of kin ties that, in principle, ought to obviate the straightforward notion that their blood is different.[7] With such essentialist notions in circulation, conversion to Islam does not beget the ethnic fluidity that it apparently once did. In today's Malindi, for example, some imams' ledger books compel new Giriama converts to indicate their tribal membership alongside their confession of Islam, suggesting a static model of ethnic identity. Many Giriama themselves concur that a Giriama convert becomes a Giriama Muslim (Mgiriama Mwislam) rather than a Swahili. Yet these discourses that function to create boundaries do not thwart Giriama mobility, for they are also occasionally enlisted by Giriama in their efforts at self-empowerment. Giriama sometimes stake a defiant claim to a timeless, independently potent ethnoreligious and linguistic identity.

Evidently, converting to Islam no longer leads a Giriama in a straight line to "becoming Swahili." How, then, do Giriama in Malindi relate to Islam, and how do Swahili interpret these interactions? The answers to such questions can be understood only by examining them against a broader religious backdrop. In principle, Giriama in Malindi may align themselves with any one of three religions: Islam, Christianity, or Traditionalism (dini ya kienyeji). In practice, however, religious alliance is bound up with ethnic identity politics. Christianity enjoys perhaps the most straightforward status of the three religions. Just as its Western advocates bill it as a universal religion that welcomes all converts, so do Giriama generally feel free to convert to Christianity. Perhaps as many as a third of Giriama in Malindi have converted, though these alliances are often partial and shifting. Islam and Traditionalism, however, are framed in more ethnically focused terms. Giriama tend to consider themselves deeply linked to the forces of Traditionalism in an ethnically exclusive fashion. The notion of an outsider converting to Traditionalism would seem odd to most Giriama because they accept that this stigmatized system of powers is yoked to their basic identity rather than being a universal religion. Islam brings with it powerful ethnic associations as well, for many Giriama seem to believe that both the Arabs and the Arabo-African Swahili groups are proprietors of the religion. Giriama certainly invoke the symbols of Islam in their divinatory and healing rituals, but some Swahili express skepticism at the ways Giriama convert to and practice the faith, while Giriama themselves, in ways both stark and subtle, sometimes hold at arm's length the very Islamic powers on which they draw, as though such powers were not really theirs.

Giriama orientations toward Islam, and Swahili reactions to these, speak to the broader question of how various communities have imagined Islam and its boundaries. As Varisco (2005) has eloquently demonstrated, in the past scholars tended to essentialize Islam, representing locally inflected versions of the faith as if they instantiated a singular, organic religion. Others too have challenged the notion that Islam has any consistent identity, given the manifold ways in which cultures strategically appropriate and manipulate its terms (Al-Azmeh 1993; Asad 1986; El-Zein 1977). The ethnographic literature on Islam in sub-Saharan Africa has increasingly focused on the ways Islam is locally imagined (see, for instance, Boddy 1989; Brenner 1993a; Holy 1991; Kresse 2003; Lambek 1993; Launay 1992; Masquelier 2001; see also Kritzeck and Lewis 1969; Lewis 1966/1980). Different African societies, for instance, play up or down specific aspects of the faith, such as the role of the Prophet, the calendar feasts of Islam, and male and female circumcision. In some locales the Islamic pillar of almsgiving (*sadaqa*) is translated into animal sacrifice to petition God for assistance (Lewis 1966/1980: 73); in others, prayers may be directed "for or through" (though not to) ancestors (62). Spirit beliefs, mediumship, and possession figure heavily in the lives of Muslims in many African societies (Giles 1989a, 1989b; Lambek 1993; Masquelier 2001). Some of these local ways of imagining Islam pose no significant religious dilemmas for their practitioners. Boddy (1989) has demonstrated that in the Sudanese village of Hofriyat, Islam and indigenous elements have been reconciled to the point that Zar spirit possession practices are seen as compatible with the principles taught by the Quran. Accordingly, tropes of *syncretism, adaptation, indigenization,* and even *symbiosis* have figured heavily in discussions of African Islam, emphasizing the assimilative, permeable qualities of the religion (Holy 1991; Launay 1992; Lewis 1966/1980; Ryan 2000; Van Hoven 1996).

At the same time, however, Islam's heterogeneity is often a source of anxiety and controversy within Muslim communities. Across sub-Saharan Africa Muslim scholars have positioned themselves as arbiters of Islamic ideals. Often such community experts find a conflict between traditional customs and what the Quran, the Hadith (the record of the Prophet's actions and speech), or sharia law seem to recommend (cf.

Lienhardt 1966/1980). According to some local experts, practices such as divination and witchcraft must "derive their validity from a Muslim source," for if they are regarded as sources of power in their own right they threaten the supremacy of the Muslim God (Lewis 1966/1980: 65). These tensions have been particularly acute in the domains of spirit beliefs and possession, for while the Quran concedes the existence of angels, demons, and *jinn* spirits, many community authorities regard these and their ritual invocation as potential threats to piety. Such debates are alive and well on the Kenya coast. Many Swahili acknowledge that practices such as spirit belief, divination, and ritual healing are customary (*mila*) in their communities, yet they also evince great uneasiness about whether and when these practices are acceptable (*halali*) or forbidden (*haramu*) in the eyes of Islam (see Middleton 1992; Parkin 1985b: 235).

The landscape of judgment is further complicated by the rise in recent decades of Wahhabist adherents (who sometimes call themselves Ahl al-sunna [Brenner 1993b: 60] or, as it is often pronounced and spelled on the Kenya coast, Ahlul Sunna), who look to Middle Eastern reformists for guidance about proper Islamic practice. While Wahhabism has been diversely interpreted across space and time (Delong-bas 2004), reformists generally wish to see stricter interpretations of the Quran and Hadith, firm implementation of sharia law, and elimination of so-called innovations (*bid'a*) in religious practice. Across Africa Wahhabist movements have tensely coexisted with versions of Islam that are informed by indigenous spiritualism and by Sufist traditions such as ecstatic forms of worship (Brenner 1993a; Kane 2003; Kresse 2003; Launay 1992; Rosander and Westerlund 1997). In Malindi a vocal and influential minority of Swahili (perhaps one in five or six, by my informants' estimates) are self-professed Ahlul Sunna who object to such Swahili ritual traditions as the ecstatic celebration of the Prophet's birthday (Maulidi).

Clearly, Islamic practice in Africa is both heterogeneous and contested. Scholars have tended to focus on two aspects of this heterogeneity: the interpretation of Islam through preexisting cultural categories and the tension between custom and the judgments handed down by Muslim authorities and reformists. Less explored, however, have been the ways Islam is negotiated *between* ethnic groups in a context of socioeconomic hierarchy and tension. Islam in Malindi is complicated not only by the debates about *mila* and the presence of reformism, but also by the presence of Giriama, many of whom live on the geographic and economic margins of areas dominated by Swahili in the core of town and who maintain an ambiguous and difficult relationship with Islam. The culture of Islam seems significantly more problematic when Islam is engaged by both a lower status group that envies and resents Islam's power and a higher status Muslim group that wishes to remain separate despite long-standing kin ties.

Such dynamics lead not only to contests over what counts as proper Islamic practice and acceptable conversion, but also to idiosyncratic uses of Islam by Giriama that mark the religion (through language choice and other semiotic devices) as ethnically Other. While official Swahili ideology welcomes any and all converts into the fold, Swahili discourse and sometimes their interactions with Giriama in Malindi suggest that many Swahili regard Giriama converts as unsuitable Muslims. It is a description of which many Giriama are aware. Admittedly the very fact that some Giriama aspire to count themselves as Muslims suggests that at least some see the religion as available to them. Nevertheless, Giriama also routinely align Islam with Arab and Swahili ethnicity, as witnessed in the recurrent conflation of the terms *Muslims* and *Swahili* or *Arabs* (a term that sometimes encompasses Swahili and Arab communities) in Giriama discourse. Among Giriama we see tensions between the hope that they might be accepted as converts and strong currents of cynicism and insecurity about their relationship to Islam. It is not unusual for Giriama approaches to Islam to look like a kind of poaching, in which Giriama reach from a social and metaphysical distance for powers to which they do not necessarily feel entitled. In fact, their use of Islam in Traditionalist divination and healing rituals cannot be characterized as syncretism in the sense of a reconciling or harmonizing of different religious traditions. Rather, Giriama maintain a metaphysical distance between Islam and Traditionalism. In some regards, then, this book is influenced by the approach of Masquelier (2001: 8), who explores the ambivalence toward Islam on the part of *bori* spirit possession practitioners in Niger and the ways Islamic and *bori* identities "overlap despite concerted efforts, on both sides, to reaffirm distinctive forms of knowledge, practice, and morality."

The tensions between hope and resentment, the belief that Muslim powers are real but linked to Other ethnicities, inform an array of Giriama spiritual practices and experiences. For instance, the animus that Giriama feel toward their wealthier Swahili and Arab neighbors is present in elaborate narratives about Muslim *jini* (Kiswa., Kigir.) spirits who are said to collect money for their masters, sometimes pouncing on Giriama and drinking their blood to sustain themselves. Other Muslim spirits routinely possess Giriama and attempt to force them to convert to Islam, often by making them vomit traditionally Giriama foods such as bush rats and palm wine—an experience Giriama respond to with attitudes ranging from accommodation to resentment and resistance. Meanwhile in Giriama divination and healing rituals Islam is yoked to the high prestige, ethnically Other languages of Kiswahili and Arabic, which Giriama wield to tap Islam's power even as these languages reinforce the sense that Islam is an ethnically distant force. This ambivalence between aspiring to partake of Islam and feeling it to be a distant or potentially oppressive power culminates in dramatic cases of madness in the Giriama community. One of the most common symptoms of madness among Giriama is babbling in a spirit version of Arabic, sometimes even emitting Arabic calls to prayer, suggesting, perhaps, that the ethnically Giriama person has been utterly quashed and supplanted by an Islamic form of agency. To the extent that one can seek meaning in madness, such tragic cases might be interpreted as a perverse parody of Giriama aspiration or a personified cautionary tale about Giriama interactions with a dangerous supernatural force.

While ethnoreligious boundary work is a prominent theme in my findings, so too is the theme of ambivalence toward such boundary work. Dogmatic claims about the way the social world is may come to the fore in Giriama and Swahili discourse at strategic moments, but these tend to mask the heterogeneity and confusion of opinion and experience in the wider community. Some Swahili and Giriama in Malindi still define *Swahili* in permeable terms, even while members of the same Swahili family debate the very definition of the ethnic category. A residue of ethnic fluidity thus coexists with currents of ethnic absolutism, just as Giriama relationships with Islam vacillate ambivalently between aspiration to participate and doubt about full acceptance. Many Giriama shift back and forth between cultivating ties with Swahili and repudiating them, between longing for access to the privileges associated with Islam and claiming to despise Muslims. Their liminal status is brought into sharp relief in tales of Muslim spirits colonizing their bodies and forcing them to reject the very foods associated with Giriama identity. The spirits' demands imply that Giriamaness is incompatible with, even polluting to Islam, and yet it is not clear that an alternative ethnic identity is available to these individuals.

Personhood and Hegemony: The Shaping of Religious Practice
and Its Implications for Social Hierarchy

Two prominent concepts, *personhood* and *hegemony*, can help to illuminate the boundary-making dynamics among Giriama and Swahili in Malindi. The term *personhood* has been widely applied in the anthropology of African societies and beyond, encompassing an astonishing breadth of concerns that include cultural variation in the domains of exchange, kinship, and gender (Piot 1999; M. Strathern 1988, 1992, 1999); aesthetics, affect, and morality (Rasmussen 1995); embodiment, epistemology, and religiosity (M. Jackson and Karp 1990; Lambek and Strathern 1998); materiality and the ontological composition of persons (M. Strathern 1988); ritual, death, and memory (Battaglia 1990); and understandings of the human condition in response to forces of modernity (Ahearn 2003; Piot 1999). In this volume I use the term *personhood* as a way of indexing culturally specific expectations and ideologies about people's relative independence or interdependence, the qualities of their agency, and the extent to which they are expected (or not) to cultivate introspective, internalist modes of being-in-the-world.

An early and well-known articulation of these themes comes from Mauss (1938/1985), who suggested an analytical distinction between selfhood (*moi*), or awareness of one's own individuality, and personhood (*personne*), in which one plays out a social role as part of a collectivity.[8] Mauss suggested that the self-consciousness that seems utterly natural to Westerners is actually a relatively recent product of a long and shifting history. While subsequent scholars have criticized Mauss's evolutionist stance, his insight that different social organizations are bound up with different ideas of selfhood and personhood has been highly influential. More recently Dumont (1985: 93) has contended that "modern individualism . . . is an exceptional phenomenon," with roots in classical and Judeo-Christian heritage. He suggests that while some societies treat the monadic individual as a paramount value, many others center instead on interdependent, hierarchical, and complementary relations between people.

In recent decades there has been a profusion of scholarly explorations of interdependent and fluid forms of personhood in non-Western contexts (Geertz 1973a; Lamb 1997; Shweder and Bourne 1991). In many African societies, for example, sociocentric ideologies are deeply bound up with customary forms of economic exchange (Bohannan 1959; Shipton 1989). In some Asian and other contexts, the interdependence of the person is thought to extend to an ontological consubstantiality with the communities, places, and objects with which the person interacts (see, for instance, Daniel 1984). In her ethnographies of Melanesian attitudes toward gender and material relations, Marilyn Strathern has developed the notion that persons are "frequently construed as the plural and composite site of the relationships that produce them" (1988: 13; see also M. Strathern 1992). Similarly, ethnographers working in Africa have repeatedly described folk ideologies of the person that stipulate ontological interdependencies between persons and the material and spiritual domains (Comaroff and Comaroff 1991; M. Jackson and Karp 1990; Piot 1999). In many societies persons are seen as enmeshed in and emergent from relationships and from the material, narrative, mystical, and other transactions that establish and modify these relationships.

Societies also vary in the way they attribute intentions or motives behind actions and in their valorization of will and introspection. Every human being has agency in the sense of an ability to act upon the world, but cultures differentially prioritize intentional action as a vital, even a moral element of the person (cf. Taylor 1989). In classically liberal and capitalist contexts, persons are seen as autonomous beings with the ability to affect the world through their own free will and the capacity to (re)construct themselves through introspection. According to Giddens (1991), "self-identity" in the modern order is an ongoing, reflexive, and introspective endeavor in which persons continually strive to achieve a cohesive narrative or "story" of self. Yet in other cultural contexts the source of a person's effectiveness may be external or ambiguous (see, for instance, Piot 1999), and there may be little stock placed in objectifying the self in order to scrutinize, fashion, or express it. These variable models of agency and interiority inflect religious ideals as well. Keane

(1997a: 679; 2007) details the tensions that surfaced between Dutch Calvinist missionaries and Sumbanese ritualists in Indonesia: the former expected prayers to express the inner sincerity of the individual, whereas the latter regarded ritual speech not as emergent from an egocentric locus, but as having been "handed down unchanged from the ancestors."

Keane's findings resonate with the theme of this book, in which different understandings of personhood compose a subtle backdrop for many of the differences between Swahili and Giriama, informing their respective understandings of religion and Islam and the felt distance between them. Customary Giriama notions of personhood are inflected by some of the interdependent mores I have described, whereas Swahili ideas of the person tend to place more emphasis on the individual, the result of the reverberation of ancient Islamic theological traditions, an influential Islamic reformist movement that stresses interiorism and rationalism, and Swahili participation in the modern, urban economic marketplace. I should make clear, however, that in suggesting that Swahili and Giriama tend to be subject to different prevailing models of personhood, I do not wish to create an artificial binary between modern Swahili and premodern Giriama, nor to suggest uniform consciousness in either community, for Giriama and Swahili culture mutually permeate one another, creating dilemmas and ambiguities within these communities. Both are perpetually in flux, subject to cross-cutting global and religious influences as well as shifting economic and political exigencies (cf. Piot 1999). Swahili possessive individualism is mitigated by an emphasis on charity, while Giriama sometimes wring their hands about the tensions between customary forms of communalism and the temptations of personal accumulation (Ciekawy 2001; S. G. Thompson 1990). Furthermore, as Leinhardt (1985: 145) reminds us, "One can lay too much one-sided stress on the collectivist orientation of African ideas of the person. . . . The recognition of the importance of an inner, mysterious individual activity [inside] a person is attested by many proverbs." To this I would add that while prevailing cultural notions of personhood have a role in shaping subjectivity, they surely do not wholly determine it (see also Jacobson-Widding 1985). Nevertheless, it is the case that urban Swahili these days are subject to a number of ideological forces and expectations that do not circulate so prominently in Giriama communities, and vice versa. And these differences inform some of the tensions between these groups.

One such tension is in the economic realm. Giriama have historically endorsed long-term reciprocal economic relationships between people and the redistribution of wealth on a regular, even ritualized basis. Giriama entrepreneurs have challenged these values for decades (Parkin 1972), yet it is nevertheless the case that Giriama in Malindi emerge from a tradition that values an interdependent model of economic personhood, causing unease in their encounters with contemporary capitalist accumulation, which many regard as exploitive and hence potentially devastating to a community's very humanity (Ciekawy 2001). Meanwhile, among Swahili in Malindi capitalist values of individual effort and prosperity are considered largely compatible with Quranic messages and have taken hold of the consciousness of many (cf. Masquelier 2001). Almsgiving and charity are also crucial to their Islamic ideology, but these practices tend to signify affirmations of the individual's piety and compassion rather than obligatory forms of face-to-face reciprocity designed to level the economic playing field. As will be seen in chapter 2, such differences have a profound influence on Giriama envy of Swahili wealth, as well as Giriama cynicism about Swahili norms and values.

Two other elements of personhood that I explore in this book are the intertwined values of agency and interiority; these have particular importance in Swahili and Giriama modes of religiosity. Swahili versions of Islam in Malindi, particularly under the influence of reformism, tend to valorize individual choice and interior states such as belief and intention as crucial elements of piety. To be a good Muslim it is important to exercise self-control and to direct one's state of mind in pious ways; pious actions will follow. Giriama too value certain forms of agency; their strenuous critiques of their contemporary situation as a new form of slavery attest to that. But Giriama religiosity has not tended to valorize internal states such as belief and intention; one does not need to prove oneself a good Traditionalist, for instance, through the intensity of one's inner devotion. Furthermore, Traditionalism places less emphasis than does contemporary Swahili Islam on the role of individual choice. Instead, much Giriama religious practice involves making pragmatic decisions in response to outside forces, whether these are spirits possessing the body and making demands, ancestors appearing in dreams to offer directives, or the witchery of others that must be counteracted under the direction of a ritual specialist. To some Giriama appropriate personhood is located in a person's very grounding in customary Giriama practice, which includes prosocial and reciprocal ritual activities designed to ensure the wholeness (-*zima*) of society. Social relations that have been "disordered, muddled, or broken" by one person have the potential to bring suffering not only upon that person but upon the community as a whole (S. G. Thompson 1990: 49). Giriama actions, particularly desirable actions, are thus not customarily modeled in terms of individual free will, but instead are seen as stemming largely from outside forces and potentially reverberating far beyond the individual.

This relative disregard for internal states has several implications for Giriama interactions with Islam. Because religion is not for them centrally about belief, Giriama often attempt to draw pragmatically upon the potency of more than one religious locus at a time, a pluralistic practice that dramatically violates the Swahili expectation that only one religion can have a monopoly on Truth. And because conversion to another religion need not stem from an individual's choice or will, many Giriama convert to Islam because, they say, possessing Muslim spirits have forced them to convert, a claim that Swahili tend to regard critically. Indeed, Swahili receptions of Giriama converts are sometimes influenced by the essentialist presumption that Giriama are intrinsically incapable of practicing Islam with inner conviction (being unable to shuck off the rural ways of "palm wine and women," as one Swahili put it, "to turn their minds to God"). Models of personhood also influence Giriama and Swahili interactions with the Arabic language in their divinatory rituals. While many Swahili diviners pride themselves on their literate, exegetical skills, Giriama are comfortable sharing agency with a possessing spirit who reads and writes Arabic through their bodies, prompting Swahili critics to see such attempts as superficial and mimetic rather than authentic, sincere, and grounded in self-command. Different understandings of personhood also inflect Swahili and Giriama interpretations of the relationship between wealth and the supernatural. Whereas Swahili tend to regard good fortune as a result of individual effort in combination with God's blessing, Giriama tend to regard Swahili wealth as emerging not from human agency but from the intervention of malevolent Muslim spirits who collect money for those already rich. Ultimately, Giriama and Swahili models of personhood help to sustain a social force field in which Giriama use spiritual intermediaries to appropriate an

Islam they find distant and Other, and Swahili cast doubt upon the legitimacy of Giriama interactions with Islam.

This interplay between personhood and religiosity reinforces common ideas in Swahili and Giriama communities that contribute to their ethnoreligious separation. Although Swahili and Giriama have different reasons for thinking so and different means of reinforcing these notions, the following ideas circulate through both groups: that Giriama and Swahili are categorically (and, to some, essentially) distinct ethnic and religious beings; that Islam and its accoutrements (especially Arabic) are intrinsically and supernaturally potent; that Swahili enjoy a more privileged connection to the forces of Islam; and that Giriamaness is essentially distant from and, in some respects, even toxic to Islam. These ideas are not shared by everyone in Malindi's Swahili and Giriama communities, but they are sufficiently prevalent and so often taken for granted that where they take hold they achieve what Bourdieu (1977: 164) has suggested every social order must: "the naturalization of its own arbitrariness." Ironically, this naturalized social order subordinates the very Giriama who subscribe to these ideas, creating a painful tension for many Giriama. Indeed, the fact and feeling of subordination inflect virtually every dimension of Giriama life discussed in this book, yet Giriama also articulate their anger at and defiance of this state of affairs. I have found it useful to discuss this duality, as well as other aspects of the power relations between Swahili and Giriama, by drawing on two related but distinct theoretical concepts that Jean Comaroff and John L. Comaroff (1991: 22) call "the two dominant forms in which power enters—or, more accurately, is entailed in—culture," namely, hegemony and ideology.

While the social scientific literature offers many definitions of these terms (see, for instance, Althusser 1971; Gramsci 1971; Hall and Jefferson 1976; Williams 1977; Woolard 1998a), Comaroff and Comaroff (1991) provide particularly useful interpretations that I draw on here. The Comaroffs' understanding of hegemony is inspired by multiple intellectual sources, including the work of Antonio Gramsci and a Foucauldian concern with the presence of power in the unrecognized corners of social life. According to Williams (1977: 108), prior to Gramsci, hegemony was defined as "political rule or domination, especially in relations between states." Gramsci enriched this definition by drawing on Marx's emphasis on relations between ruling and subordinate classes. At the same time, however, he departed from a traditional Marxist understanding of power in which ruling classes secure and exert power largely through the materialist means of the base, including coercion. Gramsci never fully specified what he meant by hegemony (indeed, J. Comaroff and Comaroff [1991: 19] refer to it as a "relatively empty sign" subject to numerous interpretations). One widely held understanding of hegemony, articulated by Williams and elaborated by the Comaroffs, is as a system of meanings and values that expresses and more or less ensures the success of the interests of a particular class, typically the dominant one. In this understanding, hegemony permeates all class groups in a particular system, infusing the entire culture by organizing it around such meanings and values. Through the spontaneous consent of all class groups to assimilate the worldview of the dominant group, hegemony thus makes opposing ideas harder to think. While Gramsci spoke to Marxist hopes of revolution with his assertion that subordinate groups can secure the spread of their own worldview through persuasion and in so doing build up a counterhegemony to the ruling class, most scholarship since Gramsci has used the term hegemony to refer to a system that supports the status quo in power relations.

A close cousin to hegemony is ideology, a concept with such a complex and varied intellectual history (see, for instance, Eagleton 1994) that I will treat only a few elements of it here. In the most general sense ideology means a way of looking at things, but its relationship to mind, materiality, and social hierarchy varies from one definition to the next. Some theorists have placed ideology in a largely material context or as instantiated in "lived relations" (Althusser 1971; see also Woolard [1998a: 6] for a discussion of "behavioral, practical . . . or structural" definitions of ideology). Many followers of Marx have located it in ideas, primarily in the form of delusional beliefs ("false consciousness") that serve the interest of the ruling class. Giddens (1997) uses the term ideology as shorthand for widespread ideas and beliefs that shore up the interests of dominant groups, a definition that resonates with Williams's definition of hegemony. What is lost in this alignment of terms, however, is the distinction between ideas that are naturalized or taken for granted (because they are buried in practice, for example) and ideas that are more explicitly articulated (typically in discourse), as well as the distinction between ideas that serve the interest of the dominant group and those that do not.

This is why the Comaroffs' differentiation of these terms has proven particularly useful. In their view, hegemony usually goes without saying; it consists of the signs and practices that typically serve the interest of the dominant group by reflecting or justifying particular relations of power and that come to be "taken-for-granted [by all social groups] as the natural and received shape of the world and everything that inhabits it" (Comaroff and Comaroff 1991: 23). Ideology, in contrast, is an "articulated system of meanings." Thus while hegemony is so naturalized that its existence is simply understood (indeed, it is "not normally the subject of explication or argument" [23]), ideology is generally self-conscious and explicit (though I would add that hegemony need not *always* be tacit, particularly in contexts where anthropologists elicit articulations of what is ordinarily taken for granted). Furthermore, while hegemony is widely shared across social strata, ideology is "the expression and ultimately the possession of a particular social group"; hence different strata within a society may have different ideologies (24). This distinction is useful in part because it allows for the ideological expression of different worldviews and priorities of different social strata, especially when they are in conflict, while retaining the notion that the priorities of dominant groups can hegemonically infuse and (at least partly) shape the actions and experiences of subordinate groups.[9]

I find both concepts particularly important to this ethnography because Giriama attitudes toward their own oppression are so complicated. Hegemonic capitulation to Swahili and Islamic superiority coexists with defiant ideologies in many domains of Giriama life. Giriama narratives about the Muslim spirits that steal money for Swahili register an ideological critique of Swahili capital at the same time that they reiterate a hegemonic view of Islamic forces as intrinsically more potent than the forces associated with Giriama Traditionalism. Giriama experiences of possession by Muslim spirits that compel them to regurgitate customarily Giriama foods and convert to Islam seem an embodied instantiation of the hegemonic premise that Giriamaness is inadequate, even polluting; at the same time, however, the very victims of these spirits frequently voice their ideological opposition to Islam. The Comaroffs have discussed the complex relationships between power and consciousness by mapping their distinction between hegemony and ideology onto a spectrum they call a "chain of consciousness," a range of mental states from subconsciousness to awareness. They define the two poles of this continuum as

> the unseen and the seen, the submerged and the apprehended, the unrecognized and the cognized. . . . Between the conscious and the unconscious lies . . . the realm of partial recognition, of inchoate awareness, of ambiguous perception, and sometimes, of creative tension: that liminal space of human experience in which people discern acts and facts but can't or don't order them into narrative descriptions or even into articulate conceptions of the world; in which signs and events are observed, but in a hazy, translucent light; in which individuals or groups know that something is happening to them but find it difficult to put their fingers on quite what it is. (Comaroff and Comaroff 1991: 29)

Several more clarifications about hegemony and ideology and their relationship to Swahili and Giriama are in order. First, the distinction between hegemony and ideology is not absolute or fixed. The concepts occupy the extreme ends of a continuum; ideas and practices (at both individual and collective levels) may thus move between states of lesser and greater susceptibility to awareness, scrutiny, and critical thought, sometimes existing in the liminal state of "ambiguous perception" the Comaroffs describe. As I have already indicated, hegemonic notions are often built in to social life and discourse in the form of habitual practices and presuppositions, but they need not *always* be tacit, particularly in contexts where anthropologists' inquiries pull them to the surface. Finally, the Comaroffs' discussion of hegemony assumes that hegemonic premises are shared by a particular "political community" (Comaroff and Comaroff 1991: 24); in my case study, however, certain hegemonic premises circulate between two communities with overlapping but generally distinct cultural and political histories rather than within a single society. Such hegemony is possible because Swahili and Giriama live in a partially shared cultural field with recurrent points of encounter, including an ethnically based class system. As a result of this unusual case study that straddles two ethnic groups, I am faced with a special terminological lacuna. I use the term *hegemony* to describe popular premises, often taken for granted, that circulate between two ethnoreligious groups and operate in the service of the hierarchical status quo. I use the term *ideology* to characterize the articulated and conscious values that circulate within each group, particularly those that address and critique ethnoreligious politics and class relations. Yet I lack a clear term for the often tacit, taken-for-granted social norms that preside only among *one* of these groups. I sidestep this terminological difficulty by resorting to familiar vocabulary, such as *culture, custom, model,* and *expectation*.

Although there are numerous influences upon the hegemonic force field I have described among Giriama and Swahili, personhood plays a central role. For instance, customary Giriama understandings of personhood, which do not put a premium on individual agency, interiority, or inner consistency, create the conditions of possibility for the particular forms of religious practice I have mentioned: spirit possession that compels one to convert without regard for one's agency; a kind of religious pluralism that does not require the practitioner to choose between faiths (or Truths), but instead allows the practitioner to propitiate two distinct religious loci that are radically separated along ethnolinguistic lines; and divination practices in which diviners need not possess literate or intellectual expertise in order to tap into the mysterious and congealed powers of Arabic and Islam. These practices in turn subtly reinforce a hegemonic ethnoreligious divide because they involve interacting with Islam from afar, sometimes experiencing it as a domineering and ethnically alien power, even among those who do not count themselves as Muslim. At the same time, the Swahili emphases on individual choice and rationality in religious practice, on the consistency of a person's private state of faith, and on literate expertise and mentation in divination all lead to critical judgments of these Giriama religious practices, thereby underscoring the notion that Giriama do not tend to make good Muslims. Put another way, customary Giriama models of personhood undergird religious practices that reaffirm both the potency of Islam and the distinction between Giriama and Swahili ethnoreligious groups, whereas prevailing Swahili models of personhood tend to undergird negative judgments of Giriama that reaffirm the high status of Islam and the same ethnoreligious distinctions. Hence although they have different means of and reasons for doing so, both Swahili and Giriama sustain the hegemonic notions of Islamic potency and deep-seated links between ethnicity and religion.

The concept of hegemony captures well the way Giriama habitually defer to Swahili status and Islam's power. Perhaps because the Swahili promise of accepting, assimilating, and assisting Giriama is partially broken yet also partially kept, it is not easy for Giriama to see the force fields of power around them with clear eyes; Giriama thus sometimes are complicit in creating elements of the very structure that weighs so heavily upon them. At the same time, the Comaroffs' observation that hegemonic ideas can bubble up to awareness helps to account for the intermittent Giriama articulations of resentment toward this power structure. Those who collude in their own hegemonic oppression sometimes recognize what they are doing when enlightened by a resistant ideology. Similarly, those who hold more power may not experience themselves as oppressors and may have little conscious ill will toward those with less; indeed, the beneficent ideologies of the powerful may contradict the hegemonic nature of the social hierarchy that supports them. This dynamic is in clear operation among Malindi's Swahili, whose norms of charity and politeness inform such claims as "These days we are as one with the Giriama" and who express acute discomfort when confronted with Giriama antagonism. Several times I received stern lectures from Swahili men who informed me that it was treacherous to ask so many questions about ethnic difference. "We don't want Kenya to turn into another Rwanda," said one. "It's better to focus on how well we get along." Other Swahili insisted that their feelings toward Giriama are totally well-meaning and benevolent, even though the institutional distribution of charitable funds tends to follow well-worn tracks that lead to other Muslims and bypass needy Giriama. Most Swahili also adhere to conventional ideology regarding the Islamic brotherhood: namely, that it warmly accepts all comers. Yet almost in spite of themselves, many seem to associate piety with proximity to Arabness, while their cynicism toward Giriama's suitability for piety can make it difficult for them to embrace Giriama as true Muslims. Indeed, in some Swahili rhetoric, Giriama seem doomed to the no man's land described by Homi Bhabha (1994: 153), in which colonizers pressed their subjects to imitate them so as to become "normalize[d]" or "civilize[d]," at the same time they treated such assimilative efforts as pale forms of mimicry that revealed the colonized as "almost the same, but not quite." Yet most Swahili I spoke to did not appear to recognize the difficulties encountered by would-be Giriama assimilates to their religious and ethnic fold. Apparently hegemonic force fields can operate in such a way as to occlude the vision not only of the subordinate, but of those in power.

Marginalization in Malindi and Beyond:
Giriama and Swahili Predicaments

When Vasco da Gama's fleet arrived in Malindi in April 1498 they found an elegantly built town on the shoreline dominated by Arab traders and settlers and a unique Muslim Arabo-African culture called Swahili that had emerged from centuries of settlement and intermarriage. The economy thrived on the agricultural labor of African slaves and through a lively trade in gold, ivory, tortoiseshell, and other goods that circulated around the African coast, Arabia, and India (Strandes 1899/1961: 92). Malindi's rulers extended hospitality to the Portuguese, but they soon learned that Portuguese intentions were less than noble. The Portuguese monopolized most Indian Ocean trade, exacted tribute from various coastal towns while deposing and replacing some of their rulers, established numerous customs stations, and razed the city of Mombasa (south of Malindi) twice, in 1505 and 1528, with great loss of life. Not surprisingly, Malindi withered under Portuguese influence; by 1606 its Arab population was living in poverty (Martin 1973: 41; Salim 1973).

After the Portuguese chapter came to a close in the late eighteenth century, Malindi's fortunes lay dormant until its late nineteenth-century rebirth as an agrarian center. Numerous Arab and Swahili families migrated to the town from Arabia and other areas of the coast, rebuilding and vastly extending the agricultural industry dependent on African slaves, many of them Nyasa and Yao imported from the Kilwa area of what is now Tanzania (Martin 1973: 58). Town culture once again centered on a thriving Swahili way of life fed by multiple ethnic influences, including Hadrami, Omani, and Bantu. Coexisting with Swahili and Arabs, but living slightly inland or on the periphery of town, were members of nine closely related coastal groups known today as the Mijikenda, of which Giriama are the largest group and by far the most predominant in the Malindi area. Mijikenda in the nineteenth century were mutually dependent on the Swahili through paternalistic patron-client and trade relationships that sometimes led to intermarriage and the assimilation of Mijikenda into Swahili society. A relatively small number of Mijikenda were also among the Africans enslaved by Swahili and Arabs, a fact that Giriama today repeatedly emphasize, if not inflate, in their discussions of contemporary Swahili power.[10]

Slavery was ended in Kenya in 1907 under British colonial law, but the transition did not lead to any straightforward condition of freedom for African workers. Instead, the colonial government engaged in a series of complex interventions that attempted to control African labor, with implications for former slaves and all Mijikenda in the Malindi area (Cooper 1980). The colonial state's primary interest was in enforcing the rights of landowners, many of them Arabs and Swahili, and creating an African working class committed to full-time wage labor. But a combination of shifting policies and what Cooper calls "governmental timidity" (224) resulted in a more complex arrangement than this. Stung by a Giriama uprising in 1914 and, later, wary of another Mau Mau revolt, this time on the coast, the colonial administration was reluctant to evict people with no land titles. Mijikenda and others squatted on land they did not own, sometimes remunerating the landlords and finding ways of avoiding steady work (225).

Mijikenda may have sustained some degree of autonomy, but they were hardly prosperous. Particularly in Malindi, Mijikenda remained vulnerable to market fluctuation and population growth (Cooper 1980: 289). Meanwhile the formerly paternalistic relations between Arab and Swahili landowners and their Mijikenda peasant tenants had been largely erased by colonial policies, heightening the vulnerability of squatters (276–77). By the time the transition to independence was complete, most Giriama in the Malindi area found themselves squatting on land owned by Arabs, Swahili, other ethnic groups, or the government. Some squatters became chronically indebted to Arab and Swahili traders and landowners, and what was once a symbiotic relationship became one-sided (S. G. Thompson 1990). In the Malindi area most squatters protected themselves against the fluctuations of the cash economy through subsistence cultivation, though they were on others' land.

Since independence the Kenyan state has created new tensions by attempting to bolster landowners' rights, sometimes implementing dubious "resettlement schemes" for squatters. Cooper (1980: 293) describes the position of Mijikenda and former slaves since independence as "less independent, less secure, and more exposed to the vagaries of markets and politics. . . . Food shortages have become chronic . . . wage labor is more often a necessity, and a job something that cannot be jeopardized by frequent returns to a farm." Today many Giriama squatters outside of Malindi rely on subsistence agriculture, but many also commute into the town center in hopes of getting a job, often from Muslim, upcountry, or European employers. Some build mud-and-wattle dwellings on the margins of town, sacrificing their access to larger plots of land for the prospect of intermittent wage labor.

While Mijikenda have suffered the brunt of economic disenfranchisement in Malindi, Swahili too have reason to feel marginalized on both national and global scales. The British colonial government tended to favor upcountry ethnic groups, and as the move toward independence accelerated in the early 1960s, coastal Muslims, fearing subjugation by an upcountry-dominated and Christian administration, instigated the so-called Mwambao movement in favor of self-rule along the ten-mile-long coastal strip. Although Muslims were granted a degree of autonomy, including freedom of worship and the protection of Islamic Kadhi courts, the coastal strip was assimilated to the Kenyan national government in 1963, and since then coastal Muslims have felt persistently aggrieved by their relationship to the state. In 2002 the Muslim Task Force on Constitutional Review argued, "The Constitution and laws of Kenya reflect the Judeo-Christian origins and beliefs of the colonial masters. Indeed the conduct of state is manifestly Christian in nature" (Hashim 2005: 25). Coastal Muslims have been largely marginalized from ministerial and cabinet positions, while much of the country's power and wealth remain concentrated "in Christian rather than in Muslim hands" (O'Brien 1995: 201; see also Oded 2000). Muslims' political indignation was stoked in the early 1990s, when the Kenya African National Union (KANU) government helped sponsor a violent campaign designed to suppress the unregistered Islamic Party of Kenya on the coast (Human Rights Watch 2002). After Al Qaeda bombed U.S. embassies in Nairobi and Dar es Salaam in 1998 the Kenyan government shut down numerous Muslim NGOs, prompting cries of opportunistic discrimination. Such political and economic forces have conspired to focus Swahili's orientation overseas, sharpening their investment in and alignment with religious, social, political, and economic networks in the Middle East (O'Brien 1995).

In Malindi itself, both Swahili and Giriama are repeatedly confronted with other evidence of their marginalization. While most urban Swahili enjoy clear socioeconomic advantages relative to most Giriama, both groups agree that upcountry Kikuyu and Luo are disproportionately represented in managerial positions, and both have accepted the presence of European landowners, hoteliers, and tourists with ambivalence. In the decades since independence Anglos and Italians have bought up many shoreline plots, building private residences and luxury resorts and shepherding in what seemed, for a time, like a booming tourism industry that brought jobs and commerce to town residents and Mijikenda on the outskirts. In the 1990s, however, Malindi's tourism industry suffered a steep decline in the wake of the catastrophic weather brought by El Niño, the politically sponsored tribal clashes on the coast in 1997 (during which disgruntled Mijikenda, most of them Digo, were encouraged to target nonindigenous residents suspected of voting against the ruling KANU Party), and the 1998 embassy bombings, which were loosely tied to coastal Muslim communities. The tumultuous violence after the 2007 elections struck another blow to a town economy that had been rebuilding itself. Many Giriama living near Malindi are dependent on petty wage labor provided by the volatile tourism industry, yet many also decry how the dynamics of tourism have brought prostitution, drug use, and fragmentation to their community. Meanwhile, although Swahili benefit from tourism's overall effect on the town economy, many feel excluded from the managerial tiers of the tourism industry (Eastman 1994) and aspire to financial autonomy through landholdings, businesses, and capital received from friends, relatives, and sponsors in the Arab world. Most Swahili also resent the moral decline brought by Malindi's casinos and traveling sybarites. And the presence of so many wealthy whites in Malindi has heightened Swahili and Giriama awareness of global racial divides and the precariousness of their own economic security. Indeed, their constant exposure to national and global flows of people, capital, and images has made both Swahili and Giriama keenly aware of the fantastic advantages enjoyed by those with greater ethnic, racial, national, or class privileges (cf. Appadurai 1991; Weiss 2002).

The discontent of both groups is frequently expressed in tribal terms. After independence in 1963 Kenya did not shake the sharp ethnic divisions carved so deeply by its colonial officials. The colonial administration encouraged the formation of political districts along ethnic lines, and each of the eight elections since 1963 has been informed by ethnically oriented electoral practices, a tendency that has been unofficially institutionalized by politicians who persistently appeal for ethnic support (Adar 1998: 71) and that sometimes comes violently to the fore, most notably in the disastrous aftermath of the December 2007 elections.[11] In Kenya's crucible of inequality, the word on everyone's lips these days is the possibility of *majimbo* (Kisw.), an ethnically based federalism that has been hotly debated across Kenya and has been defined and redefined since the 1960s to suit every ethnic group's fantasies of entitlement to land and resources. Some coastal Swahili and Arabs have pinned their hopes on *majimbo* as a means of uniting and protecting the interests of Swahili-speaking peoples, and some Giriama versions of *majimbo* are freighted with fantasies of retribution against Swahili and Arabs who have encroached on territory they say is essentially theirs. The political history of East Africa has thus reified and exacerbated ethnic difference; it is perhaps not surprising, then, that Giriama find it more difficult than ever to attain acceptance if they try to assimilate into Malindi's core Swahili community. This sense of exclusion has ramifications in many domains of Giriama experience.

These historical complexities pull Malindi's Giriama and Swahili residents in several directions at once. Swahili, for instance, increasingly grapple with how to incorporate modern forms of personhood and material practice into their identity (P. Caplan and Topan 2004), even as many are oriented to the Middle East as an esteemed locus of kin ties, status, wealth, and Muslim solidarity. Depending on political exigencies, Swahili may define themselves as Africans entitled to be on the Kenya coast (A. M. Mazrui and Sheriff 1994; McIntosh 2001a) or focus on the essentialized cachet of Arabian blood from far away, as did many colonial administrators in their dealings with coastal peoples. As I have already indicated, Islam itself is contested, for local ritual innovations in Swahili societies, some of which emerged from contact with other ethnic groups in the region, are increasingly challenged by reformists who encourage a more orthodox, text-based, and interior version of the religion in which one's state of mind is paramount to one's piety. The ritual practices of divination, herbalism, and spirit possession long practiced by Swahili up and down the coast and overlapping to some degree with Mijikenda Traditionalism are regarded by elite and reformist Muslims in Malindi as heretical and are discouraged by many in mainstream Swahili society. Overall the converging forces of modernity and Islamic reformism have heightened the salience of self-determination, agency, and carefully controlled intentions in Swahili personhood, though these ideologies hardly determine a uniform practice in Malindi.

Giriama are also subject to many cross-cutting forces. Customary social structures of the past, revolving around patriarchal, polygynous family units and ancestor propitiation, have deteriorated among residents of the Malindi area as much of their energy is focused on improvisational strategies for survival. The advantages associated with Westernization lure some youth into the tourism industry, usually as low-paid hotel workers, "beach boys," or tour guides. Christianity, which is loosely associated with the Kenyan state and the Western world, has gained a substantial number of converts, but Islam maintains a special status as a highly visible, high-status religion that Giriama associate with the wealth and privileges of their Swahili neighbors and that many Giriama look to with mingled resentment and hope. At the same time, customary Giriama models of personhood continue to shape modes of religious experience, as well as Giriama's judgments of the perils of modernity and the ills of capitalist hierarchy.

Malindi Today: Spatial Hierarchies of Ethnicity, Religion, and Language

It is by now an anthropological commonplace that ethnic communities premise their identity not only on contrasts with other groups (Barth 1969), but also on particular spatial relations (Gupta and Ferguson 1997b). Spatial experience is a privileged dimension of social contrast between Malindi's Swahili and Giriama, in part because their domiciles, places of worship, and languages tend to be concentrated in different locales. Yet the spatial quality of Giriama-Swahili relations is as much a product of social imagination as of demography (cf. Appadurai 1991; Gupta and Ferguson 1997a), and ideologically loaded spatial fantasies play central roles in Swahili's and Giriama's sense of identity. For instance, while many Swahili aspire to root their religious faith and identity in the Arabian peninsula (indeed, many have claimed an Arab heritage, sometimes on tenuous grounds), Giriama understand their most authentic identity to be grounded in the Kaya; these are circular clearings in the hinterland forest that, now almost empty, are said to have once been inhabited by entire Giriama communities and tightly administered by revered elders with sacred powers (Parkin 1991a). Swahili define themselves as an urban and civilized (*mstaarabu*, a term derived from the word for Arab) people, in contrast to the Nyika, the pejorative label they sometimes apply to Giriama, which can be loosely glossed as "people of the bush." Giriama in Malindi often reflect bitterly on the limited scope of their travels compared to Swahili abilities to tap into supernatural forms of flight and speed.

The imagined quality of space in Swahili and Giriama discourse also makes itself plain in a semiotic pattern Irvine and Gal (2000) have termed "fractal recursivity," in which the same conceptual opposition is projected at various levels of scale. Among Swahili, for instance, not only is the Muslim, urban coastal strip contrasted with the supposedly primitive hinterland, but even within Malindi the central sections of town numerically dominated by Swahili are sometimes rhetorically contrasted with the primitive depredations of impoverished outlying Giriama areas. The inner sanctum of Swahili houses tends to be guarded against low-status visitors such as non-Muslim Giriama tradesmen, who, if they are considered too redolent of the bush, are typically obliged to remain outside; indeed, the valorization of private, enclosed, and pure spaces has a long history in Swahili architecture (Donley-Reid 1990). The same opposition between civilized and less civilized spaces is thereby imagined with both broad and fine-grained brush strokes.

Spatial tropes also provide metaphors for religious ontologies in Giriama discourse, preserving the conceptual separation between Giriama-ness and Islam. For example, Giriama in Malindi tend to divide spirits into those hailing from "the Giriama side" and those from "the Muslim side." Giriama Muslims sometimes refer to conversion to Islam as a kind of "arrival" or "going in" and claim that Swahili "will never come out" of their religion, as if it were a privileged space. Spatial metaphors figure too in Giriama apprehensions of their disadvantage and marginalization. The young man discussing the disappointments of conversion in my opening vignette alludes to Giriama "trying to get to the Muslim side" who will "find themselves sweeping cake off the floor of the mosque at the end of the day." His reference to the floor picks up on his friend's image of Muslims touching their foreheads to the floor in prayer, but transforms the floor from a site of piety to one of debasement and servitude.

While tropes of spatiality are central to Swahili-Giriama hierarchies, these find much inspiration in the demographic facts and the physical layout of Malindi town. The township of Malindi extends in a seven-kilometer strip from north to south along the Indian Ocean. From a small roundabout at the center of town, paved roads radiate in several directions, partitioning and crisscrossing the various town divisions (*mitaa*, sing. *mtaa*; Kisw.). One road encircles the densely packed shops, eateries, Swahili and Arab residences, madarasas (Kisw.), and schools that make up the central division known as Barani; another passes Shella, the division housing several mosques and much of Malindi's Swahili and Arab population in buildings constructed with stone. A popular thoroughfare runs from the north, passing tourist rental cottages, cafés, insurance agencies, tiny medical clinics, Internet kiosks, casinos, and discos, ultimately arriving at the bustling heart of town. From there it deposits travelers and tourists at banks, grocery stores, gas stations, Malindi's fishing club, and dozens of curio shacks, eventually tracing the beachfront south of the town center and the large European expatriate mansions and luxury hotels so important to an increasingly fragile town economy. Still another route branches off the roundabout to the southwest, past the mud dwellings and makeshift cement houses of Ngala and Kisumundogo divisions, where migrant laborers from many ethic backgrounds live. This road passes the small landing strip that is the Malindi airport, until it eventually veers south to Mombasa. Back in town, unpaved routes weave through several residential areas, the roads pitted with rocks that ruin the axles of Malindi's decrepit fleets of three- and four-wheeled taxis. Some of these routes can be traced into the heart of divisions such as Majengo to the west and Maweni and Muyeye to the south, where so many Giriama live. Muyeye is a particularly impoverished region, and increasingly crowded as well. During a bad rainstorm the water sluices along the muddy paths between dwellings, carrying plastic bags and empty tin cans to someone else's doorstep.

Malindi's town center fairly throbs with the hum of bus engines and commercial activity. At the outdoor market just outside of town, near the piles of fresh fruits and vegetables, the cassava stacked on the ground like tree branches, and the glittering heaps of dried fish for sale, an astonishing diversity of people circulate each day. Barefoot Giriama women come from their rural homesteads to sell surpluses of mangoes, bananas, and greens; these they balance on their heads in large woven trays that complement their carefully tied, matching *kanga* cloths in bright colors. Many of the older Giriama women wear the customary *hando* bustles of grass and cloth that enhance their hips and buttocks, and small talismanic pouches around their upper arms, waists, or necks that announce their affiliation with the spirits and diviners of Giriama Traditionalism. They circulate amid Christian men and women of various ethnic backgrounds (including Giriama), some of whom take advantage of the trade in secondhand clothes from the West to buy patterned synthetic dresses with shoulder pads, pumps, or dress shirts and slacks.

Muslim Swahili and Arab men sometimes wear Western-style clothing, but many also wear their white *kofia* cap every day, and on Fridays most don the full-length white *kanzu* robe. Swahili and Arab women are hard to mistake, draped in their head-to-toe *bui bui* veils, usually of black polyester. Their feet, exposed to public view, can reach heights of expressiveness. Some women have stained their toenails with henna or painted them with red toenail polish; many wear open-toe shoes whose straps, heels, and sparkling vinyl declare an expensive and precious femininity. These groups comprise most of the marketplace crowd, but every so often others stroll past: a lone Maasai draped in his red cape, on his way to a hotel where he and his peers have been hired to sing and dance for a largely Western audience; a Somali immigrant from the war-torn north; a Bohra Muslim of Indian descent, perhaps walking to the fabric shop he owns; a finely shod Kikuyu office worker; a Kamba from the hinterland, come to sell his carvings to tourists or in search of wage labor. Occasionally a group of white backpackers—usually English, German, Italian, or American—strides through the marketplace looking for a soda and gazing curiously at the scene.

Beyond the market, Christian churches and Muslim mosques are scattered throughout Malindi's divisions. The construction and maintenance of Malindi's large mosques are often funded by organizations from the Middle East, while a handful of missionaries, most of them American, have been instrumental in the efflorescence of small churches around town. In 1998 I found twenty-eight churches and fifteen mosques in the approximately fourteen square kilometers of Malindi township, some of them sitting almost cheek by jowl. The mosques, while fewer in number, have the advantage of beauty and size; their tall, bulbous minarets are visible from a distance, their cavernous central spaces are encircled by long, crenellated walls, and their ornate pastel paint jobs seem designed to broadcast both purity and wealth. Calls to prayer are typically announced through loudspeakers, filling the town with melodious Arabic. Most churches, on the other hand, are humbly and rapidly constructed; small, one-room cement structures provide no distractions from their intended spiritual message. Many were built in the past few decades as a renewed postcolonial surge of missionary effort and competitiveness with Islam washed across the Kenya coast (cf. O'Brien 1995). As if to compensate for their unprepossessing appearance, they announce their presence to potential members with numerous small, hand-painted signs mounted on stakes and driven into the soil along the main roads of town.

Walking through Malindi town, passersby can hear a *muzzein* intoning the call to prayer from a mosque loudspeaker or the sound of children reciting Quranic prayers in the madarasa. On Sunday morning the church just a few doors down might resound with Christian songs accompanied by the tambourine or the tumult of an entire congregation speaking in the voice of the Holy Spirit. The presence of Giriama Traditionalism is more muted, for it stakes no claim to land in town or to formal educational institutions, and its shrines are tucked away in rural spaces. Many Muslims and Christians consider it a backward form of religious practice, one that they have transcended with their connections to transnationally validated faiths. Yet Traditionalism's presence in the town center is nonetheless broadcast through small, subtle cues: the talismans on the arms of Giriama women, the occasional sign advertising traditional healing (*uganga wa kienyeji*), and the tiny kiosks named after some element of Traditionalism (such as *kiraho*, a supernatural spell that protects against theft).[12]

The material accoutrements and spatial layout of Malindi's religions point to and reinforce the steep hierarchy between Islam and Traditionalism. A related hierarchy can be found in the linguistic domain, which is central to the ethnoreligious dynamics I describe. The four most prominent languages in Malindi are Kiswahili, Kenya's national language and one of its official languages; English, the other official language; Kigiriama, the Giriama mother tongue; and Arabic, vital to Islamic religious life. Of these, Kigiriama, Kiswahili, and Arabic are most central to the ongoing struggles of Swahili and Giriama to define and protect their ethnic identities. And each language tends to be associated with certain spaces that are more or less valorized in coastal society.

Swahili see Arabic as broad in its extension, connecting them to the wealthy and sacred Arab lands and to the pan-national sites of the global Muslim community. Arabic also extends vertically in the sacred imaginary, as the language not only of the Quran, but also of Allah and all the souls in heaven. Those Swahili who have the opportunity and the motivation study the language in madarasa, and some travel to Arabia to master it.

The national language, Kiswahili, has a more truncated spatial reach and a correspondingly lesser status among coastal Muslims, but still enjoys prestige for several reasons. For noncoastal Kenyans, Kiswahili represents an element of panethnic national identity and, for those who have learned the standard forms in primary and secondary school, education. The language is spoken by millions in East Africa, offering a degree of local cosmopolitanism to its speakers. Among coastal residents local versions of Kiswahili, which is strongly associated with their ethnic heritage and with Islam, constitute the mother tongue of the Swahili people. While Kiswahili has many Bantu elements, with syntactic and semantic cognates in Kigiriama and the other Mijikenda languages, about 20 to 30 percent of its lexicon originates in Arabic. The meanings that Swahili themselves impose upon these linguistic facts are a matter of cultural and political contingency (Khalid 1977; A. M. Mazrui and Shariff 1994; A. A. Mazrui and Mazrui 1995; Russell 1981). Some nationalists have emphasized Kiswahili's Bantu roots to underscore its essential Africanness, while others have cited its Arabic components to support an Arabocentric model of Swahili identity. Regardless of where the ideological and spatial emphasis is placed, Kiswahili retains a dual connotation on the coast as both the language of urban Muslim Swahili and a language of education and East African commerce.

Kigiriama, by contrast, suffers as the least valued and most spatially marginalized language in the wider linguistic marketplace. Considered atavistic and nonliterate by Swahili and Arabs, upcountry folk, and representatives of the Kenyan state, Kigiriama is sometimes associated by cultural outsiders with the bush (*msitu* or *nyika*) rather than with town life. It has been neglected by scholars and state agencies, is virtually never used in print media, and, unlike Kiswahili, Arabic, and English, is not offered as a subject of study in state or private schools. While some non-Giriama pick up elements of the language through proximity, the idea of setting out to learn Kigiriama would strike most coastal residents as peculiar, if not outlandish. Underscoring this stigma, many coastal schools forbid the use of Kigiriama in primary school classrooms once students have begun the study of Kiswahili and English. The opprobrium associated with Kigiriama works against elderly and unschooled Giriama who speak little to no Kiswahili or English; they are isolated from employment opportunities, from communication with medical professionals in town (most of whom come from upcountry), and from interaction with most bureaucrats. Giriama themselves recognize the stigma some apply to their language and the limits of its extension into the wider world, yet many associate it with the potencies of Traditionalism and defend it as the repository of an authentic Giriama identity. "Those old Giriama diviners in the hinterland," say some Giriama youth with reverence, "they speak the original Kigiriama, the pure version." The Giriama deployment of Kigiriama, Kiswahili, and Arabic in divination and healing rituals sometimes reinscribes the ethnoreligious links between Kigiriama, Giriama people, and Traditionalism, as well as the hegemonic ethnoreligious links between Kiswahili, Swahili people, and Islam.

In the Field

Every field experience brings its own complications. My own, carried out over eighteen months in 1995, 1996, 1998–1999, and 2004, was shaped by the contingencies of studying two communities that live in a fraught relationship with one another. Giriama and Swahili alike were intrigued by my research into their relationships, an interest that opened up many conversations about the perceived shortcomings of the other group and, in some cases, anxiety that my study might exacerbate ethnic tensions. Nevertheless, I found many informants to be forthcoming, particularly as people grew accustomed to my presence. I gathered information through a combination of interviews with both Swahili and Giriama and participant observation in households and public areas, where I could listen to daily chat among family and friends and witness interactions between Swahili and Giriama. I have altered the names and other identifying characteristics of most of my informants to preserve their anonymity; exceptions include my primary research assistant, Maxwell, and certain well-known individuals who did not object to being identified, such as the famous Giriama healer Charo Shutu (now deceased).

Finding a suitable place to live proved to be more complicated than finding conversation with willing informants. I worried that members of each community might look at me askance if they thought I was living with the other ethnic group. Choosing a home was also complicated by the economic hardships in Malindi; a precipitous drop in tourism in the late 1990s had resulted in heightened violent crime that made outsiders (especially those assumed to be wealthy on the basis of race) potential targets. When I first arrived in town I found quite a few well-to-do families scrambling to set up security alarm systems for their homes. The tensions between Mijikenda and Swahili, fomented by the politically motivated ethnic clashes of 1997, fed an undercurrent of discontent among Mijikenda youth, among them Giriama who contemplated rebellion against Swahili and Arabs and sometimes, in my presence, discussed the possibility of another violent uprising. When the embassies in Nairobi and Dar es Salaam were bombed in August 1998, FBI agents swarmed through Swahili communities up and down the coast (eventually arresting one individual from Malindi), and some of my Swahili friends and informants participated in rallies where American flags were burned. Some Swahili, particularly those with ties to the controversial and as yet unregistered Islamic Party of Kenya, wondered aloud if I might be a CIA agent with anti-Muslim intentions.

Seeking a safe space that would not obviously align me with either Swahili or Giriama causes, I eventually spent the greater part of my fieldwork house-sitting for an East African of British descent whose gated home was equidistant from some of my primary field sites: the Swahili communities in Shella and Barani and the Giriama communities in Muyeye and Maweni. My home base may have aligned me initially with the white colonial community, but it also helped me present myself as neutral in the matter of Swahili and Giriama disputes, and I hoped that my extensive contact with Swahili and Giriama friends and informants would eventually make it clear that I was a *mzungu* (white person) of a different stripe. By day I walked or rode a bicycle to Swahili or Giriama communities, socializing at length with certain families I came to know well, accompanying family members on their errands, joining in leisurely conversations on public verandas in town or in clearings in more rural areas, and engaging in prearranged interviews. Sometimes I would live in a Giriama or Swahili household for several days during special occasions, such as a Giriama funeral or Ramadan. I also ventured into communities several kilometers away from Malindi town, living with Giriama friends in Ganda and Swahili in Mambrui. Much of my attention was directed toward religious practitioners, including Giriama diviners and healers (*aganga*), Muslim leaders (imams and other pious individuals), and the Swahili diviner healers known as *walimu wa kitabu*. I came to know some of these people fairly well, observing as numerous Giriama *aganga* practiced their craft and studying Arabic with one Swahili *mwalimu wa kitabu*. As a woman I was not allowed access to certain ritual contexts, particularly within Malindi's mosques, but I also came across as a more benign figure than I otherwise might have, able to ingratiate myself fairly easily into households and many social situations.

My field situation involved speakers proficient in Kiswahili, Kigiriama, and occasionally English or Arabic. I interviewed some Giriama in Kiswahili and, less often, English. When spending time with Giriama who were speaking Kigiriama, I required the help of an assistant, who performed simultaneous translations and went over recordings of interviews and less formal (often multilingual) discussions in detail with me. I interviewed Swahili in Kiswahili and occasionally in English, and I used a Swahili assistant to help me translate Arabic when necessary. Most of the quotations in this book come from transcribed recordings of conversations carried out in Kiswahili, Kigiriama, or English.

Overview of Chapters

In chapter 1 I discuss Giriama and Swahili ethnicity from two angles: the historical and political, and the contemporary and discursive. I offer a brief overview of the rise of ethnic categories on the Kenya coast, describing the precolonial fluidity between Swahili and Giriama in the nineteenth century and the colonial policies that attempted to crystallize divisions between these groups while allocating resources asymmetrically. This divisiveness lives on in the tribalist rhetoric of today's politicians and has been heated to the boiling point by politicized ethnoterritorial contests over land and resources that blight much of Kenya. I then discuss contemporary ethnic discourse among Swahili and Giriama in Malindi, focusing on widespread (though not unanimous) currents of ethnic essentialism and on Giriama frustrations at perceived Swahili prejudice. This chapter sets the stage for my subsequent discussions of a hegemonic divide that is not only ethnically but also religiously framed.

In chapter 2 I lay out a more detailed portrait of current economic discrepancies between Swahili and Giriama, explaining how Giriama experience and translate these discrepancies into models of the world. I describe how economic differences emerge from and reaffirm core differences in Swahili and Giriama understandings of personhood. Swahili increasingly emphasize individual discipline and accumulation (supplemented by a flow of resources from Middle Eastern communities), while Giriama tend to apprehend these orientations with some suspicion, valorizing instead more reciprocal modes of the economic person. I further explain that Giriama tend to model Swahili wealth in terms of tropes of mobility, speed, and transport to faraway locales, qualities Giriama perceive as both enviable and dangerous, and qualities that they contrast with the rootedness in local land to which many Giriama aspire. Finally, I detail the popular Giriama narratives about Muslim *jini* spirits that live off the blood of innocents, including Giriama, so that they may fly to Arabia to bring money to their Swahili and Arab owners. I suggest that these spirit narratives constitute a critique of Swahili capital, consolidate the association between money and mobility, and contribute to a hegemonic naturalization of the perceived relationships between ethnicity, religion, and supernaturally obtained privilege.

In chapter 3 I focus on Giriama attitudes toward Islam and the contrasts between Swahili ideologies of conversion to Islam and Giriama spirit possession experiences that compel them to convert. These religious differences among Swahili and Giriama hinge on the different notions of personhood that prevail in their respective communities. Swahili notions of ideal conversion target inner states such as rationality, free choice, and intention. In contrast, Giriama tend not to focus on these mentalistic notions; their model of personhood privileges practice and embodied experience as crucial components of religiosity. This orientation can be seen in the Giriama spirit possession phenomenon in which Muslim spirits overtake Giriama individuals and force them to regurgitate the food and drink considered quintessentially Giriama while demanding their conversion to Islam. I suggest that this possession experience, far from constituting an act of resistance, as it is commonly described in the literature on spirit possession, is an embodiment of a hegemonic premise, namely, the notion that Giriamaness and Islam are intrinsically incompatible and that Giriamaness is polluting to Islam. Still, although some possessed Giriama convert to Islam to mollify the spirit and end their own torment, many also give voice to their anger against Muslims and Islam. Embodied hegemony and articulated ideologies of resistance can therefore coexist within the same individual. Finally, I discuss the fact that Swahili sometimes deride what they see as flawed Giriama agency in their spirit-forced conversions. Their different assumptions about personhood thereby score an even sharper line between these already ruptured ethnic groups.

Chapter 4 details Giriama healing rituals in which practitioners seem to tack back and forth between distinct, linguistically grounded loci of power, one Traditionalist and the other Islamic. I argue that the religious and linguistic pluralism in such rituals is grounded in a Giriama model of religious personhood in which mental states such as belief are neither scrutinized nor discussed, and hence consistency of belief is not particularly important. As a result, Giriama appropriation of Islamic symbolism in these rituals is not best described in terms of standard notions of religious blending or harmonious syncretism; indeed, I suggest that we need a more refined term, *polyontologism*, to take account of a mode of religiosity that deliberately moves between discrete supernatural ontologies. I further argue that code switching in some Giriama rituals both emerges from and helps to sustain a hegemonic model of ethnoreligious essentialism in which particular ethnolinguistic groups, in this case, Swahili and Giriama, are intrinsically linked to particular religious forces: Islam and Traditionalism, respectively. Even when Giriama appear to be mixing religious influences, many ritual practitioners nevertheless mark them as not only ontologically but ethnically separate.

Chapter 5 explores the politics of language in greater depth, with a focus on power and personhood in interactions with Arabic. Both Giriama and Swahili consider Arabic a repository of supernatural power with divinatory and curative abilities; this is another instance of hegemony that Giriama tend to accept. But Swahili and Giriama uses of Arabic texts in divination ceremonies are quite different, in ways that speak to their different models of personhood. While Swahili tend to treat Arabic as a rich repository of hidden meaning that can be accessed only through mental mastery and intellectual agency, Giriama tend to access its potency through spirit possession, in which they relinquish personal agency and defer to the powers of the Muslim spirits. This pattern consolidates the Giriama mystification of Islam and reinforces Swahili suspicions that Giriama "don't know what they're doing" with Arabic texts. At the end of the chapter I analyze the fact that a common symptom of madness among Giriama is being taken over by Muslim spirits that speak (spirit versions of) Arabic. Apparently the ultimate dissolution of Giriama personhood is represented by its colonization by this ethnolinguistic identity.

The epilogue discusses Giriama responses to the politically driven ethnic violence that tragically divided Kenya in the wake of the December 2007 presidential elections. In early 2008 some Giriama and other Mijikenda retreated to the Kaya, the mythic locus of their autochthony, to plot a war against those coastal residents who have profited in a geographic region where they supposedly do not belong. In this latest national conflict, it seems that all sides have turned to ethnoterritorialism in some of the starkest terms Kenya has ever seen.

Chapter 1

ORIGIN STORIES
The Rise of Ethnic Boundaries on the Coast

In 1997 the Kenya coast was wracked by a series of violent, politically orchestrated clashes over land ownership and economic opportunity. The events that gained the most publicity from local media and scholars were the upheavals south of Mombasa between Digo, a Muslim Mijikenda group, and the *wabara* (Kisw.), or upcountry tribes, who in recent decades have laid claim to many economic advantages on the coast. But north of Mombasa, in the Malindi area, the ethnoreligious dynamics of resentment were somewhat different. Some Giriama (and, to a lesser extent, other Mijikenda represented in Malindi) arrayed themselves not only against *wabara*, but against Arabs and Swahili who had been living on the coast for centuries. Their grievances sounded old themes, ranging from the accusation that Muslims enslaved their ancestors in large numbers, to the furious charge that Arabs and Swahili maliciously grab the land of hapless Giriama squatters and rightful landowners. Many young Giriama men in Malindi joined a loosely organized underground movement dedicated to exacting some form of revenge on their oppressors, and though the violence in Malindi never reached the levels in the Likoni area to the south, it simmered just beneath the surface.

One Giriama elder named Samson, who helped administer oaths to Mijikenda youth to secure their allegiance to the cause of potential guerrilla warfare,[1] told me that in early 1997 he went with another elder to seek the counsel of a powerful Giriama *mganga* diviner (singular of *aganga*, Kigir.), hoping to learn more about the origins and outcome of the ethnic tensions. The men asked the *mganga* the question that dogs so many citizens of the coast: Why are the Mijikenda so oppressed? The *mganga* told the men that long ago there was a fight between an ancestral Mijikenda and an Arab, who killed each other in the struggle. Their bodies were buried together in a configuration that would seal their destinies. First, the Mijikenda body was wrapped in a *bui bui*, the long covering that swathes the bodies of modest Muslim women, and was placed in the earth facing downward. Then the Arab body was laid to rest facing upward, its weight resting on the back of the Mijikenda.

In many origin stories of ethnic groups around the world, some critical moment in the past is thought to fix the destiny of the group in question. In the burial configuration described by the *mganga*, the corporeal body of the dead Mijikenda man becomes a stand-in for the Mijikenda social body. Mijikenda and Arabs are bound together forever in a wretched and degrading hierarchy in which Mijikenda must bear the weight of Arab advantage on their backs for eternity. Pain is also encoded in the orientation of the Mijikenda corpse. Traditionally Giriama dead are buried on their right side, sometimes with their feet pointing to the west and their faces to Shungwaya, a mythical point of migratory origin to the north, and sometimes oriented toward the Kaya, the customary Mijikenda capitals in the hinterland forests. While the spatial arrangement varies according to regional differences and competing ideologies, the orientation of a corpse connotes "social and cosmological as well as physical direction" (Parkin 1992: 22). Every Giriama understands the claustrophobic and shameful symbolism of the collective Mijikenda body relegated to staring down, away from the comforting sites of social life and social identity, into the cold, lonely earth. And if the Mijikenda soul is stolen through such a gesture, the humiliation is further ground in as the male corpse is swathed in a *bui bui*, a Muslim woman's garment, forcing upon it a degrading feminization,[2] as well as some kind of inchoate relationship to Islam.

Several issues invoked by this story set the stage for the discussion of ethnoreligious and ethnolinguistic relations in the rest of this book. Aside from the theme of personhood, the force field behind current understandings of ethnicity among Swahili and Giriama in the Malindi area is made up of shifting contests over resources, prejudices and perceptions, and currents of ethnic essentialism that have a complex colonial and postcolonial history. In a partial hegemony of ethnoreligious distinction, numerous, albeit not all, Giriama and Swahili share the assumption that Giriama are categorically distinct ethnic and religious beings from Swahili. Their rationales range from essentialist presumptions about the deepest nature of ethnic groups to Giriama observations of Swahili prejudice that, they contend, makes it all but impossible for Giriama to assimilate.

There are ironies in these ethnoreligious divisions, for the very category "Swahili" is a historically flexible appellation that, at least in some contexts, has readily assimilated newcomers. Such permeability has led to much head scratching as some scholars have sifted through an immensely complex history of Indian Ocean migration and intermarriage while striving to answer the question once framed by Eastman (1971): "Who are the Swahili?" As mentioned in the introduction, scholars lately have shifted from attempting to pin down Swahili identity to emphasizing instead its "openness and permeability" (Askew 1999: 73). This approach captures some important truths about Swahili history and resonates with contemporary theoretical models of ethnicity, yet it also risks glossing over the quality of some of the current ethnic tensions on the coast. From an analytic standpoint Swahili identity is indeed historically contingent and dynamic, but we must also recognize that cultural insiders on the coast do not always regard their ethnicity in the same way. Indeed, I suggest that situations like that in Malindi present us with a tension between currently fashionable analytical models of ethnicity as fluid and negotiated and the more absolute ethnic boundaries represented and understood by those on the ground. Folk representations of ethnic fixity may hide the shifting and socially constructed qualities of ethnicity that contemporary scholars seek to unmask, but in Malindi the rise of essentialist models of ethnicity among some coastal players has had concrete and sometimes painful effects. And Malindi is hardly the only place where such concerns are pressing; numerous scholars have noted the rise of ethnic differentiation in the face of globalizing trends and political liberalization (see, for instance, Gupta and Ferguson 1997: 39; Meyer and Geschiere 1999). Indeed, Parkin (1991a: 161) regards new essentialisms on the Kenya coast as local versions of a global trend toward "cultural, ethnic, and linguistic separatism . . . of a kind that in Europe was once called Balkanization."

Of course, as Comaroff and Comaroff (1989/1992: 50) remind us (and Parkin would undoubtedly agree), essentialist models of ethnicity "always [have their] genesis in specific historical forces, forces which are simultaneously structural and cultural." So too, I would argue, do more fluid models of identity. In fact, the structures of incentive for *both* ethnic fluidity and ethnic fixity deserve to be examined; arguably, neither should be taken for granted as the default state of affairs. In some contexts both can coexist, for elements of ethnic fluidity, such as shifting or ambiguous definitions of ethnic boundaries, may be overlaid by folk convictions that ethnic identity is nevertheless deep-seated and intractable, as is the case among some Giriama and Swahili in Malindi.

The "structural and cultural" history of these developments takes fine-grained form in various locales and historical moments along the East African coast, yet one can nevertheless trace a broad arc of developments in which earlier patron-client relationships that encouraged ethnic fluidity gave way in the colonial and postcolonial eras to political developments that have contributed to an increasing rigidification of ethnic categories on the Kenya coast (Cooper 1980; Glassman 1995; Willis 1993). This rigidity is not absolute; there are differences of opinion in Malindi about whether or not outsiders such as Giriama can become Swahili. But most important to my discussion is that by far the majority of Giriama in Malindi see "Swahili" as an exclusive category that is deeply, ontologically distinct from them and that would not welcome them if they attempted to assimilate. While some Swahili describe the category as relatively open, this ideology of fluidity is often contradicted by hegemonic patterns of compartmentalization and boundary making. In fact, the history of social fluidity that predated the arrival of Europeans gives the present situation a special piquancy, for Giriama are still mindful of their past kin relationships with Swahili, making their cynicism about their current predicament especially bitter. Paradoxically, these social memories coexist with currents of essentialist discourse about both Swahili and Giriama ethnic identity.

Religion plays an important role in this force field. If conversion to Islam is a sine qua non of Swahili assimilation, it is telling that the Islamic *bui bui* garment in the origin myth is equated not to the possibility of upward mobility, but to the loss of dignity of the Giriama person. Status and socioeconomic advantages are supposed to accrue to Islamic converts but, Giriama claim, rarely do. Furthermore, many Giriama seem to have internalized the hegemonic notion that although their customary religious ways are inadequate and conversion might redeem them, Islam nevertheless belongs in some deep ontological way to Arabs and Swahili and not to Giriama. Many Giriama thus find themselves caught between the promise of uplift and possible assimilation that attaches to Islamic conversion, and the flouting of that promise as they are rejected, in their view, by their Muslim neighbors. It is perhaps no wonder that in this origin story an index of Islam is treated not as a badge of status but as part of the overall humiliation of the Mijikenda.

Coastal Dynamics until the Nineteenth Century:
Social Fluidity and the Importance of the Arab World

In his overview of Swahili culture, the anthropologist John Middleton (1992: 1) writes that Swahili and Mijikenda have been entirely distinct groups for a very long time: "[The Mijikenda are] closely related to the Swahili in language, live next to them, and indeed often intermingle with them on the ground, and have for centuries been linked to them by trade, clientage, and mutual military protection. Yet neither they nor anyone else have ever argued that they are Swahili, and intermarriage has been rare."

Intermarriage between Swahili and Mijikenda is indeed fairly rare in contemporary Malindi. Yet the work of scholars such as Cooper (1980), Glassman (1995), Parkin (1989), and Willis (1993) suggests that to extrapolate the past from the present pattern is to portray the groups as more discrete and homogeneous than they historically have been. Indeed, says Willis, before the twentieth century the unifying ethnic term *Mijikenda* did not even exist, being an invention of the 1930s that swept nine culturally related peoples under the same rubric as part of the British effort to classify all their subjects according to ethnicity. Before then, Swahili, Arabs, colonials, and others tended to refer to the population of Mombasa's and Malindi's hinterland as Nyika, a pejorative term that can be roughly translated as "people of the bush." Nyika referred to a "wider grouping of people than does the term Mijikenda," says Willis; it "connotes uncivilized life as against the life of the town, and is in a sense a definition of the peoples of the hinterland by what they are not rather than what they are" (19, 28). (Although Willis uses the term Nyika to refer to Mijikenda before they were so named, I prefer to avoid it because its connotations are so offensive to Giriama today. I therefore use the term Mijikenda to index the loosely related hinterland cultural groups, including Giriama ancestors, that in the nineteenth century were not yet called by that name. When I do invoke the term Nyika I am alluding to its use by some other group of coastal players.) Meanwhile oral histories have shown that the category "Giriama" was a permeable category in the nineteenth century, incorporating outsiders from other lineages who came from varied circumstances (Spear 1978; Willis and Miers 1997).

Not only was "Giriama" a relatively permeable identity and the category "Mijikenda" a twentieth-century invention, but careful histories of coastal relations have also demonstrated that the interdependence between coastal groups prior to European colonialism often translated into fluidity of group membership. Mijikenda enjoyed incorporation into Swahili life by way of several idioms, including patronage, intermarriage, the forging of putative descent ties, and affiliation with Islam.

To begin to understand the intersection of Swahili and Giriama lives, we need to go back to the tenth century or earlier. The first Arabs apparently arrived on the coast to consolidate trade routes for the commodities of the African interior, including ivory and slaves. Arab caravan routes ranged from north of what is now Mombasa, down through the Zanzibar and Dar es Salaam area, and as far south as Mkindani (Bennett 1968). Arab settlers intermarried with Africans and built towns of various sizes, and over the centuries a loose category known as "Swahili" emerged on the coast, assimilating people of African, Arab, Persian, and Indian origins. In medieval times the term Swahili was fluidly applied, and even those deemed Swahili had important other tribal or clan affiliations, such as Wafamao and Watikuu (Tolmacheva 1991, cited in Eastman 1994). In the nineteenth century Omani and Hadrami Arab immigrants flocked to the coast, resulting in a second major infusion of Arab influence into Swahili culture and politics. Arab power was consolidated in formal structures of Omani sultanate rule, governed alternately by Mazrui and Busaidi lineages, in Mombasa and Zanzibar.[3] In 1887 the Busaidi sultan leased Mombasa to the East Africa Company (which in 1888 became the Imperial British East African Company), and in 1895 the coast became a British protectorate under the nominal authority of the sultan of Zanzibar. According to Willis (1993: 63), governors from the Mazrui and Busaidi lineages left most administration in the hands of Arabs and Swahili living on the coast, reserving for themselves a mediating role. Meanwhile Arab-owned plantations and business ventures enlisted Swahili, Mijikenda from further upcountry, and other African groups, some of them as slaves and, later, as wage laborers. These events, which locate Arabs as governors, extractors of resources, and negotiators with colonial powers, broadly indicate the importance of Arab prestige on the coast, a prestige that has lived on in various forms with implications for ethnic self-identification.

From an early date, acquired markers of Arabness carried unmistakable status in Swahili culture. Constantin (1989) contends that from the tenth century onward, during the formation of Swahili settlements, the material, symbolic, and military resources of Arab immigrants impressed their local hosts. Arabization was "feverishly sought among the subordinate groups, who engaged in various kinds of mythical construction in order to integrate with the power elite" (148). Sometimes this amounted to a kind of ethnic remodeling as Swahili attempted to "become—or be considered as—Arabs" (145). These attempts at integration included taking on the markers of high Islam, claiming access to Arabian forms of magic, and purporting to have Arab blood and ancestry. Conscious of the strategic nature of these alignments, Allen (1993: 118) casts a skeptical eye on many Swahili origin stories, contending that the number of immigrants from Arabia was originally so small that before the eighteenth century or the nineteenth, most Swahili claims to Arab lineage were designed primarily to create a mystique around Swahili business, enabling patricians to bolster their power through such means as withholding magical Islamic items for their exclusive use.

In the nineteenth century, while Swahili attempted to Arabize, many of those in the African group now called the Mijikenda oriented in the direction of Swahili, some holding out their own hopes of assimilation. Several centuries earlier, according to Brantley (1981), relations between the more rural Mijikenda and the Arabs and Swahili in Mombasa had been largely hostile, the former continually threatening to attack the latter. Afro-Arabs in Mombasa began to pay tribute to Mijikenda to curtail this threat, forging an alliance that endured until the advent of European colonialism. During most of the nineteenth century the relationship between Swahili and Mijikenda was one of mutual dependence and relative fluidity (Brantley 1981; Willis 1993). Mijikenda occasionally defended the poorly armed Mazrui from overseas threats coming from Portuguese and new waves of Arab imperialists. When the Mazrui went to war with Busaidi on the island of Pemba in the early nineteenth century they called on Mijikenda as allies (Willis 1993: 61). As agriculturalists with access to more fertile land than the coastline itself, Mijikenda supplied grain to coastal peoples in exchange for tribute and some participation in Mombasa politics (Brantley 1981: 12). Giriama, as one of the largest subgroups of the Mijikenda, played a dominant role in Mombasa's trade routes (Willis 1993: 61), soliciting ivory, cattle, and other goods from inland peoples such as the Waata and Oroma for exchange with urban Swahili and Arabs.

In turn Arab and Swahili patrons living in Mombasa supported up-country migrants with food during famines like the one in 1837, sometimes receiving children or services in exchange. As trade expanded in the nineteenth century, so too did the available credit to Mijikenda. Through patronage and clientage, newly forged kinship relations, dance societies, and other means, wide networks of interdependence between hinterland people and the coastal city of Mombasa were created. This blurring of boundaries resulted in a general braiding of Muslim and Mijikenda customs along the coastline, an interpenetration visible in nineteenth-century coastal rituals (Willis 1993: 61). Migration into Mombasa and other towns by Mijikenda was common; it allowed them to avoid the demands of their homestead elders for redistribution and to become more deeply inserted into patron-client networks that afforded newcomers certain forms of security. For many Mijikenda clients this movement was accompanied by a conversion to Islam and the adoption of other cultural habits (97–98).

From this new vantage point, migrants could "become Swahili," constructing a position from which they too could serve as patrons even as they retained dependent status (Willis 1993: 67). In fact, the very term Swahili, instead of describing a relation of consanguinity, captured an orientation toward the patron-client networks in the town, networks that in turn were based on Arab societies in coastal towns and across the Indian Ocean. In the nineteenth century the category Swahili was "potentially vast and permeable . . . [serving] to obscure rather than define the origins of the heterogeneous populations which could lay claim to it." According to Willis, ethnic terminology in Mombasa was so fluid that many new arrivals in the city "had no general or agreed label for themselves." Some used their Mijikenda names, whereas others borrowed names from their Muslim patrons or referred to themselves as "slave of" or "follower of" so-and-so. In late nineteenth-century Mombasa, "[to] identify oneself as belonging to a clan, a town group, was more important than to claim membership of some larger ethnic group" (75–76).

Further south, on the coast of Tanganyika, nineteenth-century social categories were also fairly fluid. State officials appointed by the Zanzibar sultanate and Swahili notables in local positions of rank vied for power (Glassman 1995: 146), usually by means of attempted assimilation into the Arab world. Swahili Shirazi governors sometimes deemed themselves Waarabu or Arabs,[4] priding themselves on their knowledge of Islam and their civilized qualities (*ustaarabu*), insulating their identity by terming newcomers from the hinterland *wageni* (foreigners or visitors), and pursuing elite Arab-associated activities such as literacy in Arabic and elite or magical forms of Islam. At the same time underlings such as Mijikenda were still able to shift their alliances and partake of some advantages of Swahili identity. Traders and entrepreneurs from disparate backgrounds, such as the famous ruler of Saadani, Bwana Heri, competed for power and clients by appropriating the markers of the Shirazi gentleman, particularly by wearing Arab goods. Meanwhile, some slaves and Mijikenda in other menial positions managed to successfully "shar[e] knowledge of *ustaarabu*," by converting to Islam, marrying into patrician families, and going on to secure or enhance their commercial opportunities within Shirazi communities (117). In Zanzibar beginning in the first decade of the twentieth century, the former slaves who numerically dominated the island began to self-identify as "freeborn coastal Swahili" (Fair 1998: 65). For many, the term Swahili became "a euphemism by which slaves and others of low status could eschew their upcountry origins and identify with the Muslim culture of coastal towns" (Glassman 1995: 25; see also Fair 1998: 66, 75; Glassman 2000; Prins 1967). In fact, by the 1930s on Zanzibar island Swahili came to imply a euphemism for a common individual of slave origins, a pejorative connotation that sometimes still applies today in that area, though the term generally retains higher status connotations elsewhere (see Eastman 1971, 1994).

Slavery (*utumwa*) among Arabs and Swahili is an important theme in this ethnography because Giriama in Malindi frequently invoke the concept as a rhetorical device when discussing their subordination in the past and present. But their use of the term as an index of Swahili brutality toward Giriama cloaks a history of more complex social arrangements. First, most coastal slaves were extracted not from Mijikenda in the neighboring hinterland but from more distant groups, such as Nyasa, Yao, Manyema, and Zaramo (Cooper 1980: 159; Fair 1998: 65), and many Swahili who were not members of the bourgeoisie did not own slaves (A. M. Mazrui and Shariff 1994: 42). Second, among Arabs and Swahili slavery incorporated diverse arrangements that involved varying degrees of autonomy and possibility for the slave. In fact, the Kiswahili term for slave, *mtumwa*, can index any kind of servant or laborer, building ambiguity into the very category, while in some areas the lines between a slave and a client or even a kinsman were blurred (Cooper 1977, 1980; Glassman 1995; Willis 1993; see also Miers and Kopytoff 1977). Although newly imported slaves (*washenzi*) were considered very lowly indeed, all slaves engaged in "drawn-out struggles to assert their humanity" and to shift their status (Glassman 1995: 85). Unhappy slaves frequently resisted their condition through disobedience and flight; flight was particularly common in Malindi (Cooper 1980: 22). Female slaves could gain a degree of upward mobility through concubinage (90), and the possibilities for autonomy varied considerably for others. Some slaves were "able to trade and buy land on a modest scale" (75), and the *wazalia*, slaves born into coastal culture and religion, were sometimes left free to cultivate on their own while paying regular tribute to their masters (Glassman 1995: 86). Slaves on the coast prodded their masters to acknowledge them as members of Swahili communities and to treat them as clients in a patron-client relationship rather than as mere chattel (Cooper 1980; Glassman 1995; Willis 1993). Conversion to Islam in particular allowed a slave to appeal for new treatment as a member of the Islamic brotherhood, sometimes proclaiming his or her new status as a "civilized slave" (*mtumwa mstaarabu*) or even as Arab (Glassman 1995: 92). Ultimately, says Cooper (1980: 22), slave owners "had little choice but to allow some [slaves] to rise" in stature, particularly those who learned Islamic customs.[5]

This is hardly to minimize the forms of hierarchy and oppression under which some Mijikenda suffered. Rather, I suggest that the intricacies of history have a way of being erased as history is retold in the present (Cohen 1994). Among other things, recurrent Giriama claims that they have been slaves to Swahili and Arabs (past and present) obscure the complex demography and definition of slavery, as well as the fact that nineteenth-century Giriama themselves incorporated marginal newcomers into their families through an idiom of kinship in which subordinates became a "child of the house," sometimes with few freedoms (Willis and Miers 1997).[6] Such claims also reify ethnic difference between Giriama and Swahili, glossing over the fact that for many slaves, becoming Swahili or even becoming Arab was one route to upward mobility. Apparently ethnicity then did not mean precisely what it does today on the Kenya coast.

The Colonial Era: Shoring Up Ethnic Lines

The British incursion into East Africa profoundly affected this ethnic fluidity by establishing new structural antagonisms that "crystallize[d] people into rigidly defined ethnic groups, economic roles, and social classes" (Brantley 1981: 64; see also A. M. Mazrui and Shariff 1994). The fundamental force behind this shift was the colonial desire to control labor after slavery ended. Although there were strong antislavery ideologies circulating through the metropole and to some extent in the colony as well, many British representatives of the Imperial British East African Company and the protectorate were opponents of abolition, fearing that it might cause economic chaos, jeopardize their alliance with the Arab landowning class, and enable Muslim landowners to mobilize the workers themselves through ties of clientship and debt (Cooper 1980: 178–82). After abolition was decreed by officials in the metropole in 1907, the British on the coast made a sustained effort to mobilize and control the African labor force to produce surplus for the colonial economy. In the nineteenth century and early twentieth, new European-owned plantations had sprung up on the coast around Mombasa, and with the decline of slavery there was a large demand for contracted labor from the hinterland on the plantations and the Mombasa docks (Brantley 1981; Cooper 1980). Europeans envisioned the transformation of Arab and Swahili slave owners into capitalist farmers, and slaves and other Africans into an agricultural proletariat (Cooper 1980, 1992).

But social networks on the coast, including the mobility of former slaves and Mijikenda, made such a transformation unlikely. Following abolition many Mijikenda took up long-term residence on lands owned by Arabs, Swahili, and Asians, growing their own crops and providing occasional harvests in exchange for squatting privileges. Squatters could also earn cash by harvesting coconuts and growing food for the Mombasa market (Cooper 1980; Willis 1993: 87) or by trading palm wine in the hinterland. With these living arrangements, squatters did not need to contract themselves out as regular workers. Now and then Mijikenda and former slaves appeared as casual laborers, working one day and disappearing the next.[7] Meanwhile Mijikenda migrants continued their influx into Mombasa and other towns, motivated by a desire for more clothing and food, the search for bridewealth, the wish to be free of homestead demands, and, for some women, a desire to "renegotiate the terms of their participation in the domestic economy [in part through Islamization] and so do less work" (Willis 1993: 169). Their ready incorporation into the category Swahili made individuals hard to identify, confounding colonial systems of control such as tax and labor laws. This permeability was especially vexing for administrators who wanted pure Africans with a rural, "tribal mentality" who might easily be relegated en masse to a native reserve (Allen 1993: 4).

Labor thus became a matter of intense concern for British administrators, who initially targeted freed slaves for disapproval, but soon set their sights on the Mijikenda (Willis 1993: 81). The fact that Mijikenda would work for Arabs and Swahili but refused to be disciplined in colonial terms prompted the colonial state to intervene. To facilitate their agenda, colonials took steps to solidify the categories of Swahili, Arabs, and Mijikenda (then, Nyika) and to seal them off from each other. In breaking up the preexisting social networks of incorporative patronage and "atomizing" economic roles along ethnic lines, the state hoped to facilitate the kind of class formation colonials envisioned (Cooper 1980: 158). As Cooper demonstrates, coastal dynamics ultimately took a far more complex turn, for the state's economic and social categories were often ambiguously defined, allowing considerable room for manipulation by coastal players. In the end the state never succeeded in establishing the rigid landowner-worker class dynamic it had hoped for. But its efforts along the way did a great deal to heighten the salience of ethnic identity, to intensify the hierarchy between Swahili and Mijikenda, and to consolidate the notion that everyone falls into one category or another.

In 1910, for example, the administration passed an ordinance that divided the population into landowners and nonlandowners. Nominally designed to protect hinterland people from fraud, the ordinance in fact barred Mijikenda (Nyika) from claiming Swahili identity, allowed Arabs and Swahili to sell land, and prohibited Mijikenda from claiming or selling land (Willis 1993: 125–27). Another 1910 decree, the Hut and Poll Tax Ordinance, identified Swahili as "natives" and subjected them to a battery of colonial tax and labor laws, while exempting supposedly nonnative Arabs. Because status was defined by descent, many Swahili scrambled to establish Arab ancestry and to align themselves as closely as possible with Arab communities to achieve nonnative status. Often property owners won the nonnative status they sought, more by virtue of wealth than descent (Constantin 1989; Willis 1993).

Swahili also sought to redefine Swahili identity to more clearly signal entitlement to advantages granted by the colonial administration. According to Swartz (1991), many men from the Twelve Tribes—divisions internal to Mombasa Swahili—joined the coastal Arab Association in the early 1920s.[8] Within the Twelve Tribes, Arabicized clan names were increasingly used to separate the Swahili into entitled upper-class and lower-class hangers-on. Meanwhile some of the Twelve Tribe leaders attempted to strengthen the boundary around the Twelve Tribes category to exclude Nyika, former slaves, and recent immigrants. Concerns about ethnic categorization were reflected in coastal census results and indicated a pervasive pattern of attempted upward mobility. Ironically, while coastal residents jockeyed to place themselves in the most advantageous category they could, it was during this era that categories of identity were increasingly treated as discovered rather than invented, as intrinsic qualities with strict consequences for a person's rights and entitlements.[9]

In summary, to speak of the Mijikenda and the Swahili as discrete groups before 1920 does not take into account the fluidity of coastal society prior to that time. By 1920, however, the groups were increasingly defined in terms of "separate area[s] of residence and separate rights" (Willis 1993: 173). By the 1920s those from the hinterland who found work in Mombasa did so firmly as Nyika, while Swahili had reason to draw a boundary between their ethnicity and that of Mijikenda, sometimes by emphasizing their supposed Arab roots. Individuals strategically shifted their own ethnic classification when they could, but such practices further pointed up the importance of ethnicity as a badge of identity. Colonial policies also foregrounded the notion that essential qualities such as blood, birthright, and autochthony attach to ethnic categories. And as ethnic categories were defined and redrawn, economic and social policies progressively disenfranchised the Mijikenda, setting a precedent for decades of disadvantage. The history of ethnic interpenetration on the coast lives on in residual form, but today the possibility of Giriama mobility into Swahili ranks is contested and regarded by many Giriama in Malindi as a fantasy.

Postindependence Politics:
Tribal Tensions and Ethnoterritorialism

Kenya gained independence in 1963, but it did not suture the sharp ethnic divisions carved so deeply by its colonial officials. The colonial administration encouraged the formation of political districts along ethnic lines, and since then national as well as local politics have underscored the kinds of ethnically based classification that colonial policies encouraged. Each of the eight national elections since 1963 has been informed by ethnically oriented electoral practices, a tendency that has been unofficially institutionalized by politicians who persistently appeal for ethnic support (Adar 1998: 71). The explosive ethnic conflict ensuing from the December 2007 national elections, concentrated primarily (but by no means exclusively) among Kikuyu and Luo and framed from the outset by politicians themselves in terms of ethnic favoritism and ethnic cleansing, attests to the power of this legacy.

It is by now a given in Kenya that different ethnic groups, referred to in common parlance as "tribes," see themselves as having different interests. The original constitution of 1962–1963 allowed for a regional federalism (*majimbo*ism) that encouraged a number of ethnically based secessionist movements, including the Mwambao United Front (*mwambao*, Kisw., means "autonomy") formed by coastal Arabs and Swahili. Coastal Muslims pinned their hopes on Mwambao as a means of protecting the interests of Swahili-speaking peoples while facilitating political unification between the Kenyan coastal strip with the Swahili- and Arab-dominated Zanzibar to the south. A central concern of coastal groups was the economic domination of upcountry ethnic groups; the hope (on the coast, as elsewhere) was that ethnically based land claims and loyalty to ethnically aligned political parties could help protect their interests. This brief moment of federalist experimentation was brought to a halt in

1964, when the influential leader Tom Mboya persuaded leaders that a strong single-party state would provide greater stability.[10] But after 1991, when Kenya shifted to a multiparty state, Kenyan politicians and voters colluded to score political choices along ethnic lines. In the 1997 presidential elections Daniel arap Moi (a Kalenjin), Mwai Kibaki (a Kikuyu), and Raila Odinga (a Luo) each swept their ethnically dominated provinces, the Rift Valley, Central, and Nyanza, respectively, while the disastrous 2007 elections also pit Kibaki's and Odinga's supporters against each other largely along ethnic lines. By now Kenyan politicians and laypeople alike see "tribal thinking" as an inevitable ingredient of multipartyism. Although politicians do much to encourage the translation of political interests into ethnic terms, some political commentators, such as Peter Okondo (1995), regard the situation as natural and inevitable, contending that Kenyans have an intrinsic allegiance to their tribes and feel at home in autonomous ethnic states. Such rhetoric sometimes factors into ethnic essentialisms on the coast.

Yet tribalism is typically merely a cloak for political machination, and nominally ethnic conflicts in Kenya have been no exception. President Moi's political party, the Kenya African National Union (KANU), in an effort to assure the Rift Valley's allegiance to the Kalenjin president, sponsored a *majimbo*ist agenda of ethnic cleansing against non-Kalenjins in that province as multipartyism loomed in 1991 (Human Rights Watch 2002). As the elections of 2007 approached, President Kibaki was widely accused of Kikuyu ethnic cronyism. The Luo presidential candidate Raila Odinga claimed that Kikuyus were at the root of poverty in Kenya and embraced a segregationist, *majimbo*ist stance that fomented ethnic clashes in Molo, Sondu, and elsewhere. Such preconditions set the stage for the horrific violence that followed the election.

Most relevant to Mijikenda and Swahili were the clashes a decade earlier (between August and November 1997), when the incumbent political party KANU apparently sponsored a wave of violence based largely in the Likoni area just south of Mombasa that pit gangs of Mijikenda— including some Giriama and many Digo, a Muslimized Mijikenda group —against civilians who appeared to be of upcountry origin. According to A. M. Mazrui (1998), KANU had several motives for fomenting these clashes, most of them rising from its attempts to shift coastal demographics to secure an advantage in the upcoming national elections.[11]

The political leaders who encouraged the conflict did not have to work hard; Mijikenda and Swahili alike had long nurtured resentment toward upcountry business owners who leached profits away from coastal peoples. At the time of the violence, approximately 80 percent of small- and large-scale businesses in Kwale district (south of Mombasa) were owned by nonlocals, including upcountry people, Asians, and Europeans.[12] Money from the tourism industry is rarely reinvested into coastal areas, and much local administrative control in that area is in the hands of upcountry people, creating a widespread feeling that "the Coastal people have not been treated fairly when they have applied for business licenses, for jobs, or in the provision of educational and health facilities" (A. M. Mazrui 1997: 13). Meanwhile coastal peoples' efforts to recoup political ground have been continually thwarted.[13] Muslims in districts south of Mombasa have complained about their lack of representation on the Electoral Commission, which they have deemed "a clear reflection of domination by a 'Christian fraternity'" (12).

Such disappointments culminated in violence and in a more general, loosely organized underground *majimbo* movement for ethnoterritorial control that exacerbated tensions between Giriama and Swahili in the Malindi area. The main impetus for this movement was, initially anyway, for coastal peoples to mobilize against the economic incursions of upcountry folk. According to A. M. Mazrui (1998: 25), by the end of July 1997 word spread among Mijikenda as far south as Lunga-Lunga (just north of the Tanzanian border) and as far north as Vipingo (about midway between Mombasa and Kilifi) that "oaths were being administered for a coastal *majimbo* cause." Indeed, word may have spread still farther north than this; some of my interlocutors told me that oaths were administered in secret areas between Kilifi and Malindi. Swahili diviner healers from Tanzania apparently administered some oaths to Swahili and Mijikenda Muslims, while other oathing rituals were arranged by non-Muslim Mijikenda leaders such as Samson, mentioned at the beginning of this chapter. All of those enlisted vowed their allegiance to a *majimbo*ist approach to coastal resources.

But while everyone on the coast talks about *majimbo*ism, no one is quite sure what it means; articulations of *majimbo* thus have a way of saying a great deal about the particular concerns of the speaker.[14] The oathings and clashes of the late 1990s pointed to ethnically framed conflicts between coastal and upcountry peoples, yet other cross-cutting grudges came to the surface at this time. A. M. Mazrui himself (1997) observed what he terms "Digo *sub-majimboism*"; Muslim Digo attackers appeared to make decisions about whom to kill and whom to spare along religious as well as ethnic lines. Some Digo apparently attacked non-Muslim Giriama during the clashes, and authorities found that some of the raiders' shirts were inscribed with an Arabic excerpt from the *shahada* (the Islamic creed, which must be recited daily) "There is no God but Allah" (30). But neither scholars nor the national media reported the incidents in Malindi in which some Giriama, particularly young men, unleashed their anger against Arabs and Swahili. For just as coastal Muslims feel disenfranchised and threatened by the Christian-dominated state and by upcountry individuals who hold economic and political power on the coast, so too do many Giriama in Malindi feel that Swahili and Arabs have dispossessed them of what is rightfully theirs. Thus while some Swahili champion a version of *majimbo* that harks back to the sultanate, many Giriama versions are freighted with fantasies of retribution against Swahili and Arabs who have encroached on land they say belongs essentially to Mijikenda.

Many Giriama clearly told me that in their vision of *majimbo*, Swahili and Arabs (the terms are sometimes used interchangeably in Giriama parlance, as if to point out Swahili alignment with the Arab world while marking them as interlopers) will have to relinquish territory that ought to belong to a Mijikenda state. As one man put it, "If *majimbo* comes the Giriama should fight for justice in the matter of land first. So the Arabs will be forced to leave the land, if not the country. . . . God created every tribe and put them in a place that suits them." Other Giriama told me that 75 percent of jobs currently in the hands of other ethnic groups would have to be given to Mijikenda, while upcountry tribes and Arabs would be required to relinquish their lands, remaining in residence only through leases, heavy taxes, or an agreement that they would leave within some number of years. Both Giriama and Swahili informants in Malindi told me that in the fall of 1997 threatening letters were pushed under the doors of certain Swahili families, commanding them to "go back to Arabia." The imminent threat of violence has faded, but the sentiments endure. In 2004 I overheard a conversation among several young Giriama men in Muyeye, the impoverished Giriama area bordering on

Malindi town, in which one complained to his friends that his mother had sold a bad coconut to a Swahili and the Swahili had returned the next day to insult her, calling her a "dog." The speaker's anger became an ethnically based rant: "If I had been there this guy would have regretted the day he was born. The Swahili have insulted our women for a long time now." His friend chimed in, "The police would have to separate us if I'd been there. We can't be mocked by these people." A third added, "This is why we're calling for *majimbo*—they have to leave and go back to their grandfathers in the Persian Gulf." The group laughed at this point, perhaps acknowledging the improbability of such a scenario, perhaps taking pleasure in this fantasy of retribution.

Contemporary Giriama resentment toward Swahili and Arab landowners in Malindi, and the heated wish by some Giriama to expunge them from the land, has its roots in a century's worth of disenfranchisement. Giriama economic success in trading crops at the end of the nineteenth century and in the early twentieth century was largely contingent upon rights to land, and these have been in question since the European colonial era. The 1910 colonial ordinance ensured that only "subjects of the Sultan," Arabs and Swahili, were allowed to register land as private property. Thus dispossessed along the coastal strip, Giriama in some areas were further destabilized by various resettlement schemes and restrictive legislation. The success of Mijikenda as cultivators was considered one key to their reluctance to work on British terms (Brantley 1981), so in 1913–1914 masses of Giriama were expelled from the fertile lands north of the Sabaki River, where they had been growing crops. The act precipitated a Giriama uprising that was violently contained by the British. Meanwhile colonial administrators controlled the palm wine and maize trades in ways that proved disastrous to Mijikenda's ability to access cash (Willis 1993). Such regulations, in combination with taxation and compulsory labor on public works, lowered the fortunes of thousands of Giriama (S. G. Thompson 1990).[15] With most Giriama in the Malindi area now squatting on land owned by Arabs, Swahili, or others, the single most raw political issue today between Giriama and Swahili is the charge that these groups have grabbed land out from under Giriama living on the coastal strip, a phenomenon I discuss in greater detail in chapter 2.

Their wariness of Swahili and Arab privilege makes many Giriama anxious about the possibility of a return to Muslim rule. In recent years

Giriama have been alarmed by reports that at least some Swahili and Arab proponents of *majimbo*ism nurture hopes for the creation of an Islamic state in which sharia laws would prevail. In recent years many Giriama have regarded the Shirikisho Party as their greatest hope for a version of *majimbo* that would prioritize their needs. Shirikisho Party meetings often feature prominent Giriama politicians who decry their neglect by the ruling politicians and expand on the urgent needs of coastal people, especially Mijikenda. At some of these rallies antagonism toward Swahili and Arabs has come to the fore. In a 2002 rally leading up to the December elections, one Malindi-based Giriama man proclaimed that although some Mijikenda had once pinned their *majimbo*ist hopes on the Swahili-dominated Islamic Party of Kenya (IPK, denied party registration in 1992 on grounds that it violated the "secular principle" of Kenya's constitution), the era of joining forces with Swahili seemed to be over:

> My people, our friends the Swahili are not with us. . . . Most of you joined the IPK not because you're Muslim but because you're coastal. Our youth were killed during innumerable riots organized by that party, and many were jailed in the name of IPK. We were willing to fight hand in hand with our fellow Swahili. Eventually that party was burned because it was working under religious grounds, which was said to be illegal. Now that it's time for them [Swahili] to join hands with us, they have turned and befriended KANU [the ruling party in 2002]. This shows how unfriendly they are. Now we know we need to fight alone to have this freedom, but let me tell them this: once we win, we won't count them as part of us![16]

How paradoxical, but telling, are these opening words: "Our friends the Swahili are not with us." The mixed legacy of interdependence and perceived betrayal is palpable; clearly some kind of former alliance has been ruptured. This speech was discussed for days afterward, as many Giriama vowed to vote for the Shirikisho Party and expressed dismay and anger that they did not have Swahili voters on their side. Said one Giriama man, "The Swahili aren't with us, but after the voting they'll pretend to be with us. We know that the day is coming when they will bow at our feet."[17]

The suffering and dispossession of Giriama have generated myths and narratives that suggest explanations for their current predicament, provide a modicum of hope for the future, and consolidate the notion of an autochthonous, essential, and distinct Giriama ethnicity. The origin story I relate at the beginning of this chapter explains Giriama's miserable lot. Yet there is another class of origin story involving spatiality, both real and imagined, that aspires to recoup what is seen as Giriama's (and other Mijikenda's) authentic identity. Some Mijikenda origin stories of the early twentieth century looked to the northern area called Shungwaya as their locus of geographic origin (see Spear 1979). Willis (1993: 30) contends that Mijikenda in the Mombasa area adopted the story to justify and explain their relationship and "coincidence of interest" with Swahili who claimed that region as the site of their own mythic origin. But just as the idea of Shungwaya origins caught on among Mijikenda, Swahili apparently dropped it to isolate themselves from these socially inferior people (190). By the mid-twentieth century political and economic exigencies had shifted for Giriama in many areas, influencing their own accounts of their roots. In the rural area of Kaloleni (southwest of Malindi) in the 1960s, Parkin (1991a: 38) rarely heard the Shungwaya narrative; instead, he repeatedly encountered "the Kaya concept" as the spatial locus of Giriama origins. The Kaya and Shungwaya narratives need not be mutually exclusive; Spear's oral histories depict Shungwaya as a place of distant origins and the Kaya as a locus of more recent origins. But as Parkin notes, the question of where emphasis falls seems crucial. In the narratives Parkin elicited the Kaya figured far more prominently as a social and psychological locus of Giriama authenticity, and while the Shungwaya narrative aligned Giriama with Swahili, the Kaya narrative presumes an essentially different core identity.

Kaya were fortified forest villages inland of the towns on the Kenya coastline, and some Mijikenda claim that they housed all the members of the Mijikenda groups, each group with its own Kaya, until overpopulation led to their abandonment in the nineteenth century. According to popular narratives the Kaya social system was highly structured, run by committees of male and female elders who enforced the traditional courts, ritualized social structure, medicinal practice, and political decisions. Kaya life, as it is idealized in collective Giriama memory, was also characterized by reverence toward the ancestors (*koma*) and the creator Mulungu. Parkin (1991a) contends that to Giriama today the Kaya symbolize an authentic Giriama essence that is nostalgically regarded even by those who have been corrupted, in the eyes of some, by modern and worldly town ways, including exposure to Islam.[18] A. M. Mazrui (1997: ii) agrees: "[Kaya have come] to assume a sacred function and [become] symbolic of Mijikenda culture, history, and identity." This connection is so intense that some of the oaths for the ethnically framed 1997 clashes were administered in one of the Kayas (Kaya Bombo).

But agitation over land rights has generated a third and more diffuse origin concept, one widely available among Giriama in Malindi. This additional origin claim probably stems from the practicalities of access to land, for the nationally protected Kaya areas now house only a handful of elders, and while dispossessed Giriama can invoke the symbolic importance of these sites they cannot settle in them en masse.[19] Hence Giriama repeatedly told me that they have occupied "since time immemorial" the same coastal lands on which they now live, including urban areas founded over a millennium ago and dominated by Arabo-African architecture. The implication is that Giriama (and other Mijikenda) are the proper owners of coastal lands by virtue of precedent and, in some of these stories, God's will. God is said to have intended the coastal land for Mijikenda, and upcountry land for Luo, Luyah, and Kikuyu. Whites should go "back to Europe" and Asians to Asia, while Swahili, aligned rhetorically and geographically with Arabs, belong properly in Arabia.

This essential linkage between land and ethnicity is dramatically played out in an oath that Samson, the elder warlord mentioned at the beginning of this chapter, administered to Mijikenda youth intending to join the *majimbo* rebellion in 1997. A self-professed Christian, Samson had much to say about land grievances, and his oath, as he narrated it to me, encapsulated his ideology:

> We say this and it is eating our heads. These are the principles of war. God created people. After that he divided them by different languages. After each group had been divided by language, each was given a place to live. The Indians were given the language of Kihindi and placed in India. God ordered them to stay there. Arabs were given the language of Arabic and placed in Arabia. God ordered them to stay there. The Kikuyu were given their language and placed in Kikuyu land. God ordered them to stay there. . . . If they oppress us,

I can't go to India, or Arabia, or Kikuyu land to build a house or a farm, or I will be killed. It is better that we all die so that they take empty land.

Samson's oath underscores Giriama grievances not only toward upcountry peoples and Asians, but also toward Arabs. It is also a culmination of colonial and postcolonial political rhetoric, for like others on the coast Samson has adopted the essentialist notion that ethnic groups are natural, absolute categories with intrinsic entitlements. Indeed, the reasoning in his oath is redolent of the European ideology described by Irvine and Gal, in which European linguists and ethnographers "discovered" language boundaries and relationships in non-Western areas and assumed that languages "[identified] populations and territories that could be suitably treated as political unities" (2000: 50; see also McIntosh 2005b).

In the thick of these currents of divisiveness, where do everyday relationships between Swahili and Giriama now stand in Malindi? Giriama and Swahili encounter one another frequently; many Giriama work as wage laborers in Swahili households and shops, and whenever Giriama living on the outskirts venture into town to sell surplus vegetables at the market, to offer rides on their bicycle taxis, to use the post office, to go to work at a hotel, or to make special purchases they and Swahili routinely cross paths. While Giriama often refer to Swahili as Arabs, it is also not uncommon for them to use the term *Adzomba*, meaning "uncles" (literally, "mother's brothers"), an appellation that picks out the history of intermarriage between the groups and Giriama dependency on Swahili. To be sure, cordial interactions between Swahili and Giriama are common enough (though so too are less amenable interactions). I also found many Swahili I spoke to at pains to downplay tensions between themselves and Giriama, expressing a kind of paternalistic affection for their neighbors. One Swahili leader of a Muslim youth organization informed me, "We're more comfortable with the Mijikenda than we are with the upcountry people. These days we [Swahili and Giriama] are as one. Especially if they're Muslim; they're like our brothers [*kama ndugu*]."

But from the point of view of some Swahili and nearly all Giriama I spoke to, the divisions between the groups are undeniable. The structural differences, in fact, supersede even the good intentions of individuals. One of my Giriama research assistants, Maxwell, became friendly with one of my Swahili assistants, Ali, sustaining their friendly conversations even after I departed. "We tried to keep reaching across that wall," said Maxwell. But when Maxwell found out that Ali had gotten married without informing him, he said to me, "Come on, a Swahili in these parts can't just invite a Giriama to his wedding. It would be shameful. He would never invite me there."[20] One Swahili man told me of being taken aback when, after he attempted to engage a Giriama woman in conversation about the goods in a shop, she retorted, "Why are you talking to me? I'm not of your kind." The few Swahili families living in the impoverished Giriama-dominated areas flanking Malindi town sometimes express discomfort inflected by class anxieties; as one put it, "I don't feel secure here. The Giriama might do anything to get money. They're dirty and unmannered, they don't use toilets, they eat dirty food, they worship evil spirits, and they don't have good language . . . and they can steal. These are really poor people."

In subsequent chapters the anxieties among both Swahili and Giriama about their relationship will come into greater focus, anxieties that I argue underpin some of the most intriguing aspects of contemporary Giriama religiosity in Malindi. To fully understand these, however, it is important first to explain more about the contemporary valences of the categories Swahili and Giriama in Malindi. For if Giriama's past relationships with Swahili offered the hope of assimilation and upward mobility, today both Swahili and Giriama give ambiguous answers to the question of whether Giriama can become Swahili, with the majority of Giriama feeling barred from Swahili identity. This ambiguity is the legacy of the contradictory historical processes I have described in this chapter, and it lies at the heart of the Giriama ritual and speech practices I analyze in subsequent chapters. I turn now to the ways these contradictions are played out in contemporary discourse.

Blood Kinship and Bush Swahili: Swahili Identities in Malindi Today

We have already seen that the designation "Swahili" has historically been defined and redefined by political, economic, and social contingencies. Such variation and flux remain in the postcolonial era. Tensions between Arabness and Africanness in Swahili identity endure, and identities within Swahili communities are hierarchical and heterogeneous.[21]

The appellation Swahili also retains some permeability; Parkin (1989) has shown that in recent decades Mijikenda Digo hoping for upward mobility sometimes deem themselves members of that group. The socially constructed nature of ethnicity is further evident in the fact that the very designation Swahili is often relative to both speaker and spoken-about. Giriama living deep in the hinterland sometimes consider anyone who has converted or been otherwise influenced by Islam to be Swahili, yet many Giriama living on the fringes of Malindi town next to the core Swahili communities would consider this appellation far-fetched.

Despite the lack of coherence or homogeneity to the category Swahili, those Swahili living in urban centers such as Malindi are increasingly motivated to draw distinctions between insiders and outsiders. This group with a once glorious economic and political past now see themselves as ruled in ignominy by Westernized Christians from upcountry. As Swahili feel increasingly disenfranchised by the postindependence state, many look to their kin and contacts in the Middle East for economic support, religious validation, and an anchor for a separatist identity. A. M. Mazrui and Shariff (1994: 147) note, "The more dispossessed the Swahili become . . . the more nationalist they become about [their] identity and the more radical their response." According to Eastman (1994: 85), "In opposition to the state, people (perhaps for the first time) are now seeing themselves as belonging to a Swahili ethnic group. . . . [The term Swahili] is increasingly being used for self-identification purposes by people who previously would have referred to themselves as 'of a place' or 'of a clan.'"

Shared cultural practices and distinctively local versions of Kiswahili are vital to this self-conscious sense of identity; so too are myths about origins, what Eastman (1994: 94) identifies as "the convenient fiction that in-group members of Swahili society have Arab and freeborn roots." And if urban Swahili define themselves in contrast to the groups they least wish to resemble, in Malindi a primary foil is the "pagan" and "uneducated" Giriama who exist geographically and socially at the edge of Swahili life, looking longingly at the advantages they lack. The Swahili emphasis on insiders versus outsiders has clear implications for the residue of ethnic fluidity in Malindi. Today Mijikenda and, sometimes, members of other ethnic groups do occasionally marry Swahili or convert to Islam and call themselves Swahili, yet these newcomers often find themselves in a vulnerable position.

Swahili sometimes describe Mijikenda and others who live among them as interlopers who are merely trying to "pass."[22] Take, for instance, the pious Muslim Hassan, who lives a fairly impoverished existence on the edge of Malindi town but walks every day in his clean white *kanzu* robe and *kofia* cap to pray at a mosque in the Swahili-dominated area of Shella. Hassan and I met through a mutual Swahili friend, and he eagerly chatted with me about patterns of worship in the mosque. The next day I brought Hassan's name up with Mohammed, a local Swahili patriarch. Mohammed seemed uncomfortable: "You know, that man may have told you he is Swahili but in fact he is Pokomo. He moved here twenty years ago from Pokomo land and converted to Islam. But he's not Swahili." In an incident in the ethnically mixed division of Maweni, I heard a Swahili woman heatedly accuse another woman, "You act Swahili, but you're a Kuke [a slur for Kikuyu]!" The accused woman denied this sting vociferously, but those overhearing muttered about the truth of the claim. The pressure to have an authentic and primordial Swahili identity has clearly been absorbed by some members of society; one woman with a Swahili father and a Kalenjin mother confessed to me rather sadly, "I don't know what to call myself, because I'm not 'pure' anything." Although she had been fathered by a Swahili man and married another, spoke only Kiswahili, and followed cultural habits resembling that of many Swahili, she remained anxious that a Kalenjin maternal line might bar her from full category membership.

But it was about Giriama-Swahili relations that I had the vast majority of my conversations, conversations that exposed competing perceptions of the fixity and fluidity of Swahili identity. I spoke to many dozens of Giriama and self-professed Swahili (the latter living in the core of town) about whether or not a Giriama individual can become Swahili, something that was once clearly possible in the course of a single life span.[23] While such discussions were sometimes initiated by me rather than spontaneous, and though I do not assume that speakers' opinions are wholly consistent from one context to the next, their responses nevertheless demonstrate the circulation of powerful assumptions about ethnicity, assumptions that sometimes operate in tacit, hegemonic fashion to enforce a distance between the groups. Indeed, in these conversations I encountered a powerful but not unanimous current of ethnic essentialism running through both communities. At the same time I also found that multiple criteria for ethnicity are at play among both Swahili and Giriama, including birth and blood, patrilineality (an idea with precedent in both Arab and African cultures), religion, language, and even class. These cross-cutting discourses almost felt like a palimpsest of different historical emphases of various elements of ethnicity. It is impossible to trace precisely where or when each of these emphases originated, yet each theme has its own social life and is not infrequently pulled in to reinforce the others (and, occasionally, to compete with them).

As for Swahili responses to the question of whether Giriama can assimilate in the course of one generation, I found opinion divided approximately in half. Regardless of their responses, most Swahili acknowledge the history of Arab-Mijikenda intermarriage that was foundational to their community and agree that this occasionally still takes place. Some refer to this history in support of their contention that Swahili identity remains permeable. In one conversation with a Swahili educator in which I mentioned some of the Giriama resentment I was encountering, he said, "Some Giriama have had bad experiences with their neighbors, but we can't deny history, and the fact is that in every Swahili family there are Giriama intermarried somewhere in their past. In fact we remain a big melting pot on the coast." His friend agreed. In response to my claim that some Giriama feel barred from assimilation, he groused in an English idiom, "The problem is that you're talking to every Tom, Dick, and Harry. The more sophisticated Giriama know that there's no real problem between us. They are welcome in our community if they are willing to change. Conversion to Islam is the first step." Other Swahili also described their group identity as permeable enough to embrace Giriama comers. "Swahili isn't a tribe at all," said Zeinab, a fortysomething woman who lives in the Swahili-dominated division of Barani. "It's a religion and a language. So if a Giriama converts to Islam and speaks Kiswahili, they can be counted as Swahili." Hamisi, a thirty-year-old Swahili living in Shella, said, "Religion is what makes a Swahili a Swahili. Giriama can become Swahili by coming and joining the religion."

Yet in numerous other conversations with Swahili living in Shella and Barani about their identity, I also encountered powerful currents of discomfort and denial at the prospect of Giriama assimilation. These expressions ranged from general prejudice against Giriama to essentialist claims about ethnic identity. In fact, approximately half of Swahili I spoke to contended that Giriama simply cannot become Swahili, either through conversion or marriage. Concepts of blood and birthright figured prominently in many of these arguments. A young mother named Amina, for instance, argued, "Giriama can't become Swahili because Swahili are the offspring of an Arab male and an African female. So a Giriama can't become Swahili any more than a Swahili can become Giriama." Said Muhammed, a wealthy restaurant owner, "Swahili have Arab blood. Giriama don't. They can't be one of us." Said, a Swahili living in Muyeye and married to a Giriama woman, insisted that even his wife can't become Swahili: "Swahili identity is about blood; the nature of a person comes from their blood kinship [*urithi wa kuzaliwa*]." Some of these informants contended that the *offspring* of a Swahili father and a Mijikenda mother could indeed be deemed Swahili because such individuals would have Swahili blood and, by implication, Arab ancestry. This admission picks out the essentialism that underwrites such models of ethnic identity.

Other Swahili contended that Swahili identity revolves around such seemingly pliable or intangible characteristics as culture, religion, language, or character (*tabia*). Yet as the conversation progressed it sometimes became evident that the definitions would shift to exclude Giriama aspirants from Swahili category membership. When I asked Aziz, a young store clerk, what makes the Swahili who they are, he replied, "Culture—my greetings, my praying, my games, and even my eating habits—all of these make me a Swahili." Asked what makes a Giriama a Giriama, Aziz said again, "Culture." I asked, "Can a Giriama practice Swahili culture and become a Swahili?" Aziz looked vexed and replied, "They can practice the culture, but [they] won't become a Swahili." Fareed, the owner of a small shoe store, explained, "A Swahili is [defined by] language [Mswahili ni lugha]," but when I asked whether Giriama can become Swahili, he said, "No. They don't speak Kiswahili." I countered, "What if they decide to speak only Kiswahili?" Fareed contemplated this. "It's a matter of parentage. You get your tribe from your father." Occasionally I encountered more idiosyncratic and prejudicial claims about Swahili identity, such as the restaurant owner Ibrahim's class-based definition of ethnicity: "Giriama aren't as intelligent as Swahili. That's why you'll see most of the Giriama are beggars and Swahili are not. Swahili can't beg; they have money. Sometimes Giriama try to become Swahili, mainly by getting money, but they aren't real Swahili."

Fareed's claim that language is an important component of Swahili identity was echoed by others I spoke to. On the face of it, an emphasis on language as an ethnic criterion might seem to make the category Swahili particularly permeable, for Kiswahili is spoken as a lingua franca by most coastal residents, including Giriama (despite Fareed's initial erasure of this fact). Yet Kiswahili as a marker of ethnic identity is not as democratic as it may seem, for Swahili sometimes find ways to preserve it as an exclusive kind of patrimony, often through intricate distinctions that indicate mastery of the language (A. M. Mazrui and Shariff 1994: 77). One Swahili friend confided that "the problem with Giriama" is that "despite the fact that Swahili people understand Kigiriama, Giriama people just don't know Kiswahili." At the time this statement baffled me, since in my experience few Swahili speak or understand Kigirama well, yet many Giriama in and near Malindi speak Kiswahili on a daily basis. But this man's claim probably emerged from an ideological investment in the idea that, as Mazrui and Shariff put it, "a person does not become Swahili merely by speaking just any variety of the language. To qualify for Swahili identity one has to acquire, as a first language, an in-group variety of the language" (77; see also Eastman 1994).

Many Kiswahili dialects mark speakers as hailing from one or another region of the Swahili coast: Kibajuni from the north, Kipemba and Kiamu from Pemba and Lamu, Kimvita from Mombasa, Kiunguja from Zanzibar, and so forth. Those who learn Kiswahili in school or through multiethnic contact on the Malindi streets, like many Giriama, are unlikely to pick up a regional Swahili dialect, mode of pronunciation, or conversational idiom. Furthermore some Swahili deride what they consider the sloppy and crude versions of Kiswahili spoken by other folk and pride themselves on the precision with which they use a standard version of grammar, mastering, for example, archaic or complex idioms and the many Kiswahili noun classes with their associated prefixes and infixes (though it should be said that plenty of native Kiswahili speakers also speak in nonstandard grammatical forms).

Some also locate the essence of Kiswahili in a register of obscure speech known as Kiswahili *ndani* (literally, "inner or internal Swahili"), treated by many as a repository of Swahili traditions and values. Considered unintelligible to outsiders (Russell 1981), Kiswahili *ndani* includes aphorisms (*jina* or *methali*), slang terms, archaisms, obscure metaphors, and riddles (*mafumbo*). In at least some Swahili communities since the nineteenth century command of Kiswahili *ndani* has been an important factor in constructing an Mswahili *sana* (literally, "a very Swahili Swahili"): a cultural sophisticate and expert in local language and culture (Pouwels, 1987: 73). Such ideologies help to reinforce a boundary around the Swahili community since these elite registers are largely unmastered by Giriama at the margins of Swahili culture.

The prejudices against would-be Giriama assimilates are evident in the sobriquets Swahili have invented for them. In one Swahili household in Shella I sat with the women on a cement platform, preparing lunch near the gate at the front of the home while watching passers-by. I caught sight of an elderly woman wearing a ragged *kanga* cloth over her head and wondered if she might be Giriama. I turned to Mariamu, who sat on a stool low to the ground while grating a coconut, her hair in neatly pinned curlers.

> McIntosh: About how many Giriama live in Shella?
> Mariamu: There are some Giriama here. Not so many. Some have converted to Islam.
> McIntosh: If they've converted to Islam, are they Swahili now?
> Mariamu: Ah-huh! (laughing and looking at her friend, who was smiling) No. They aren't Swahili.
> McIntosh: Okay, so who are the Swahili?
> Mariamu: It's about language.
> McIntosh: Okay, so if they leave Kigiriama and adopt Kiswahili only, are they Swahili then?
> Mariamu: No, because their parents are Giriama.
> Mariamu's friend: Maybe we'll call them "Waswahili Wasitu" (literally, "bush Swahili").

The two of them then laughed together, glancing at me, perhaps to see if I was shocked or amused.

In another conversation, a middle-aged man named Fuad offered a similar assessment of what becomes of Giriama converts:

Fuad: There's a . . . difference between Swahili and Giriama who convert to Islam. Swahili themselves refer to converts as "a Giriama who's converted to Islam [Mgiriama *wa kuslimu*]." And there are others who are called "meek Swahili [Mswahili *pole*]" or "bush Swahili [Mswahili Msitu]."[24] So even if a Giriama has converted, still they're not a Swahili. They'll be a Giriama still, but a Giriama who has converted. Even if their deeds and their [linguistic] pronunciation [are assimilated to those of Swahili]. Any Giriama can cleave to Swahili custom.

McIntosh: But if the Giriama converted a long time ago and lived on the Swahili side for about thirty years, can they be called Swahili?

Fuad: No, they'll still be termed a bush Swahili. . . . For a Mijikenda— maybe they'll be a Swahili by deeds or by words, but in their character, from the point of view of the Swahili group [*katika kundi la* Waswahili] they can't be counted as a proper Swahili. . . . Swahili have the temperament of removing themselves from other tribes. . . . If you look hard, you'll find a tribe that's hidden itself in between Mijikenda and Swahili. If you take [a Mijikenda] who has converted to Islam, and if you really scrutinize, you really look into it, you'll find there's a tribe in between Swahili and Giriama. . . . They aren't accepted [by Swahili], even if they've lived as a Muslim for a long time. This is how I see it in Malindi, but in Mombasa or Lamu it could be different.

It would seem that for Giriama in Malindi looking at the Swahili community from the outside, there is a tantalizing yet slight hope of becoming part of this more privileged community, a hope that is offered with one hand and revoked with the other. While some Swahili admit the possibility that Giriama can become Swahili, just as many do not, and many agree that those who attempt it will be marked as outsiders or pretenders by a stigmatized classification ("bush Swahili") that invokes that other pejorative, Nyika. True, children born to Swahili-Mijikenda marriages (particularly when the father is Swahili) have a much greater chance of acceptance, as their bloodline and the possibility of social amnesia about their origins combine in their favor. But Giriama in Malindi are so pessimistic about assimilation that to them this hardly feels like the fluid and flexible precolonial social dynamic described by Willis (1993).

Also striking is that in all of these conversations, religion is cited by some Swahili as a means by which Giriama can assimilate to Swahili society, but—unlike blood, birth, character, language, and culture—religion is never explicitly mentioned as a potential barrier to becoming Swahili. Presumably this is because the official ideology among Swahili is that anyone, including Giriama, can convert to Islam and become Muslim. Yet despite this widely articulated idea of universal Islam, a subtle hegemony (one that is widely, if not unanimously shared by Swahili and Giriama) seems to be at work to undermine it. For in other conversations and contexts I came to learn that some Swahili are skeptical of Giriama efforts to become Muslim, while many Giriama are pessimistic that they can be accepted as good or true Muslims—and even more pessimistic that they can be accepted as Swahili. It is the Giriama point of view that most concerns me, because their perspective on Swahili ethnicity as compelling yet Other is intimately bound up with their perspective on Islam and, ultimately, with the occult practices and experiences I recount in the remaining chapters.

Essence, Aspiration, and Disappointment:
Giriama Perceptions of Ethnoreligious Identity

Swahili are not alone in perceiving a boundary to Giriama assimilation. Many Giriama perceive Swahili discrimination as a crucial barrier to their becoming Swahili. At the same time, like some Swahili, many Giriama in Malindi traffic in essentialist notions of ethnic identity, an essentialism that shapes their religious lives in ways that further reify the perceived ethnic division. When Giriama subscribe to the notion of a deep and natural separation between Swahili and themselves, they contribute to a hegemonic force field in which members of both privileged and disenfranchised groups entrench the status quo—in this case, a social structure that makes Giriama assimilation and upward mobility particularly difficult.

While essentialist thinking among Giriama is surely influenced by the colonial and postcolonial ethnopolitics I have described, it also has an indigenous precedent. The Giriama notion of a group's ethnic purity (*ueri*) can be traced to the Kaya era, when young men had to demonstrate their pure Giriama heritage in the male line to learn the secrets and folklore of the Kaya elders (Parkin 1991a: 31). Since colonialism Giriama themselves have imputed different degrees of ethnic authenticity and purity to different segments of the Giriama population; the western cattle-herding Giriama are regarded by at least some easterners as "independent of the 'contaminations' of the largely Muslim coast" (12). Pure Giriama identity, then, is instantiated not only in Giriama bloodlines but also in the spaces through which they move. Indeed, it resides powerfully in the Kaya themselves, the traditional forested capitals of Mijikenda life referred to by some as the "pure village" (*mudzi mueri*; Parkin 1992; S. G. Thompson 1990) and thought by some Giriama to be "the source of their cultural essence and the moral safeguard against complete politico-economic encapsulation" (Parkin 1991a: xv). True to Parkin's findings, Giriama in Malindi often told me that if I wanted to understand the "real Giriama," I ought to speak to an elder associated with the Kaya, or at least to travel west to the hinterland, away from the influences of towns that have so altered Giriama culture. One of my Giriama interlocutors explained that the Kaya need to be kept pure of such influences:

> In the past it was easy to dwell in the [Kaya] homesteads because urban life was uncommon among the Mijikenda. People could live in the Kaya their whole lives. But the influx of rosewater and aspirin [references to Muslim and Western healing traditions, respectively] weren't in the Mijikenda air then; we relied on the forest and on the foliage there for everything. Today, people want to be part of the urban life. When a person is in the Kaya they should not contemplate urban life. When Kaya elders go to the Kaya, they dress themselves in the traditional way—and when they leave, they perfume themselves [a habit associated with both Muslim and Western influences] and change into trousers.

At this point in the conversation, a younger man made a striking addition: "When a person gets used to hygiene, perfume, and other forms of medicine like the Western-style medicine and [the medicine] from the Muslim side, those things get into their blood. So if a person goes into the Kaya, they might even die."

The first man's remarks suggest that Giriamaness, represented by the Kaya, *should not* be combined with lifestyles from other ethnic groups. The second man suggests an even deeper incompatibility: one *cannot* combine these lifestyles with impunity. The markers of Western and Muslim lifestyles, encapsulated in physical substances such as perfume and medicinal traditions that compete with Giriama traditions, can actually "get into your blood" and may cause a fatal clash of essences if an individual, polluted in these ways, enters the Kaya. In these narratives we see a paradox that arises elsewhere in my conversations with Giriama: on the one hand, people are malleable (even, in this case, at the level of their blood), but on the other hand, there is such a thing as an essential ethnic identity that stays with them. In the conversation just related, the locus of the essential ethnic identity is the space of the Kaya. In other conversations I had, however, Giriama interlocutors located ethnic purity in blood-borne identity.

The trope of pure blood actually hampered the efforts of one of my research assistants, Charo, as he sought to arrange my interviews with Giriama diviners living on the outskirts of Malindi. Charo's father is Giriama and his mother is a Luyah. He grew up in the impoverished Giriama-dominated section of Malindi called Muyeye, speaks Kigiriama as his first language, and is fully enough integrated into the Giriama community that most people never doubted his ethnicity. Yet these surface traits were not enough to allay the suspicion of one elderly neighbor of his, John, who repeatedly insisted, "We know you're not a fully bred Giriama . . . you're half-bred. You don't have our blood. You're doing this research to alter yourself to be more like us and pretend to be pure bred, but you're fooling yourself."

If Giriama sometimes conceptualize Giriamaness in terms of an essence (located in blood, in sacred spaces, or both), how do they conceptualize Swahiliness in relation to their own identity? Giriama from Malindi say that if they head inland into the rural areas far from the coast, they might be referred to by their upcountry Giriama peers as Swahili simply because they live in an overlapping cultural field with urban Swahili. But within Malindi most Giriama agree that the category Swahili is adjudicated by, or at least established in comparison to, the denizens of the town center, and most see that category as one that they cannot be part of. In fact, despite the great heterogeneity of Swahili origins and the distinctions Swahili themselves make between (for instance) those from different geographic regions, or freeborn Swahili versus those with slave origins, Giriama discourse tends to portray Swahili as a more or less homogeneous block of people who enjoy the privileges of both Arab roots and Arab loyalties. Giriama explanations for the perceived ethnic barrier between Swahili and themselves include both essentialist arguments about ethnicity and bald accusations of racial, religious, and linguistic prejudice.

Still it is important to acknowledge that not every Giriama feels that the path of assimilation is closed off. A small minority of Giriama not only convert to Islam but also attempt a wholesale ethnic shift that they hope will allow them to be incorporated into the Swahili community (see chapter 3). In conversation, only a minority (about a quarter) of the many Giriama I spoke to about this issue contended that the category Swahili remains permeable. (A few considered themselves Swahili, but I found it telling that most of them do not live in Shella or Barani, and so are not confronted on a daily basis by the question of whether or not the core Swahili community embraces their new identity.) Several informants argued that becoming Swahili through intermarriage is possible for Giriama women but not for Giriama men. Others felt that religious conversion alone is sufficient to merit reclassification. Hamisi, a resident of the ethnically mixed Maweni area on the edge of Malindi town, was born Giriama but has converted to Islam and now considers himself Swahili, though he prays at the Maweni mosque and does not socialize much with the Swahili who live in Malindi's core. He said, "Religion is what makes a Swahili a Swahili and a Giriama a Giriama. Swahili can't become Giriama because it's difficult for them to change religion, but Giriama can become Swahili because Islam is the true religion. People from the local religion come to the true religion and become Swahili."

Mi-Dama, a middle-aged woman who works at a butcher's shop in ethnically mixed Maweni, agrees that assimilation is possible, claiming that her sister has become a "true Swahili": "She married a Muslim and converted to his faith. She likes speaking Arabic [Kiislam]. She lives without trouble among the Swahili, and she's very well educated; she even went to college. She works at a hotel in the reception department." Mi-Dama said this with evident pride, highlighting the connection between Swahili ethnicity and upward mobility and, perhaps, factors of learnedness and professionalism that figure into the question of whether a Giriama aspirant can be assimilated. A young Giriama man named Kadenge who drives a bicycle taxi in Malindi town center spoke in coded terms about the Islamization of Giriama, suggesting that it has resulted in the reclassification of Giriama and the ruination of Giriama culture: "Sure, Giriama can become Swahili. Look at how many of the people around here have inherited Swahili ways of dress and behavior. Actually, the Swahili have destroyed our culture." The diviner Kashutu, who lives in the impoverished, Giriama-dominated area of Muyeye, suggested (like Hamisi) that there is a semipermeable membrane between Swahili and Giriama, in which ethnic assimilation can flow in one direction: "The difference between the two groups is religion and blood. A Giriama is Giriama by birth and blood, but a Swahili is Swahili by religion. A person can change religion and not their birth, so they can become Swahili but they can't become Giriama."

Despite these accounts of ready ethnic recategorization, I also encountered narrative after narrative infused with essentialist premises about ethnic identity or pessimism that Giriama aspirants can be accepted into the Swahili fold. In conversations, formal interviews, and informal group discussions with many dozens of Giriama, I found that a strong majority (about three-quarters) believe that a Giriama cannot become a Swahili. A number of rationales emerged for this claim, many based on the ontological impossibility of transforming an ethnic identity that is essentially fixed by birth or blood. Asked what differentiates Giriama and Swahili, a young Giriama woman named Mary replied, "Birth. You just find out you're born Swahili or Giriama. You don't choose the tribe of your parents." Many others indicated that one cannot become Swahili without "Arab blood."

Other Giriama accounts of ethnic category membership did not allude to blood but simply asserted that ethnic identity is absolute and fixed. "Of course a Giriama can't become Swahili—he's a Giriama," as one woman put it. Others chided me when I raised the possibility of assimilation: "What are you talking about? No one can change their tribe." One local Giriama politician argued, "If you are a particular tribe, you cannot be changed to be another—if you are Giriama, you are Giriama. If you are Kikuyu you cannot be changed. . . . Tribes are given by God. How else can you explain where [any of these] people came from?" Some Giriama contended that ethnic identity is instantiated in a person's "character" or "culture," but talked about these characteristics as if they are intractable. For instance, when asked whether Giriama can become Swahili, the young diviner Jane replied, "No, that's impossible. The two are different in the way they solve problems." Chengo, a young barfly in Maweni, said, "We're different in so many ways. We eat rats; they don't eat rats or pork. We inherit wives; they don't. We dance during funerals; they don't. . . . We're afraid of towns and they like owning shops and servants. . . . What a Swahili wears isn't what a Giriama puts on. The faith a Giriama takes isn't what a Swahili takes. The Giriama business, palm wine, isn't for Swahili. I don't think a Giriama can become a true Swahili."

Jumwa, an elderly woman, agreed: "The total way of life makes these two groups different. A Swahili can't become a Giriama, and a Giriama can't become a true Swahili." Even Haluwa, a twenty-year-old Giriama woman married to a Swahili, said, "The difference between me and Swahili is culture. We will never be the same, ever, nor will one be what the other is. I can never be Swahili and Swahili can never be Giriama." A few informants referred to Giriama wishing to Swahiliize using the cynical appellation "Adzomba Achungani," a phrase that originally referred to upwardly mobile Giriama who converted to Islam on Swahili plantations (*chunga*) and were made headmen of other Mijikenda workers, but whose origins continued to mark them as different because they "still ate rats [*udzora*]," as one put it.

These conversations evoked not only ontological but also moral claims about ethnicity. Many Giriama interlocutors asserted that Swahili exclusiveness and discrimination are the forces that bar them from membership. Salim, a self-described Muslim Giriama who lives in Muyeye, expressed this tactfully, focusing on the linguistic differences that trigger Swahili discrimination: "Swahili isn't really a tribe. It's about lineage [*ukoo*]. But it is still exclusive. If you convert and go say 'I'm Swahili' they won't agree. This is a matter of language; the real Swahili speak like a dictionary, with very very hard words. You can't get their words, and they know you don't have [those words]."

A young Giriama Muslim named Abdalla suggested that deep forms of discrimination work even against those whose ancestry is only half Giriama (notice how Abdalla conflates Swahili and Arab actors in his account): "Even if someone has a Giriama mother and a Swahili father, when they go to those Arabs they'll say: 'No no, he's not a Swahili; his mother's a Giriama.' They'll still disown you. You see, you're a burden to them; they can't fully abandon you but you'll suffer, for they still can't fully accept you. Many years will elapse and you'll never get to their level. They'll accept fully only their fellow Arabs." Another Giriama made his point vividly as we stood together in Shella. A slender young woman passed in a black *bui bui*, carrying an enormous bag of coal on her head. "That one is a Giriama," said my companion. "Maybe she works for a Swahili household, or maybe she married a Swahili, but a real Swahili woman would never be made to carry such a load on her head."

Some Giriama defend traditional Giriama life in the face of perceived Swahili prejudice, explaining that Giriama cannot become Swahili by virtue of the improbability that Giriama could swing so radically from one cultural and moral center of gravity to another. Katana, a taxi driver who lives in Shella among many Swahili, said, "A Giriama can't become a Swahili. Their character is totally different. The idea that Giriama could become Swahili is a joke, and a big insult to Giriama!" "What makes me a Giriama," said a middle-aged woman named Hedza, "is the way that I was brought up. Our way of life is the thing that makes me what I am. The way of our ancestors is good. The Swahili are also controlled by the way they were brought up. Neither one can change into the other." A Muslim Giriama named Sidi explained, "The difference between Giriama and Swahili stems from Swahili habits. They like to abuse people." A non-Muslim Giriama named Tsenga described the double bind of Giriama who wish to climb the social ladder but risk being marginalized by both Giriama and Swahili: "Giriama character is one of sharing and loving. . . . Swahili think they're high in value when of course they aren't, while in our culture people who engage in such behavior are stigmatized. A Giriama might pretend to take on Swahili prejudice, but the Swahili themselves will discriminate against him!"

In one gathering of young Giriama men in Muyeye, a non-Muslim named Kapembe Ngumbao went on an impassioned tear about Swahili ethnoreligious prejudice against those who aren't "real Arabs." Speaking in an emphatic crescendo, to the great enthusiasm of his friends, Kapembe said:

> You know that the Swahili call us Nyika. Do you understand what that means? Nyika refers to a very rural, remote, uninhabited place where wild animals can devour your flesh and no one cares about your death. Here we are in Malindi, yet they call you Nyika. . . . Those

converting to Islam are fools. How can you leave your own tribe to join another? Aren't you stupid? For instance, I'm Ngumbao. If I convert I might be called "Said Ngumbao." Why can't I be called "Said Mohammed" or "Said Bakar"? I'm called "Said Ngumbao." Or something like "Omar Chome." What's the meaning of this—a Swahili name and a Giriama name? Don't you understand that this is a sign that you don't belong there? . . . They deceive you by calling it a religion, but it's a tribe, and you'll never be accepted. If they need to make use of you they'll have you be their *muezzin* [caller to prayer] so you can call the REAL Arabs to come and pray to their god!

Kapembe's narrative bespeaks his longing to be considered part of urban coastal life; the pejorative Nyika and the suggestion that he and other Giriama might come from a remote, unsocialized part of the bush clearly rankle. He resents the difficulties of assimilation into elite Swahili society. He has encountered the claim that conversion to Islam can allow one to be adopted as Swahili, but he uses the naming practices that follow conversion to argue that this apparent permeability is a sham, that the retention of Giriama clan names among converts indicates that in fact Swahili is "a tribe," one that, he charges, operates according to an essentialist logic in which some members are "real" and others are not. Tellingly, Kapembe also implies that this rejection obtains not only at the ethnic level but at the religious level; after all, the god in question is "theirs."

Indeed, matters of ethnic and religious exclusion often arise together, for many Giriama claim that when they attempt to join Islam their Swahili counterparts pull up the drawbridge surrounding the religion. In principle anyone can convert to Islam and become Muslim; this, indeed, is the ideology that Swahili hold to, saying that they welcome converts from all sides. Unofficially, however, Swahili hegemony asserts itself in the fact that many Swahili apparently feel that Giriama are not disposed to become good Muslims, while many Giriama seem to have internalized the idea that Swahili are the proprietors of Islam. If Giriama cannot be accepted into the Islamic religion they certainly cannot be embraced by the Swahili community as Swahili insiders, for being a Muslim is widely considered a sine qua non of ethnic assimilation (among those who think it is even possible).

Giriama narratives about their religious rejection by Swahili sometimes claim that new forms of slavery are at the root of such patterns. The concept of slavery, and its accompanying trope of race, is widespread among Giriama in Malindi, as it is among Mijikenda elsewhere (Ciekawy 2001).[25] Like Ciekawy, I find that Giriama commonly use metaphors of slavery to discuss new forms of exploitation. As one Giriama man put it, with poetic flourish, "To be Giriama is to be a slave to the white skin [a category that includes Arabs and sometimes, rhetorically, Swahili], a beggar to those in authority." As I have already indicated, in Malindi today many Giriama are persuaded that their ancestors were enslaved almost wholesale by Arabs and Swahili, a claim that most historians would view as overstated. Nevertheless the Mijikenda scholar Mkangi (1995: 110–11) insists that Mijikenda continue to share memories of forced conscription and of "tricks which were used by the slave-raiders into luring the unsuspecting Mijikenda victims into slavery." The history of slavery is remembered by Giriama not as a condition from which mobility and ethnic assimilation were possible, but as emblematic of the economic immobility and helplessness that has weighed upon them for decades. This discourse seems to be influenced by transnational currents, for many Giriama in Malindi are keenly aware of the history of race-based slavery and discrimination in the United States and occasionally asked me questions about this history. Slavery and race are also common themes in Kenya's national newspapers and occasionally arise in local controversies; in 1998, during a debate about whether and how to commemorate the five-hundredth anniversary of Vasco da Gama's arrival in Malindi, Europeans and Swahili volleyed accusations about whether Portuguese or Arabs had historically been the more racist culprits in enslaving Africans (McIntosh 2001a).[26]

The trope of slavery makes its way into some Giriama Muslims' perception of their subordinate religious status.[27] According to the young Muslim Abdalla, when the small mosque in Muyeye was built, an elderly sheikh opened a madarasa for Giriama boys and girls in order to win converts. "They pressed on well until they could read in the Arabic alphabet," said Abdalla, "but later on that habit of discriminating against Giriama came up." According to Abdalla, the sheikh began to insist that the Giriama pupils clean up the school after hours but didn't place the same demands on the few Swahili children who were there. When the

Giriama pupils complained, he said, "that sheikh would say: 'Go your way, you Nyika!' Something like that makes a person lose their faith pretty quickly. There's still hatred and discrimination in there. And to think that they sold us for silver, molested us, and such things. Maybe a quarter of Giriama in this area have agreed to convert to the Arab's religion, but they have still not yet been fully accepted."

Race too is often invoked in such narratives as a coded way of speaking about power. In Giriama invocations of race, "black" is set against "white," the first corresponding to Giriama and the second, often, to not only Arabs but also Swahili. Such rhetoric underscores the imagined dimensions of racial discourse; race is often ostensibly grounded in appearance, but racial discourse just as often ignores the subjective dimension of physiognomic judgments (cf. Glassman 2000: 396) and, in this case, overlooks the fact that some high-ranking Swahili are dark-complexioned. Said one Giriama Muslim, "The black Giriama Muslims do the caretaking of the mosque. . . . The high ranks are given to the white Muslims. They just won't accept me." In the following conversation, two young Giriama converts to Islam use tropes of skin color and slavery to discuss their frustration at being unable to break into the inner sanctum of Muslim life:

> Hamisi: Let's say on my plot of land I build my own mosque. I'll get very few Muslims. Even if I inform the Muslims at the biggest mosque of the town, very few people would come. They can't leave the big mosques and come enter a mosque in Maweni—"That was built by so and so. What does he know about the religion? Let's go this way." They'll go to the other mosques. . . . There's that division and segregation, because I'm a Giriama converted to Islam. But if I were born an Arab and I came to build a mosque here, it would be absolutely filled with Muslims.
>
> Kijanaa: Wait a minute, I want to add to that. Do you know why? Here we are now, but in ancient times, you know, Arabs came. They didn't make the Wagunya [a Bajuni group with a reputation for being light-skinned] their slaves; they mainly picked the Giriama. Right?
>
> Hamisi: Yes. PRISONERS!
>
> Kijanaa: Prisoners. Weren't they badly harassed? Slaves! That tradi-

tion continues up to our times. . . . They say this religion is of the Arabs. Islam comes from Arabia. So they treat us accordingly. If you go to Sheikh Salim's place seeking assistance, it will be very difficult to be helped before he helps another Arab. Even if you're in the middle of important discussion and a fellow Arab comes—

Hamisi:—someone white—

Kijanaa:—someone white, you'll be abandoned and he'll attend to the white Arab first. That's all going on still. Of course they have to despise us. If you're a Muslim but you just converted [rather than being born into the Muslim community], then no matter how much you learn the religion you're not going to be accepted by them.

Hamisi and Kijanaa draw a striking contrast between the lack of respect "whites" allegedly accord Giriama converts and the favors they grant to those of Arab descent. Meanwhile they treat the historical memory of slavery as analogous to the contemporary treatment of Giriama converts: "Slaves! That tradition continues up to our times. . . . They say this religion is of the Arabs. Islam comes from Arabia. So they treat us accordingly." A subtle kind of spatiality undergirds these felt impediments: "Islam comes from Arabia," marking it as inaccessible to indigenous Africans; meanwhile the Muslims in the center of town snub and deride the Giriama settlements on the outskirts. The overall portrait is of Giriama spatially marginalized and generally thwarted, constrained, even "imprisoned" by their more privileged Muslim neighbors, who simply "will not accept" them.

Another young man, Khassan, was born of Muslim Giriama parents and lives in Muyeye. He wears a metal locket on his neck shaped like a tiny Quran; on the front the name "Allah" is etched in silver Arabic letters, and on the inside he carries pictures of his parents, one on each side. He explained:

I am a Giriama who's a Muslim, NOT a Swahili. If I go way inland, other Giriama will call me a Swahili because I've forgotten the deep Giriama ways. In fact, even if I go to Arabia they might call me a Swahili, just like they will call a coastal Arab a Swahili! But I'm not. I don't speak the Kiswahili full of Arabic; I just speak Kigiriama. There's not much acceptance of my type in Shella; the gap is wide between black

Muslims and Swahili and there's a lot of discrimination [*ubaguzi*]. I pray here in Muyeye, if I go to pray in the mosque in town they'll say I've just turned up for the coffee and dates and I'm not a real Muslim.

Khassan's friend Salama, sitting next to him, also cited racial discrimination as a factor in ethnoreligious boundary making on the coast:

A Giriama can't become a true Swahili; we are still denied. . . . Even if you go toward the Islamic religion they will not accept you—it's very hard work. They'll still keep some things hidden. . . . They won't agree you're a regular Muslim [Mwislam *wa kawaida*]. They won't let people know everything about them—they keep secrets. They are the original, authentic [*asili*] Muslims. They think Mijikenda are black instead of brown. If an Arab comes along and says "I've got a billion shillings I want to divide among these people" and gives it to Sheikh Omar and Omar divides it, the ratio will be different for a Swahili woman and her Mijikenda husband. They won't give you access to their wealth. Anyhow, it's rare for a Giriama to marry in.

These discourses of racism, and suggestions that Swahili and Arabs are "original" Muslims while Giriama are perceived as vaguely fraudulent if they convert, indicate that Giriama perceive essentialism in Swahili prejudice. But this perception sometimes slides subtly into acceptance of the essentialist premise that Giriama are not full Muslims. Indeed, Salama's locution "They are the original, authentic Muslims" hovers vaguely between reported Swahili opinion and an internalized statement of fact. We see the same blurring of the lines between observed prejudice and internalized hegemony in the words of one female diviner: "Those who convert to Islam have to ignore their friends and relatives, and may cheat [their friends and relatives, by telling them] that if they convert they'll be given good food, nice clothes, and wealth—but this is not true. These people aren't correct Muslims—they just lie somewhere between simple Traditionalists and correct Muslims."

Evidently, coastal social dynamics have instructed Giriama in Malindi that Islam is not a universal religion one can fully belong to at will. Indeed, certain aspects of Giriama ritual and linguistic practice reinforce the notion that Swahili and Arabs are in fact the proprietors of Islam— and not necessarily because of a socially constructed, historically contingent hierarchy of power and knowledge, but sometimes because Swahili and Arabs are ontologically connected to mystical Islamic power in ways that Giriama are not. Many Giriama in Malindi find themselves covetous of the occult potencies that attach to the Islamic religion, yet at the same time they are morally appalled by these powers and insecure about their own access to them. Swahili ethnicity is off-limits, but so too is Swahili's enviable depth of connection to the powers of Islam. Even among Giriama who do become Muslim tensions remain, for conversion tends to involve renouncing practices and qualities fundamentally associated with Giriamaness, an option that some find abhorrent. Conversion to Islam can thus mean being caught between renouncing a fully Giriama identity (because one has embraced the religion of an ethnic Other) and being renounced by the Swahili community (because, say many Giriama, they cannot become Swahili for reasons of either human prejudice or ontological essence or both). Some find a way to deal with these dilemmas by poaching the powers associated with Islam without themselves becoming Muslim. Others live in a state of chronic ambivalence about Islam and the ethnic groups who command it.

Chapter 2

BLOOD MONEY IN MOTION
Profit, Personhood, and the *Jini* Narratives

Nyevu is a female diviner in her fifties who lives about ten kilometers inland of the center of Malindi town with her elderly husband, her sister, and several children and grand-children. The mud-and-thatch dwellings on her compound are in dire need of repair, but Nyevu has been reluctant to put money or labor into them for fear that the Arab landowner may soon drive her family off the land they are squatting on. The family survives largely on the meager crops Nyevu and her female kin harvest, but they are also in continuous contact with town life. Nyevu's twenty-year-old son, Juma, works at a low-budget guest house on the outskirts of town, bicycling home every weekend to share some of his salary and stories about the array of characters he encounters there: the European backpackers playing card games on the veranda; the handful of furtive local men who arrive, he suspects, with prostitutes; the occasional businessman from Nairobi. Nyevu herself walks or takes a *matatu* minivan into town about once a week to sell a few baskets of surplus fruit and vegetables. She positions herself on the edge of a tarmac road at the fringes of Malindi's large outdoor market with several other women from her home area; together they lay their mangoes and bananas on a colorful cloth and sit on the ground in their grass and cotton *hando* skirts, their bare legs stretched straight before them.

As the buses, *matatus*, and Land Rovers speed past, the women chat among themselves in good humor and watch the flow of people along Malindi's roads. Arab and Swahili men hold mobile phones to their ears as they make their way to the mosque; Swahili women wearing *bui buis* go about their errands; office workers stride to a small restaurant for lunch. On Fridays, Nyevu says, she sometimes hovers at the entrance to one of Malindi's mosques in hopes of receiving alms, but she has found that the giving is patchy and wonders aloud whether she would garner more if she wore a head scarf to indicate that she considers herself a Muslim, having converted to please the Arab spirit Pepo Mwarabu with whom she works in her divination practice. Nyevu keenly notes the material privilege that seems to envelop so many of the people who emerge from the mosque but never alights on her, and while she suspects the mosque-goers of stinginess, she has an additional explanation for this imbalance. Nyevu, like so many Giriama in the Malindi area, is convinced that Swahili and Arab capital comes from money-gathering, bloodsucking *jini* spirits who fly to Arabia and bring back riches to their Muslim masters.

Giriama translate economic inequalities between them and Swahili in contemporary Malindi into distinctive models of the social and occult worlds. The ethnoreligious class system that structures their lives has become a dense point of cultural production in which narratives about *jini* spirits serve as an idiom of emotional expression and moral condemnation. Giriama notions of moral and economic personhood—particularly their notions of independence, reciprocity, and agency—are central to their interpretation of urban Swahili wealth. Although Giriama envy the rich, their *jini* narratives contain an implicit critique of the way Swahili accumulation appears to abstract value by exploiting helpless others while violating customary Giriama ideals of exchange and social obligation. What might be described as a Giriama moral economy is a set of (sometimes conflicted) assumptions about the moral content of particular economic lifeways (Scott 1976; E. P. Thompson 1971).

The *jini* narratives are hardly the only expressions of a people's moral economy. Across many cultures, folk narratives about supernatural entities—assorted spirits, vampires, witches, and bogeymen—have been interpreted as veiled critiques of the transformations caused by modernity, capitalism, and social inequality (Comaroff and Comaroff 1993; Mills 1995; Taussig 1980; Weismantl 2001; White 2000). Much work in this vein has focused on critiques of Western socioeconomic arrangements imposed by colonial and neoliberal economic orders. The Giriama critique addresses a somewhat different structural logic and another form of sovereignty: that of a Muslim community that has lived in coastal Kenya for centuries and that increasingly looks to the Middle East for its capital as it participates in globally recognizable forms of modernity. *Jini* narratives hence do not merely critique the cultural logic of late capitalism; they also focus on the concept of travel, for the advantaged social group in this context is seen as having a deep historical association with long-distance trade and transport and an increasingly transnational cultural orientation, both to the larger Arab world and to international commodity markets. Giriama *jini* narratives are thus shot through with tropes of long-distance movement and velocity, forces that, in Giriama understanding, both instantiate and create forms of agency and value for Swahili and Arabs. These qualities of mobility are enviable yet suspect for the way they potentially run against the grain of Giriama efforts to root themselves more firmly in territory they are at risk of losing. The *jini* narratives thus bring together folk critiques of capital and its suspicious mystical qualities with representations of spatiality and spatial mobility in sub-Saharan Africa.

The narratives discussed in this chapter not only express Giriama concerns about personhood, inequality, and mobility; they also shore up the increasingly hegemonic ethnoreligious boundary between Swahili and Giriama. *Jini* narratives bespeak a complex separatism, reifying the notion that Swahili and Arab privilege is not so much the result of effort as it is a windfall conferred by money-gathering supernatural forces that are accessible only to Swahili and Arab Muslims. Giriama may yearn at some level for the privileges enjoyed by Swahili, but the tales they tell in contemporary Malindi suggest that the differences between them and Swahili are virtually insurmountable. Giriama see Swahili as oriented toward and possibly belonging in another geographic setting, at the same time that Giriama increasingly conceptualize themselves as the primordial and fixed residents of the coastal zone. *Jini* narratives, then, subtly reinforce the hegemony of ethnoreligious separation by asserting a social, metaphysical, and spatial distance between Swahili and Giriama ethnicities, a distance often encouraged (albeit in different terms) by Swahili themselves. Even as many Giriama wish they could share the advantages of urban Swahili, their own narratives often suggest that achieving this through assimilation is but a remote possibility.

Mobility and Prosperity among Swahili of Malindi

The Giriama *jini* narratives circulate among contrasts between urban Swahili and periurban Giriama economic life in Malindi, and the tensions between accumulation and reciprocity, and mobility and rootedness in land. Many Swahili in Malindi enjoy material and institutional advantages of which Giriama are keenly aware. In particular Swahili men, who have more social leeway than women, aspire to and often achieve two kinds of mobility: upward economic mobility through the accumulation of capital and material goods, and mobility through space, typically up and down the coast and overseas to the Middle East. Giriama perceive the link between capital and movement through space in Swahili's ability to buy money-generating commodities such as buses, *matatus*, and taxis. This capital facilitates what some Giriama regard as the impersonal transactions of urban life, travel, and long-distance connections.

Swahili life in Malindi is composed of a creative and uneasy blend of cultural influences. For middle-class Swahili who live in the core areas of town, such as Shella and Barani, such a life is also increasingly expensive. In the stone and cement Swahili and Arab houses that line the streets of Shella and Barani, many live at a standard that requires at least ten to twenty times the paltry income of eighty shillings a week brought in by Nyevu, and a much broader range of socioeconomic contacts. Over the past two decades perhaps half or more of Swahili homes in the center of town have managed to attain electricity, though not without great persistence and the occasional reluctant bribe to the clerks at Kenya Power and Lighting Company. Once electrical connections are in place, many families set about acquiring a series of coveted imports: refrigerators, television sets, and VCRs or DVD players. In one representative middle-class Shella household the television set is nestled in an ornately carved, glossy wooden display cabinet in the living room. The sofa across from it, purchased from a Swahili workshop on Malindi's main road, is lavishly upholstered in deep red, velvet-textured cloth and the cushions sport bold tiger stripes. The air of prosperity reaches even the floors: the kitchen is paved with smooth cement painted a bright green, the hallways are laid with a thin layer of linoleum, and the living room floor is covered by a Persian-style rug made in India and purchased in Mombasa. On the walls, next to a plastic clock, framed prayers from the Quran in

Arabic calligraphy hang over a tapestry of the Ka'aba shrine in Mecca, the ultimate pilgrimage site. These displays index several forms of symbolic and literal capital; they indicate the family's faith and their aspirations to a faraway locus of Islam, while marking the contemporary salience of financial well-being, "modern things" (*mambo ya kisasa*), and development (*maendeleo*) in urban Swahili life (cf. P. Caplan and Topan 2004; Walley 2004).

Indeed, contemporary aspirations and transnational connections saturate the lives of many of Malindi's Swahili residents, sometimes clashing with and sometimes intersecting with the ways of the older generations. While elderly women who never went to school bemoan the brash and shameful (*aibu*) comportment of today's girls, twenty-year-olds aspire to get degrees in secretarial work, teaching, or nursing. Yet these young women pin their most fervent hopes on a well-to-do husband, the social security of motherhood, and the monogamous marital pattern that increasingly supplants polygamy among Malindi's Swahili. Those already married show off wedding albums with white-clad American bride models on the cover; in the photos they pose seductively, wearing heavy lipstick and impossibly shiny colored dresses imported from the Middle East, their hands decorated with henna arabesques. Young men use the profits from their business to buy new and noisy motorcycles, and use the same vehicles to get to the mosque on time for prayers. Many Swahili rent Disney and Schwarzenegger videos from a Swahili-owned store in Barani that displays a large poster of Osama bin Laden holding a machine gun—a reflection of the pan-Islamic sympathies (and, in a few cases, the radicalism) of many town-based Muslims. In the eyes of some, the most alarming changes in Malindi have stemmed from Western influences, particularly the presence of tourists, who are blamed for encouraging lax behavior and the decay of virtue. The Malindi Council of Imams and other community leaders continually struggle against what they term the "decline of morals" and have spearheaded the closure of brothels and the arrest of heroin peddlers while championing the ideals of self-control, restraint, and piety.[1] Some Swahili organizations in Malindi, such as the Malindi Education and Development Association (MEDA), attempt to reconcile the tensions of contemporary town life by proposing new institutions to integrate religious and secular education. As the MEDA chairman Attas Sherif Ali told me, "We want to prove that there is no contradiction between being modern and being Muslim" (cf. Beck-erleg 2004; P. Caplan and Topan 2004).

Part of that modernity in Malindi involves making a living in a com-petitive capitalist zone. While many Swahili and Arabs in the precolonial era subsisted as merchants, traders, and plantation owners, today Swahili and Arabs are situated in a complex urban economy that is partly domi-nated by upcountry ethnic groups (Kikuyu, Luo, Luyah, and others) who occupy some of the more lucrative office jobs in town, by South Asian business owners, and by Europeans (including British ex-colonials and Italian expatriates) who live in beachfront mansions and own a number of hotels and tourist-related businesses. For Swahili, avenues to accumu-lation vary widely. The least wealthy individuals, and indeed, some Swa-hili suffer in relative poverty, subsist as fishermen or small kiosk owners. Still, many urban Swahili men aspire to greater profits by working as clerks or owning shops, restaurants, and other small businesses such as Internet cafés, hardware stores, printing presses, butcher shops, and bakeries. Others pursue skilled technical work as electricians, mechanics, or furniture makers or make a profit from renting out buildings in town. Employment options for Swahili women are more limited, but growing numbers of young women pursue secretarial work, primary school teach-ing, or clerical work, often until they have their first child. Families with kin in the Persian Gulf may receive occasional remittances, and some aspire to get temporary jobs in Saudi Arabia (though apparently all too many of them have been bilked by duplicitous employment agents).

Many of Malindi's Swahili are widely connected in several senses of the word, and all of these connections can facilitate accumulation. Among Swahili entrepreneurs start-up capital is obtained from loans, personal or family savings, local and international Muslim organizations, and kin in the Middle East. Those men and women who work as clerks in Internet cafés, post offices, and banks also participate in global circuits of knowledge, social contacts, and money. The association of Swahili with another kind of circuit, travel, is secured by their domination of the transportation business in Malindi. Since the year 2000 a popular form of taxi owned by many Swahili has been the *tuk tuk*, an open-sided, three-wheeled diesel vehicle imported from Asia that sputters along the street as it ferries passengers economically between one end of town and the other. But Swahili and Arabs also own many of Malindi's Toyota taxicabs, *matatu* minivans, and long-distance bus lines, and they hire other Muslim men as drivers. The business is lucrative, highly visible, and semiotically elaborate; many buses and *matatus* brashly announce Islamic pieties ("Bismillahi"; "Yaa Allah") in large painted letters on the windshield and their articulation with sensibilities at once self-consciously modern, transnational, and cheeky ("Bad Boy"; "Monica Lewinsky") on the rear window. While all ethnic groups use these forms of transport, Swahili themselves are prominent customers, frequently traveling for business or to visit family members elsewhere on the East African coast. Giriama interpret long-distance journeys as an index of wealth; as one woman put it, "If they go to Dar es Salaam and Zanzibar—that's money! Do you think they can live in a place where they aren't known without money?"

Yet accumulation is hardly Swahili's only goal, and many Swahili in urban Malindi live in a perpetual dialectic between ideologies of prosperity and religious communitarianism. On the one hand, many Swahili regard entrepreneurship and piety as compatible.[2] On the other hand, in the eyes of some, Swahili enthusiasm for upward mobility poses a potential threat to their ideals of integrity (Saleh 2004). Religiously framed acts of charity thus help to assuage the anxiety of prosperity, at the same time that such acts benefit the spiritual capital of the individual and rally the community around itself. Fundraising (*zakat*) through mosques is common, with special drives during Ramadan that culminate on the eve of Idd-ul-Fitr. Giving alms, a pillar of Islam, is sometimes framed as a kind of exchange, the payoff being heavenly salvation or God's blessing (*baraka*). The Council of Imams, for instance, has pressed members of the community to open their pockets to others: "If you give, your reward is eternity [Ukitoa kile ambacho kitawanafaisha wengi faida yake ni ya milele]." One Swahili philanthropist in Malindi overtly models charity as a kind of spiritual investment: "Giving is like foreign currency invested with God."

Many Swahili donations feed into Malindi's umbrella organization Star of Hope, whose well-orchestrated charities have substantial ties to the Middle East. In the activities of these charities one gains a sense of how Swahili life in Malindi is influenced by both a global and a local sense of the *umma* (Muslim community). Tawfiq Muslim Youth, which is supported by the World Assembly of Muslim Youth of Saudi Arabia and similar organizations in Pakistan and Abu Dhabi, has been raising funds locally for a hospital and other social services. The Tawheed Muslim Association runs a dispensary and a maternity unit at the Malindi District Hospital. The four-decades-old Al-Islam Society, which owns rental properties on the coast and has received millions of shillings from a Saudi Arabian NGO, has eleven madarasa under its umbrella. The Malindi Islamic Centre of Orphans empowers widows and orphans in income generation and runs an interest-free lending facility for these individuals and the orphans' guardians. The rapidly growing Malindi Education and Development Association holds local fundraisers in the Swahili and Arab community, using the proceeds to promote job training and career guidance, academic excellence (particularly in the sciences), scholarships, HIV/AIDS education, and access to library services. In these initiatives one can clearly see communitarian impulses coexisting with possessive individualism among Swahili.

Ethnoreligious Resentment and Economic Constraint:
Giriama Impoverishment in Malindi

Giriama are aware of the flow of resources between Muslim individuals and organizations and can't help but observe how little of it reaches their own communities. Indeed, most Swahili philanthropy in Malindi reaches needy Sunni Muslims rather than Mijikenda Traditionalists, Christians, or the small number of Indian Shi'ites, such as Bohras and Ismailis. Such patterns of exclusion are generally byproducts of Muslim communitarianism rather than deliberate discrimination; MEDA's spokesman, for instance, emphatically stated that non-Muslims are eligible to partake of many of their programs. Yet in practice those who know of and benefit from these charities are nearly always Swahili and Arabs. The Giriama diviner Kadzo Fondo noted a similar trend in informal patterns of almsgiving: "It's not easy to receive alms if you're not a Muslim. . . . Islam is a religion of selfishness. It's like a club; it's confined to Muslims only, because it's encouraged for Muslims to give to Muslims. . . . Muslims give Muslims alms, and there's a great deal of help."

Another Giriama, John, told me of hearing about a meeting on microcredit opportunities run by the Swahili-led Coast Development Authority. When John and three of his friends arrived, they were surprised that the small hall was filled with Swahili men and women, attentively listening to the Swahili directors of the organization describe the program over a microphone. "We suspected prejudice," says John, "because members of our community had not been notified. The program even listed a special time for midday prayers. They knew this would be a meeting for their own kind." Ironically, many Swahili in attendance left the meeting disgruntled at the small quantities of credit on offer: up to Ksh20,000 (about US$250 at the time). "The Giriama in Muyeye really could have used that money," said John, "and the Swahili didn't even need it!"

John's experience of marginalization is common among Giriama in Malindi, whose interactions with Swahili are routinely marked by boundaries both economic and spatial. While Swahili numerically dominate the central areas of town such as Shella and Barani, Giriama tend to be concentrated in low-income areas (particularly Muyeye) that cluster around the edges of town. The geography of core versus periphery is replicated in microcosmic form even for those Giriama who pass through Swahili neighborhoods. Swahili architecture famously demarcates private, restricted interior spaces from public verandas where communication with outsiders is far more likely to take place (Donley-Reid 1990). For many Giriama, the sense of being barred from the interior of Swahili homes is palpable. One day soon after I arrived in Malindi in 1998 I sat in the front room of a Swahili house in Shella watching an elderly Giriama man move from house to house, offering to sharpen the blades Swahili women use to grate coconut. He shuffled down the muddy path between the dwellings in bare feet, wearing a long *kikoi* cloth wrapped around his legs, a secondhand button-down shirt, and a *kofia*, the white flat-topped cap typically worn by Swahili men to emphasize their piety. As he approached each house he shouted the customary Kiswahili salutation to announce his arrival, "Hodi!," and I noticed that the Swahili women at home that afternoon replied with the acknowledgment "Hodi!" but never the more welcoming "Karibu!" ("welcome"; "come in"). Instead, the Giriama man waited on each stoop while the women fetched their graters. I had seen Swahili tradesmen invited inside the same houses, so when he approached I went out and asked him why he never entered the Shella homes. "You have to be Muslim to go inside the house," he replied. "But I just do my work outside on the doorstep so it isn't necessary."[3] He scraped the serrated edge of a blade against a sharpening stone, extended his hand for a ten-shilling payment from the lady of the house, and moved on. Eventually I would learn that many Giriama men who work for Swahili wear a *kofia* regardless of their religious affiliation, to "show respect," as they put it. Evidently this semiotic gesture is not always sufficient to guarantee access to household interiors, let alone acceptance by the core Swahili community.

Such disappointments have a particular sting, coming as they do at the end of a long history of Swahili and Giriama and Mijikenda interdependence. As I discussed in chapter 1, nineteenth-century urban Swahili and hinterland Giriama on the East African coast lived in reciprocal patron-client relations in which Giriama provided grain, military support, and trade assistance to Swahili, often enjoying credit from Swahili patrons and upward mobility through conversion to Islam and intermarriage into Swahili families. The blurring of boundaries between these groups was reflected in nineteenth-century coastal rituals, and the category Swahili was so permeable it said little about the consanguinity or origins of the populations that laid claim to it. Swahili and Arabs did own slaves, some of them Mijikenda, but it was not unusual for slave converts to Islam to urge their masters to accept them as members of Swahili communities (Cooper 1981; Glassman 1995; Willis 1993). Bids for Swahili citizenship were often successful, as even the lowest status Mijikenda became members of the Islamic brotherhood. An avenue of upward mobility, in other words, was available to Giriama through their interactions with and sometimes entrance into Swahili lives. The climate of ethnic divisiveness that emerged in the colonial and postcolonial eras, however, has severely dampened such possibilities.

The twentieth century brought other negative changes in Giriama economic prospects. Giriama in the western hinterland have long subsisted as cattle herders or, in the case of those closer to the coast, on growing palm, cashew, fruit trees, and assorted other crops. Prior to colonialism local and upcountry palm wine sales provided a vital element of the Giriama economy in times of crisis. Yet the British colonial government banned this trade, fearing it would detract from their ability to secure a labor force. In postindependence years palm wine has been repeatedly, often capriciously, made illegal (then made legal again) in the name of fighting poverty and backwardness; these bans have been to the advantage of Kenya's commercial breweries (Willis 1998, 2002). Tapping and local selling often persist despite these injunctions but provide only an irregular and risky source of income. Subsistence agriculture too has become precarious near Malindi, where landownership is contentious and squatters can be displaced at a moment's notice. Giriama in and near Malindi are no longer able to live wholly off the land, yet the vast majority are unable to earn enough cash for a comfortable life. It seems that Swahili capitalists are situated within what Marx (1867/1967) called the "money-commodity-money" circuit, making profits by exchanging their money for commodities that are transformed (or held) and sold for yet more money; at the same time many Giriama are trapped within the "commodity-money-commodity" cycle, entering the market with only limited commodities, such as their labor or a small harvest, the money from which must immediately be converted to a different commodity, such as medicine or thatch for a leaking roof. There are, of course, exceptions to this rule; Giriama in the Malindi area sometimes purchase goats, bicycles, or other commodities that might be able to bring in a small profit. For the most part, however, their economic prospects are extremely limited.

Cash is so elusive for most Giriama that the expenses of a reasonable life in the squatters' area of Muyeye are terribly hard to cover with the pittance most households actually bring in. Even if they are able to grow maize, *sikuma wiki* (a dark green leafy vegetable), or fruit, most households pay for at least some of their food and basic household necessities, such as bread, milk, sugar, salt, firewood, small cooking stoves, and dishes. Those building new homes usually must buy the long, thin poles and palm fronds necessary for a mud-and-wattle dwelling; a fortunate few are able to purchase cement blocks for a sturdier house. Innumerable costly necessities add up: *matatu* fares, clothing, school fees, hospital bills, divination and other ritual payments, mobile phone points, bride-price (usually tens of thousands of shillings, in Malindi), even attending funerals, at which community members are expected to pay for the feast, the coffin, and the future needs of the deceased's family.

With so many living expenses in and near town, improvisation is often the key to economic survival. Money and goods are often distributed by kin and friends to those in need. Entrepreneurship too plays an important role. In the Giriama-dominated area of Muyeye, vendors set up tiny stands to sell handmade brooms, firewood, charcoal (*makaa*), surplus crops, ground nuts, deep-fried dough balls, palm wine, mobile phone refill cards, batteries, and newspapers. Others set up more substantial lean-to stores that provide their neighbors with bread, milk, a few vegetables, cigarettes, aspirin, and gum; some circulate the paths of the village with rickety wooden pushcarts, hawking plastic bowls, forks and spoons, sandals, and secondhand clothing. Many young men work as manual laborers on construction sites or commercial farms, and in recent decades many have taken work as beach boys, offering tourists souvenirs, a tour of the town, drugs, or sex. Women and girls have turned to prostitution, to the great consternation of the older generation. Many women also sell surplus produce, chickens, or goats or, like Nyevu, take up work as diviners (although the profession is not particularly lucrative for most, especially since many diviners charge next to nothing). Other common sources of income are making beds in beach hotels, cleaning Swahili, Arab, Indian, or European houses, or wiping tables at Swahili-owned restaurants. Indeed, Swahili businesses and households frequently employ Giriama, typically in the capacity of servers or cleaners. Most of these men and women earn between Kshs1,000 and 4,000 per month (roughly between US$15 and $60), which may not cover the basic requirements of survival in a mud dwelling without electricity. It certainly does not provide the basis for regular medical care, secondary school fees, or savings. Many Giriama saw their already minimal income dry up when the ravages of El Niño and the several Al Qaeda–sponsored terrorist acts in the late 1990s nearly killed coastal tourism and the town's entire economy. There have been exceptions to this grim pattern of Giriama disadvantage: a handful of Giriama earn advanced degrees and become professionals, and others make a success of political or entrepreneurial careers. But for the most part the relationship between Swahili and Giriama in the Malindi area has shifted from relatively fluid patronage and clientage into an ethnically based class system.

While the term *class* approximates the economic relationship between these groups, Giriama frequently model their position instead through the trope of *slavery*. As noted in chapter 1, many Giriama have re-visioned the history of Mijikenda slavery; instead of a historical label for several complex categories that allowed some degree of integration into Swahili households, slavery has become a stark, unitary emblem of their contemporary economic helplessness. "They treat us like slaves" is the repeated refrain, a claim that encapsulates the sense that Giriama are chained to the spot by servitude that is so poorly paid it might as well be coerced.

Transportation and Groundedness: Conflicted Longings

The economic constraints of Giriama life parallel a relatively truncated mobility through space. Although Giriama have a history of migrating from hinterland areas to coastal towns for wage labor and later returning to their homesteads, this fact is largely erased from Giriama discourse in Malindi, which plays up their relative lack of mobility in contrast with the seemingly extravagant journeys some Swahili are able to take within East Africa and abroad. Certainly Swahili tend as a whole to be able to travel faster and farther than Giriama, and with greater profit in the process. In fact, to many Giriama the economic division between these groups is encapsulated in the dynamics of Malindi's transportation business. While Swahili run profitable bus lines and own fleets of *matatus* and taxis, it is rare for Giriama to have the capital to buy such vehicles themselves. One research assistant of mine used the wages I gave him to try to break in to the taxi business, purchasing a Toyota in 1999 (just before the arrival of the more economical and popular *tuk tuks*). It broke an axle before he had mobilized any savings for repairs, and he had to sell the car at a steep loss. Around the year 2000, dozens of Giriama men created a new, if lowly tier of the transportation business by ferrying other low-income town residents on *boda bodas*, bicycle taxis with a long narrow seat behind the driver, who earns about Ksh20 (about US30¢) for a short route.[4] For these urban youth, older ways of locating value in agriculture and animals have been supplanted by transport; as one *boda boda* driver explained, "We Giriama in Malindi don't collect cows; we collect bicycles." Around 2003, however, the supply of *boda bodas* began to outstrip demand, with the result that bicycle owners have sometimes had to wheedle customers. As I walked the streets in 2004 many begged me to take even a short ride, some putting their hands to their mouth in a sign of hunger.

Under such conditions fantasies of travel and transnational contact have become a salient part of Giriama life. In Malindi these are no doubt exacerbated not only by Swahili privilege but also by the presence of so many tourists, whose obvious wealth colors faraway places with the tint of lucre. Allusions to foreign celebrities and locales adorn Giriama schoolbooks, T-shirts, and even the walls of houses.[5] The next best thing to travel, it seems, is the mobile phone, increasingly widespread in Malindi. The wide availability of "scratch cards," used to load prepaid minutes into one's phone, means that one needn't have a home address or even a post office box to lay claim to a telephone number. As a result it is not uncommon to see young men in villages on the outskirts of Malindi sitting in front of a mud-and-wattle dwelling and conversing on a mobile phone. Since 2000 text-messaging has become a popular medium of communication for young Giriama in Malindi as they coordinate the logistics of their workdays and rendezvous with friends traveling in from outlying areas. Some elders whisper that this new technology is a kind of *uganga* (supernatural power), though they are uncertain as to whether it is a good force or a form of witchcraft. The many stories about *uganga* practitioners who can magically transport themselves from one locale to another in the blink of an eye betray Giriama's ambivalence toward travel, for such powers are alternately enviable and frightening.

According to one thirty-year-old Christian man who works as a clerk at Malindi hospital, the power of travel is suspect, for the forms of transportation that make up urban life are matters of the Devil: "Satan has taken hold of this world, and Satan can take hold of you. Did you know that when the Devil enters into your body and stays in you for a long time, he turns your body into a town? He constructs roads, houses, offices, and even buys cars and travels in your body. He travels through you using cars he has bought. So he turns your body into a town like Malindi." In this vision a morally suspect town life is associated with houses and offices but also, emphatically, with new technologies of transportation. While the speaker does not discuss Arabs or Swahili per se, it is telling that the act of buying cars, widely associated by Giriama with Swahili entrepreneurial efforts, is here imputed to an evil power. Yet such narratives hardly deter Giriama from aspiring to travel, or to control travel, themselves. Many Giriama, particularly the younger generations, resent the limited circuits of their own mobility and speak longingly of what it would be like to own their own taxi or even to go abroad, perhaps in the beneficent care of a European or American lover. All in all, the ambiguity lingers in the Giriama community: Are speed and transport primarily desirable kinds of potency, or are they dangerous and suspect?

The unresolved question has special weight for Giriama because mobility has become associated with value making in precisely the era that Giriama feel the most displaced from the lands that, according to their narratives, once grounded and defined them. As in many sub-Saharan African contexts prior to colonialism, in Giriama areas land was not primarily an object waiting to be commodified by buyers or appropriated as property by the state. Uncleared land was said to belong to Mulungu, the Giriama godhead (Udvardy 1990: 64), or to the spirits. While an individual might acquire rights to use land through exchange (men could own land; women could own land only jointly with their husband), it was also common for men to inherit property rights through the male line in a practice called *lukolo* (53–54). Giriama today argue fiercely for their right to the land they had grown accustomed to cultivating by the time British colonials arrived. Invoking the Giriama rebellion of 1913–1914 in which Giriama north of the Sabaki River attempted to derail British colonial plans to displace them, one elderly farmer said to his grandson, "You young men don't know. We fought wars over this land and we won the wars. When we died, our blood sank into this earth." Giriama, he implies, are essentially linked to the earth by virtue of a blood connection, established through their self-sacrifice. Ultimately, however, colonial efforts successfully displaced numerous Giriama from their territories, while colonial ordinances decreed that only those with bloodlines traceable to Arabia were allowed to legally own land (Cooper 1980; Willis 1993). As discussed in chapter 1, to be indigenous on the coast became a liability; to have an invisible yet essential thread reaching across the oceans to a faraway place was the key to advantage. Giriama and other Mijikenda were reduced to squatting and, in some cases, applying for permits from their local chiefs to till the land.

Today Giriama are legally entitled to buy land, but most in the Malindi area squat on land owned by Arabs, Swahili, other ethnic groups, or the government. One of the most vexing political issues for Giriama all over the coast is land grabbing: the charge that the wealthy, frequently Swahili and Arabs, have appropriated land out from under Giriama and other Mijikenda who live there. Land grabbing takes several forms. In some cases, land-grabbing charges emerge from the mishandling of post-independence settlement schemes ostensibly designed to assist the landless. Elites connected to central state politicians received much of the land in these arrangements; they, in turn, sold the land—sometimes to Arabs and Swahili, sometimes to hoteliers—or gave it to their cronies, some of them from upcountry (cf. Kanyinga 1998). In other cases, say Giriama, a schemer appeals to older modes of generosity by asking to borrow a small area of an individual's territory, then falsely claims to the commissioner of lands that he was sold the entire plot. In still other instances, individuals may apply for title deeds to lands that are not privately owned; the squatters on such land can contest these applications once the allotments are listed in the *Kenya Gazette* (as they must be by law), but few squatters have access to this publication or know about this procedure. Sometimes squatters don't realize the land they live on is privately owned by Muslims who were given the title deeds by the sultanate at the turn of the century; they are surprised when long-absent Arab and Swahili landowners return to claim their title deeds or to sell the land (a popular move in the 1980s as tourism picked up and coastal real estate gained value). Giriama who actually own land sometimes sell the title deeds on the cheap to Swahili and Arabs, but they usually do so out of financial desperation (A. M. Mazrui 1997).

In their own defense Giriama sometimes adduce laws that take account of squatters' having built permanent structures or planted valuable trees on the plot in question. Some Muslim landowners, in fact, have allowed squatters to remain, provided that they do not grow cash crops or trees, which might be used to support legal ownership claims (Kanyinga 1998: 15). In the worst cases, landowners have bulldozed entire Giriama villages without warning. For decades many Giriama have demanded compensation for these disruptive and sometimes calamitous developments (S. G. Thompson 1990: 112), but rarely have they met with success. The anxiety about land grabbing is so great that when a group of archaeologists based at Fort Jesus Museum in Mombasa recently traveled to the Sabaki River area (just north of Malindi) to conduct a survey of ancient settlements, some Giriama in the area who noted the light complexion and Muslim surname of one of the archaeologists refused to cooperate with the team, fearing they represented Arabs scouting the land for appropriation.

The dispossession of Giriama from coastal lands has resulted in a surge of Giriama interest in the ancestral Kaya compounds. Some Kaya are today inhabited by a small handful of elders considered ritually potent repositories of Mijikenda authenticity; these individuals are sometimes called upon in times of acute crisis, for instance during the coastal clashes of 1997 and the anxious months in early 2008 when the country seemed on the brink of an ethnoterritorial civil war. Yet the Kaya are not the only lands Giriama (and other Mijikenda) lay claim to; as noted in chapter 1, many Giriama in Malindi assert their rights by claiming that they have lived along the *entire* coast, including the urban areas long occupied by Swahili and Arabs, "since time immemorial." In a meeting with politicians over land rights, one man called upon the trope of slavery to make his point about land rights: "How come a stranger owns our property while we are made slaves in our ancestral land?" (Kanyinga 1998: 13).

If Giriama wish to be rerooted in the land they have lost, their narratives sometimes contrast this longed-for groundedness with the forces of mobility that so often accompany modernity. Such a contrast undergirds the tales told to me by a number of male elders about mystical Mijikenda powers that have thwarted the advance of developers. One such story involves a cluster of magical black stones in land occupied predominantly by Chonyi (another Mijikenda group, closely related to Giriama) near Chasimba. "That place is impassable," explained a Giriama elder. "No one has been able to build a road through it." He continued:

> First a water company tried to break their way through the stones. The old men who live there challenged them to try but they couldn't bulldoze them; they had to bend the water main. Then some developers were trying to build a road to get access to a secondary school, and they encountered a big black stone. They tried to break it, and it regrew again and again. They blew it up again and again! Another engineer tried and still the stone failed to explode. Finally an old man called Tzonga Wako came and said "Call your own God— you can't beat ours. Ours is making the stone grow." He told the engineers: "Even if the president comes, you can't break it!" So they called Kenyatta [Jomo Kenyatta, president of Kenya from 1964 to 1978], and he witnessed the magical stones. He was amazed, and designated the place for a museum. But the elders said: "No; this is a place where we pray. Leave it alone."

Numerous contrasts appear in this astonishing tale: the modern, scientifically minded engineers, powerless against the challenging Mijikenda elders, who represent timeless customary forces; the museum of (nationalized? secularized?) wonders dismissed in favor of the implied authenticity of (ethnically based) prayer; the feeble developers' god versus the potent Mijikenda god. It seems too as if the invocation of Kenyatta's awe might bespeak a fantasy about the national respect Mijikenda have never received. But most germane to this discussion is the implacability of the black stones that vex all things flowing and changing. Water, roads, traffic, even modern schooling—all must stop or bend to accommodate these rooted Mijikenda powers.

Another tale of mobility versus stasis describes the most famous, and final, oracle of the nineteenth-century prophetess Mipoho. While there are many versions of this narrative, a common assertion is that Mipoho stood bolt upright in the center of a circle of drummers and began to descend vertically into the ground as she prophesied that a people as white as butterflies would soon arrive, bringing craft that soared across the sky and great traveling machines that would roll across the land. Mijikenda youth would scorn their elders and abandon their old ways. In one telling, Mipoho is swallowed by the earth in an area of Kaloleni "just where the tarmac road ends"—at the limen, in other words, of the old ways of the hinterland and the new, speeding forces of urban development. This prophetess is now a heroine of Giriama ethnic revivalists, having foreseen the forms of lightness (butterflies and other flying things) and velocity that would uproot young Giriama and so radically threaten customary Giriama life. How appropriate, then, that as she foretold these changes she defiantly drove her body into the ground like a stake marking territory.

Property, Possessive Individualism, and Personhood

Mipoho was right. The people as white as butterflies arrived and brought with them not only the Mombasa railroad and tarmac roads, but also a paper bureaucracy that emphasizes private property. Most Giriama know they must play the game of rights and resources in contemporary terms, but many wend their way through the world of title deeds, acquisitiveness, and the legalities of landownership with tortured ambivalence. Such tensions are hardly new; Parkin (1972) has written of the conflicts in mid-twentieth-century Kaloleni between Giriama elders and their entrepreneurial sons, whose economic lives ran against the grain of older distributive values. In today's Malindi too the Giriama population is host to competing models of ownership and entitlement.

Before the colonial and postcolonial eras of title deeds, say my Giriama informants, rural land was shared generously among Giriama; there was plenty to go around. Rights to land could be inherited through the male line, but the traditionally valued model of ownership was a kind of patrimonial stewardship in which land was overseen by Mulungu and the spirit world rather than dominated strictly by humans, and beneficent caretakers, elders, would have a sense of the boundaries of their ancestors' lands. If those who moved into the area wanted to use the land, they would introduce themselves with the presentation of palm wine and request use of the territory from the elders. When the elders agreed, the arrangement would be sealed by gift giving, followed by the public consumption of palm wine by all parties and sometimes a feast. The original steward might even help the new party to clear the land, and the newcomer would maintain these social relations, sometimes holding a feast for the previous owner and others in the community at the time of harvest. Such transactions involved the spiritual world as well. If any large trees, particularly baobabs, were disturbed in the clearing of the land, the spirits who lived there would require palliative offerings of palm wine. "You owed those spirits a debt," as one elder explained it. In such narratives the transfer of lands was a matter of interdependence with and long-term recompense to both the spirits and the original landowners.

Almost no one in Malindi talks anymore about spirits or Mulungu as the custodians of the land, nor do Giriama elders have much power over territory. As landownership has shifted to a matter of impersonal transactions and battles over land tenure rights, title deeds have become the cause of generational tensions. Some younger Giriama fight with the Municipal Council for their legal rights, while elders sigh, saying, "These matters of paperwork are foreign to us." Some still talk about a speech President Moi delivered decades ago on the Malindi showground in which he announced that squatters should not be turned off their land; many Giriama listeners assumed that the president's spoken word should be legally binding and have been dismayed to find, repeatedly, that it is not. Nostalgia for an older kind of authority underpins the lecture one elderly man gave to one of my Giriama research assistants who had recently finished high school. "In school," he said, "you can go a long long distance [notice his metaphorical equation between education and travel], but if you return home you must ask your elders, not the Municipal Council, about the land boundaries. Yet you young people don't see the reason behind this." Tensions about how to apprehend land conflicts have even given rise to conflicting stereotypes about an intrinsic Giriama character. I have heard a few boast, "How fierce we Giriama are," as they describe throwing stones at Arab landowners threatening to bulldoze their property. Yet others announce with a degree of resignation, "You know, we Giriama are very generous and trusting. If a Swahili asks to borrow our land, it's in our nature to capitulate. We're accustomed to sharing."

Such remarks invoke the patterns of Giriama reciprocity that stand in tension with urban possessive individualism. Traditional Giriama sensibility emphasizes distribution rather than accumulation; Giriama funerals, for instance, provide a regular, ritualized means of dispersing cash, food, and palm wine among hundreds of guests (Parkin 1972), and elders expect wage laborers returning to their large rural homesteads to share a portion of their earnings. Even in today's improvisational homesteads near Malindi, those who earn more money are expected to give generously to their neighbors. Swahili too believe in communal support, yet their generosity is not based on equality of distribution but, in many cases, is to assuage the embarrassment of riches while engaging in a kind of investment in the afterlife. Furthermore Swahili donations to community projects usually support the advancement of other Muslims, a pattern of exclusivity that Giriama note with resignation, having once been recipients of Swahili patronage. And so, while Swahili tend to construe their own relative wealth as the result of hard work, community support, and divine approval (*baraka*), many Giriama find Swahili accumulation a distasteful negation of the value of reciprocity. Yet this revulsion is twinned with envy, as many, particularly the young, express frustration at being unable to attain such a standard of living. One Giriama owner of a small but successful guest house complained of the tension he felt: "It's hard to make a profit when everyone [in the community] is eating at you."

Another source of unease in Giriama life emerges from the fact that their customary notions of personhood are not bound up with the kinds of privately cultivated desires and motives that are idealized in modern capitalist settings. While their discourse on slavery makes clear that Giriama value the ability to live their lives without being subjugated by other ethnic groups, it is nevertheless the case that they have not traditionally cultivated a folk ideology of self-determination, free will, or individualism. Indeed, as Parkin (1991a: 215–16) has written of Giriama personhood, "The person and his or her desires seem most likely to be defined in response to events affecting them from the outside, so to speak. One does not start from one's own desires and work outwards, but, rather, one seeks and devises the means to combat the ill-effects of other people's desires." Agency for many Giriama is thus construed as a relatively distributed affair; one's desires and activities are interdependent rather than emergent purely from a private locus. This orientation to the desires and actions of others is coupled with a tendency to formulate plans with the help of intermediaries from the spirit world. It is not unusual, for instance, for Giriama to make important decisions on the basis of directives from their deceased grandparents, who have appeared in their dreams. Many also call upon diviners to learn about the forces, often supernatural, impinging on them so that they may counterbalance bewitchment with the appropriate antidotes. Adjudication of disputes is sometimes put into the hands of aleatory devices operated by diviners (such as elaborately configured gourds on a string) that provide yes-no responses to determine a course of action. While some Swahili also draw upon the spirit world, divination, and other such forces, in Malindi this is usually frowned upon by religious authorities as a distraction from ideal forms of Muslim piety. Among Giriama, however, acting in concert with these other agents is a widely accepted norm. Rather than cultivating an ideology of self-determination and individualism, many Giriama monitor the forces that impinge upon their fate and use other agents to alter the world to their advantage.

Many of these agents are mystically empowered forces and are a primary means of interpreting and dealing with the tensions caused by capitalism and accumulation. As in many parts of sub-Saharan Africa, social hierarchy tends to be associated with jealousy and accusations of witchcraft—in both directions, for the poor may bewitch the rich out of envy, while the rich may bewitch the poor out of spite. Anxieties about the toll exacted by less fortunate, jealous neighbors are rife (Parkin 1972,

1991a), and Giriama elders, as they lose control over old patterns of resource consolidation and social arrangements, are frequently subject to witchcraft accusations in Malindi.[6] Not surprisingly, witchcraft accusations against Swahili and Arabs are the most dramatic. These are commonly expressed through the distinctive idiom of the *jini* spirits that, according to Nyevu and many others, bring ill upon the powerless so that the powerful may gain. These spirit narratives emerge from Giriama understandings of personhood in at least two ways. As Giriama tend to value the qualities of interpersonal reciprocity and interdependence, so too do they use *jini* narratives to criticize what they perceive as the economic selfishness of Swahili. At the same time, just as Giriama understand their own fate as bound together with the acts of spiritual agents rather than as wholly self-determined, they demonstrate through the *jini* narratives that they understand Swahili fortune in the same way.

Greedy Jini: A Giriama Critique of Swahili Capital and Mobility

Many of the *jini* narratives I describe sound common themes in sub-Saharan Africa and elsewhere. A broad ethnographic literature has observed that witchcraft, demons, and bloodsucking vampires often serve as popular idioms for contemplation of the perils of social inequality, possessive individualism, and modern forms of personhood. Taussig (1980) contends that notions of the devil in the mines and cane fields of South America reflect the workers' abhorrence of the market economy and fidelity to principles of reciprocity. Mills (1995) describes how labor migration and anxieties associated with modernity in rural northeast Thailand have resulted in a spreading fear of sexually voracious, deadly "widow ghosts." Weismantel (2001) analyzes Andean Indians' stories about the terrifying Pishtacos, white bogeymen that hang Indians upside down to drain their fat, narratives that she says score racial and ethnic boundaries while encoding a moral critique of the economic exploitation of indigenous people by whites. And scholars such as Auslander (1993), Ciekawy (1997, 1998), Comaroff and Comaroff (1993), Geschiere (1997), Meyer (1992, 1995), Niehaus (2001), and Smith (2001) all recount ways that witchcraft and spirit beliefs in sub-Saharan Africa constitute a pointed critique of the social disruptions and asymmetries created by colonial, modern, and capitalist orders.

While *jini* narratives undoubtedly resonate with this pattern, their valence is distinctly local and deserving of scrutiny. The literature I have just cited typically casts witchcraft and spirit narratives as responses to Western economic and political orders such as colonialism and neo-liberalism, but *jini* narratives speak to modern versions of historically ancient Swahili and Arab advantages, gained through spatial mobility and long-distance ties. This recurrent trope in the narratives yokes them to another common cultural pattern in sub-Saharan Africa, namely, associations between witchcraft or dangerous spirits and transportation (Auslander 1993; Bastian 1998; Masquelier 2002; Weiss 1993; White 2000). Scholars have argued that the opportunities of urban life and development are predicated on motion and speed, yet mobility, roads, and vehicles are frequently associated with uncontrolled movement, danger, social breakdown, isolation, and marginalization. In southern Niger, for instance, harmful spirits are thought to assail travelers on the roads, encapsulating what Masquelier (2002: 831) calls "a profound ambivalence toward roads, mobility, and mass transport." Auslander (1993: 169) documents a series of tropes among rural Ngoni in eastern Zambia in the 1980s in which roadways were construed as sites of "dangerous flows of person and substances." In the *jini* narratives the ancient theme of Swahili mobility is twinned with anxieties about its contemporary forms. The witchly *jini* spirits instantiate not only a critique of Swahili movement, but also a critique of Swahili capital, much of which Giriama see as derived from transport and, they say, from the exploitation of the underclass. Swahili's long-distance travel, furthermore, is read by some Giriama as necessitating depersonalized and thus morally suspicious economic transactions. Often the same people who harbor *jini* spirits are said to be wealthy landowners who, having secured the powers associated with mobility, establish a double monopoly by refusing to grant Giriama the access to land, the rootedness, they consider their patrimonial right.

Giriama life is populated by numerous kinds of spirits, including many that assist diviners and healers and many with ethnoreligious identities in their own right (see chapters 3 and 4). *Jini* are considered a particularly malicious kind of Muslim spirit, thought to be purchased by wealthy Arabs and Swahili from other Muslims and to be the primary device for accruing financial privileges at the expense of others.[7] In some cases Swahili are said to use *jini* to bewitch a beleaguered Giriama servant who picks up a few shillings off his or her employer's floor or a hungry Giriama taking mangoes off Muslim-owned trees. Most common, however, are narratives about Arabs and Swahili who use the assistance of *jini* to magically import money from faraway places. A *jini* may fly to Arabia to retrieve gold or currency, then bury it or place the stolen money under its owner's pillow, appearing to its owner in dreams and telling him (the owner is almost always male) where to find the hidden lucre. One elderly Giriama man led me by the elbow to the Vasco da Gama pillar—a tall, whitewashed obelisk with a small white cross atop it facing the sea—and indicated, in a hushed voice, that some *jini* bring money from abroad and place it in that very spot. Ironically the pillar was erected in the early sixteenth century by Catholic Portuguese as they initiated centuries of struggle against local Muslims for control of Indian Ocean trade; it became the site of high tensions in 1997, when Swahili accused European residents of Malindi of neocolonial aspirations in their attempts to commemorate da Gama's arrival in East Africa (McIntosh 2001a). Still, the stark white façade of the pillar may index Islamic purity for at least some Giriama, while its foreign origins and oceanfront view invoke the mystique of faraway places and the privilege of long-distance travel.

In many *jini* narratives the worst offenders are Swahili and Arabs in the transportation business, including several families in the Malindi area. A prolific series of tales centers on one family in particular, the Bakhsons, who own several prominent bus lines and *matatus* in Malindi. Giriama accounts of the Bakhsons pointedly mention that the family has Arab blood on the paternal side and Mijikenda on the maternal, a lineage emblematic of the Swahili people, whose very genesis includes Mijikenda roots but whose contemporary aspirations place them (as many Giriama phrase it) "on the side of the Arabs" and in a position to renounce and betray their Mijikenda roots. The mythic status of the Bakhson family has been enhanced by its decades-old clash with the family of a prominent Giriama healer, Charo Shutu, over the ownership of several acres of land in Maweni on the edge of Malindi town. As accused land grabbers who dominate Malindi's long-distance ground transportation business, the Bakhson family is to many Giriama synecdochic for wealthy Swahili and Arab families in Malindi. While there are many variations on the Bakhson narrative theme, the most common tale portrays the family as ruthless entrepreneurs who have stolen Giriama territory, perpetuated some kind of essentialist slur against Giriama (for example, that Giriama are "too black" to be entitled to large plots of land), and consolidated a powerful money-gathering *jini* to aid the success of their bus line. Many Bakhson parables are intertwined with the personal misfortunes of the teller, crystallizing the teller's resentment and moral indignation. One such account was related by seventy-year-old Kimati Tinga. Shortly before Kenya's independence, Kimati's father was forced off his plot by a Swahili landowner when a senior member of the Bakhson family displaced him again:

> [My father's new] house was destroyed by the Bakhson family, and [he] had to go to yet another place, about four kilometers from Malindi. But when Kenyatta took the presidency he announced that people don't have to move or be forced by someone, but may stay where they are staying; no land may be grabbed. Kenyatta was powerful—he didn't want the Swahili to chase someone off their land. So my father and his friend went back to their old farm that Bakhson kicked them off. Then Mr. Bakhson employed some Giriama to cut down the palm and mango trees in my father's farm, so that the Giriama who were staying there would have nothing to survive on. He bribed the police not to do anything about this. . . . [The few] Giriama remaining on the land were forced to collect the harvest and to give it all to Mr. Bakhson. . . . My father, who is a Christian, insisted that they had many troubles during that time; they lived in fear. Then Bakhson's son was born in Malindi. . . . This son's deeds were just like those of his father; he had a supervisor who was also ruthless to his Giriama workers. And at the time, the land he was on was government owned —it wasn't fair of him to use it like that! It was around this time that Mr. Bakhson bought *jini*.

In Kimati's narrative the Bakhson family members are land-grabbing puppet masters who bribe authorities, hire other Giriama to betray their own people, and display general "ruthlessness" toward ethnic underlings, generation after generation. Kimati's brief invocation of his father's Christian affiliation rhetorically taints the Bakhsons' Islamic identity with immorality, while his emphasis on the displacement of Giriama from their land condenses a common Giriama anxiety about their deracination by precisely those people who have the freedom of mobility that Giriama lack.[8] The injustices mount, and then the young Bakhson buys a *jini*, the ultimate index of foul play.

Jini narratives frequently invoke the *jini*'s own motion and speed. The spirits' instantaneous long-distance journeys to Arabia are portrayed as awesome; as one Giriama youth put it to me, "Wow, man [Kumbe, bwana]! Can you believe they get all the way over there and back with all that gold in the time it takes you to wink your eye?" Another explained that the reason Swahili get rich so quickly is because the *jini* can fly so fast back and forth to Arabia. The link between *jini* and flight is further secured in a Giriama song that is sometimes sung at rituals designed to exorcise possessing *jini*, while sweet-smelling luxuries such as incense, fruit, and a tempting (to the *jini*) gourd of blood are used to lure the *jini* forth from various places on the body:

> *Kule manga kule—ehee!*
> *Kule manga kule—ehee!*
> *Majini yasaliako kule manga kuna madege meupe, kule manga.*

> These places, these—hey!
> These places, these—hey!
> *Jini* were staying at these places; there are white birds, at these places.

This song is striking not only for its likening of a possessing spirit to a creature with the power of flight, but also for its invocation of the color white, widely associated with Islam on the coast, and the color that Swahili and Arab men prefer to drape themselves in, particularly on Fridays. Arguably not only *jini* but Swahili themselves may be indirectly likened here to birds with the power to alight upon a Giriama victim.

The speed and ease with which Swahili themselves soar to faraway places and amass wealth index an unfettered kind of agency in which the weight of local kin ties and the associated obligation to redistribute may be shucked off. Yet this process involves a dreadful sacrifice, initiated as the *jini* begins a crescendo of demands upon its master. Usually the master must set aside an entire room in his house to accommodate the spirit, leaving the space untouched except to provide supplication— plates of food and incense—which the *jini* consumes once left alone. As the *jini* satisfies its hunger for mundane foods it ratchets up its requests, asking for the sacrifice of chickens, goats, cows, and, ultimately, human beings—sometimes impoverished Giriama or even the children of the owner himself. These victims, called the *jini*'s "seat" (*kihi*, Kigir.; *kiti*, Kisw.), are mercilessly exploited by the *jini*, who drink their blood, killing them off or meddling with their health until they succumb to physical disease, mental retardation, or madness. Here is how Kimati Tinga describes the sacrifices made by the young Bakhson after he purchased his *jini*: "They started to trouble him. If you buy *jini*, first you have to buy eggs for them, then chickens, goats, and cows—and after you've gone through all those, you must give them a person to feed on. So Mr. Bakhson had to get all those things. His eldest child is the seat of the *jini*. This child doesn't do a thing—he just talks to them, and is nearly paralyzed by *jini*." Other Giriama repeatedly told me that the Bakhson family or the Malindi Bus family have an enormously fat boy or girl locked in a special room in their home who serves as the seat for the *jini*. In some accounts the child's body is said to bloat and deflate with time, depending on when the *jini* are sucking its blood.

In another common variation on the *jini* narratives, indigent Giriama are the ones who lose blood to Swahili- or Arab-owned *jini*. Sometimes the *jini* owners are said to arrange a public feast, slaughtering a cow to attract the multitudes. The hungry crowd then becomes a sacrifice, a veritable menu from which the *jini* can select their next victim. One woman narrates this theme as follows:

> The Bakhson family get all their new lorries from their *jini*—but you know, those *jini* need to be fed a lot. Did you know the Bakhsons own land in Majengo [a slum area on the periphery of Malindi town]? They own that area where our children play their soccer matches, and some of the ticket money goes to them. When someone is setting up a match, the Bakhsons tell their *jini* when and where it will happen. Then the people start to arrive, and the people who can afford tickets get to sit in the chairs. The Giriama who are too poor to pay for tickets climb the trees to watch the game being played, and sometimes the trees can't stand the weight of them and collapse. That's when the *jini* pounce on the injured people and suck their blood. . . . In one match in 1995 a goalkeeper fell and cut his knee; he got a really bad infection and died—that was because of a thirsty *jini*.

In such narratives, harboring a *jini* is portrayed as a slippery slope to an immoral economy: the willful sacrifice of the innocent for the sake of profit. Sylvester, a Giriama man who works in the tourism industry, spoke for many when he said of the use of *jini*, "It's not acceptable. These aren't good people. It's not fair to kill your fellow man while looking for money. That's witchcraft [*utsai*]." The human seat of the *jini* is portrayed as an allegorical victim of Swahili greed, symbolizing the (alleged) Swahili willingness to murder others, often their own kin, for financial success.[9] The stories also tellingly place Giriama in the same structural position as Swahili progeny, as victims of the spirits and the spirits' masters. Giriama refer to Swahili as Adzomba (uncles) in an evocation of their historic kin ties, and their structural alignment with Swahili children in these tales implicitly alludes to an abandoned system of kin obligations. In fact, this deep sense of betrayal may be one reason that Giriama *jini* narratives nearly always target Swahili rather than the other wealthy ethnic groups in town, such as whites, Asians, and upcountry groups; after all, as Bähre (2002: 319) points out, "Witchcraft . . . tends to reveal inequalities and tensions [between those] who depend on each other, especially kin."

Not only do *jini* narratives critique what Giriama see as the Swahili abandonment of a reciprocal, morally acceptable mode of personhood; they also castigate what Giriama see as the perverted relationship between labor and accumulation in Swahili life. In customary Giriama life, and for many Giriama in town, Giriama derive money from the generalized reciprocity of others in their community or from the direct exchange of their own labor rather than from the appreciation of a vast stock of commodities or the profits skimmed from the labor of others. Consequently they seem to valorize not only the moral worth of mutual exchange but also what Marx called a labor theory of value, in which the values of goods and services are calculated in terms of the labor required to produce them. Among Swahili, however, wealth seems to arrive and compound itself without being rooted in reciprocity or hard work; indeed, the fact that Swahili can merely wake up to find money placed under their pillow by a *jini* underscores how little they need invest. For some Giriama, such as Sylvester, the only imaginable way to achieve this is through supernatural loopholes and the exploitation of others: "We Giriama TOIL for things; how can this guy buy all these lorries in a month, *bwana?* It's not possible. He must be using a *jini.*" The contrast between generating money through one's work and insidiously extracting value from others is also implicit in the words of a middle-aged Giriama man named John in conversation over palm wine with one of my research assistants: "Listen, we're here to drink, but we drink out of our pockets. We worked for this drink. We also take our children to school; that's money WE pay. The house rent, that's money WE pay. But our Swahili depend on their family members who are abroad. They milk money from abroad to sustain their lives." John distinguishes between the integrity of Giriama earnings, grounded in their own labor and bodies ("our pockets"), and the dubiousness of Swahili wealth from relatives abroad. While Giriama too depend on assistance from kin, the key to John's objection lies in his choice of the verb "to milk" (*kuamwa*), which implies in this case an exploitive extraction of life-fluid rather than a reciprocal exchange. The same kind of accusation suffuses the *jini* narratives in which blood is drained from hapless victims. Children, who represent the very possibility of social reproduction, are ruthlessly sacrificed on the altar of production, while capital is obtained through an abstraction of social relations that disregards the humanity of one's own kin. Similarly the bodies of Giriama, whose lives were once so closely intertwined with Swahili that they still refer to them using a kinship term, become expendable commodities. This depersonalized kind of wealth, unhinged from the toil of work, from mutual exchange, and from kin loyalty, is an affront to customary Giriama ideals of personhood. Yet the *jini* narratives rarely result in a conscious conceptual connection between the drinking of Giriama blood and the exploitation of cheap labor. An exception was the response of my research assistant Maxwell, who, after a long day of eliciting such narratives, burst out, "Wake up, you Giriama: they don't have *jini,* they have Giriama!"[10]

In other narratives *jini* not only collect wealth but also affix their dangerous powers to money associated with Swahili and Arabs. If a Giriama employed by a Swahili or Arab merely bends down to pick up cash that has fallen on the floor of the home, he or she will be bewitched by these spirits. According to one frustrated Giriama candidate for town counselor, this association between *jini* and money can result in political intimidation:

The majority of Giriama think that Arabs and Swahili can do better [as politicians] just because they are white people, and because they have the *jini*. I remember in the last general election, Arabs bribed some Giriama with money, and one Giriama said to his friends: "If they give you money, just take it—then vote for whoever you want!" But others said: "No, the Arabs have *jini*, and once you take that money, if you betray them, you could die, or something terrible could befall you, so you have to vote for them." So even if they got just a glass of soda from the bribe money, they still had to vote for them. This is what people think!

In this account the money in question is both ill-gotten (by *jini*) and ill-given (as a bribe), and to succumb to the bribe is to be held in thrall by dangerous powers. Such equations between money of dubious provenance and danger appear in other areas of East Africa. Shipton (1989: 25–26) found that upcountry Luo believe that "bitter money" obtained through the sale of land, tobacco, or gold must not be used for transactions involving "permanent lineage wealth and welfare, notably . . . livestock or bride-wealth transactions." If it is, potentially disastrous consequences may ensue. Similarly, Hutchinson (1996: 84) found that according to Nuer, a cow purchased with "shit money," earned by emptying the latrine buckets of households in town, will die. Among some Giriama, to accept money associated with *jini* and Arabs or Swahili without having earned it through labor is to cast oneself into a state of supernaturally enforced obligation, at risk of death.

It is, of course, a capitalist money economy that facilitates the depersonalized exchanges and abstraction of value that many Giriama deplore. Critiques of money in small-scale indigenous societies are familiar in the anthropological literature. As Simmel (1900/1978) and others have noted, money has a way of establishing equivalent exchange values across commodities with highly diverse use values, a quality that opens new possibilities for exchange but tends to loosen the social glue and alienate people from the personalized transactions that typically make up non-monetary economies. While scholars such as Parry and Bloch (1989) have argued that indigenous societies can turn money to their own social purposes rather than being subject to its impersonal logic, it nonetheless seems the case that many sub-Saharan African societies have experienced money as a kind of rupture with their previous social and economic values. Bohannan (1955, 1959) long ago noted that money's role as an impersonal, all-purpose unit of exchange has tended to level out indigenous distinctions between kinds of value among the Tiv. Hutchinson (1996: 74) has explained how the Nuer, in reckoning with the arrival of a market economy in the late twentieth century, critique money as "an 'inappropriate' medium of exchange in certain contexts because it [cannot] bind people together like 'blood.'" According to Masquelier (1999), locals in southern Niger have compared money to wind or snakes, metaphors that capture the speed with which it changes hands and its qualities of elusiveness and fluidity. These tropes of speed are particularly relevant to the *jini* narratives, in which money and motion are implicitly linked. Money not only facilitates impersonal exchanges, but its abstractions are precisely what enable the long-distance travel of Swahili and Arabs as they purchase the means of rapid mobility (entire bus lines, airplane tickets) and buy themselves out of the social ties one needs in a new place (recall the words of the woman who remarked, "If they go to Dar es Salaam and Zanzibar—that's money! Do you think they can live in a place where they aren't known without money?"). The implicit logic of the *jini* narratives thus aligns travel itself (by *jini*, by Swahili and Arabs, and within the transportation business that the *jini* enable) with the pernicious moral effects of a capitalist money economy.

Finally, it should be pointed out that the emotional valence of the *jini* narratives allows Giriama a degree of satisfaction as well as a reaffirmation of their identity in contrast to Swahili. *Jini* narratives may contain a thinly veiled longing for prosperity, but at some level these tales are "good to tell," for there is also pleasure, perhaps schadenfreude, in the moral condemnation of greedy Swahili and the detailed stories of how their children are grimly drained by the bloodlust of the spirit. These children are socially destroyed; their paralyzed status caricatures the state of ineffectual lassitude that many Giriama associate with *all* Swahili. *Jini* narratives produce satisfying evidence of Swahili laziness in contrast to Giriama hardiness, a common theme in Giriama life in Malindi. I can recall, for instance, one conversation with a man who met me at a café during a downpour; as we began talking about Swahili-Giriama relations, he remarked with some satisfaction, "If this meeting were held by the

Swahili they wouldn't show up. . . . Do you think they can walk in the rain? They'd just pull their sheets up and curl themselves on their beds." In one Giriama song an adult admonishes any youth who would be tempted to marry a Swahili:

> Nda hagomba utu haya msinene
> Mndabagazwa
> Amisheni kamarima kamajema
> Nimikono lewelewe
> (chorus) Sendee sendee mwanangu sende undabagazea.

I'll say something here, okay. Don't tell anyone.
You [pl.] will be made lazy.
The Swahili [literally, "the missionaries"] don't cultivate their land,
    they don't tap their palm trees.
They only dangle their hands freely.
(chorus) Don't go, don't go my son/daughter; don't go. You [sing.]
    will be made lazy.

The next verse is similar but for the sardonic addition, "Walking is their [the Swahili's] job [Kutsembera ndo kazi yao]." The song righteously contrasts Giriama production with the sloth of Swahili, who just "walk" and "dangle their hands," allusions not only to idleness, but to the loose-limbed, sashaying gait of some Swahili women and men, sometimes imitated by Giriama with great hilarity.[11] Such accusations doubtless draw upon a collective awareness of colonial and contemporary accusations that Giriama poverty results from laziness but turn the tables by deflecting the charge onto wealthy Swahili, who are symbolically aligned with colonialists and, through the term missionaries (amisheni), implicitly accused of aggressively promulgating their religious faith. And while this song portrays assimilation into Swahili society as possible, it is framed not as a route to upward mobility but as potentially disastrous for the way it contravenes Giriama virtues.

The Hegemony of Ethnoreligious Boundaries

Swahili may be "lazy" in Giriama accounts, but they also benefit from the luck of the cosmic draw. Jini narratives turn Swahili socioeconomic advantage—the result of historical contingency, kin ties, class privilege, and fervent efforts on the part of many Swahili entrepreneurs—into a supernaturally secured advantage and a cosmic fact. Giriama are almost never said to be able to obtain the powers of *jini*, for several reasons. First, *jini* are assumed to trump the powers of the indigenous Giriama religious forces that Giriama might use to poach or attract them. Second, they are said to be prohibitively expensive. Here is Kagwidi, an elderly farmer in Muyeye, giving voice to both assumptions: "You know, this land belongs to our people. . . . But today the Arabs and Swahili have just taken it. We can't use witchcraft to deter them because they have stronger witchcraft than we do. Even if we plant a *fingo* [a talisman designed to ward off trespassers or thieves], their *jini* can render it powerless. The witchcraft of the Arabs includes *jini*, which we can't afford to buy." Third, *jini* are sometimes said to be available only from faraway places dominated by Swahili and Arabs and largely inaccessible, logistically and culturally, to Giriama, such as Zanzibar, Pemba, Pate, Siyu, Tanga, or Arabia itself. Fourth, some say that Swahili and Arabs simply refuse to sell *jini* to Giriama, as if deliberately barring their access to upward mobility. Finally, in some narratives *jini* are portrayed as having an intrinsic or ineluctable ethnoreligious bond with Swahili and Arabs. Occasionally one hears, for instance, "Those *jini* are for Swahili and Arabs, not us." Consider too the words of Nyevu, the diviner mentioned at the beginning of this chapter who converted to Islam to palliate her spirit: "Most of those Muslims are witches. Those Swahili use *jini* to get their money." When I asked why Giriama don't use *jini*, Nyevu replied, "You have to be Muslim; otherwise you can't get them. You have to buy them from Swahili." I had to listen to my recording of this conversation more than once to notice that Nyevu's choice of words subtly conflate "Muslim" with "Swahili," despite the fact that she deems herself a Muslim. Her use of the phrase "those Muslims," for instance, places an ontological distance between herself and those to whom she alludes. Giriama, the subtext goes, may try to convert to Islam, but they will never fully belong to the Muslim community, with all of its (dubious) advantages. Other *jini* narratives too model Swahili privilege as not only unearned but also intractable. One Giriama woman sums up this sense of futility:

> We have our own witchcraft, while the Arabs and Swahili have *jini*. We believe that our witchcraft is weaker than theirs—ours works between

us, but we cannot do anything to them. . . . We think their *jini* are stronger than our witchcraft, so once someone gets *jini*, we are power-less. So, as always, we believe that Arabs and Swahili are in the advan-tageous position for everything: in the case of money, and in the case of their witchcraft, which takes the form of *jini*—there, too, they're on top. So we continue to fear them, and we don't feel free in anything we do. . . . We feel like we are poor, we can't do anything, and whenever we try something, witchcraft brings us down.

It appears that *jini* narratives serve, however inadvertently, as a means of both expressing and naturalizing ethnoreligious boundaries between Giriama and Swahili and Arabs. They reify Swahili power by yoking it to a mystified source of potency available only to Swahili and Arabs, and in so doing they help to secure the conviction that upward economic and ethnoreligious mobility is out of the reach of Giriama. Many Swahili have come to the same conclusion about Giriama, though for different rea-sons. While Swahili and Giriama do not view Giriama disadvantage in the same way, they appear to concur that it is intractable. It is pre-cisely this kind of sociocultural formation, in which the socially privi-leged naturalize the disadvantage of others while even oppressed groups come to take for granted their own subaltern status, that Comaroff and Comaroff (1991) have deemed hegemonic.

Swahili Perspectives on Jini *and Prosperity*

What do Swahili themselves say about *jini* tales? Swahili in Malindi live with Giriama in an overlapping cultural field, one that many are at pains to deny or repress. *Jini* (*jinn*, Ar.) are certainly mentioned in the Quran, and as such must be accepted as real; the question is how to conceptualize these spirits and how to react to Giriama narratives about them. Many Swahili living in Malindi's urban core, such as this madarasa teacher, treat Giriama narratives as a half-baked excuse for Giriama pov-erty, while ascribing Swahili success to a combination of drive, work ethic, and God's blessings upon his faithful: "I've heard those stories. Giriama make those up to make themselves feel better. You see, we know how to work, we know how to mobilize ourselves. They get angry when we don't give them a good job, but why should we hire someone who has trouble moving forward, making a plan that's organized and neat [*tara-*

tibu]? So they blame spirits. It's not spirits. God will bless you if your faith is in the right place."

Others agree that their good fortune stems from a combination of self-reliance (*kujitegemea*) and faith; as the owner of a restaurant in Barani put it, "It's not *jini*. It's effort [*bidii*] and the blessing of God." Another man attributed Giriama's economic plight to their lack of business acumen and the distractions of the flesh: "We don't get rich by *jini*. We get rich through business. Giriama can't do it because their whole mentality [*nia*] is palm wine and women."[12] Swahili thus tend to deny that there is a link between their overall socioeconomic advantage and the intervention of spirits. Giriama subordination, they suggest, is the fault of Giriama themselves, particularly their inadequate inner lives and failure of character, which many Swahili discuss in essentialist terms. A naturalized, negative model of ethnically based personhood, in other words, underlies Swahili explanations for Giriama poverty, while reinforcing the popular Swahili notion that Giriama do not make good Muslims.

Still, the Swahili dismissal of Giriama *jini* stories conceals the flow of idioms that continues to move between Giriama and Swahili communities. For money-related *jini* narratives circulate among Swahili themselves, albeit in different form. Swahili *jini* narratives do not include *jini* attacks on Giriama, and the narrators nearly always insist that *jini* are hoarded only by a few individuals who are far wealthier, less pious, or more socially marginal than they. Many deny that any faithful Muslims among them would use *jini*, for such practices are *haramu* (forbidden by Islam), "undertaken only by the very rich, and bad Muslims at that." A few use *jini* as an explanation for the advantages of ethnic Others; one Swahili woman told me, "Wazungu [white Europeans or Americans] have their roots in *jini*. They have a lot of education, so much that an African can't get to the same place unless the African has studied in the white style. And the roots of white intelligence lie with *jini*." Some informants suggested that the Omani Arabs in their midst, who are sometimes said to be more acquisitive and less pious than other Arabs, tend to hoard *jini* for money, whereas those of Hadrami descent are more likely to have the blood of the Prophet running through their veins or to have "elevated themselves by studying," to be "men of religion."

Clearly *jini* demarcate the margins, the edge, of Islam in different ways for these different ethnic groups. For Giriama, *jini* mark the painful edge of a socioeconomic, moral, and metaphysical boundary, beyond which Swahili and Arabs supposedly live in selfish luxury conferred upon them by their intrinsic connections to powerful mystical beings. For many Swahili, *jini* haunt the edge of acceptable Islamic practice, a reminder of illicit engagements with mystical beings that the truly pious are meant to ignore.

I close this chapter on another edge: on the eastern border of Muyeye, close to Malindi town itself. A grand house owned by a Swahili family sits incongruously beside several dilapidated mud-and-thatch dwellings occupied by Giriama. One has the sense that the owners could have bought a home in Shella or Barani but discovered they could get more luxury for their money by venturing beyond a few fields of maize into the outskirts of town. The mansion has whitewashed outer walls, a gated enclosure for two shiny cars, and a conspicuous satellite dish for television reception. On either side of the black gate, beneath a row of protective iron spikes, the owner has written two Quranic prayers in large white letters:

SURA BANI ISRAIL
Nasema ukweli umefika na uwongo umetoweka.
Uwongo mwishowe huwa ndio wenye kutoweka.

PRAYER OF THE CHILDREN OF ISRAEL
I say the truth has arrived and the lie has vanished.
Lies are what vanish in the end.

SURAT-AL JINN
Sema imefunuliwa kwangu yakuwa kundi moja la majini lilisikia
    (Quran) likasema: Hakika tumesikia Quran ya ajabu.

PRAYER OF THE JINI
Say it has been revealed to me that one group of jini heard (the
    Quran) and they said: Truly we have heard an amazing Quran.

Giriama who live near the mansion do not focus on the theological register of these prayers. Instead, ever alert to socioeconomic tensions, they remark that the male head of household must have penned these lines on his gate as a defense against robbery. The allusions to *jini* and to *uwongo*, which can be interpreted in colloquial Kiswahili to mean either "lies" or more general kinds of dishonesty, are taken as a reminder to the impoverished neighbors that if they should steal from the home, the owner will unleash the spirits of the house upon them. While this interpretation is plausible, I wish to highlight the almost ingenious polysemy of these prayers. The prayers remind Giriama of the (potential) presence of malevolent and dangerous *jini*, but they can also be read by the homeowners' fellow Muslims as a testament to their piety. After all, the second prayer mentions *jini* in theologically correct fashion as subordinate to and awed by the Quran. The first prayer, taken in theological context, does not concern stealing per se, but the Islamic emphasis on Truth prevailing over falsehood, as well as the immanent spread of the religion. Islam, it seems, can have one face for Giriama and quite another one for those who consider themselves its faithful followers.

Chapter 3

TOXIC BODIES AND INTENTIONAL MINDS
Hegemony and Ideology in Giriama
Conversion Experiences

Giriama accounts of Islamic *jini* that subsist on the
blood of innocents to fuel their journeys to Arabia so
that they can bring wealth to their Swahili and Arab owners imply a
geography of Swahili and Giriama relations in which Swahili wealth and
people circulate over long distances to magnify their advantages, while
Giriama struggle with their feelings of exclusion from the empowering
flow of buses, cars, capital, and persons. Superimposed upon this map of
mobility and wealth is another kind of geography: that of Swahili and
Giriama ethnoreligious orientation. For while many Swahili increasingly
turn away from the ostensibly African flavor of certain local Islamic
practices and orient themselves toward Middle Eastern affiliations and
forms of religiosity, Giriama in Malindi exist uneasily at the edge of
Islam, tacking back and forth between attempted alliances with Swahili
religiosity and expressions of loyalty to their natal group. Unlike some
other Mijikenda, such as the Muslim Digo in Mtwapa (an area north of
Mombasa) who thoroughly renounce non-Muslim Mijikenda customs as
they aspire to become more acceptable to Arab and Swahili clerics (Parkin 1989), most Giriama in Malindi are far more ambivalent about their
ethnoreligious position.

Indeed, the oppositional force fields that make up Giriama's subjective
ethnoreligious lives are sufficiently complex to merit a detailed examina-
tion. Social memories of assimilation into Swahili society are vexed by a
nagging contemporary suspicion that Swahili live in a world essentially
different from and inaccessible to Giriama. And while many Giriama are
put off by what they see as the selfishness of Swahili, some apparently

internalize the hegemonic notion (one that also circulates in Swahili society) that their Giriamaness is polluting and offensive to Islam. Wariness and anger compete with awe and longing, while the pressures to assimilate to the Islamic *umma* (community) stand in tension with two Giriama discourses, one of ethnoreligious essentialism and the other about Swahili discrimination, both of which mark the *umma* as a relatively closed system, accessible primarily to those with nominally Arab roots, including Swahili. If the fundamental question for Giriama is how much social mobility is available to them, the answer is terribly fraught. Their spectrum of ambivalent social and psychological orientations toward Swahili is displayed with particular drama in Giriama apprehensions of Islam.

A conversation with an elderly diviner named Kashutu depicts one form of Giriama's encounter with Islam. Kashutu began our discussion of her religious life with a proud announcement of her identity: "I'm completely Giriama, completely Traditionalist [*dini ya kienyeji*]. When I do divination, I pass the exams [her powers meet her objectives], so I don't need to convert! Besides, if I converted I'd have to fast during Ramadan and I don't want to fast." Yet as our conversation proceeded, the apparent clarity of her position was soon confounded. "Yes," she said, "I'm a Traditionalist. But when the month of Ramadan comes, I just don't feel like eating until the evening comes." I was trying to process the significance of this confession—she doesn't *want* to fast during Ramadan, but she doesn't *feel* like eating?—when her son pulled up a stool and interjected, "Yes, she can't eat pigs, bush rats, palm wine, or animals that haven't been properly slaughtered. If she does, she's laid low by bouts of vomiting."

Kashutu's symptoms, it turns out, are shared by a significant number of Giriama in the Malindi area. They attribute the cause to possession by a Muslim spirit or spirits who colonize Giriama bodies and force them into mimetic Muslim behaviors, including the rejection of the kinds of foods Giriama associate centrally with Giriamaness (bush rats and palm wine). Several decades ago Parkin (1970, 1972) undertook a pioneering study of the economic advantages gained by young, rural Giriama entrepreneurs when they were compelled by Muslim spirits to convert. As I explain, however, the demographics and dynamics of such spirit encounters are different in and near today's Malindi and require a less economically based interpretation. My own interpretation is motivated in part by the range of responses from Giriama beset by these spirits. Some Giriama seize the opportunity to align themselves as fully as possible with Islam; others capitulate minimally to the demands of the spirit but hold fast to their stated alliance with Traditionalism, declining to call themselves Muslim; still others dig in their heels and refuse altogether to accede to the spirit's demands. A struggle is clearly taking place upon the site of Giriama bodies in Malindi, and its meaning seems to extend beyond the notion that Giriama are seeking economic uplift or prestige. For these possession experiences speak to Giriama's conflicted perceptions of Islam, Swahili, and Arabs and their anxieties about the possibility of their assimilation to the Islamic *umma* or Swahili society. Just as important, these spiritual encounters are also grounded in subtle cultural premises about what religion is to begin with: its ontological status vis-à-vis ethnicity, its purchase on the body, and its relation to personhood.

Similarly Swahili reactions to would-be Giriama converts, including those possessed by spirits, cannot be grasped without a discussion of how Swahili understandings of religiosity emerge from models of the person quite different from those implicitly held by many Giriama. For although Swahili Islam is contested and internally diverse, there are nevertheless identifiable currents of rationalism and intentionalism among Swahili in the Malindi area; these are cultivated forms of self-awareness that are heightened by transnational connections and by local interpretations of modernity and that are foregrounded in prevailing models of ideal conversion and ideal Islamic practice. Giriama personhood, however, is not customarily focused on internal states such as intention and self-scrutiny, and Giriama spirituality and ritual practice focus on pragmatic outcomes rather than faith. Many Giriama thus model Islam in a way that pushes inner states such as belief and intention to the background, while focusing instead on dietary practices, dress, linguistic code choice, and other public semiotic markers. This disjuncture opens a space for Swahili to deride what they see as flawed Giriama agency in their spirit-forced conversions, thereby scoring a sharper line between these already ruptured ethnic groups.

The difference between prevailing Swahili and Giriama models of the person creates one layer of complexity in Giriama conversion experiences. Another layer obtains in the possession experience itself, in which bodies are wracked by the presence of Muslim spirits while, at a conscious level, Giriama resist or even revile the spirits' demands that they convert to Islam. I have found it useful to analyze these dynamics in terms of the concepts *ideology* and *hegemony*. As explained in the introduction, I follow Comaroff and Comaroff (1991: 23) in taking hegemony to mean the signs and practices that typically serve the interests of the dominant group and come to be "taken-for-granted [by members of all social groups] as the natural and received shape of the world and everything that inhabits it"; ideology, by contrast, is an "articulated system of meanings." Thus while hegemony is so naturalized that it may exist tacitly (indeed, it is "not normally the subject of explication or argument" [23], though it can become so under prodding from the ethnographer), ideology is generally self-conscious and explicit. Furthermore, while hegemonic notions and forms circulate across social strata, different strata within a society may have different ideologies (24). This distinction is useful in part because it allows for the ideological expression of different worldviews and priorities of Swahili and Giriama, while retaining the notion that the priorities of dominant Swahili may hegemonically infuse and (at least partly) shape the actions and experiences of subordinate Giriama.

My account of Giriama spirit possession helps this distinction between hegemony and ideology gain traction because the difference between these theoretical concepts can be seen even within the same conflicted person. Individuals may be possessed and thereby compelled to regurgitate and reject foods coded as Giriama—a bodily expression of the hegemonic premise that Giriamaness is toxic and polluting to the forces of Islam. Yet in these very same individuals this hegemonic force field may be countered by a vector of ideological resistance, which impels the rebellious individuals to deride both their own possessing spirits and the community of Swahili and Arab Muslims they feel have shut them out. This complex antithesis between the signs of the body and resentful discourse in the same person encapsulates the tension between lure and resentment, the hope of change and the impossibility of assimilation, that characterizes Giriama attitudes toward Swahili and Islam in Malindi.

Ethnoreligious essentialism also plays an important role in spirit possession. While plenty of Giriama convert to Islam, they also entertain a lingering suspicion that Swahili and Arabs are more connected to that religion than they are, not merely because most Swahili and Arabs are born and raised Muslim, and not only because Giriama perceive currents of discrimination against Giriama Muslims in Swahili society, but also because Swahili and Arabs are constitutionally, essentially linked to Islam. In some Giriama discourse Swahili are said to be literally poisoned by Giriama foods forbidden by Islam, and the possession experiences I describe are predicated on the notion of a deep ontological incompatibility between Islam and Giriamaness. These Giriama notions of natural, essential links between certain ethnicities and certain religions dovetail with common, if not unanimous Swahili assertions that Giriama do not make good Muslims. Ethnoreligious essentialism thus helps to sustain a hegemonic hierarchy between Swahili and Giriama in Malindi.

I contend, furthermore, that contrary to many prevailing models of spirit possession, these Giriama possession experiences do not constitute an example of resistance against power; instead, the possession itself instantiates oppressive, hegemonic power, while Giriama ideological *responses* to their possession are themselves resistant. At the same time, Swahili skepticism toward Giriama conversions that do not obviously involve agency or rational choice emerges in part from the different prevailing models of personhood and ideal religiosity among Swahili and Giriama. I suggest that these Swahili reactions further underscore the social boundaries between ethnoreligious groups in Malindi.

Regimenting Intentions: Rationalism and Interiority
in Swahili Ideologies of Religiosity

In their public pronouncements Swahili say they welcome any and all who seek to convert to Islam and join the *umma*. As we sit over tea discussing ethnic tensions in Malindi, a Swahili educator named Salim tells me that any Giriama convert will be embraced by Swahili with open arms. "Converting to Islam is a green card with us," he says in his impeccable English. I nod in recognition; I have heard generous assertions like this from many Swahili religious leaders and laypeople. In defense of his claim, Salim points to the Giriama converts who pray at his mosque in Shella, the heart of Malindi town, and the Giriama children— admittedly, only one or two—who study with Swahili at a nearby madarasa. But when pressed, he has difficulty naming any single individual who has converted to Islam and has been so completely assimilated as to be deemed Swahili. He agrees that not all Swahili are as welcoming as he is to the Giriama converts who pray and study in the mosques and madarasas in the center of town. "There are some Swahili who reject Giriama," he admits, "and there are some Giriama who feel rejected. But this is the result of communication gaps and misunderstandings. What we need is better communication."

Yet the tensions noted by Salim stem from more than a communication gap; they emerge from the ethnoreligiously framed socioeconomic and political tensions I described in the preceding chapters and are enhanced by divergent cultural premises about what it takes to become and be a good Muslim. Swahili notions of Islam, in brief, are increasingly focused on autonomy, introspection, and self-fashioning, qualities of personhood that have been associated with post-Enlightenment forms of modernity (see Taylor 1989), but that are hardly restricted to secular life (see, for instance, Keane 1997a, 2007, for discussions of Christian missionaries' models of religiosity in Indonesia).

Swahili up and down the coast acknowledge certain basic premises of Sunna Islam, including submission to the will of God as laid out in the Quran and the Hadith (a record of the Prophet's life, action, deeds, and words). Concerns about physical and symbolic purity play a crucial role in daily religiosity. Yet Swahili versions of Islam also emphasize a hierarchy of scholarly expertise, agency, and rationalism. A widely accepted dictum is that comprehension (*fiqh*, Ar.) of God's will and the "right path" are best attained through effort (*ijtihad*, Ar.); such effort follows guidelines laid down in the Quran and in the way (Sunnah, Ar.) of the Prophet (cf. Pouwels 1987: 66–67). Ideally this effortful process will involve Islamic education (*elimu*, Kisw.) that attends closely to the Quran and the Hadith. The most prestigious roles in Swahili society are occupied by the Islamic scholars and functionaries with theological and jural expertise (see Knappert 1970: 132; Middleton 1992: 162), but since the late nineteenth century religious expertise has been sought by more and more Swahili townspeople (Pouwels 1987: 192–93). In Malindi many of those without much theological knowledge or Arabic literacy speak longingly about gaining more; *ijtihad*, after all, is a process of contemplation and transformation rather than a static state. Islamic education in Malindi begins in primary schools (*vyuo*, Kisw.), where students first learn the Quran in Arabic by rote through musical chanting and ideally graduate to the madarasa for Quranic studies that, unlike those in some other Muslim communities across the world, frequently emphasize comprehension in Kiswahili and ultimately in Arabic as well, rather than mere rote memorization in Arabic.[1] In short, much Islamic education in Malindi tends to encourage the application and development of the intellect in the pursuit of piety.

Yet Swahili Islamic ideals cannot be treated as monolithic, for Islam-as-lived takes many forms and has been subject to internal tensions on the coast. For instance, Swahili versions of Islam have long been characterized by ecstatic, Sufist strains in their rituals, particularly during celebrations of the Prophet's birthday, Maulidi. Maulidi celebrations on the island of Lamu, a locale considered by many Swahili to be a repository of authentic Swahili culture, involves tambourine music, singing, drumming groups, and famous dances, such as the men's *goma*, in which they stage mock fights with walking sticks and Arab swords. Versions of these practices infuse many other Maulidi celebrations on the coast. Other Swahili ritual forms have long had an indigenous flavor, overlapping with Mijikenda practices such as herbalism and spirit mediumship. For instance, Giles's mid-1980s study of spirit possession among Swahili (primarily in the Mombasa area) found evidence of cult ceremonial activity that, though admittedly on the wane at the time of her findings (Giles 1989a: 82), involved the propitiation of spirits of varying ethnic backgrounds, including Arab, Pemba, Somali, Maasai, and even Mijikenda. The spirit propitiation she witnessed combined ceremonial forms from Islam such as songs, prayers, and chants, with forms more marginal to Islam such as offerings, animal sacrifice, and dramatic patterns of possession.

Orthodox Swahili and Arab Muslims on the coast have long been skeptical of such activities as a distraction from the primacy of Allah (see, for instance, Knappert 1971; Giles 1989a). Since the nineteenth century revivalist and reformist movements sponsored by Arabian interests have gained ground (Kresse 2003; O'Brien 1995; Pouwels 1987). According to Kresse, in recent decades coastal reformists have tended to "act as the executive agent for the external ideological interests of the institution by which they are funded," institutions that include welfare organizations based in numerous Middle Eastern countries (281). Proponents of reform, sometimes called Wahhabists (Bakari 1995; Parkin 1989), *watu wa Sunna* ("people of the Prophet's way"; Kresse 2003: 303), Halali Sunna adherents (Beckerleg 19941), or, as some of my informants in Malindi call them, Ahlul Sunna adherents, have criticized local Swahili versions of Islam for "innovations" (*bid'a*, Ar.; *bidhaa*, Kisw.) thought to deviate from the original tenets of Islam laid out in the Quran and the Hadith.[2] These innovations include practices such as the reverence of Sharif clans (believed by some Swahili to be imbued with supernatural powers because they are directly descended from the Prophet), the use of tambourine music in mosques during Maulidi, and the singing of prayers when carrying a body from the mosque to the graveyard.[3] Ahlul Sunna adherents contend that the Prophet wished such rituals to be reverently silent and wanted mosques to remain quiet and peaceful "even when the rosary is counted," in the words of one. Similarly many reformists scoff at those who tell fortunes using mystical geomancy techniques or spirit possession, emphasizing instead the importance of understanding the contents of the Quran and respecting its total authority. Kresse (2003: 301) has aptly termed this reformist movement the "Swahili enlightenment," a phrase that captures its emphasis on the rational and self-governing individual.[4]

While Ahlul Sunna reformism is a minority movement in Malindi,[5] it has succeeded in recent years in cultivating insecurity along the coast about indigenous versions of Maulidi and other practices (Kresse 2003: 282; O'Brien 1995). Many Swahili laypeople are vigilant about the perils of *shirk* (Ar.) or *ushirikina* (Kisw.), practices that distract from monotheistic piety and the total authority of the Quran. Anxiety about *ushirikina*, which predates Wahhabist movements but is exacerbated by them, has distanced some Swahili from practices with cognates in Mijikenda life, such as mystical divination techniques and heavy reliance on singing and drumming (*ngoma*; Kigir., Kisw.). The least apparently indigenous or African forms of worship, in other words, are becoming for some Swahili the ones with the highest status. Meanwhile the currents of strict rationalism espoused by Ahlul Sunna adherents align with certain strands of Western thought increasingly available on the coast through tourism, travel, and media outlets, including rationalism and the forms of economic individualism described in the previous chapter. These accreting forces have heightened the salience of rationality and understanding among Malindi's urban Swahili, concepts already immanent in Islamic texts and Islamic law and now prevalent in Malindi and elsewhere.

In fact, although only about 15 to 20 percent of Malindi's Swahili (by the informal reckoning of my contacts) call themselves followers of the Ahlul Sunna movement, the focus on rationalism and introspection is regarded as important even by those who do not consider themselves adherents. Take, for instance, a middle-aged taxi driver named Ali, who could hardly be considered a stringent reformist; every day, in fact, he affably drives pleasure-seeking tourists to and from the discos of Malindi in his Hawaiian shirt. Ali explained the Ahlul Sunna movement this way:

> In Lamu, the custom was to carry a Sharif from a boat to the shore; the Ahlul Sunna refuse this. There's also the tendency at Lamu and Mambrui for people to pray at the grave of a Sharif for their personal desires—like to get a girl baby or a boy baby. They might even leave food for that Sharif! But the Ahlul Sunna reject this—and so do other people like myself. This is an ordinary person [mtu wa kawaida]; why pray to him? The Ahlul Sunna also believe in understanding the meaning of the prayers; the Sharifs liked to do everything in Arabic without translation, but the Ahlul Sunna know that if you study the Quran in Kiswahili you will come to understand that Sharifs are just normal people. The important thing is to pray and to UNDERSTAND [kufahamu] the religion. We've got to get rid of this overwrought respect [heshima ya hali ya juu], kissing their hands and so on.

In Ali's portrayal the fetishization of the Sharif clans looks faintly ridiculous, while a demystified, nominally more egalitarian model of persons takes the fore. In his view a more enlightened approach to Islamic education will support this perspective, as individuals cultivate a rational grasp of Quranic messages. Notice, too, that Ali invokes an implicit geography in which Lamu and Mambrui, Swahili towns to the north that many consider repositories of authentic Swahili culture, come to seem confining and atavistic to a more transnationally oriented Islamic self. Some Swahili attempt to resolve the conundrum of ushirikina by invoking the ever-contested conceptual divide between religion (dini) and custom (mila), explaining that the more African-seeming ritual patterns are intended merely as benign custom rather than as religious practice that could threaten their piety. The same logic, incidentally, that goes into prescinding dangerous Swahili acts from acceptable ones is often used to disparage Mijikenda ritual acts as insufficiently religious; as so many

Swahili put it to me, "They don't have religion. They just have custom [Hawana dini. Ni mila tu]."

A common idiom of piety that circulates among Malindi's Swahili is the concept of *nia* (Kisw.) or *niyya* (Ar.; the word is also sometimes spelled *niya*), meaning "intention." Islamic scholars in the Middle East and elsewhere have for centuries highlighted the salience of intention to faith, to the relative worth of one's actions, and to legal determinations (Messick 2001). The importance of the concept is apparent in a canonical hadith that states, "Works are rendered efficacious only by their intention [*niyya*]." While *niyya* can attach to works in general, it is most commonly used across Islamic contexts to refer to the intention in prayer and other ritual acts (153). In Malindi many Swahili believe that anyone can go through the motions of prayer or fasting, but the *nia* behind an act is a, or perhaps the critical factor that makes it pious. The supplicant must wholeheartedly intend, during prayer and at other moments, to subordinate his or her will to God. The emphasis on appropriate *nia*, though sometimes highly rationalistic, is not particular to Ahlul Sunna reformists. Maalim Hussein, whose madarasa walls in the heart of Malindi are decorated with Maulidi tambourines (thereby clearly marking him as an adherent of a practice condemned by the reformist movement), delivered a series of moralizing speeches (*hotuba*) about *nia* in the Shella mosque in 2004. "The Prophet himself said," Maalim Hussein emphasized, that "everyone will be punished before God according to the *nia* behind his deeds [Ndiyo mwanadamu atakwenda kuadhibiwa mbele ya Mwenyezi Mungu kulingana na nia yake juu ya amali yake]." Some Swahili living rooms in Malindi have a plaque on the wall reading "He who prays with *nia* will have his prayers agreed to by the Lord [Aombe kwa nia Mola humtakabalia (*sic*)]." According to one Swahili man who works at a printing shop for Islamic texts, intention is central to receiving God's blessing:

> The first priority in Islam is belief—you see this in the *shahada* when the convert says "I believe God is only one." The second thing is your deeds, particularly your prayers. But *nia* is crucial, because if you do anything without the proper intention, you don't get God's blessing [*baraka*]. If you go through the motions of Islam you must believe and think to yourself: "I'm doing this because of God." If you have

sexual intercourse and you wash yourself afterward, the ablutions must be done with the intention of self-purification for the sake of God, not just to clean yourself up. Even if you swim in the ocean, it won't do the job unless the *nia* is there.[6]

This highly interior focus on *nia*, and the type of personhood it projects, is rather different from that described by Rosen (2002) in Morocco. Rosen contends that *niyya* in Morocco is considered publicly observable in a person's acts, in keeping with his general assertion that "in Arab culture, another's mind is regarded as directly evident in words and acts and therefore as neither significantly private nor inscrutable" (118). Yet folk models of a gap between evident behavior and inner state can be found elsewhere in the Muslim world; for instance, Mahmood (2001: 843) describes the distinctions Muslim women in Cairo make between the act of prayer and their state of mind as they perform it, in which "disparity between one's intention and bodily gestures is . . . considered to be a sign of an inadequately formed self that requires further discipline and training to bring the two into harmony."[7] While there are distinct differences between ideologies of prayer in Cairo and among Swahili, it is nonetheless the case that discussions of *nia* among many Swahili in Malindi also stipulate the possibility of a gap between one's acts and the intentions that drive them. Because the same physical act of prayer may be performed with or without the appropriate *nia*, the criterion for acceptable piety is driven into a private sphere that can be adjudicated only by God or those who feel themselves qualified to assess a person's sincerity. In Malindi Swahili frequently make guesses about Giriama sincerity in prayer, and these are not usually flattering. Many express the same kind of skepticism about Giriama conversion.

While *nia* should drive prayer and worship, Islamic leaders in Malindi also emphasize that prayer and worship should double back upon oneself to have a permeating and altering effect. One brochure distributed by a Muslim youth group in Malindi explains, "Islam does not think much of mere rituals when they are performed mechanically and have no influence on one's inner life."[8] Importantly, *nia* is not strictly located "in the head," but sometimes is "in the heart [*moyoni*]," a term that indicates a more encompassing form of interiority. Indeed, Hirschkind (2001) has described how young men in Cairo, as they listen to sermons on cassette tapes, are enjoined to "hear with the heart," a concept that is not strictly mentalistic but that enlists a complex set of bodily disciplines. Swahili do not cultivate such an elaborate folk ideology of embodied devotion, yet the concept of *nia* does not seem neatly reducible to pure cognition, for it is an inner state enlisting the whole person, passions and inclinations included.

The Swahili internalist focus becomes particularly evident in discussions about conversion. Successful conversion is thought to be grounded in a constellation of material and ritual acts, felicitous performatives, and, crucially, an inner transformation that accompanies these. In one Swahili household in Shella the grown daughters of my host brought their Giriama maid over to the couch where I was sitting. "You're studying the Giriama, right? You should meet Halima. She works for us." Halima was young, perhaps nineteen or twenty. The women flocked around her and adjusted her head scarf approvingly as she looked with apparent embarrassment at the floor. "Oh, it looks like she might be a Muslim?" I asked tentatively. "No, no, not yet," the women answered for her. To become a Muslim she would need to formally appear before a kadhi to recite the *shahada*, after which she would be tutored in Quranic education to learn the pillars of Islam and prayers, "taking them to heart," the women explained. The head scarf was a gesture, an index in the right direction, one obviously sanctioned (and most likely initiated) by Halima's employers, but it was nowhere near enough. Halima had to cultivate the arts of prayer and inner dedication to be counted a successful convert.

The moment of the *shahada* confession, so powerful in Muslim communities across the world, has special salience to my discussion because it exposes some of the differences between Swahili and Giriama religiosity and personhood. For some religious officials a spoken *shahada* is sufficient, but in the heart of Malindi town the favored technology of conversion is the signed testimony. Some kadhis and others who work closely with them keep a registry of these testimonies with a permanent record of their converts. In one such book, shown to me by a madarasa teacher in Shella, each page is entitled "Certificates of Confessing Islam." At the top the *shahada* confession is written in Kiswahili, English, and Arabic. Confessors recite the *shahada*, usually in Kiswahili (recent converts are unlikely to know Arabic), then they or the kadhi fills in the rest of the form, listing the place and date of the registration, the confessors' age and tribe, their original name and religion, and their adopted Muslim name. Their state identification card number and address finalize the form, subtly aligning the authority of Muslim leaders with that of the state itself, while enveloping the convert in a contract with legal force. The Giriama convert, who signs at the bottom along with the kadhi, is simultaneously reified as a Giriama by tribe, classified as a new Muslim, and encompassed in the broad bureaucratic forces indexed by three languages: English, representing the state; Kiswahili, representing both the nation-state (in its capacity as a lingua franca) and the Swahili people (in its capacity as their first language); and Arabic, representing the authority of Islam and Islamic law, to which the convert is now subject in such matters as marriage, divorce, inheritance, and death rites.[9] Importantly, the confessor's final written word is his or her signature, the performative that presumes the unity and consistency of the person, making manifest his or her (ostensible) inner conviction while securing an absolute change of state. Yet Giriama experiences of Islam do not tend to be predicated on such a unified or internalist model of the religious person.

Another variation on the theme of internalism in Swahili Islam can be found in the hyperrationalism championed in a series of didactic booklets and pamphlets about Islam that circulate through Malindi's bookstores, classrooms, and households. The genre of texts is not new; according to Pouwels (1987), it emerged on the coast in the nineteenth century during the Busaidi period, encouraged by the sultans and heightened by Swahili nationalist pride during Busaidi times. In more recent decades the East African Muslim Welfare Society has printed informative pamphlets by the lauded Swahili scholars Sheikh Muhammed Quasim Mazrui and Sheikh Al-Amin bin Ali Mazrui, the latter of whom established a printing press and newspaper devoted to teaching and preserving the faith (132). Today many of the dozens of texts that circulate through Malindi originated in the Middle East but are reprinted by Muslim organizations in Zanzibar, Mombasa, or Nairobi. Written in Kiswahili or English by a combination of Swahili scholars and internationally known Middle Eastern champions of Islam, the texts presume a national or international audience, and many explicitly pit Islam against Christianity—a reflection, no doubt, of the widening competition between the religions on the global stage, the influence of Christianity in postcolonial Kenyan politics, and, more locally, the surge of Christian missions on the coast in recent decades (cf. O'Brien 1995). While these didactic texts are overtly aimed at Christians, I discuss them here because they contain ideological strains familiar to many Swahili that help to inform the conflict between prevailing Swahili and Giriama understandings of Islamic personhood.

The authors of these texts, all of them men, share a number of rhetorical strategies. They tend to introduce their case with gestures of humility and adjurations that their conclusions emerged from a searching, rational pursuit of Truth over a long period of time, a pursuit enhanced by extensive familiarity with the Quran and the Bible. Readers are urged to match the writers in applying their intellectual faculties. Deedat (n.d.: 27), for instance, entreats his readers to join him: "O Learned People! Come let us reason together!" Baagil (1984: 24) repeatedly invites his reader into the next stage of his argument with the phrase "Let us now use our reason." The Bilal Muslim Mission of Kenya in Mombasa has inscribed the dust jacket of Joommal's (1965/1992) book with a reminder that Islam is an intellectual, not an emotional, faith: "Do you know that . . . Islam welcomes you to think and reason and not to succumb to any religion purely by emotional outburst?" Once the reader begins to engage in the reasoning process, these texts imply, the path to conversion has already begun, for rational thought leads one inexorably to the conclusion that Islam has discerned the only accurate model of the cosmos. The reader's reasoning process is often steered and enforced through a textual format that targets the critical faculties. In Baagil's (1984: 10–11) text, a Christian interlocutor (c.) poses skeptical questions at first, but gradually comes around after a Socratic-style interchange with his wiser Muslim tutor (M.):

> M.: Suppose one verse [of the Bible] states that a certain person died at the age of fifty years and another verse states that the same person died at the age of sixty years, can both statements be right?
> c.: No, both statements can never be right. Only one can be right or both are wrong.

M.: If a holy book contains conflicting verses, do you still consider it holy?

C.: Of course not, because a Holy Scripture is a revelation from God and it should be impossible to contain mistakes or conflicting verses.

M.: Then it's not holy again.

C.: Right; its holiness disappears.

M.: . . . If there are conflicting verses in the Bible, do you still consider it Holy?

As the Muslim sets up this syllogism for the Christian, organizing their turns so that the Christian will neatly see the error of his ways, the reader is placed by analogy in the Christian's position and so put through his or her corresponding paces. Notice too that according to the Muslim's reasoning, logic and consistency are not merely crucial devices for conversion, but markers of holiness itself.[10]

As the persuasive interchange between Baagil's (1984: 11) Christian and Muslim interlocutors continues, the Christian articulates what the text frames as a central value of Islam: "I am looking for a belief that I can rely on, that can give me peace of mind, [be] scientifically acceptable, and not just believe in it blindly." The notion that blind faith is flawed faith recurs in several other didactic texts. According to Joommal (1965/1992: 3–4), for instance, "Every single Christian . . . accepts everything blindly because his priest has drummed the very fear of Eternal Hell in[to] his heart if he disbelieves one single word." The Bible's messages, he claims, are often logically untenable, particularly the notion of the Trinity. But the good Christian is not supposed to question such tenets because the officials of the Church discourage it:

[They tell us] NOT to use our reason in trying to understand the dogmas of the Church. So *that* is the crux of the matter. We are not supposed to use our God-given power of reasoning in order to understand that which we are asked to believe. Our belief in these doctrines must be BLIND, UNQUESTIONING, ABSOLUTE!! . . . Does not one's common sense tell one that most certainly there must be something awfully wrong, something terribly wrong, something unspeakably ridiculous about this doctrine that even those who profess to "understand" it and who preach it, do not understand it at all? (6)

Not only are reason, knowledge, and contemplation upheld as the keys to conversion, but so too is free will. The convert must come to the conclusion that Islam is the right path through his or her own volition, without coercion. Hence many texts exemplify the values, already culturally familiar to Swahili, of temperance and patience, emphasizing that they are designed to persuade rather than to cudgel the reader. In Baagil's (1984: 8) text, Muslims refuse to proselytize too aggressively or even to tempt the prospective convert: "We are not allowed to [lure] anyone. We propagate only to those who want to listen to us. . . . There is no compulsion in religion."

The importance of understanding and free will complement the theme of *nia* popular among Malindi's Swahili; taken together, these injunctions require the self-conscious internalization of the doctrines of Islam and the application of one's inner self to the external performatives of ritual. Yet, as many scholars have noted, the notion of a self-conscious, inwardly held creed or doctrine is important only to certain religious systems, particularly the Abrahamic ones (Asad 1993; Needham 1972; Tooker 1992). Even within these religions, the concept of belief has not been static. Ruel (1982) traces the historical shift from Hebrew notions of belief that emphasized relational trust in God rather than an interior conviction about ontology to the concept of an inward-looking faith in Reformation Christianity. The contemporary demand that converts fixate on their inner lives, popular among Christians and Muslims alike in Kenya, is one factor that resulted in painful tensions between early Christian missionaries and the Africans they wished to transform. In fact, some scholars have argued that the appeal of Christianity in Africa has sometimes been grounded not in its focus on the inner self so much as its ability to be adapted for healing, purification, and other pragmatic rituals (Comaroff 1985; Sundkler 1948). In Malindi today the churches led by African preachers and filled with Giriama and other Mijikenda congregants encourage converts to testify to the pragmatic efficacy of Christ in healing and bringing them good fortune, mystical changes with cognates in Mijikenda ritual. The most successful missions, furthermore, are those that have allowed singing, dancing, being filled by the Holy Spirit, and speaking in tongues—again, familiar practices to Mijikenda comfortable with ecstatic celebration and spirit possession. While converts to Christianity learn the discourse of belief (and deploy it in a fashion too complex to relate here), it remains the case that Giriama come from a tradition of religious personhood that fixates not on inner devotion, but on the material and symbolic pragmatics of ritual performance and ritual outcomes.

Bodies and Ethnoreligious Essences: Modeling Purity

I will return presently to the matter of conversion among Giriama, but some further ethnographic context will help to illuminate the symptoms Giriama display when possessed by the Muslim spirits who demand their conversion to Islam. For Swahili discourses about interiority and re-flection, though they may be omnipresent in their sermons, in the max-ims displayed on Swahili walls, and in the didactic texts that circulate through Swahili communities, are rarely taken up by Giriama themselves. Instead, a different kind of Swahili discourse seems to penetrate Giriama apprehensions of Islam more keenly. Giriama are exquisitely sensitive to Swahili accusations that they are too polluting to make good Muslims, a charge that condenses their marginalization, feeds into ethnoreligious essentialism, and plays a key role in Giriama possession experiences.

One reason that Giriama are so keenly aware of Swahili discourses about purity is that the issue sometimes becomes painfully evident in their encounters. On one occasion I was strolling with a research assis-tant through Maweni, an area on the outskirts of Malindi town where Swahili, Giriama, and other groups live in dwellings that range from lean-tos to elegant three-story cement apartment buildings. We noticed a Swahili shopkeeper opening the large wooden doors to his store. As he began to place racks of *kangas* and other clothing in the doorway for passers-by to see, he spotted a boy on the road who looked about thirteen years old and called him over with a familiar air. From their interaction it became evident that the boy knew the shopkeeper, who soon began to upbraid the youth: "How long ago did you bathe?" The boy looked stricken. "How long ago did you bathe?" repeated the shop-keeper. "I don't know," mumbled the boy, "maybe a few weeks ago." The shopkeeper made a sound of disgust. "I'm not calling you 'Salim' any more; you're 'Katana' [a Giriama name] again." With that the boy was demoted from his acquired status as a Muslim to a wholly Giriama iden-tity, with all its connotations to Swahili of paganism and primitiveness.

Purity (*ueri*) is a concept built into Giriama metaphysics, but Giriama tend to define it rather differently than do Swahili. In Giriama tradition people, things, and places periodically require ritual cleansing to rectify their social and metaphysical balance and wholeness (Parkin 1991a; S. G. Thompson 1990). As Parkin has noted, such rituals generally occur in special locations; in fact, "place and purification are necessarily part of each other. . . . To talk about purification, which we may translate as repairing or sustaining sacredness, is inevitably to talk about the space in which the operation occurs" (221). The purest place is the originary Kaya stronghold, which is essentially yoked, in Giriama ideologies, to Giriama identity. Needless to say, Swahili do not honor Giriama ritual modes of purification, which are often effected through the herbalist's *vuo* bath or animal sacrifice; in fact, some consider such rites to be forbidden by Islam (*haramu*), and as such polluting. Swahili do not consider the Kaya to be pure spaces, but part of the bush (*msitu*): hinterland territory that in the Swahili imagination is not only uncultivated but uncivilized.

Among Swahili, then, purity tends to mean something altogether different. Linked to Islamic holiness and moral goodness, purity is a spiritual notion that is grounded largely in the body of a person. Purity is instantiated in and signaled through ablutions, visible cleanliness (such as a sparkling white *kanzu* gown), comportment (such as chastity among women and marital fidelity in both sexes), and dietary practices. A brochure titled "Concept of Worship" circulated by a Malindi youth group explains the moral importance of fasting during Ramadan: "The main function of fasting is to make the Muslim pure from 'within' as other aspects of Sharia make him pure from 'without.' By such purity he responds to what is true and good and shuns what is false and evil."[11] Crucially, several emblematic Giriama foods are considered intrinsically impure and *haramu*. These include the bush rats that provide a free source of protein for Giriama living in rural areas and the palm wine that has historically been a central source of Giriama income, a popular beverage, and a crucial element of Giriama rituals ranging from libations to the ancestors to exculpatory payments in cases of wrongdoing.

Many Swahili, in fact, regard palm wine not only as a polluting substance, but as synecdochic for Giriama identity. Swahili stereotypes of Giriama sometimes portray them as sitting idly beneath a palm tree, sucking down one bottle after another, contaminating their bodies while ruining their minds. The habit is generally perceived as intractable; I heard several Swahili intone, "For those Giriama to be good Muslims they would have to give up that palm wine, and they will never agree to do that." This discourse applies as well to Giriama hygiene. In unguarded moments, when straying from their normative standards of politeness, many of my Swahili friends and acquaintances made it clear that they consider Giriama a "dirty" people who "never wash"; they were aghast to hear that I had stayed with Giriama friends in the bush for a week at a time. Swahili women express revulsion at the thought of Giriama households—their dirt floors, their unclean surfaces, the rats that supposedly squat under their beds—while the rural Giriama custom of wearing no clothing above the waist (less common, admittedly, as one approaches urban areas) is an affront to Swahili eyes. The Giriama diet is a matter of particular horror. "What do you even eat when you stay with them?" asked one young woman, her eyes wide with what seemed like mingled disgust and curiosity.

Giriama are keenly aware of this critical discourse surrounding their habits; as one rather bluntly put it to me, "The Swahili can't spend time with us because we eat dirty foods." This simple statement belies the semiotic and ontological complexity of food in Giriama life. For Giriama, as for so many other ethnic groups, the consumption of food is not only about commensality, but is also partly constitutive of the category of ethnicity, thereby blurring the line between habitual culture and biological nature (cf. Bell and Valentine 1997; L. K. Brown and Mussell 1984; Van den Berghe 1984; see also Lambek 1993 for a discussion of how food taboos can be constitutive of the person). The naturalization of the relationship between ethnic groups and foods takes a striking form in Giriama discourse about Swahili. A significant number of Giriama have heard so often about Swahili intolerance of their food that they consider Swahili ontologically incompatible with the foods that both represent and constitute Giriamaness. Hence Giriama take it for granted that, while they might attempt to shuck off their former identity and assimilate into Swahili society, Swahili would never emerge from their ethnoreligious sanctum to join Giriama society, in part because of their foodways. The membrane that surrounds Swahili society in such discourse is modeled as semipermeable; Giriama can try (with uncertain success) to get in, but Swahili cannot get out—in some discourse, for quasibiological reasons. One Giriama diviner who recently converted from

Traditionalism to Islam told me, "A Swahili cannot change his religion, but a Giriama might try to convert to Islam [*kujaribu kuingia kule*, Kisw.; literally, 'to try to enter there']. But it's very difficult for a Swahili to convert [*kutoka*, Kisw.; literally, 'to go out/come out'] to enter into the ways of the Giriama. It's terribly hard for a Muslim to begin to eat rats, or to eat pigs. A Swahili will hate that. He just won't agree to do it." The locative indexicals in this account—as if Islam occupies a separate and bounded space, somewhere over there—indicate the mental geography that separates Giriama ways and Islam. In this diviner's reckoning the boundary between these Muslim and non-Muslim fields is defined in terms of what the body will and won't accept; the Swahili "just won't agree" to eat foods like rats and pigs that are *haramu*. This speaker's choice of words suggests that Swahili aversion to Giriama ways could be a matter of preference, yet other Giriama clearly express their conviction that Islam is part of an embodied Swahili ethnoreligious essence. Nyevu, the diviner we encountered in the preceding chapter, and her young counterpart Tresea explained to me why Swahili do not abandon Islam for Giriama Traditionalism:

> Nyevu: It's about the food. That food just isn't possible for a Swahili.
> Tresea: Even [their] skin will change [if they abandon Islam].
> Nyevu: Yes, their skin will change to look like a Giriama's.
> McIntosh: How will it change?
> Tresea: Eating rats and pigs just doesn't do for a Swahili.
> McIntosh: What will happen?
> Nyevu and Tresea (overlapping and echoing one another): It will completely ruin their skin. They'll get blemishes and sores, they'll scratch themselves—they'll even have to take a lancet [*kijembe*, Kisw.] to scratch themselves.

The assertion that Swahili will become ill or break out in pustules if they consume Giriama food circulates widely. In the logic of these accounts, eating *haramu* foods is not merely distasteful to a Swahili, but constitutionally, biologically poisonous. This putative illness reaction suggests that Swahili ethnoreligious identity is not just a cultural overlay of beliefs and practices, but part of their deepest constitution. Islam permeates Swahili bodies, and Giriama habits are toxic or polluting to Swahili and Islam. To the extent that this discourse makes stipulations about the innermost nature of ethnoreligious groups, it is essentialist; to the extent that Swahili have perpetuated this discourse and Giriama have internalized it, it is hegemonic.

Yet not all Giriama accept this hegemony without complaint. Consider, for instance, the words of Sylvester, a Giriama working as a doorman in a Malindi hotel whose conversations about Swahili often took a conspiratorial tone:

> Those Swahili, they say we're dirty, but when they're sitting around eating, they'll pick up some rice and mash it around with their hand, then they'll put it right back down where they got it! For a Giriama it's dirty to put food back onto the public platter after picking it up, but not for the Swahili. . . . And those Swahili kids also use some awful swear words. Even to the district commissioner; they'll say it right in his face. A small Giriama child can never never do that in his life. Okay, now maybe in Malindi, because people are all mixed together here. But normally a Giriama child can never be so disrespectful or filthy with their words.

Actually, there is one context in which Giriama are expected to let loose with their words: the liminal space of funerary ritual (McIntosh 2001b, 2005c). It is also a context in which antipathy toward Swahili understandings of pollution has a public outlet. In the Malindi area many Giriama funerary songs (particularly those termed *kifudu* and *kihoma*) are bawdy, profane, and irreverent, sung primarily by women but written by male and female songwriters. Many of the songs focus on tensions between the sexes, but songs of fresh political relevance are occasionally added to the repertoire. One of these heralds a future in which Giriama reclaim the land taken by Swahili, concluding with the refrain "I have raised the flag—now it's time, Africans, for the Swahili to eat rats!" In contrasting Africans with Swahili, the song makes an implicit ethnoterritorial claim: that Giriama, unlike Swahili, are truly African and are preparing to plant their territorial flag in the earth. Then the song taunts Swahili with the image of a dietary role-reversal. The consumption of rats becomes a synecdoche for social subordination, an especially powerful insult given that at least some Giriama believe that rats are not only offensive to but also ontologically polluting for Swahili. Another song cries, "The Swahili eat vagina-rice," derogating the rice cooked in coconut milk that is a staple of the Swahili diet by invoking the feminine pollution so important to Islamic prohibitions. There is surely some satisfaction to be had in imagining Swahili forced to ingest the substances they so vilify. These articulations of anger and resentment point to more profound ideologies of resistance among Giriama.

Complexities of Conversion

The ideological backdrop I have presented suggests that conversion in Malindi today is a complex and potentially fraught notion for both Swahili and Giriama. Yet most scholarship on Giriama conversion has focused on the strategic nature of affiliation with Islam and the ebb and flow of Mijikenda converts in response to fluctuating political, economic, and social conditions. Most accounts portray Mijikenda transitions to Islam as straightforward and pragmatic matters of affiliation. According to Sperling (1985: 50), the first Mijikenda conversions came about through trade and cultural contacts: "Commercial interests created common affinities, which in turn gave rise to personal relations favorable to conversion." Sperling documents numerous historical moments in which coastal Muslims formed close relations with Mijikenda groups; in the late nineteenth century, for example, Mazrui living in villages north of Kilifi Creek frequently traded with local Giriama, who sometimes converted to Islam (63).

Accounts of conversion from the historians Willis (1993) and Cooper (1980) confirm the strategic nature of conversion and suggest that conversion often led to social advantages that sometimes included assimilation into Swahili society. When Mijikenda clients of Swahili patrons converted, they sometimes benefited from incorporation into another social field that provided the excuse to avoid the gerontocracy of their natal homesteads, which many experienced as oppressive (Willis 1993: 55, 73). According to Willis, Mijikenda who converted in the nineteenth century in Mombasa were usually fully assimilated, accepted as kin and part of the household by their Swahili patrons. As Willis describes them, these conversions were total and resulted in full "removal of social barriers" (98). Some patrons took on a paternalistic obligation to converts whose transition they had facilitated, such that, in Cooper's (1980: 225) words, conversion to Islam among freeborn Giriama could serve as a "religious idiom of dependence." Slave owners also tended to encourage or compel their slaves to convert, with complex results, for slaves some-times used their new identity as a "challenge to their owners' notions of religious superiority" (22). After abolition former slaves sometimes claimed a Swahili identity and blended successfully into Muslim coastal culture (165). Parkin (1970, 1972) found that Giriama conversion re-mained strategic in nature decades later, in the 1960s in Kaloleni; spirit-forced conversion, he argues, allowed young entrepreneurs to distance themselves from their natal households and justify their nonobservance of Giriama redistributive norms.

Today conversion remains the sine qua non for acceptance by and assimilation into Swahili communities, however difficult and unusual that has become in Malindi. "Occupational conversion" is usually man-datory for Giriama men and women who wish to work in a Muslim business or home. Periodically there has been a rush to convert among Giriama men when they get wind that a Muslim-owned bus line is seeking drivers. Others convert because it is a precondition of marrying a Muslim man or woman, though many Swahili, particularly women mind-ful of their social status and economic prospects, scoff at the prospect of marrying a Giriama. Some Giriama nurture inchoate hopes that they will benefit from financial favors if they convert, particularly in light of ru-mors of extravagant payoffs to Giriama converts in the form of "cars and such things," as one taxi driver put it. Almost no Giriama nurture the conceit that conversions are primarily motivated by piety or religious preference. "One in a hundred convert because they actually like Islam," says Sylvester. "Usually people have a material reason. They want money or a spouse."

While the strategic nature of conversion is important, the dynamics of conversion are more problematic and less absolute than some scholar-ship suggests. I describe three complexities of conversion here because they are important to the spirit possession phenomenon to which I turn after this. The first of these is a religious relativism that emerges in part from Giriama models of personhood and informs many Giriama inter-actions with Islam. The semantics of conversion in coastal Kenya suggest an all-or-nothing state; the question "Umeslimu?" (Kisw.) or "Wasi-limu?" (Kigir.), "Have you converted to Islam?," requires a yes or no answer. Yet few Giriama regard Islam, or any religion, as a repository of absolute Truth, and only some regard the religious person as beholden to a single faith. Instead, many consider each religion—Islam, Christianity, and Traditionalism—to be a locus of discrete, ontologically real powers that one might or might not draw from and that might or might not make demands upon the person. In other words, one can use and interact with Islam without converting to it. Such relativism throws into question the categorical absolutism of Swahili and Western ideologies (including some scholarly depictions) of conversion.

Another complexity arises because Giriama approach conversion to Islam with a range of improvisational and largely indexical semiotic strategies, flummoxing Swahili models of standardized, internalized conversion. Among the most wholehearted Giriama converts, who are few in number in Malindi, the shift to Islam is accompanied by an attempt at ethnic and class assimilation. Beyond such acts as prayer and the rejection of *haramu* foods, they may attempt to rent a stone apartment in or near Shella or Barani, hubs of Swahili life in Malindi. The lucky few will intermarry with Swahili in the urban core. If they can afford it, they forgo the simple Giriama staples of maize meal and beans and begin to eat Swahili-style food that is religiously neutral but ethnically indexical, such as rice cooked in coconut milk and curries prepared with spices. Along with taking up overtly religious outer garb such as the *kofia, kanzu,* or *bui bui,* these converts seek out the more polished button-down shirts of well-to-do men or the housedresses and high-heeled sandals worn by Swahili women. "It's like one is trying to become upper class," explains one Giriama man of such women. "If you compare Swahili women to Giriama women, you see the Swahili know how to take care of their appearances; these Giriama are hoping to become Swahili by acting fancy." Indeed, these would-be assimilates, particularly women, may affect gestures they associate with Swahili, such as smiling more, swinging their hips flirtatiously, and gesticulating more while talking. One woman was excoriated by Giriama onlookers as she sashayed back and forth between Muyeye and the town center: "She thinks she's a real city girl now. . . . Look at the way she holds her wrists." Perhaps most galling of all, a few would-be assimilates refuse to speak a word of Kigiriama, replying even to customary Kigiriama greetings in Kiswahili. Because the majority of Giriama in Malindi believe that a Giriama cannot become Swahili in the course of one generation, whether because of Swahili prejudice, blood, ineradicable cultural differences, or other factors, some of them considered intrinsic and essential to identity, such attempts at total transformation often meet with obstacles.

The continuum of Giriama approaches to conversion also involves more partial stances. Some converts, such as the middle-aged Ali who lives in Muyeye, are sent by Giriama diviners to Swahili healers when they have been diagnosed as bewitched by a Muslim; these healers sometimes convert their Giriama clients and train them in habits of worship. Ali has taken an Islamic name but still lives in Muyeye and drinks palm wine regularly while working as an assistant to a Giriama Traditionalist healer; both are behaviors considered anathema by pious Swahili. Ali prays, though not on a daily basis, in the modest local mosque in Muyeye and periodically goes into town mosques as well. He tells me he has been hoping for some recognition by a group of Swahili who assisted in his conversion; they have given him alms but have been unable to promise him a job. Like Ali, other converts make erratic use of the indices of conversion; to them, shifts in clothing or dietary habits, or the mere fact of announcing their new religious affiliation, can count as conversion. Nuru and Sophia, for instance, are two young Giriama women living in Muyeye who converted when they worked as domestic servants in a Swahili house in Shella. Today they practice subsistence agriculture on the outskirts of town, and while they both consider themselves Muslims and wear head scarves, neither wears a *bui bui* or spends much time in prayer, and both eat an ordinary Giriama diet that includes *haramu* foods. I still remember my surprise when one young man who had assisted me in meeting local Giriama families casually noted the reason he considered himself a Muslim: "Because I never eat pork." Then there are converts such as Hamisi, the only Giriama I encountered who spoke continually of his devotion to reading the Quran, as well as of his frustration that he has not been well enough respected by town Muslims to join their social circle.

Hamisi's dilemma brings me to the third complicating factor in Giriama conversion. While historians have portrayed conversion to Islam and assimilation into Swahili ethnicity as relatively straightforward, in today's Malindi would-be converts vacillate between hope and frustration about the prospects for their acceptance by Swahili living in the center of town. Not only is acceptance into the ethnic category Swahili very difficult to achieve, particularly in the first generation, before memories of a person's origins may become blurred, but many Giriama also contend that Swahili consider them unfit for Islam, atavistic, and even intrinsically polluting. Some Giriama, in fact, regard Islam as so socially and onto-logically distant that they encourage other Giriama to reject Islam before it can reject them. For those who do convert, the question lingers: Who or what have they become, ethnically, religiously, and socially?

In one conversation with a Giriama man in late middle age I noted the *kofia* cap he wore, sometimes an index of Islamic piety, and I asked if he was a Muslim. "No," he replied. "Oh, I've been told to convert, but I won't have it." He then embarked on a bitter diatribe:

> Those Muslims promise they'll make someone a member of their family, they'll give him a plot to till, they'll build him a house—but these are all empty words. They may even promise him a Swahili wife, but he'll never marry a rich one or a pure, proper Swahili [Mswahili *sanifu*, Kisw.], because he's still like a slave. A person can even wear a *kofia*, but he can't live with them! They won't eat the animals he slaughters. If there's a wedding or a Maulidi, the real Swahili [Waswa-hili *sawasawa*, Kisw.] do it separately, and [a convert will] be told to wash and sweep up the mosque after them. He'll be left outside; he's "dirty," he's "Nyika." If he converts he'll be like a servant to them and he'll die. They'll toss him out and he'll have no home. He'll end up on his own, just on his own, all alone. He might beg from them and get two shillings one day, or three the next. They cheat him and treat him rudely.

The sense of exclusion in this narrative is palpable. Being "left outside" seems not only a remark about the spatial relations of Swahili households vis-à-vis Giriama, but also a metaphor for a more general sense of mar-ginalization. The theme of exclusion also appears in the tropes of slavery and skin color I discussed in chapter 1. Several Giriama insisted that it is only the "black people" who do the custodial work in the mosques in town, while high-ranking positions are invariably given to the "white Muslims." "It's black versus Arab," as one informant put it, a striking claim given that so many dark-skinned Swahili are accepted as core to the Muslim community in the town center. But as in so many cases of racial thinking, physiognomy does not neatly map onto social strata; rather, ideas about skin color emerge from anxiety about hierarchy. In this case, those with claims upon the faraway lands of Arabia, including dark-skinned Swahili, have the upper hand against those rooted, by dint of both autochthony and relative immobility, in Africa. The recurrent notion that Giriama are still controlled like slaves or servants contributes to the sense that Giriama cannot be embraced into the *umma* and also to their spirit possession experiences.

Some Giriama are stung by accusations that they have converted to Islam for free meals or other tangible rewards. Several Giriama Muslims who live in Muyeye told me they prefer to pray in Muyeye's small mosque rather than go into Shella or Barani and face the suspicions of the regulars. "If I go into that mosque," one explained, "they say I've just come for the food—the coffee and dates." The implication is that Swahili treat Giriama as if they are driven by appetite rather than piety. In some cases, of course, there is a degree of truth to this; poverty, after all, has a way of anchoring people to bodily exigencies. But such narratives also reinscribe the Giriama's sense that they are seen as ignominious scroungers rather than legitimate Muslims.

The dilemma for many is just what kind of identity they have once they have converted. Giriama have a history of assimilation into Swahili communities, yet today there is only a tenuous possibility that Giriama converts will be considered Swahili by Malindi's self-defined core Swahili communities. The records of conversion kept by some Swahili religious leaders treat ethnicity as a fixed rather than a labile identity marker, one that does not change with conversion to Islam. As described in chapter 1, many Swahili in Malindi refer to Giriama converts derisively as Waswahili Wasitu, "Swahili of the bush," while many Giriama refer to converts as Mgiriama Mwislam, Muslim Giriama. One Giriama community advocate, Phillip, discussed the complex tension between conversion and assimilation, portraying conversion itself as an effacing kind of slavery:

> We're being enslaved. I'm not afraid to say it—it's just like the way it used to happen before independence. I'm bitter about that. The Muslims are seizing their chance again, preaching that if you're employed [by] them you must become a Muslim. . . . If you drive for a Swahili *matatu*, after a while you'll become "Ali" and wear a *kofia*. But you haven't left your tribe; you're not a Swahili. You're just captured into the religion. You'll be "Ali Chai" or "Ali Mumba" [Giriama surnames],

and you're not allowed to do anything related to your culture because it's "barbaric" [*shenzi*, Kisw.] and "pagan" [*kaffiri*, Kisw.] and they say we don't have religion. I'm telling you, even if the ancient Giriama had invented the telephone, the Swahili would reject it. So your culture is erased, and so is your personhood, because personhood is culture [*utu ni mila*, Kigir., Kisw.]. You erase yourself, but you aren't considered a full Swahili. So where are you?

Phillip's vividly drawn portrait indicates what he sees as the capricious nature of Swahili rejection of Giriama culture. So gratuitous is their aversion to things Giriama, he said, that anything associated with Giriamaness is tainted with barbarism, no matter how ludicrous the rejection.[12] Phillip described the depredations of Giriama conversion, in which Giriama are lured halfway to Swahili life, then abandoned in a kind of limbo between Giriamaness and Swahili identity: "Your culture is erased, and so is your personhood, because personhood is culture." In Giriama ideologies, after all, personhood is not located primarily in private internal states but is constituted through the very kinds of public practices that Islam prohibits, such as the consumption of certain foods and the practice of indigenous rituals that ensure the wholeness of the community. Phillip also claimed that converts are "captured into the religion." The sense of subordination in this telling phrase evokes the kinds of encounters with Muslim spirits to which I now turn.

Reluctant Muslims: A Giriama Spirit Possession Complex

Phillip's idiom of capture may not intentionally allude to spirit possession, but it is indicative of an experience common to many Giriama. Over the past few decades the pressures to convert to Islam have taken mystical as well as social forms. A substantial number of Giriama— women and men, young and old, diviners and laypeople—say they are tormented by possessing Muslim spirits who hold their bodies hostage until they agree to capitulate to the spirit's demand that they convert. The most common and striking symptoms of possession are somatic reactions of the sort described by Kashutu earlier. The possessed complain that they lose their appetite in daylight hours during the month of Ramadan, that they experience illness if they do eat during these hours, and—one of the most common symptoms—that if they eat certain foods at any time, including the palm wine and bush rats that are emblematic of Giriama culture and *haramu* to Muslims, they vomit. Such conditions may endure for months or years in a chronic state of possession-induced discomfort in which the spirit's host is continually reminded, often through regurgitation, of the toxic clash between the dietary emblems of Giriamaness and the spiritual emissaries of Islam itself. I argue that these patterns of possession reflect certain essentialist premises that circulate among Giriama, that they speak to the different models of what counts as legitimate conversion and, in turn, of personhood among Giriama and Swahili. At the same time they exemplify the complex relationship between hegemony and ideology that can obtain in a conflicted society. These possession experiences also challenge prevailing models of possession as a form of resistance.

Some context for understanding Giriama spirit possession will be helpful. Giriama and other Mijikenda regard the earth as populated by numerous spirits, though their description varies somewhat from one locale to the next. Like their Swahili neighbors, Giriama use a cluster of terms (all of them found in Kiswahili as well), such as *pepo, sheitani, rohani,* and *jini,* to mean "spirits," and while some people differentiate carefully between these categories there is no consensus on the definition of each term.[13] However, among Giriama some definitions are fairly consistent. The term *jini* is used to refer either to Muslim spirits in general or more specifically to the class of Muslim money-gathering (and sometimes possessing) spirits discussed in chapter 2. *Sheitani* has a pejorative connotation to many speakers; it is sometimes translated as "little devil." *Pepo* is by far the most common term used by Giriama diviners and healers to talk about the spirits they encounter and work with. The possessing spirits I discuss in this chapter are usually referred to as *pepo* or *sheitani,* though occasionally they may be called *jini.*

In many parts of sub-Saharan Africa, indeed, in cultures across the world, spirits often stand in a complex, partially mimetic relationship to human society and history (Boddy 1989; K. M. Brown 1991; Lambek 1981). It is not unusual, for instance, for a community to define its own ethnicity through juxtaposition with ethnically Other spirits (see Giles 1995) or to construct a spirit pantheon that reflects and reworks its history of ethnic contact or social hierarchy (Lambek 1993: 62; Masquelier 2001; Sharp 1993; Stoller 1984, 1994). Spirits are not merely shadowy reflections of social reality; indeed, scholars such as Rosenthal (1998) have insisted that they not be thus reduced. It is nevertheless the case that spirits and society are in vivid dialectic in Giriama life. As part of that dialectic, the range and classification of Giriama spirits are extremely telling.

Giriama have no fixed pantheon of spirits, yet certain spirits, including Muslim ones, have endured in collective consciousness for decades or longer. Noble (1961) and Parkin (1991a), who carried out major portions of their ethnographic work among rural Giriama in the 1950s and 1960s, describe numerous spirits still known to Giriama today. These include animal spirits (a lion, a dog, and others), a catalogue of less easily classifiable spirits, such as Katsumba Kazi (an ethnically Giriama female spirit who coaches diviners-in-training) and Zikiri Maiti (the "walking corpse"), and, crucially, spirits of ethnic groups Giriama have interacted with, including Arabs.[14] Noble (1961: 52) insists that Giriama regard Muslim spirits variously as "a devil," "the devil," or "the Devil's spokes-man." Parkin (1991a: 168) notes that Muslim spirits are regarded by Giriama who live near Muslim towns as "very powerful and potentially harmful."[15] Ethnographic research in the 1980s in hinterland Kaloleni (Udvardy 1990: 27), Magarini (S. G. Thompson 1990), and Giriama communities north of Mombasa (Giles 1989b: 243) indicates that in all of these areas Arab or Muslim spirits featured prominently as especially potent or even fearsome supernatural agents.

Muslim spirits are recognizable by the languages they speak when they possess diviners, Kiswahili and Arabic, and for their names. Some of the most popular are Pepo Mwalimu ("Teacher spirit," the term *mwalimu* being the Kiswahili word for "teacher" and a shorthand for *mwalimu wa kitabu*, Kisw., a Swahili diviner healer, literally "teacher of/by the book"); Pepo Ijumaa ("Friday spirit," the term "Ijumaa" being the Kiswahili word for "Friday," the Muslim Sabbath); Pepo Mwarabu ("Arab spirit"); Pepo Quruani ("Quran spirit"); and Pepo Msomali ("Somali spirit," whom Giriama presume to be Muslim like the majority of Somalis they encounter).

For Giriama everywhere, spirits of various kinds play a crucial role for spirit-medium diviners (*aganga a mburuga*), who commonly summon their helping spirits to bring them oracles. Most spirit-medium diviners are initially called to their trade by possessing spirits who make them recurrently ill, bringing headache, fever, dizziness, or any number of other symptoms until they strike up a kind of working contract with the spirits, agreeing to propitiate them from time to time (for example, through *ngoma* drumming dances to summon the spirits into their hosts) in exchange for the spirits' gifts of prophecy. Laypeople are frequently possessed as well. Sometimes the spirits simply make demands for attention and material offerings before they quit the host; sometimes, however, they have more sinister effects, making a person ill or inflicting misfortune upon them. Under such circumstances a formal exorcism by a ritual healer (*mganga wa kumbo* or *mganga wa kuhundula*) may be required. Spirit possession among Giriama may thus be either undesirable, bringing illness or bad fortune, or desired, such as the possession invoked by diviners during their divination sessions and dances of propitiation.

The presence of possessing Muslim spirits has been documented in several Mijikenda communities, though the dynamics of possession appear to vary across time and space. Giles (1989b) found that among her Giriama informants living north of Mombasa, possession by powerful Islamic spirits had "pervaded society at large." In fact, in comparing her own findings to Parkin's, Giles contends that the high frequency of possession by Muslim spirits is a "fairly recent phenomenon," said by her informants to be on the rise (253). (It is hard to know just how general this trend is since Giles does not specify whether her primary field site was more urban or rurally based, but given that much of her research was conducted not far from Mombasa, where many Swahili and Arabs live, Islamic possession may have been more prevalent there than in hinterland areas such as Kaloleni.) Giles also reports that those so possessed undertook certain Islamic behaviors, such as refraining from working on Fridays, attending more fastidiously to personal cleanliness, and, of "primary importance," following Islamic dietary prohibitions. Giles does not, however, discuss spirit-forced conversion per se, nor does she detail her informants' reactions to these Muslim spirits, focusing instead on these spirits as part of the "symbolic construction of the other [and] a simultaneous construction of the self," while noting that their presence "appears to reflect the hegemony of Swahili socio-political, religious, and cultural forms within the coastal area" (259).[16]

In her research among hinterland Giriama of Magarini (approximately thirty kilometers northeast of Malindi), S. G. Thompson (1990) found a subset of possessing spirits associated with the seaboard (*pwani*, Kigir., Kisw.) who are generally considered to be Islamic. These can possess a person and make what Thompson calls "prestige-enhancing" requests for costly items, such as Islamic clothes and rosewater. Furthermore, non-Islamic diviners sometimes "incorporate Islamic elements in their daily lives" and, she argues, may benefit from Islamic spirits because the "Islamic elements used in diviners' rituals are . . . seen as increasing the efficacy of their practice." While Islamic spirits sometimes "demand Islamic dietary restrictions" (77), Thompson does not mention pressure from spirits to "convert" to Islam per se. She explicitly notes, "No diviners I knew in the northern hinterland actually converted to Islam" (205), perhaps because this Giriama community does not experience daily encounters with Swahili and Arabs or the powerful tension between longing and resentment that such encounters precipitate. Nor do any of her informants appear to resent or reject the presence of Islamic spirits. Instead, it would seem the primary social role of the Islamic spirits she describes is to demand prestigious objects and acts or confer on their hosts reflected glory, thereby earning their hosts a modicum of social uplift (cf. Lewis 1971). Social ascendancy also seems the primary force behind the spirit-forced conversion Parkin (1970, 1972: 41–46) documented in young male Giriama entrepreneurs in the 1960s in hinterland Kaloleni. These young men gained an economic and social advantage from their conversions, unlike some, if not most of my informants in Malindi.

Possession by Muslim spirits thus appears to be a largely advantageous, prestige-enhancing phenomenon in the hinterland Giriama communities examined by Parkin and Thompson. But among the Giriama I spoke to living in and near Malindi, much discourse about possession has a different valence because it reflects more immediately the fraught social dynamics between Giriama and Swahili and Arabs. To be sure, all things Islamic are generally considered powerful among Giriama (and I wholly agree with Giles that this phenomenon is a reflection of Swahili and Arab hegemony). Among spirit-medium diviners, furthermore, short-term, voluntary possession is a welcome and prestige-enhancing aid during their divination trances. However, many laypeople and diviners alike are also chronically possessed by coercive Muslim spirits, such that the hosts go about their lives in a state of ordinary awareness while their bodies and actions are subject to the spirit's intervention, which is generally interpreted as pressuring the host to convert. Many Giriama so possessed comment on the experience of vomiting when they attempt to participate in customary Giriama foodways, suggesting that this unpleasant act has become a salient part of possession discourse, one that implicitly comments upon the impurity of Giriama foods from an Islamic vantage point. The condition of possession thus blurs into the conditions of ordinary life, suffusing the latter with new meanings (cf. Lambek 1993: 316; Masquelier 2001: 121), such that the host is forced to confront and grapple with the meanings of Islam to Giriama culture. In that grappling, we see a range of reactions suggesting that for some Giriama in Malindi the pressure to convert is resented rather than embraced.

The breadth of Giriama experiences with possessing Muslim spirits can best be introduced through the words of several Giriama themselves. Even among those who do not resent the spirits, the sense of being overtaken by forces beyond one's control is clear. The following diviner, a woman in her thirties, considers her symptoms an indication of her inevitable conversion: "I'm planning to convert soon because of my Muslim spirits. . . . I know it's going to happen in the future. . . . I already have some of the signs. There are certain foods I don't eat, like bush rats or dead animals that haven't been properly slaughtered. If I eat those, I vomit and become ill for several days. And during Ramadan, the spirits force me to fast; I just don't feel hungry during the daytime, and get my hunger back at night. And if I work on Fridays, I get sick."

Those diviners who agree to convert to Islam typically enter a contractual relationship in which the host becomes a Muslim and obeys the spirit's prohibitions; the spirit then ceases to provoke discomfort and assists the diviner with fortunetelling. But not all of those who are possessed convert. Some, in fact, experience recurrent somatic reminders of the presence of the spirit, even as they decline, sometimes vehemently, to align themselves with Islam or to obey Islamic prohibitions. The following female diviner, like Kashutu, asserted that she does not consider herself Muslim but that she is physically compelled to obey Muslim dietary conventions because of an Arab spirit whose assistance she uses when she divines: "In terms of religion, I'm neither a Muslim nor a Christian—I'm Traditionalist—but during Ramadan I don't feel like eating during the day; I only get hungry around evening time. I never drink palm wine or eat dead animals that weren't slaughtered [properly], or pigs. Even a chicken has to have been slaughtered by a Muslim, or I get very sick for a while if I eat it, an illness that feels like things rushing through my body. . . . All this is because of the Arab spirit."[17]

The vomiting of bush rats and palm wine signals an acute rejection of foods considered constitutive of Giriama ethnicity. The inability to drink palm wine can mark a profound social rupture in a culture whose rituals and gatherings so frequently revolve around this substance. But the narratives of these individuals, who often use the passive tense to describe their symptoms, attest that these bodily changes are beyond their control. Notice, for instance, the lack of agency in the following diviner's description of the first stages of her possession experience: "I just found myself not working on Fridays and not eating during Ramadan, during the daytime." A middle-aged male diviner who was forced to convert described the fugue-like state that initiates the process: "You might start to wash yourself, to wear a *kofia*, that sort of thing. That's how you'll know [you've been possessed by a Muslim spirit]." Those who refuse to convert often do not make the transition from passively experienced symptoms to willful adoption of the prohibitions of Islam; with this refusal, they may condemn themselves to years or even a lifetime of inconvenient somatic symptoms and behaviors.

Diviners are not the only ones to experience this form of possession; a significant number of laypeople have experienced the same cluster of symptoms as their bodies reject Giriama foods and other behaviors considered forbidden by Muslims. Occasionally individuals experience the symptoms of forced conversion just prior to applying for a job in town with a Muslim employer, a convenient rationale for shifting one's religious allegiance to "the Muslim side." Plenty of others, however, are subject to these spiritual demands during the ordinary course of village life in Muyeye or other areas on the outskirts of Malindi and receive no obvious material reward. Several men whom I knew to be out of work habitually wore a *kofia* and were said to have done so for several years because of their Muslim spirits. Sometimes symptoms take the form of generalized illness and are only recognized by diviners as the result of Muslim possession. The diviner Nyevu's son, for instance, told me of being felled by a vague ailment as a teenager. When he did not respond to the medicine from the clinic, his parents took him to a diviner friend of Nyevu's, who informed them that he was possessed by Muslim spirits. The spirits demanded that he wear the clothing of pious Muslim men, including a long white *kanzu* robe. He grudgingly complied but never wore the clothes outside of his home, mortified by what he saw as a subjugation. After he recovered he threw the clothes away and returned to his former life.

Nyevu's son was never internally committed to Islam, nor did the spirits enjoin him to believe. Indeed, the Muslim behaviors reported by those possessed are striking for their exclusive grounding in the body and the material world. Foodstuffs, dietary patterns, habits of ablution and clothing: these are the demands of the Muslim spirits. In dozens of conversations with those who had experienced spirit possession, not once did I hear of Allah, prayer, or belief in relation to the symptoms of possession or demands of a Muslim spirit.[18] These encounters with Islam are characterized not by the self-conscious choice, intention, and rationality championed by Swahili religious experts, but by a set of embodied practices that are foisted upon the unwitting individual, who is sometimes dismayed to be reminded that his or her cultural habits are polluting to the forces of Islam. This possession does not seem anything like an Abrahamic religious revelation, nor does it always bear the positive connotations that it does in the hinterland communities described by Thompson and Parkin.

To be sure, Giriama have a range of reactions to these confrontations with Muslim spirits. Some, such as Changawa Thoya, eagerly submit to the demand to convert to Islam and are pleased with the outcome: "I don't have nearly as many problems now that I'm a Muslim," she told me. These enthusiasts willfully engage in the Muslim prohibitions enforced by the spirits and tend to distance themselves from the stigma of Giriamaness. One old woman who has so embraced her transformation that she speaks only Kiswahili said, "I like Giriama, but their deeds are not good," using the third-person possessive to suggest she no longer wishes to consider herself Giriama. Another woman emphasized that her affiliation with Islam is so strong that she does not want to be buried in the Giriama style. Others, like Nyevu's son, comply with the spirits' demands, but only temporarily, to rid themselves of the torment of possession.

Many subject to the whims of possessing spirits, however, respond with overt resentment. They refuse to tout Islam as a part of their identity, they state their reluctance to distance themselves from other Giriama, and they loathe the message that Giriama are inadequate compared to Swahili. They may grudgingly take minimal steps to keep the spirits at bay—avoiding certain foods and perhaps fasting during Ramadan—yet when asked about their experience they express anger at the forces holding them hostage. Some take no steps at all and are recurrently sickened when they eat certain foods, even as they castigate the spirits' complicity in Muslim domination in ordinary social life. For them, the experience of chronic illness is preferable to capitulating to the demands of a domineering Muslim spirit.

Many of these resentful hosts couch their responses in terms of ethnoreligious loyalty; the struggle between the Giriama individual and the possessing Muslim spirit becomes analogous to the social struggle between Giriama and Swahili and Arabs. Some explicitly say they refuse to cross over to the Muslim side, a spatial metaphor for ethnic abandonment. Said one woman, "I don't want to ignore my people by converting to Islam." Some of those who do convert use their forced conversion as a platform on which to announce their allegiance to other Giriama and denounce Muslim snobbery. As one woman described her feelings, "I was forced to convert because of those problems [sickness], but I don't really like the religion. If a person really puts [Islam] into their mind they have to ignore and scorn all Giriama, which is not good." The following female diviner accepts (as do many) that Muslim spirits have special power—they are, she says, "high"—yet power, in her calculus, is not the same as the moral "goodness" of Giriama: "I don't like being a Muslim. I refuse to change my name and I don't pray—in fact, I don't even like Muslims; they just scorn Giriama and call us 'Nyika.' I'm a Muslim by job only. I like my low spirits, the Giriama ones. They're good and they work faster than the high Arab spirits."

Even Giriama who have not been beset by Muslim spirits may use them as a touchstone for their ideological opposition to Muslim power. This elderly healer, for instance, expressed relief that Muslim spirits have not afflicted him, for he sees Islam as morally tainted by the historical acts of Muslim ethnic groups: "I don't want anything to do with that religion. I work on Fridays, and I don't see any ill effects on my healing. I eat straight through Ramadan, and I eat everything the Muslims don't.

Those who convert to Islam take on Muslim habits—I don't want that. I can't forget the way the Arabs handled Giriama during the era of slavery."

As I have noted, forced conversions in rural Kaloleni have been analyzed extensively by Parkin (1970, 1972, 1991a). Parkin first noted the phenomenon while researching the gaps between redistributional and capitalist lifeways among Giriama in Kaloleni. The palm wine industry that burgeoned among young Kaloleni men in the mid-twentieth century threw traditional Giriama communitarianism off balance, creating tension between older and younger generations. In this context some young male entrepreneurs were possessed by Muslim spirits who made their hosts ill until they converted in a gesture Parkin (1970: 225) terms "therapeutic" because the ostensible aim of such conversions was to regain health. Some converts separated themselves from non-Muslim kin, refusing to eat with them and sometimes moving away from their natal village closer to town. According to Parkin (1972: 42), these new Muslim entrepreneurs could thereby distance themselves from their intimates and allies and hence "stave off [the] repeated requests for financial help" that accompany proximity. They could also keep malicious efforts at retribution at arm's length; then as now, jealousy was a common response to new inequalities occasioned by economic changes. By eating separately, entrepreneurs could lessen the chances of being "poisoned by a jealous neighbor or relative" (Parkin 1970: 225).

Despite the similarities between the spirit-forced conversion found by Parkin in Kaloleni and that in Malindi, these geographically and historically specific complexes deserve different readings. First, Kaloleni forty years ago was a profoundly different social site from Malindi today; the area was Giriama-dominated and not nearly as ethnically heterogeneous as the coastal towns. Tensions between Swahili and Giriama of the sort I have found in Malindi were almost nonexistent (Parkin, personal communication, 14 April 2004), and those possessed in Kaloleni did not voice antipathy toward their possessing spirits.[19] Furthermore, in Malindi today the demography and dynamics of spirit-forced conversion appear different. In the areas where I worked quite a few forced converts are diviners, and while they may gain some cachet by working with "high" Muslim spirits, their financial position does not usually lead to the obvious accumulation of Parkin's entrepreneurs. Most of those possessed by Muslim spirits have little money to protect, and even if they had more, their enactments of Islam do not seem effective means of fending off covetous friends or kin because in the Malindi area relatively few converts separate themselves socially. Nor is forced conversion noticeably male-dominated; both men and women experience it, and in Malindi itself women make up the majority of forced converts because women are considered more vulnerable to spirit possession and because nowadays most Giriama diviners who work with spirits are female (McIntosh 1996; see also S. G. Thompson 1990). I also found no discernable generational trend to forced conversion; it seems fairly evenly distributed among old and young. It is true that, as suggested by Giles (1989b), Parkin (1970, 1972), and S. G. Thompson (1990), Giriama consider Islam a locus of economic and supernatural privilege, and conversion may offer proximity to that privilege in principle. But most converts do not reap economic benefits, publicize their new religious standing, or go beyond perfunctory concessions to Islam. Among those who are not diviners and do not stand to gain from the epistemological advantages of working with Muslim spirits, there seems little obvious advantage to their condition.

In fact, I suggest that in Malindi many of these possession experiences run against the grain of a dominant trend in the recent ethnographic literature of interpreting spirit possession, particularly possession involving the mimesis of more powerful social groups, as a kind of resistance against or strategic response to oppression. For several decades studies of spirit possession have been heavily influenced by the work of I. M. Lewis (1971), who argued that possession tends to be a strategy used by marginalized or peripheral people to achieve a degree of status enhancement, exact redress against their social superiors, or otherwise gain an advantage. In a 1994 review article, however, Boddy notes that in recent years scholarly interpretations of spirit possession have become increasingly subtle and complex. Scholars such as Boddy (1989), Masquelier (2001), and Rosenthal (1998) have emphasized the capacity of possession to generate "shifting, contested, and at times contradictory" meanings (Masquelier 2001: 124–25; see also Boddy 1989: 8). Nevertheless, as Boddy (1994: 419) herself notes, the view of possession as "an embodied critique of colonial, national, or global hegemonies" is "widely held," suggesting that Lewis's legacy lives on in new forms. Scholars such as Jean Comaroff (1985), David Lan (1985), Aihwa Ong (1987), Paul Stoller

(1984), and Janice Boddy herself (1989) have treated possession as a means of articulating and energizing opposition to Western incursion, capitalism, and other forms of oppression. To highlight the difference between their interpretations and my own, I briefly summarize two accounts of spirit possession elsewhere in Africa that also involve the mimesis of a powerful social group, then contrast those cases with the Giriama case.

According to Boddy's (1989: 126, 233, 129) account of women's Zar possession in a patriarchal society of northern Sudan, Zar rituals sometimes involve foreign spirits, including Western doctors, lawyers, and military officers; gypsy spirits; and an Ethiopian prostitute. As they take on such personae during possession, women may threaten men, swear, flail, dance wantonly, and engage in numerous behaviors ordinarily considered unacceptable to them. Zar thus provides women with expressive possibilities they do not enjoy in ordinary life, particularly since female roles are heavily overdetermined and circumscribed in that society. The "anti-language" of Zar, Boddy argues, allows women to "play with" and "reassess" their experiences (156–57).

Another interpreter of possession, Paul Stoller (1984, 1994), focuses on the possessing Hauka spirits among the Songhay of West Africa. In the "horrific comedy" of the Hauka spirits, possessed men and women mimic European army generals and other members of the colonial administration in a mocking and often ghastly manner, frightening children while amusing the adults who look on. Hauka burlesque includes exaggerated, two-minute-long salutes and other forms of bombastic formality, embellished by verbal sparring between the spirits and audience members. This form of spirit possession, says Stoller (1984: 177), offers "clear and boldly critical statements about the nature of the colonizer and his behavior." Indeed, Hauka possession emerged after Songhay military resistance failed around the turn of the century, much like the farce and theatrical paradox that emerged among groups lacking political and military power in royal France (167–68). According to Stoller, these parodic commentaries create a sense of comprehension and mastery that helps the living move into a new relationship with the encounters of the past.

Both Boddy's and Stoller's interpretations render possession a form of mimesis through which understanding may be achieved and objections phrased. As social critique, they imply, these possession experiences do not merely represent powerful social groups, but articulate something critical *about* a representation. Hence the overtly parodic elements of Hauka possession do not simply mirror colonialist behavior; they reframe it in such a way that it is configured as the brunt of mockery. Zar similarly offers exaggerated and peculiar representations of society; through their very distortion, these representations suggest a metacommentary upon their content. In the Hauka and Zar cases, furthermore, possession occurs in a demonstrative, ritualistic setting that, if Boddy and Stoller are right, engenders reflection in onlookers and participants much as theater or storytelling can.

Should we conclude that Giriama possession by demanding Muslim spirits is also a case of resistance? On the one hand, the Giriama case involves some of the same components as the others. The possessing spirits hail from a powerful, dominant social group, and the symptoms of possession involve a degree of mimesis of that powerful group's behavior. Yet forced conversion is not theatrical or demonstrative in nature; it is a mundane, protracted, and largely private matter, often involving uncomfortable sickness or inadvertent behavioral changes that may endure for months on end, a diagnosis in a private divination session, and a capitulation to or rejection of the spirit's demands. There is no clearly established audience for these dynamics, no public ritual in which to consolidate their significance, and no obviously subversive message borne by the possession itself. Many of the symptoms of forced conversion iconically mimic Muslim habits (fasting, food avoidance, not working on Fridays, donning a *kofia*) without altering them in a way that might be construed as parody or critique. Giriama *responses* to possession are laced with critique, but the embodied possession experience itself does not seem oppositional.

Nor does Lewis's (1971) framework of possession as strategic and beneficial seem to apply neatly here. In fact, it is striking how many Giriama in Malindi do not obviously benefit from their possession experiences. To be sure, it is not uncommon for spirits cross-culturally to announce themselves through illness and for hosts to resist or resent possession when it first happens to them. Yet in many such cases this initial period of suffering is transformed through a ritual process in which the spirit is exorcised, or the host accepts the spirit's demands and enters into a salubrious contractual routine with the spirit, thereby becoming healthy again. In some cases, concessions to spirits help individuals to move up the economic hierarchy or to prosper as shamans or priestesses (Ben-Amos 1994; Lewis 1971). In other cases, the host's desires and frustrations may be expressed obliquely through the spirit (Lambek 1981; Lewis 1971; Obeyesekere 1977), which serves as a therapeutic or communicative device. These patterns of advantage are relevant to some Giriama experiences with spirits, especially to those diviners who work closely with powerful Muslim spirits to tell fortunes. But in many cases I encountered, Giriama experience possession as inconvenient or downright humiliating, while their avid critique of the spirits may translate into an enduring rejection of the spirit's demands and even enduring illness or manipulation at the hands of the spirit. In such cases, no amicable contract is embraced or frustration vented, and the experience of possession does not appear to offer social or psychological benefits.

I return, then, to the concepts of hegemony and ideology and to my contention that at least some of these Giriama possession experiences can be read as an instantiation and reinscription of a system of oppressive meanings. These Muslim spirits seem to put their hosts through a somatic recapitulation of Islamic hegemony on the coast. Some scholars of possession have focused on the incorporation of the spirit into the host's body as a kind of corporeal epistemology. Masquelier (2001: 183) has argued that possession lends itself to "the primacy of bodily techniques over verbal expression to effect understanding of, and literally grasp, the world." Giriama experiences of possession are certainly a somatic form of understanding, but what is grasped is hardly illuminating knowledge; instead, it is a punishing social truism about Muslim disapproval of Giriama ways. If, as Foucauldian scholars insist, hegemony routinely imprints itself on the body, and if illness and other forms of embodied dis-ease can reflect broader forms of social injustice (Scheper-Hughes and Lock 1987; A. Strathern 1996), then Giriama possession can be read as a physical instantiation of their beleaguered socioreligious status. Muslim spirits might even be construed as a device for the kind of self-surveillance theorized by Foucault (1995) as they inflict the punishing disapproval of a higher authority, in this case Swahili and Arab Muslims. The experience of being dominated by Muslims in the human world is paralleled by the experience of being controlled, puppet-like, by possessing spirits, while the humiliations of socioeconomic and cultural oppression are mimicked by punitive physical symptoms to which some Giriama strenuously object.

Furthermore the symptoms of possession seem to somatize the widespread discourse about the polluting qualities of Giriama lifeways and the essential clash between Islam and Giriamaness. The disruption of Giriama bodily habits, sometimes through the physical extremes of regurgitation, is not merely an expression of the spirits' disapproval but a rupture with some of the most fundamental markers of Giriamaness. By making Giriama vomit bush rats and palm wine, the invisible agents of Islam invoke a fundamental, constitutional incompatibility between Islam and the nominal impurity of Giriamaness. Apparently some Giriama have adopted these concepts and collude in Swahili and Arab hegemony by structuring their ideas of ethnic difference in essentialist and unequal terms. Possession symptoms, in other words, appear to reflect a set of hegemonic ontological presuppositions: that Giriama traditions are polluting and toxic to Islam (as personified by the spirits).

And yet this hegemonic domination is only partial, for Giriama *responses* to their possession can hardly be said to align with Swahili messages. We have seen Giriama resentment coursing through the accounts in this chapter: in the angry funerary songs that fantasize about Swahili consuming pollution, in the diatribes of those who insist that they will never be accepted by Swahili as full Muslims, and in the defiant statements of those possessed. It would seem, in fact, that these reluctant Muslims are caught somewhere between hegemonic internalization of their own subordination and articulated, resistant ideology. Their responses might usefully be located on the spectrum Comaroff and Comaroff (1991: 29) term a "chain of consciousness": somewhere between subconscious hegemonic oppression and conscious ideological resistance, in that in-between state in which "individuals or groups know that something is happening to them but find it difficult to put their fingers on quite what it is." In this state many of those possessed have at least a partial recognition of the link between their symptoms and Muslim domination (though, in the eyes of this outsider, what they do not recognize is that they themselves have internalized certain elements of Muslim power). The embodied symptoms of possession may intensify and heighten the experience of being oppressed for some, raising it to a level where it invites contestation. Hence, unlike Foucauldian "docile bodies" (Foucault 1995) that wear the stamp of hegemony without complaint (or so the phrase implies), many Giriama apprehend their possessing spirits with resistance, usually articulated in moralistic terms.

The phenomenon of spirit-forced conversion among Giriama thus allows us a glimpse of several points along the chain of consciousness stipulated by the Comaroffs. At one level, below their own awareness, Giriama somatize and recapitulate hegemonic messages about Muslim power and the intrinsic incompatibility between Islam and Giriamaness, the latter being toxic to the former. Yet the experience of possession allows them to discern these messages about Giriama inferiority and to respond to them as conscious agents. Not every possessed Giriama responds to Muslim spirits rebelliously, but many do, and in so doing they articulate a defiant Giriama ideology about the worth of their own ethnicity and the perceived moral shortcomings of Muslims. This lamination of concession to and rebellion against Muslim power is yet another instantiation of the force fields that make up Giriama experience in Malindi today. Giriama are in an impossible situation: instructed that their lifeways are intrinsically polluting but thwarted from assimilation into another community. They continually tack back and forth, orienting at once toward and away from the Swahili ecumene.

Meanwhile, in these possession experiences we are reminded of a quality of Giriama understandings of personhood, namely, their relative lack of emphasis on interiority. In customary Giriama life a person's actions are believed to be highly responsive to external forces, while the notion of independent free will is not highly valorized. In ideal Giriama society humans respond reciprocally to others' needs, making the social world and the person within it "whole" (-zima; S. G. Thompson 1990). In customary Giriama religious life a person is subject to the demands and whims of external agents, including ancestors and spirits, who have great control over fate and fortune. This opens the Giriama person to vulnerability at the hands of mystical agents associated with ethnoreligious Others, agents who may bring messages that threaten the coherence of the Giriama community. Personal choice is not involved in the arrival of these emissaries, and while individuals evidently choose how they will respond to them, an inner faith does not seem to be at stake among many Giriama who convert. Religion, it turns out, can be a force that alights upon the body, sweeping it into social currents whose force is more powerful than the will of the individual.

Swahili Skepticism and Ethnoreligious Boundaries

Interestingly, not all Swahili are aware of spirit-forced conversion (some express surprise at the very concept), nor of the embittered Giriama discourses I have described. But among those who are aware, what reactions do we see to such patterns in Giriama life? The answers speak to the tension between models of Swahili and Giriama personhood and to the matter of hegemonic ethnoreligious boundaries.

It is important first to explain that Swahili in Malindi tend to be embarrassed by Giriama cynicism when they get wind of it, and are deeply distressed when accused of slavery in the past and bigotry in the present. As Giriama ratchet up their claims about the extent to which they were enslaved in the past, Swahili and Arabs are placed in an increasingly defensive position, at pains to debunk prejudice against Islam as they strive to persuade a transnational audience of the righteousness of their faith (cf. McIntosh 2001a). Furthermore some Swahili insist that they are nothing but kindly and concerned toward their Giriama employees; plenty of them tithe to indigent Giriama (particularly on Fridays), and some lament the sorry state of Giriama socioeconomic development. In fact, despite the currents of tension I have described, Swahili point to the fact that many interactions between Swahili and Giriama on the streets of Malindi are perfectly cordial, even overtly friendly. What Giriama interpret as brutal discrimination or outright exclusion is sometimes intended as nothing more than pious caution, they say, though this stance unwittingly contributes to the structural hierarchy Giriama so resent.

Yet hegemonic hierarchies need not be the outcome of conspiracies of the powerful; they can be supported, even inadvertently, by those who benefit from them. When it comes to Giriama conversion to Islam, Swahili may intone the official ideology that anyone can join the *umma*, yet at the same time many Swahili tend to regard Giriama efforts at conversion as faltering or half-hearted. Often this disapproving commentary revolves around the apparent Giriama disregard for the rationality, lofty intentions, and literate sensibility that Swahili consider so important to high Islamic practice. One Swahili woman named Fatma distinguished converts' behavior from their state of mind: "Inside themselves, those Giriama just convert to get favors." A Swahili printing shop owner in Malindi refuses to sell copies of the Quran to Giriama customers, insisting that "they do not know what they are doing" with it, and that their misuse will constitute heresy. Remarks along these lines range from skepticism that Giriama are really thinking of God when they pray, to doubt that Giriama are sufficiently clear-headed or literate to grasp the noble central ideas of Islam.

Spirit-forced conversions have the potential to raise this set of critiques to an acute pitch. It is ironic that, in their unconscious recognition of Swahili hegemony, possessed Giriama wind up practicing a version of Islam that stands in stark opposition to contemporary Swahili ideals of conversion and good Islamic practice. Instead of emerging from individual choice, forced conversion defers agency to the spirit. Instead of emphasizing intellection, intention, and rationality, forced conversion involves the unwitting body. Instead of focusing on the supreme will of God, forced conversion neglects God altogether, treating a minor spirit as supreme controller. And instead of taking the form of an absolute transformation, an interior shift externally indexed by a signature in a kadhi's ledger book, forced conversion often places the host in an ambivalent state.

Among those Swahili who have heard of spirit-forced conversion, disapproval takes several forms. Some indicate that there might indeed be spirits who wish Giriama to convert, but the legitimacy of that conversion would depend entirely on the belief and intentions of the host. One imam I spoke to said he has agreed to convert spirit-possessed Giriama "in hopes that their *nia* will change." Similarly Ali, the taxi driver who extolled the virtues of comprehending Islam, told me there are two major dangers in Giriama conversion: "For a Giriama to convert because of a woman is not acceptable [*ni kosa*]. If a spirit converts him, well, it depends. If he is taught well and comes to understand the religion, okay. Otherwise, it's not acceptable." The Swahili educator Salim said, "The best kind of conversion is one where there is awareness before implementation. In the implementation stage it is much better if you know what you are implementing before you do it. Before becoming a Muslim, you had better know the face of it before following it. In terms of spirit conversion—how many people will end up following Islam in its true picture, its true image? I think the possibilities are fifty-fifty of really understanding it. Otherwise the Giriama will end up a cultural Muslim who doesn't really understand what he's doing." Salim's phrase "cultural Muslim" conjures a definition of culture as superficial practices of dietary habits and dress, contrasting these to the crucial inner state of understanding that consolidates the legitimacy of a would-be Muslim. In another conversation, the women in a Swahili family in Shella insisted that people should not reveal they converted because of a spirit: "You are supposed to decide this for yourself. You can't be forced [*huwezi kulazimishwa*] to convert. You mustn't. Because conversion is about belief [*uamini*]. If people know you've been converted by a spirit they won't accept you as a good Muslim."

This emphasis on belief recurred in a conversation with a madarasa teacher who invited me one day to look on while he instructed twenty rows of adolescent boys as they recited the Quran, interpreted the prayers he wrote on the chalkboard, and took turns coming to the front of the class to write phrases in Arabic. Of all his students, only one is a Giriama boy from Maweni, just outside the Malindi town center; the rest are born Swahili. After class we began to discuss Giriama conversions to Islam, and I raised the issue of Giriama being forced to convert by spirits. The teacher shook his head, cutting me off:

> There are no "Islamic *pepo*." There are no "Islamic *jini*." There are no "Islamic *sheitani*." There are no Muslim spirits at all. People who talk about these things are caught up in *itikadi* [Kisw., Ar., a term that sometimes connotes beliefs held by virtue of pure ideology or traditional persistence over time; "blind faith" or "superstition"]—they've put something in their heart, even if it's not true. If you say you've been converted because of *pepo*, you have not been converted. You're just under the spell of *itikadi*. If a Giriama comes along complaining of possession by a Muslim spirit, they are sick and you must give them a *kombe* preparation [Kisw., Kigir., a prayer from the Quran, written on paper and dissolved in rosewater, then drunk] because the Quran is the only medicine, and he is sick. Then if he wants to be converted you must TEACH him, so that his *itikadi* will stop. A true grasp of

Islam will chase away the *itikadi*. Conversion is a matter of believing [*kuamini*] and an acceptance of the idea that Mohammed is the Prophet and there is no god but God himself. [He then recited the *shahada* in Arabic.]

The same didactic impulse was evident in one Swahili intellectual, Abdul, who attended a talk I gave at a local museum society. I was discussing Giriama uses of Islam in their rituals and described some rituals in which Giriama diviners and healers appropriate the symbolism of the Quran while still appealing to the forces of Traditionalism. Abdul raised his hand during the question-and-answer period and expressed his dismay at these acts. He knew that this sort of thing goes on, he said, but such acts constitute a hopelessly misguided form of *ushirikina*. He continued (in English):

> You know, all of my relatives believe firmly in spirits, and nothing I can say to them will shake this belief. But these things are really bad among the Giriama. I had a Giriama boy working in my house, whose sister came to me and said she wanted to convert to Islam. Why? Her *sheitani* told her to! Well, I talked to this girl and it turned out she knew nothing about the religion itself, and had no good reasons for wanting to convert. I said: "You come back next week; I'll give you some books to read, some small small things in Kiswahili, and then you can read about Islam and decide for yourself." [laughing] She never came back!

Abdul greeted this girl's report of spirit-forced conversion as an example of her credulity. His solution was to give the would-be convert some "small small" books to read; his use of the double adjective is a structural device borrowed from Kiswahili grammar that underscores a connotation of diminutiveness. A capacious text about Islam would overwhelm this girl, he implies; he will therefore start her off with just a little literature, designed to foster her comprehension of the religion. Importantly, he requires her to "decide for herself" so that she might have a "good reason" for wanting to convert. These themes of comprehension and choice disregard the embodied epistemology that brought the girl to him seeking a transformation. (Strikingly, in fact, Abdul translates what was almost certainly an embodied experience of conversion into a linguistic interaction that is perhaps easier for him to assimilate: "Her *sheitani* told her to.") Thus competing models of religious personhood, one hinging on embodied compulsion from without and the other on individual will from within, confront each other in Abdul's narrative. Apparently Abdul's well-meaning offer did not speak to what this girl was seeking. She never came back.

Abdul's discomfort is directed at the Giriama girl's spiritual encounter, yet it emerges from anxiety about the role spirits sometimes have played in Swahili society as well. As he himself says, "all" his relatives "believe in spirits," a fact he evidently sees as a blight on their rationality. The most thorough documenter of spirit beliefs and spirit possession among Swahili is Giles (1989a, 1989b, 1995), whose study of Swahili possession cults in several places on the Kenyan and Tanzanian coast in the mid-1980s brings with it several ironies worth highlighting here. Giles found that these cults, although fairly secretive, comprise a wide range of individuals of both sexes, including a significant number of elite and prosperous individuals, as well as (surprisingly) those with ties to orthodox Islam.[20] Cult membership is not voluntary but is precipitated by chronic illness or adversity, which is interpreted by ritual experts as the result of spirit possession, remediable through cult attendance. Most striking is that the possession by ethnoreligiously Other spirits that Giles documents is similar to the Giriama patterns I have described, but the ethnicity of host and spirit is switched. A small minority of the Swahili cult members she studied were possessed by so-called *kinyika* spirits who demanded that the Swahili consume palm wine, an offensive request that the hosts typically deflected by protesting that none was available (1989b: 251). Giles describes possession by Muslim spirits among Giriama in the 1980s as "much more pervasive and important" than possession among Swahili by *kinyika* spirits (253); indeed, she contends that Swahili possession by *kinyika* spirits constitutes but a "grudging acknowledgment" of Miji-kenda culture (259), while some of my Swahili informants in Malindi say they have never even heard of Mijikenda spirits. Nevertheless, the parallels to forced conversion by Muslim spirits among Giriama are striking.[21]

Still, even Giles (1989a: 299) notes that cult worship was on the wane at the time of her research; ceremonies for certain spirits that were "formerly prevalent in the Malindi-Mombasa area" had largely been "replaced by more orthodox Islamic ritual forms." The use of non-Islamic spirits was on a path of decline at the time of her research (Giles 1995), and these spirit activities were seen by many as existing in uneasy tension with orthodox Islam. Neither I nor Beckerleg (personal communication, 20 January 2007), who lived in the heart of Shella for several years, encountered the presence of such cults in contemporary Malindi, and pious Swahili are generally dubious of ritual spirit possession. In the face of powerful ideologies of rational choice in religion, Swahili in Malindi do not generally valorize Giriama's spirit-forced conversion as legitimate unless it is accompanied by and ultimately superseded by a thoughtful and sincere choice to become Muslim.

In fact, if Swahili recognize a glimmer of their own cultural heritage in the spirit possession practices of the Giriama Other, they have even more reason to react against it. Not only is spirit-forced conversion almost totally antithetical to the Swahili ideals of bureaucratically sanctioned and inwardly sincere conversion, but it may also remind them of elements of Swahili practice that many would prefer to exclude from their identity. As Swahili police the legitimacy of aspirational Giriama converts, they assert a kind of local monopoly on nominally correct Islamic practice. As Bhabha (1994) might predict, the mimetic efforts of the subaltern meet with rejection; in this fashion, the elite preserve their distinctiveness.

Both Swahili and Giriama thus sustain the hegemonic notion of deep-seated links between ethnicity and religion, albeit in somewhat different ways and with somewhat different emphases. Swahili tend to focus on personhood and the apparent unsuitability of Giriama for introspective and reflective faith, while Giriama have deeply elaborated the notion of an essential ethnoreligious separation that involves a naturalized link between Swahili and Islam and an ontological distance between Giriamaness and Islam. These discursive and experiential threads create a hegemonic field in which some members of both groups support the notion of a divide between Giriama ethnicity and Islam. Giriama patterns of pluralistic worship and ritual propitiation reveal still more distinctions between prevailing Swahili and Giriama approaches to Islam, further underscoring the notion of an ethnoreligious divide.

Chapter 4

RETHINKING SYNCRETISM
Religious Pluralism and Code Choice in a Context
of Ethnoreligious Tension

Islam looms large in Giriama consciousness in Malindi. Ruthless Muslim *jini* are thought to suck Giriama
blood to sustain themselves while bringing lucre to their Arab and Swahili masters. Other Muslim spirits possess Giriama and force them to
regurgitate their customary foods, holding their bodies hostage until
they convert to Islam. Yet Giriama do not perceive the power of Islam
as a solely adversarial force. Many, in fact, strategically mobilize Islamic potency in their efforts to transcend the material and epistemological limits of their own station, particularly when the mystical forces of
Giriama traditionalism seem inadequate to the job. Still, Giriama appropriations of Islam do not resolve their enduring ambivalence toward the
religion or toward the Swahili and Arabs who frame themselves (and
tend to be framed by Giriama) as its coastal proprietors. In fact, like the
possession experiences I described in the preceding chapter, the ritual
interactions with Islam I describe in this one sometimes reinforce the
hegemonic notion that Islam is distant from Giriamaness and is more the
province of Swahili than of Giriama.

In ritual practices, especially those involved in healing, Giriama interact with Islam in order to appropriate its perceived power. Once again
we see that Giriama understandings of personhood inform these interactions, for just as Giriama conversions to Islam reflect a model of
religious personhood that downplays belief, so too do some Giriama
rituals run against the grain of the Abrahamic emphasis on consistency of
faith. Indeed, in some rituals Giriama appeal to both the powers of Islam
and the powers of Traditionalism, treating them as if they are totally

distinct but equally real supernatural loci. The distinction is emphasized by the fact that ritual practitioners tend to map the respective religions onto different languages. Since these languages have ethnic valences in Malindi, each religion in turn becomes more vividly associated with a different ethnicity. The preservation of ethnoreligious difference in some of these rituals is so striking I contend that they are not well characterized in terms of syncretistic blending or cultural hybridity. Instead, understood in folk theological terms, some of these religious practices foreground the conflicted Giriama notion that while Islam may provide supernatural assistance under the right conditions, it is nevertheless an ethnically distant force that does not intermingle seamlessly with forces from "the Giriama side." The ritual practices I describe thus reinforce the hegemonic notion of a separation between Islam and Giriama people, even among those Giriama who appropriate the religion.

I had an early glimpse of Giriama religious pluralism during one of the first visits I paid to a Giriama shrine (*mzimu*), this one located in a rural area about twenty kilometers inland of Malindi.[1] The three elderly female spirit-medium diviners (*aganga a mburuga*) who tend the shrine have all converted to Islam—"We have arrived [Tumefika]," they say in Kiswahili—and cover their heads intermittently with brightly colored *kanga* cloths. Their shrine is a large and impressive coral rock formation, carved by the sea thousands of years ago, before the shoreline retreated, now set on a rise that looks out over relatively flat farmland and Giriama homesteads. The entrance is so covered over in creepers it is invisible to passers-by, and as we climb the steep slope together, I carrying a recording device and they a white chicken and other offerings for the spirits, I find myself doubting there could be a cave up there as the women have promised. Suddenly one of the *aganga* entreats me to remove my shoes, common practice among Giriama when approaching a sacred site. She pulls aside a tangle of vines and we stoop low in single file, entering a dimly lit, cavernous space writhing with bats that squeak and flit past us. The ground beneath our feet feels cool and light; desiccated bat droppings, accumulated over the years, have created a soft, powdery texture that the women sweep flat from time to time.

Near the entrance to the cave I notice the glint of coins and several half-empty rosewater bottles; I know enough about the preferences of

Muslim spirits to recognize these as their propitiatory gifts. In a corner one of the women lights three sticks of incense and plants their ends in the earth so the smoke curls upward. A second woman unrolls a bottle of milky-looking rosewater from the cloth around her waist, sprinkles some upon the ground, and embeds the base of the bottle in the soil. Shifting into Kiswahili, the three women begin to call out together, overlapping one another as they address the Muslim spirits in the fashion of apologetic supplicants:

Hodi hodi![2] *Hodi masheikhe! Hodi wazee wetu! Hodi! Tuaja na wageni! Hodini! Habari ya asubuhi? Salama! Hodi. Hodi wenyewe hodi! Salama tu, sijui nyinyi? Pole poleni. Poleni poleni poleni. Msipige wageni! Tuna wageni, poleni!*

Greetings, Greetings, sheikhs! Greetings, our seniors! Greetings! We've come with guests. Greetings! What news of the morning? Peace! Greetings. Greetings, owners of this place, greetings! We're just peaceful; how about you? Sorry, sorry. Sorry, sorry, sorry. Don't beat the guests! We have guests, sorry!

The *aganga* begin to carry on simultaneous individual conversations with these spirits. My recorder captures the eldest *mganga* (sing. of *aganga*) explaining her absence:

Ilikuwa nafasi sina. Eeeh, ni kitambo. Juzi tukapata hawa wageni; tukawaleta. Ilikuwa nafasi, tu. Tulikosa na nini? Nafasi yangu ili-kuwa sina. Hakuna ubaya. Sina chuki na nyinyi. Hakuna chuki kabisa. Lakini ilikuwa nafasi sina. Hakuna vita. Naogopa sana—nataka hu-ruma. Eeh, ni kitambo lakini ilikuwa ni mimi sina nafasi. Mnisamehe. Hakuna vita kabisa kabisa. Siwezi kumtupa hata kidogo. Nilikuwana kazi nyingi nyumbani. Basi mniletee baraka, mniletee baraka kibandani kwangu.

It was that I didn't have a chance. I know, it's been a while. The other day we received these guests; we brought them [here]. It was just a matter of [not having the] opportunity [earlier]. Whom have we offended? It was just that I didn't have a chance. There's no badness. I don't have any hatred for you [pl.]. There's no hatred at all. But it was that I didn't have a chance. There's no war here. I'm very afraid—I want [your] compassion. Yes, it's been a while but I just didn't have time. Forgive me. There's really no war at all. I couldn't renounce you, not at all. I had a lot of work at home. So then, bring me blessings; bring me blessings at my little hut/store.

The urge to mollify the Muslim spirits, bordering on obsequiousness, is striking in this monologue, as this *mganga* linguistically adopts the role of a subordinate wishing to please a group of demanding and potentially angry spirits to assure them that "there's no war" between them. When we move into yet another section of the shrine, a clearing with sunlight shining from overhead, one of the *aganga* reaches under a lip of the rock and produces a pristine white ceramic plate with a border of delicately painted pink flowers. I have occasionally seen such plates in Swahili households, but never in a Giriama one. (Most Giriama near Malindi use mass-produced plastic plates, though a few elders still use hand-carved wooden bowls.) "This is the favorite plate of the sheikh spirits," she says. "When I have food to offer them I place it on here." She apologizes to the spirit in Kiswahili that the lovely plate is bare: "I know, it's empty! But we'll go prepare something and bring it back here later." Even the Muslim spirits, it seems, enjoy the luxuries of Swahili domesticity, provided by the hands of the Giriama who tend to them.

We move deeper, into another cavern, stooping to avoid the convoluted coral formations overhead. The women speak again, this time using the familiar Kigiriama greeting uttered upon approaching a home: "Enye! Enye!" I see a row of wooden stakes for the Giriama ancestors (*koma*), tied with strips of red, blue, and white cloth. The women have brought bottles of palm wine, which they open and pour onto the cave floor, appealing to the ancestors in Kigiriama for their favor, promising a chicken sacrifice, and generally paving the way for their requests. Here is one *mganga* speaking to the Giriama spirits:

Haya, haha, nadza, athumia, nadza. Poreni; ne muda sidzaaona na gago gosini—ni sababu ya shuhuli haha na haryahu. Bai rero nidzire na— nidzire na fungu renu. Ptu salama salimini navoya vidzo na vidze. Uwe Bi Kahindi Chengo nakudzirira. Nyosini halani yuyu kuku mwaruhe. Dzire mimi, mwana wa Mbodze na Matsezi. Dzire ni shere; dzire ni male kuluhiro; dzire ni aone.

All right, I'm coming, old men, I'm coming. Sorry, it's been a while since I've seen you—it's because of several preoccupations here and there. So today I've come with—I've come with a gift for you. *Ptu salama salimini* I ask for good things to come.[3] You, Kahindi Chengo's father, I'm coming to you. All of you—take this white hen. I've come; I, an offspring of Mbodze and Matseze.[4] I've come to sweep; I've come in search of hope; I've come to see you.

Looked at one way, the propitiations in this shrine might be read as a kind of religious hybridity or blending, in which Islamic influence has been intertwined with the spiritual forces associated with Giriama Traditionalism. Yet such a reading would fail to attend to the subtle ways in which distinctions between Islamic and Giriama Traditionalist forces are preserved, in this context and in some other Giriama rituals. As Stewart (1999: 56, following L. Caplan 1995) has cautioned, ethnographers of syncretism must distinguish between "perceptions of anthropologists or other outside observers" and "actors' expressed acknowledgements of [religious] mixture." Stewart refers to the differences between cultural outsiders' and cultural insiders' perceptions as "a problem of 'frame'" (56). Indeed, while an outsider might frame Giriama ritual practice as a means of reconciling two religious traditions, Giriama ritual officiants sometimes retain rather than reconcile the distinctions between religious loci, framing them as different through a variety of semiotic devices.

In this particular shrine, for instance, Giriama and Muslim spirits require different forms of supplication performed in separate spaces, with spatial separation apparently iconic of the ontological distance between these sources of power and the social distance between the ethnoreligious groups with which they are associated. The women later insisted, "They don't get along; the Muslim spirits don't get along with Katsumba Kazi [a popular Giriama spirit who assists diviners]. They don't stay in the same place together, so the Muslim spirits and the indigenous kind of spirits each have to have their own space in the cave." Apparently the Muslim spirits awaiting their rosewater would be driven away by palm wine, considered *haramu* in Islam. The Muslim forces are also marked as having more expensive tastes than the Giriama spirits, mirroring the ethnically based economic hierarchy on the ground; both kinds of spirits, for instance, like to be paid in currency, but the Muslim spirits require costlier libations (rosewater is far more expensive than palm wine), while the Muslim spirits prefer cooked foods served on a decorative platter to animal sacrifice. Furthermore, Muslim spirits, not Giriama ones, are in a position to confer *baraka*, an Arabic and Kiswahili word that generally refers to blessing from the Muslim God, implying that the two spirits tap different sources or different kinds of mystical potency.

The distinction between these two sets of powers is further marked through the speakers' stances toward their mystical interlocutors. While Giriama ancestors and spirits are certainly not framed as benign (they too may exert their capricious will upon hapless humans), in this ritual and several others I witnessed there is a contrast between the self-effacement and trepidation some *aganga* demonstrate in the face of Muslim forces ("I'm very afraid") and the relative comfort evinced in the face of the Giriama spirits, a comfort marked by the *mganga's* invocation of her ancestral link to the Giriama spirits ("I, an offspring of Mbodze and Matsezi"). Crucially, the *aganga's* linguistic shifts between Kiswahili and Kigiriama map each set of spiritual forces onto different codes, which are conceptually yoked to different ethnic identities. The Giriama forces are thereby aligned with Giriama ethnicity, while the Islamic forces are accessible only in a linguistic medium that, on the Kenya coast and especially in the context of Islamic symbolism, is associated with the Swahili people. In this instance of religious pluralism elements of difference are preserved within different frames rather than reconciled or blended.

The Giriama *aganga* of this shrine are among many in the Malindi area who invoke the assistance of Muslim spirits and other forces associated with Islam in their divination and healing work. Some of these *aganga* call themselves Traditionalists (that is, affiliates of *dini ya kienyeji*), a small handful consider themselves Christian, and others consider themselves Muslim, usually having converted under pressure from the Muslim spirits they work with. Yet, as noted in the preceding chapters, many Giriama in Malindi tend to regard the Muslim Swahili community (and certainly the even more elite Arab community) as socially impenetrable, while a prominent hegemonic discourse among Swahili and Giriama portrays Islam itself as a force distant from Giriama and anchored (in some discourses, intrinsically) to the Swahili and Arab people, as well as to their associated languages, in a conflation I term *ethno-religious essentialism*. The recurrent Giriama discourse in Malindi that presumes deep, intrinsic links among religions, ethnicities, and languages is reflected in certain appropriations of Islam by Giriama ritual specialists, in which they do not attempt to harmonize the two religious systems into one, but draw upon what they regard as discrete, ethnically specific loci of power.

Ethnoreligious essentialism is reinscribed by linguistic code choice in some Giriama rituals. For just as the *aganga* switch from Kigiriama into Kiswahili as they approach the areas of the cave dominated by Muslim spirits, so too do many Giriama ritual officiants use Kiswahili and Arabic when appealing to Islamic forces and Kigiriama to appeal to forces considered Traditional. When different codes are used in Giriama ritual to evoke different sets of religious forces, different religious forces are implicitly treated as though they are essentially yoked to different ethnicities.

This mode of religious pluralism emerges from and reinforces essentialist ideas about ethnicity, religion, and language, but it also emerges from widely shared, implicit Giriama premises about the relationship between religions and persons. Indeed, just as Giriama model conversion rather differently from many of their Swahili neighbors, so do prevailing Giriama notions of what religion is in the first place differ fundamentally from prevailing Swahili models of religiosity. This pattern of assumptions about personhood in turn enables religious ritual among Giriama to be structured in such a way that it feeds back to enable the essentialisms I have just described. For unlike most Swahili, most Giriama do not customarily treat religion as a deep, internal commitment to a single, consistent, and universal model of the cosmos. Religion among most Giriama is not centrally about the truth (or Truth) of one religious ontology and the falsehood of others; rather, each religious tradition, with its various forces and instantiations clustered around a label ("the Muslim side" or "the Giriama side," for instance), represents a distinct locus of mystical potency. To be sure, some Giriama in Malindi have internalized the Abrahamic notion that one must demonstrate absolute fidelity to, "faith in," one religion to the exclusion of others, but many have not. For those Giriama who consider Islam and Traditionalism distinct loci of mystical potency rather than competing sets of Truth claims, the powers of Islam can conceivably be appropriated using the right language(s) and symbols, even from a virtual spatial distance: from the nebulously conceived and potentially threatening arena Giriama refer to as "the Muslim side."

To the consternation of some Swahili, they and Giriama in Malindi live in a partially shared cultural field of mutual influence. Just as Giriama interact with Swahili and Arab spirits, so too have Swahili historically interacted with Mijikenda spirits, though in Malindi they now do so infrequently and with attenuated interest. Among Swahili diviners and healers, some, particularly women, engage in spirit possession and propitiation. However, many Swahili religious authorities in Malindi (and elsewhere) have an ideological center of gravity that leans away from such similarities with Giriama religiosity. High Islam proscribes any ritual practice that might detract from Allah's total power, while strengthened ties to the Arab world provide further incentives to Swahili to differentiate their religious and ritual lives from those of the Mijikenda. Swahili ideologies of faith, which base religiosity upon internal states of commitment and dedication to a universal Truth, run against the grain of the Giriama tendency to impute mystical agency to multiple sources and accept multiple coexisting models of the cosmos. Swahili thus are generally disapproving of Giriama religious pluralism when they hear of it, and perhaps even more uneasy about ritual practices in their own community that remind them of their historical ties to Mijikenda (and other indigenous) cultures.

Syncretism and Boundaries in Religious Pluralism

The ethnographer who has attended most closely to Giriama religious pluralism is Parkin (1970), most specifically in his essay "Politics of Rural Syncretism," which presciently attends to Stewart's concern about emic versus etic framing. Whereas anthropologists, Parkin says, ordinarily describe syncretism as "an ethnographic phenomenon observed by themselves but not claimed as such by the people of a society" (218; see also Baird 1991), he describes Giriama uses of Islam in Kaloleni as a self-conscious, self-professed form of "cultural diversity" (219). Giriama are unusual, he suggests, in self-consciously, explicitly modeling their religious practices on two different traditions and two different sources of power, one more powerful than their own (220). My ethnographic observations also indicate that many Giriama in the Malindi area view Giriama Traditionalism and Islam as different and asymmetrical sources of power. Yet I suggest that syncretism is a potentially misleading appellation for Giriama practices. In fact, Giriama modes of thought and practice provide a rationale for scrutinizing the very concept of syncretism and proffering an alternative theoretical tool for understanding their religious lives.

Syncretism is a relatively common, if historically problematic concept in the study of religion today. Historically the term has had pejorative connotations to members of the clergy who have used it to designate supposedly disorderly and illegitimate forms of religious mixture that have compromised the nominal purity of Christianity (Leopold and Jensen 2004; Shaw and Stewart 1994). Yet the word remains in wide circulation, in part because of its relevance to the now popular exploration of cultural *creolization, hybridity,* and *boundary crossing.* Such pursuits have been vital to dismantling older social scientific assumptions of cultural boundedness, fixity, and homogeneity, and to redefining, even celebrating, the flux and bricolage that make up cultural life. Indeed, a common rejoinder to earlier conceptions of syncretism is that religious practices, like cultural practices in general, are always already porous, and hence every religion is fundamentally syncretistic (Leopold and Jensen 2004; see also Apter 1991; Benavides 2004; Stewart 1999). Some scholars thus continue to use the term to draw attention to the blending of formerly distinct religious practices, but with the premise that syncretistic conditions are normative rather than exceptional.

However, the intensified scholarly interest in hybridity has not always done justice to the fact that, particularly in the postcolonial era, essentialist folk notions of cultural and religious distinctness are frequently vital political and rhetorical strategies of social groups large and small and driving forces in their religious and linguistic lives. Hence even when syncretism, in the sense of cultural blending, is quite evident to the outsider, it may be ideologically irrelevant or even anathema to cultural insiders, who may insist upon (for instance) the nominal purity or authenticity of their religious actions. Considerations like these prompt Stewart to write, "The study of how a people contest, negotiate, and act on attributions of syncretism . . . requires a switch from theology to the ethnography of theology (in both its official and popular forms)" (1999: 55; see also Shaw and Stewart 1994: 7).

The concept of syncretism also risks conflating the myriad forms that religious pluralism can take. Although some scholars define syncretism in terms of the combination of disparate religious elements into inconsistent and conflicting new configurations (see, for instance, Baird 1991),[5] more commonly the term refers to the mingling of religious material that might once have been incompatible but is now rendered whole and compatible, or at least is pushed in that direction. The Oxford English Dictionary defines syncretism as "an attempted union or reconciliation of diverse or opposite tenets or practices." The implied trajectory of syncretism in such models moves from conflict and discrepancy to consilience, harmony, synthesis, integration, "cross-fertilization," and other concepts that imply the fusion of difference into a new whole (cf. Stewart 1999). The teleological assumption that divergence must be reconciled into coherence in religious systems is so powerful that in Pye's well-known acknowledgment of ambiguity in syncretism, he insists that "the ambiguous clash of meanings demands some resolution," that, in other words, the plurality of meanings in some mixed religious formations is "intrinsically temporary" and will eventually be lost to "assimilation" (2004: 66; see also Vroom 1989). Even in Kraemer's (1938/2004: 9) acknowledgment of what he calls "religious pragmatism" in Eastern cultures, in which individuals may participate alternately in Buddhist, Taoist, or Confucian rites with apparent indifference toward doctrinal difference, he contends that such contrasts are ideologically permissible because of an underlying belief in a "sphere of absolute pure Essence," a sphere in which the "illusory relative existence" of the phenomenal world is neutralized and religions are ultimately one, fundamentally aiming at the same premises. Kraemer attributes this conviction to "all the naturalist non-Christian religions today," implying a ubiquitous human fixation on coherent religious ontologies.

Ironically the presumption of this preference for ontological coherence inflects one of the only conceptual alternatives to syncretism in the literature: Shaw and Stewart's (1994: 7) concept of "anti-syncretism," which they define as "the antagonism to religious synthesis shown by agents concerned with the defense of religious boundaries." This "defense," they suggest, tends to be accompanied by "the erasure of elements deemed alien from particular religious and ritual forms" (8). Zehner (2005: 587) too construes antisyncretism as a kind of cultural rigidity that "forbid[s] resort to other sources of spiritual power." The problem is that syncretism (as it is most commonly interpreted) and antisyncretism do not on their own account for all the variations on the theme of religious pluralism. In fact, they share the potentially limiting assumption of internal consistency within the religious practices of a given people, whether this consistency emerges from efforts to ban or erase other sources of religious power or from the synthesis, blending, and reconciliation of what were previously different religious traditions.

This assumption of a drive toward consistency is influenced by widespread Western and Abrahamic premises about the very category of religion, premises that are grounded in Western ideologies of personhood. The syncretistic image of distinct religions being merged into a new, coherent system is often underwritten by the presumption that religions are by definition systems of belief that are integrated, internally consistent, and preoccupied with universal Truth (cf. Asad 1993). This construal of religion in terms of universality and totality is implied or asserted even by some foundational anthropological thinkers. Clifford Geertz (1973b: 98), for example, yokes religion to "general ideas of order," and Mary Douglas (1975: 76) asserts, "The person without religion would be the person . . . content to behave in society without a single unifying principle validating the social order." But critics have rightfully suggested that Western scholars have been too ready to assume the coherence and logical consistency of belief systems (Fabian 1985; Gellner 1974). Indeed, the very concept of "unifying principles" seems undergirded by post-Enlightenment Western folk notions of the person: just as the person is frequently ideologically modeled in the West as integrated, unified, and internally consistent (Geertz 1973a; Giddens 1991; Markus and Kitayama 1991; Shweder and Bourne 1991), so too (goes the reasoning) must be the beliefs, religious or otherwise, that the person espouses (cf. Gellner 1974; Luhrmann 1989: 308). Yet as Benavides (2004: 199) reminds us, "The contents of most individuals' faiths are unstable and subject to a constant reinterpretation and negotiation. This means that the 'faith' of a 'believer' . . . is constituted by a repertoire of elements, often of a contradictory nature, which generally coexist in a state of tension." I would add that local notions of personhood influence the extent to which this kind of incoherence or instability is practiced and is ideologically acceptable, as well as the extent to which terms or concepts such as *faith* and *belief* are salient to religious practice and identity. We have already seen profound differences between prevailing Swahili and Giriama models of personhood and corresponding divergences in their prevailing religious expectations. Most Swahili in Malindi, like most ideological monotheists, tend to treat interior states of belief as "the definitive feature of a religious attitude" (Needham 1972: 20). Among Swahili, furthermore, the notion of religious belief is usually couched in terms of faith (*imani*), which entails not only wholehearted, consistent personal dedication but also the notion of absolute, universal Truth. Yet for many Giriama, as for many in societies with non-Abrahamic mystical traditions, belief and interiorized notions of ethno-religious identity (Tooker 1992) are not key structuring principles of their religious lives, except for some who have been particularly influenced by the messages of their Christian or Muslim neighbors.

It seems that our analytical tools for understanding religious pluralism ought to take account of religious practices that neither wholly deny the viability of alien religious ontologies nor attempt to reconcile them with other religious traditions to create a harmonious system. Indeed, the practices in some Giriama rituals seem to fall somewhere between syncretism (when defined in terms of the harmonization of religious traditions) and antisyncretism (when defined in terms of the denial of outside religious traditions). In these rituals overt discourses about religious pluralism and subtler semiotic and linguistic clues suggest that religious plurality is not about reconciling Islam and Giriama Traditionalism into a new, systemic whole, but about drawing on both religions while continuing to mark them as distinct. More than one religion may be used, but they are juxtaposed rather than blended. Similar forms of religious plurality have been described among native groups in the American Southwest who have drawn from two distinct, "compartmentalized" ceremonial systems based on Spanish Catholicism and their indigenous religion (Dozier 1960; Spicer 1954). Stewart (1999: 56) acknowledges the possibility of such religious juxtaposition and suggests that it does not fall within his definition of syncretism—yet it does not seem to fall within his definition of antisyncretism either. Hence as part of the project of understanding Giriama religious pluralism and the broader project of identifying "local folk ideologies of what religious mixing means" (Shaw and Stewart 1994: 7), we stand to benefit from a more fine-grained analytic category.[6]

To account for patterns such as the one I have found among Giriama in Malindi, I propose a concept that I term *polyontologism*. The term is not intended to designate an absolute category but to characterize the endpoint of a spectrum of possible religious positions on ontology and cosmology. In its clearest form polyontologism is an emic stance (an attitude recognized by cultural insiders) of religious plurality that acknowledges the mystical potency (the ontological reality) of more than one set of religious or cosmological forces; marks these religious ontologies as distinct (by, for instance, marking their respective symbols and practices as embedded in different semiotic, historical, or ethnic contexts, or even marking their premises as contradictory); and considers all of the ontologies in question eligible to be propitiated or embraced by the same person.[7] In polyontologist practice the plural ontologies engaged with are not ultimately one, nor are their associated deities or forces semiotically aligned or equated (in the way that, for instance, Catholic saints and African spirits have so often been; see, for instance, Bastide 1960/1978). Differences between the systems in question are (emically) recognized and upheld by practitioners, while potential (that is, etically recognizable) contradictions between the systems may or may not be recognized and remarked on by practitioners. Either way, these contradictions are not erased or minimized because practitioners are not expected to be consistent in their beliefs or committed to a single tradition of practice. Indeed, in polyontologist contexts beyond the Giriama case, folk models of personhood are unlikely to share the Western and Abrahamic fixation on a person's inner beliefs and the consistency of such internal commitments.

To be clear, polyontologist stances are not necessarily (indeed, not likely to be) characterized by a jumble of random, unrelated commitments to free-floating loci of supernatural power. More typical is that various deities or mystical agents are organized under the umbrella of a particular ethnically (or otherwise socially) marked tradition or ontological locus. Giriama Traditionalism, for instance, adduces numerous agents, such as ancestors, the god Mulungu, and spirits such as Katsumba

Kazi, but all of these are conceptualized and marked as being tightly associated with the Giriama people, or "from the Giriama side." Similarly, Giriama often construe Islam's powers as distributed across spiritual and material agents, including Allah, Mohammed, the Quran, and the geomancy book called Falak. Yet all of these are seen as united by a core Islamic principle and force, one associated more closely with some ethnicities than others. Language may play an important role in marking these systems as bounded and associated with particular social units, as indeed it did in the American Southwest, where Spanish was used for Catholic rituals and indigenous languages for indigenous rituals (Dozier 1960; Spicer 1954). In polyontologist systems the potential ontological contradictions between these discrete loci of power may be dealt with either through explicit insistence that there is no one Truth or, as is the case among Giriama, through simple neglect to assimilate the potentially contradictory premises of each system because there is no ideological prioritization of consistency to begin with.

The ideological fixation on the universal Truth of a particular religious system might be correspondingly deemed *mono-ontologism*, at the opposite end of the spectrum of beliefs. Mono-ontologism is in principle distinct from monotheism, for one could be a polytheist—one could believe in, say, five goddesses—and a mono-ontologist at the same time by insisting that only these five goddesses exist and that all other cosmological models, such as the neighboring group's notion of a devouring godhead, are in error. A polyontological stance, by contrast, would perceive both cosmologies as possessing their own distinct mystical potency that can be tapped or appealed to by the same person.[8] Between polyontologism and mono-ontologism one might find any number of positions, including forms of syncretism that (unlike mono-ontologism) draw on more than one religious system but (unlike polyontologism) attempt to assimilate and harmonize them into consilience and consistency, creating a kind of ontological oneness out of initial plurality.

Polyontologism treats a given religious tradition not as a comprehensive worldview but as a locus of certain mystical powers. Accordingly, for many Giriama in Malindi Islam is not first and foremost a belief system with a monopoly on the Truth, but a locus of potency that can be tapped through mimetic behaviors (penning simulacra of Arabic, reading the Quran, and so forth) that call up its magic (cf. Taussig 1993). Furthermore, polyontologism among Giriama in Malindi is sometimes bound up with the hegemonic notion that certain religions (namely, Islam and Giriama Traditionalism) are tightly, essentially bound to ethnolinguistic groups. Just as some Giriama insist upon a natural, essential distinction between Giriama and Swahili ethnicity, so too are the powers of Traditionalism and Islam sometimes construed as though these are constituted by an essential force, a force with an ethnic flavor, that can't be readily blended or merged with other ethnoreligious forces. After all, as the *aganga* at the cave shrine informed me, the spirits from the two sides "don't get along." Hence Giriama rituals do not simply merge signifiers from Traditionalism and Islam as though all of them draw upon an undifferentiated supernatural locus. Instead, when Giriama in Malindi incorporate Islamic symbolism into their rituals, this is often conspicuously described as tapping the force from "the Muslim side." Furthermore, in the Giriama case, and possibly in other cultural contexts as well, polyontologism seems a particularly subaltern strategy because its practitioners are highly conscious of the subordinate status of their own religion vis-à-vis Islam and of the monopoly that Arabs and Swahili seem to have on Islamic knowledge. Giriama don't tend to see themselves as owning or encompassing Islam; they have no authority to assimilate it fully into their communities and can invoke it only from a quasi-spatial distance. Ironically, if polyontologism emerges as a response to this perceived distance, it also reinforces it.

Yet, as I have already hinted, there are exceptions to the pattern of polyontologist worship among Giriama in Malindi. Some Giriama, for instance, have adopted the cosmopolitan and consilient claim "We all worship the same God." In such cases polyontologism is replaced by a syncretistic position in which all religions are thought to interface with basically the same metaphysical forces, only by different means and through different terms, much in the way that Kraemer (1938/2004) characterizes all non-Western forms of religious pluralism. A brief example of consilient syncretism in Giriama ritual will be helpful, for three reasons: to underscore the diversity of Giriama ritual (polyontologism, in other words, is not the only stance available to Giriama); to acknowledge that Christian symbolism does occasionally appear in the rituals of *aganga*, albeit infrequently; and to introduce the fact that linguistic codes in ritual derive their significance from the context of their use.

My example comes from a Giriama *mganga* named Tsuma who recently returned to Malindi from a lengthy stint in Kenya's Western Province, where Christianity is the religious norm and Muslims are a small minority. Upon his return, Tsuma set up a small healing practice in the division of Maweni, advertising (as do many *aganga*) with an announcement written on a board propped up outside his home. Using Kiswahili —perhaps to appeal to the multiethnic constituency of this diverse section of town, perhaps to index his culturally or religiously cosmopolitan background—Tsuma wrote:

> *Mganga maarufu wa kuombea wagonjuwa na kuondowa machawi yote yanayokusumbua. Kutana naye leo. Huomba wenye shida za uzazi. Kutokwa na damu, kifafa, wazimu, kuvute mume nyumbani, kutafuta kazi . . . na mengineyo. Yote yawezekana.*

Expert *mganga* specialist in praying for health and casting out all witchery that disturbs you. Meet with him today. He can pray for those who have trouble with childbirth. [Those with] prolonged menstrual periods, epilepsy, [those who have gone] mad, [those who wish] to attract a husband back home, [those] looking for work . . . and many other things. All is possible.

On the day I visited him with my assistant to watch his practice, I noted that Tsuma had planted ancestral (*koma*) stakes outside his hut, next to which lay a calabash with a mixture of roots and herbs he used to propitiate the ancestors. Inside Tsuma was dressed in a *kanzu*, the long white robe worn by pious Swahili and Arab men, and carried two religious markers: a set of Islamic prayer beads (*tasbihi*, Kisw.) and a necklace with a crucifix on it. He greeted us in Kiswahili, invoking the words of Jesus with a Biblical phrase: "Come all of you and I will carry your burdens and give you rest [Karibuni nyote muliolemewa na mizigo nami nitawapumzisha]." On a side table a Bible was clearly visible, as were a black stone, a heavy chain, two pieces of red cloth, another calabash (presumably filled with potent herbs), seashells, and a starfish, the last two being ingredients occasionally used in Giriama talismans.

We took our seats as he focused his attention on his client, a young woman who complained that she was disturbed at night by spirits. Unlike most who come to see a healer, she had not gone to see a diviner first to get a clear diagnosis, so she didn't know what kind of spirits they were. Tsuma requested Ksh600 (about US$9 at the time) to remove the witchcraft in her; she agreed to pay him later. He lit a red candle and instructed her to sit in the middle of the floor with a red cloth over her head. Then he wrapped the chain and the stone in the second red cloth and placed these on her head, explaining that the stone would pull out any evil talismans and witchcraft that had been planted in her, while the chain would capture any evil spirits so that they did not interfere with the prayers. Giving the Bible to the young woman to hold, he clutched the prayer beads close to his chest and began to finger the beads while praying to God (Mungu, a term that does not mark the speaker's religious affiliation) in Kiswahili for the woman to be released from her witchcraft. Finally, Tsuma opened the cloth on her head. Inside, next to the stone and the chain, were a talisman, feathers, and a bone.

In our conversation afterward Tsuma was adamant that he had not been appealing to separate gods. "God is one," he said, "and he works through Christianity, Islam, and Traditionalism. The power of God directs me to the tools I should use in a particular ritual." Thus Tsuma's stance was not polyontologism, for he treated the religious traditions he practiced as superficially different means of tapping the same, singular source of mystical potency. His use of Kiswahili in this context of mingled Christian, Islamic, and Traditionalist imagery, as well as his use of the ethnically and religiously neutral Kiswahili term for God (Mungu), foregrounded Kiswahili's valence as a lingua franca that can index cosmopolitanism and interethnic communication. Yet the significance of code choice is not fixed in advance; it hinges upon the contextual contingencies of a ritual. And in many Giriama rituals, code choice, including Kiswahili itself, is used to highlight and emphasize polyontologist premises rather than harmonizing, syncretistic ones.

Tsuma's healing ritual was fairly unusual among the many I witnessed in Malindi, both for its consilient stance and for its appropriation of Christian imagery. Giriama in Malindi have ample exposure to both Christianity and Islam, but polyontologist *aganga* practitioners are especially preoccupied with the powers of Islam (cf. Parkin 1970, 1991a), in part because Islam is conceptually bound up with the vexing advantages of their wealthier Swahili neighbors. The popularity of Islamic appropriation also stems from the fact that diviners, healers, spirit beliefs, and spirit possession can be found within the Swahili community itself, a cultural overlap that enhances the mutual relevance of Islam and Giriama ritual. By contrast, Christianity discourages divination and any ritualistic healing that takes place outside of a church. Perhaps more important, Giriama pointedly do not associate Christianity with wealth, and coastal missionaries have encouraged Africans themselves, including some Mijikenda, to become church leaders and preachers. The notion that Christianity promises upward mobility, or that any given ethnic group has privileged access to Christianity, is difficult to sustain. While Christianity certainly has associations with Western countries and with the Kenyan state, it is not conceptualized as a repository of ethnically specific privilege; as a result, it is not laden with the ethnic and affective associations —the hope for wealth and ethnic assimilation, and the frustration as these elude Giriama—of Islam.

It is important to mention that although many Giriama in and around Malindi seem to conceptualize the mystical world in a polyontologist fashion, Giriama individuals do not consider themselves a member of more than one religion. It is taken for granted by virtually everyone on the coast that an individual can be a proclaimed affiliate of only one religion; for Giriama this is usually Traditionalism, Islam, or Christianity. This practice of self-categorization may be an index of Abrahamic hegemony, and on the face of it, it runs against the grain of the pluralist Giriama ethos I have described. However, such categories sometimes offer Giriama strategic means of affiliation, however disappointing they may ultimately be. The affiliative and often transitory nature of the religious labels that accompany conversion are explained in pragmatic terms by Charo, a clerk at Malindi hospital: "If you become Christian you are promised life after death. The second reason is that in Christianity you find respect from other Christians, your fellow African Christians. And also, in Christianity you find yourself closer to the government of Kenya; as you know, it's a Christian government. People convert to Islam because of poverty. They go to Islam to get rich, but in the end they find out it's not easy to get rich so they turn again and convert to be a Christian, or they turn back to African traditional religion." Clearly alignment with one or another religion brings the hope of particular supernatural or social advantages. But an individual's publicly stated religious affiliation does not guarantee ontological commitment to only one supernatural reality. Nor does it guarantee that in practice individuals will restrict their propitiation to the god or deities of their affiliated religion. Indeed, practice on the ground is often more pluralistic than this, most typically when Giriama rituals tack back and forth between Traditionalism and Islam.

Giriama Traditionalism and Forces from the Muslim Side

Many quintessentially Giriama practices and powers are considered by Giriama to be rooted in the Kaya era, when all Giriama were thought to live in these sacred and enclosed forest spaces under the jurisdiction of elders and ancestors. Men in the community were initiated progressively into age-graded levels of seniority and into several secret societies (*mwanza*).[9] Each society controlled certain powers, such as mystical medicines, the *mwanza mkulu* friction drum that can inflict illness upon the uninitiated, and charms (*viraho*) to protect and govern the social order (Brantley 1978; Udvardy 1990).[10] At least one prominent female society was thought to control powers of reproduction and regeneration and domestic boundaries (S. G. Thompson 1990; Udvardy 1989, 1990).[11] While these societies are on the decline, their vestiges remain among Giriama communities surrounding Malindi, and they are considered the very embodiment of ethnic authenticity. Customarily, for instance, initiates are forbidden to wear items associated with the West or modernity, such as eyeglasses and watches (Udvardy 1990: 129), thus marking their distance from corrupting outside forces. Similar prohibitions are used for entry into the Kaya space itself.

The ancestors, or *koma*, have been central to the making of Giriama identity. Giriama trace their clan membership through their paternal line, and they sometimes remember their recently dead and prominent ancestors with wooden stakes placed in the ground on the homestead and tied with bright red, blue, and white strips of cloth. A related practice, still found in hinterland areas but uncommon in Malindi, is to commemorate the deceased members of the Gohu society, wealthy men celebrated for their redistributive generosity, with taller and more elaborately carved posts called *vigango* (sing. *kigango*).[12] As "the living dead," the ancestors are thought to inhabit the posts erected for them and sometimes appear to their descendants in dreams, often to request propitiation from the family. Ordinarily the ancestors expect routine acknowledgment, such as offerings of food and (above all) palm wine, accompanied by prayer. Failure to comply can result in tragedy, ranging from infertility to illness and a decline in all manner of fortune. The relative importance of the ancestors, however, has been in decline in Giriama life, in part because in the post-Kaya era so few men and women are now inducted into the age grades and secret societies that once assured the primacy of the elders (Brantley 1978, 1981; McIntosh, forthcoming).[13] In Giriama homes close to urban centers, furthermore, family structure has been disrupted by migrant labor, as many workers live atomized lives, away from the jurisdiction of senior male kin. The declining regard for elders, both alive and deceased, is considered a threat to customary Giriama life, and in the Malindi area it is not unusual for spirit-medium diviners to attribute people's bad fortune to their neglect of their ancestors.[14]

In customary Giriama ritual, invocation of the ancestors is often twinned with the invocation of the overarching god, Mulungu, in the phrase "Ancestors below, Mulungu on high [Koma tsi, Mulungu dzulu]." Mulungu is not a particularly vivid agent in Giriama cosmology (Parkin 1985b: 230), and Christian missionaries have long been aggravated by how vaguely conceived he is and how diffuse are his powers (Sperling 1985). Many of Mulungu's responsibilities tend to be environmental; he is said to determine when rain falls and crops grow and may be directly appealed to for such purposes. Yet many Giriama construe their day-to-day fortunes as controlled largely by the numerous lower forces that dwell in close interaction with people on the ground: spirits, ancestors, witchery, and nameless, faceless forces that cause illness in cases of sociosexual misconduct.[15]

The most prominent force for restoring social order now that the Kaya elders no longer hold sway over the population at large is *uganga*, the body of practices that draw upon mechanistic devices and spirit possession for divining and upon distinct patterns of ritual healing. Divination and healing are frequently sought by those dispossessed of work, money, land, or good health as alternatives or complements to secular efforts to improve their lot; the practitioners of divination and healing are the *aganga*, whom I introduced in the preceding chapter.[16] Healing rites from the Giriama side are distinctively marked by a symbolic repertoire that each healer uses in an improvisatory fashion. In one fairly representative ritual, a client diagnosed with a possessing Giriama spirit (thrown upon her by a neighbor jealous of her financial success) was smudged at her joints with the black ash of healing herbs, then daubed with the blood of a sacrificed chicken to lure out the spirit, who was thought to be tempted by the prospect of a meal. The blood of the sacrificed chicken was also sprinkled on the ground as an offering to the ancestors, as the *mganga* prayed to them for their assistance in making the spirit "run away." Next, the *mganga* drew on the ground a powder effigy of a possessing spirit and produced a clay doll to represent the "jealous woman," instructing the client to walk backward and forward over both of these, crushing and obliterating them with her feet to erase the threat they posed. The *mganga* then used the black ash of herbs and a white powder to draw seven lines (*mihambo mifungahe*) upon the well-swept ground; this is a classic Giriama ritual device that clients scuff away with their feet to "untie" (*kuhundula*) the effects of witchcraft. Finally, the client was instructed to undress so that the *mganga* could bathe her with *vuo*, a cleansing and spirit-pleasing mixture of water and herbs used in many Giriama rituals.[17] Despite the diversity of such ritual practices, all are recognized by Giriama themselves as indigenous (*ya kienyeji*) practices that invoke the potencies associated with Traditionalism.

Yet many Giriama *aganga* in Malindi today incorporate objects and agents from the Muslim side into their rituals. Just as Giriama defy the notion that a single religious system has access to a total Truth, so too do they defy the ideology, popular among pious Swahili, that Islamic power emanates from a lone source: God (Allah). Instead, many Giriama believe the powers of Islam are distributed among spirits and objects, especially texts, which are often accorded talismanic significance. Diviners and healers alike propitiate both Allah (sometimes referred to in Kiswahili as Mwenye-ezi Mungu) and Muslim spirits, using the Quran, rosewater, food such as honey, and coins and other precious metal objects. Healers may prepare talismans and treatments containing scraps of the Quran or Arabic writing, while diviners may call upon possessing Muslim spirits to help them "read" and "write" the Quran, a phenomenon I analyze in some depth in the next chapter.

Giriama polyontologism is also upheld in the Malindi area by a common taxonomy of spirits. A significant number of individuals I spoke to classify spirits in terms of the two superordinate categories, "the Muslim side" (*upande wa kiislam*, Kigir., Kisw.) and "the Giriama side" (*upande wa kigiriama,* sometimes called "the Mijikenda side," *upande wa kimi-jikenda,* Kigir., Kisw.). Spirits from the Muslim side, sometimes referred to as Arab spirits, include the money-hoarding *jini* and various possessing Muslim spirits. In Giriama healing rituals the invocation of these spirits requires a different ritual apparatus. Spirits from the Giriama side include Katsumba Kazi (the female spirit who trains new diviners), Zikiri Maiti (the so-called walking corpse spirit), animal spirits such as Pepo Simba ("lion spirit"), and a cluster of other idiosyncratic creatures.[18] Also significant is that this taxonomy is not shared by all Giriama communities, so it may be a relatively recent or local innovation, emergent from the particular relationship between Giriama and Islam in Malindi. To be sure, Giles (1989b: 243, 253) notes that Giriama spirit mediums whom she interviewed in communities north of Mombasa "listed both indigenous and Islamic spirits as their major spirit helpers," but it is not entirely clear whether these mediums taxonomized their spirits according to oppositional sides. Others who have documented Giriama spirit beliefs, such as Noble (1961), Parkin (1991a), and Udvardy (1990), do not mention such a taxonomy. S. G. Thompson (1990: 77) asserts that in the hinterland Magarini area the main taxonomic distinction between spirits is between "pepo-of-the-body" (*pepo za mwirini*) and "pepo-to-be-exorcised" (*pepo za kuomboza*); pepo-of-the-body in turn are linked either to the seaboard (*pwani*) or the bushland (*nyika*), and "pepo of the seaboard are predominantly Islamic"; Islam thus plays a role in this pattern of classification, but as a subordinate rather than a superordinate category. Regardless, Giles (1989b: 253) notes that Muslim spirits are considered "very powerful and quite effective for divination, healing, and magical assistance," while S. G. Thompson (1990: 77) describes Islamic pepo as "prestige enhancing" for their hosts.

The widespread Giriama notion that Muslim spirits are especially potent is seen in the fact that many Giriama in the Malindi area consider the spirits from the Giriama side to be "low" (*wa hali ya tsini*) or "little" (*thithe*) compared to the Muslim spirits, who are "high" (*wa hali ya tzulu*) or "big" (*bomu*). Some, in fact, refer to the Muslim spirits using the Kiswahili appellation Wachuoni, or "those who have been schooled," in a nod to the politics of literacy. Some use an English gloss that brings with it an economic inflection, deeming these spirits "high class" in contrast to the "low class" Giriama spirits. Even Giriama spirit beliefs reinforce certain elements of Islamic hegemony by taking for granted the notion that the spirits who contain the essence of Muslim power are intrinsically more powerful or prestigious than Giriama spirits. Yet true to the split between hegemony and ideology, the high/low distinction does not always map neatly onto the affective stances of the *aganga* who work with the spirits. The presumed hegemonic notion of superior Muslim supernatural power is sometimes accompanied by an impassioned ideology of Giriama moral superiority. Quite a few *aganga*, in fact, told me of their preference for the indigenous spirits (*mapepo ya kienyeji*), typically on moral grounds. One *mganga* informed me pointedly that the high Muslim spirits are "lazy" and "like bad people": "They don't care to help us very much," she said. The status of Muslim spirits is not necessarily accompanied by ascribed goodness or compassion; with such opinions, Giriama reassert a defiant ideology of their own, just as they rebel against the powerful Muslim spirits who possess them and attempt to force them to convert to Islam.

In the context of polyontologism a given *mganga*'s claim that he or she is Traditionalist, Muslim, or (less typically) Christian tends to mean relatively little for ritual practice, for *aganga* of all declared faiths invoke powers from the Giriama side and the Muslim side. Take Charo Shutu, a grand old Giriama healer who until his death in 2004 was considered the very embodiment of Giriama tradition by many living in and around Malindi. "If you're interested in our customs," Malindi residents would tell me, "you must speak to Charo Shutu. He's a very big *mganga*." Charo Shutu's prestige was enhanced by his social capital, including his prodigious number of wives (over two dozen, by some counts), his more than one hundred children, and his ongoing battle with the Swahili Bakhson family (see chapter 2) over several acres of land on the edge of Malindi town. He was famous for his knowledge of Giriama custom, dance, and traditional medicine and generously lectured me for hours on end about the fine points of herbalism. I still recall my surprise when Charo Shutu himself told me that he considered himself a Christian.

I was to be more surprised as I came to realize the plurality of the forces to which Charo Shutu appealed. On one visit I was told that Charo Shutu's elderly assistant *mganga*, Kitsao, wanted to show me Charo Shutu's shrine. Kitsao led me and my research assistant away from Charo Shutu's busy homestead to a wooded area, chatting in Kigiriama. Eventually he pointed to an enormous baobab tree in a glade and instructed us to take off our sandals and place them on the ground with the toes pointing away from the tree, marking the space as liminal and sacred. Barefoot, we walked on until we could see the gnarled tree roots poking above ground, stacked with offerings: half-empty bottles of rosewater, coins, and sooty piles of ash from incense. Kitsao fell silent and stopped. Clearing his throat and tilting his head back, he shifted from Kigiriama into Kiswahili to appeal to the spirits in a loud voice: "*Hodi hodi* to the spirits—our fine guests have come to talk to you about matters of custom, and to request your blessing [*baraka*], and to pray in the appropriate style here. *Hodi,* sheikhs!"

Kitsao then shifted into an annunciatory, keening register, so that his voice sounded like a quavering version of the calls to prayer that emanate daily from the mosque loudspeakers in town: "Allahu Akbar! Allahu Akbar! [God is great! Ar.]." He proceeded to explain to the spirits why we had come, assuring them we arrived with respect and beseeching them for their forbearance. He turned to us and explained that the spirits living at this shrine could dispense the potency of Islam: "Charo Shutu holds their power here. If he encounters a sick client whose illness is beyond his indigenous powers, he takes the client to the shrine." In this favored shrine of a renowned Christian Giriama *mganga,* the spirits are Muslims whose great potency is accessible only through appeals in Kiswahili and Arabic that mimic Swahili and Arab religiosity.

Another *mganga* named Nzingo explained how she divides her ritual practices between Islam and Traditionalism. Her ancestral history is similarly divided, and as she narrated her genealogy I realized her family has long been ambivalently connected to Islam, as the generations oscillated between the religions. "My grandfather was Muslim by birth but renounced it. My father was Traditionalist. Then I was born, just Traditionalist, but when I became a *mganga* it was clear the spirits wanted me to be a Muslim." Today Nzingo professes herself a Muslim and is one of the most active *aganga* in Muyeye. Every Friday she propitiates her "big" spirits, the Muslim ones, with a platter of food offerings ranging from milk and honey to meat. She sometimes uses the Quran to divine and heal, but this seems to depend upon her assessment of the client's needs, including the difficulty of the divination (harder cases require the stronger powers of the Muslim spirits) and the nature of the client's required treatment (possession by a Muslim *jini,* for instance, requires powers from the Muslim side). Still, one could observe her practice for days, as I did, and not see a recognizable sign of Islam aside from a few tattered sheets printed in Arabic that languish on the floor of her bedroom.

Nzingo explained to me that she invokes each system of power, Giriama and Islamic, through particular objects and linguistic patterns. Gathering leaves and roots in the forest and appealing to Mulungu, the ancestors, and the Giriama spirits are means of tapping the powers of Traditionalism, whereas appealing to Muslim spirits or using the Quran provides a route to the powers of Islam. The two are entirely distinct:

> This is how I work. Who created the herbs we *aganga* work with? It was Mulungu. So, now, if I go into the forest to collect herbs in the *mganga* style, I say: "Ptu! Greetings. Ancestors are below in the earth, Mulungu is above in the sky [Koma tsi, Mulungu dzulu]." Now, Mulungu and Allah are different. To do my Giriama-style *uganga*, I can't start talking about Mohammed; I have to return to my original religion. I mention the ancestors, I mention Mulungu, I mention various spirits we work with, I mention Mbodze na Matsesi [the Giriama ancestral couple]. It's like I go home. Then, when I do the Muslim-style routines, that's when I address Allah.

Nzingo's ritual practice is a patterned, polyontologist alternation between two separate systems of supernatural power that do not overlap or bleed into each other; each has its own spiritual forces and its own terms of address. Indeed, like other Giriama, Nzingo uses spatial terminology to allude to the gap between the systems; she "goes home" when she adduces the agents of Giriama Traditionalism. It is particularly significant that she uses this locution despite the fact that she is a Muslim convert. The ethnoreligious linking I have described has so deeply infused her concept of Islam that although she considers herself a Muslim, Islam remains Other; it is still not her "home."

This sense of a home religion, juxtaposed against a set of forces considered Other, is often marked with special precision through the selective use of linguistic codes in Giriama ritual. Indeed, although we saw in Tsuma a *mganga* who uses Kiswahili as an ethnically and religiously neutral code, other Giriama *aganga* often treat codes in ritual contexts as though they are both yoked to and evocative of ethnically particular religious ontologies. *Aganga* such as Kitsao and the women who tend the cave shrine use Kigiriama to address powers from the Giriama side and Kiswahili and Arabic to address powers from the Muslim side. So too does Hawe Baya, the *mganga* who bemoaned the fact that "the Giriama doesn't have his own Quran." Her assertion of ethno-religious essentialism, in which certain ethnic groups are presumed to have an intrinsic link with particular markers of religious potency, is further entrenched by her use of linguistic codes in ritual. "When I'm talking to Allah," she explained in an echo of Nzingo, "I have to use the Swahili language, but when I go home and talk to Mulungu, that's when I use the Giriama language."

Linguistic Codes, Religious Ontologies, and Essentialism in Giriama Ritual

The linguistic code choices in Giriama ritual seem to emerge from poly-ontologist assumptions about an ethnically grounded division between Islamic and Traditionalist ontologies. I suggest that linguistic code shifting and code switching in Giriama ritual can have two subtle effects.[19] Code choice in ritual can establish or "key" (Goffman 1974) a new frame that foregrounds the immanent presence of particular religious powers in contrast to others, while establishing the speaker's stance in relation to these. Such code choices not only reflect the idea of natural links between language, ethnicity, and religion, but they performatively reinforce such essentialisms, an idea I develop at greater length elsewhere (McIntosh 2005a). Kiswahili, for instance, is frequently used in conjunction with Islamic symbolism in Giriama ritual, thereby reinforcing the conceptual link between Islam and Swahili ethnicity, while Kigiriama is frequently used in the portions of rituals marked as quintessentially indigenous to Giriama. When the semantic content of these invocations also reinforces the notion that Giriama are on familiar terms with Giriama powers but on obsequious terms with Islam, this pattern of implied social relations further consolidates the notion that Islam and Giriamaness are distant from each other, while Islam and Swahiliness are bound together. Code shifts and code switches thus can serve as inadvertent means of reinscribing the same hegemonic divisiveness, and the same kind of distance from Islam, that Giriama resent in other contexts.

To clarify how code choice operates in Giriama ritual it is crucial to emphasize that the valence of codes varies from one context to the next.

Numerous scholars have recognized that language ideologies (in Silver-stein's [1979: 193] sense of "sets of beliefs about language articulated by users as a rationalization or justification of perceived language structure and use") associate languages with particular social valences, providing a context of presuppositions that gives code choices significance. Code switching in conversation, for instance, has been shown to draw upon culturally specific language ideologies to index ethnic identity, power and prestige, solidarity and distance, rights and obligations, and other aspects of identity and social relationships (Gumperz 1982; Heller 1988; Jaffe 1999; LePage and Tabouret-Keller 1985; Milroy and Muysken 1995). Yet if portions of the extensive code-switching literature seem to presume an a priori model of language ideology, in which the valence of each code is distinct and predetermined, a growing number of scholars have challenged such deterministic models (cf. Alvarez-Cáccamo 1990; Gal 1987; Heller 1988).[20] In Giriama talk, context is crucial to establishing which associations Kiswahili will invoke and subtly reinforce. As we have seen, Kiswahili in Tsuma's syncretic ritual did not have any special association with Islam, but in many polyontologist Giriama rituals it does.

My explorations further suggest that the phrase *language ideology*, which so permeates the linguistic anthropological literature, could use some scrutiny. If we return to the Comaroffs' distinction between hege-mony and ideology, it becomes important to distinguish between con-sciously articulated, ideological ideas about language and largely tacit assumptions about language that hegemonically cut across social groups to reinforce the status quo.[21] As the Comaroffs remind us, a given idea may move between the hegemonic and ideological poles, and indeed in my observations on the coast I found that ideas about language that are normally taken for granted are sometimes explicitly articulated and thus thrown into relief. Nevertheless, the patterns of code choice I discuss invite little metacommentary from most Giriama. They appear to ema-nate fairly automatically from ritual officiants and to require no explana-tion for onlookers, as if they are based on tacit and hegemonic assump-tions about links between particular ethnicities and particular religious ontologies. Crucially, they reaffirm existing ethnoreligious divisions by implying and thus reinforcing the notion of a tight and intrinsic yoke between Swahili and Islam and a correspondingly tight and intrinsic yoke between Giriama and Traditionalism. Hence the linguistic practices

I describe here help to undergird the hegemonic ethnoreligious essentialisms I have been discussing.

To understand how code choice operates in Giriama religious pluralism, some further background on language in Malindi is important. In the introduction I noted that the linguistic environment of Malindi is predominantly made up of Kiswahili, Kigiriama (and related Mijikenda tongues), English, and Arabic. Most Giriama living in or near town, particularly men who have had a few years of schooling, speak Kigiriama, Kiswahili, at least some English, and smatterings of other languages, but not all languages are equal in the wider linguistic marketplace. Swahili in Malindi, for instance, virtually never speak Kigiriama, and when Swahili and Giriama pass one another on the village paths and roads Swahili uniformly greet Giriama in Kiswahili or even in Arabic. This pattern hinges on their refusal to index ethnic affiliation with the Giriama people and on the ethnic politics of purity and pollution; as one Giriama woman described her impression of the Swahili attitude, "They say our language is rotten [*bovu*, Kisw.] compared to theirs." Parkin (1994c: 242, 243) also found that Kigiriama and other Mijikenda languages tend to be "shunned as contaminating" by at least some Swahili:

> Not only is [Ki]Swahili the only acceptable language of communication, but also [Swahili] will not normally respond to any of the non-Muslim Mijikenda dialects, despite the fact that in a few cases at least they must have a passive knowledge of them. They explain this by claiming that to speak and respond to such non-Muslim dialects is to lay oneself open to the contaminating practices associated with the non-Muslim speakers, namely their production and drinking of alcohol, their heavy reliance on non-Koranic divination and therapy, their lengthy funerals involving dance and drink, and the fact that their diets may include pork and other foodstuff forbidden to Muslims. To speak and know a non-Muslim language is to become consubstantial with the character and practices of its speakers.

Indeed, the presumed link between language and piety suffuses the claim of one of my Swahili informants, Mohammed: "It has not been easy to change Africans' religion; they hear Kiswahili and answer in Kigiriama." Evidently some Swahili perceive Giriama as both closer to Africa and farther away from Islam, and their language is implicated in this atavism.

Giriama have digested the lesson that Swahili are averse to Kigiriama. In fact, those few Giriama in Malindi who are invested in an ethnic change usually abandon Kigiriama if they can. One resident of Muyeye, for instance, was born and raised as a Giriama but fell in love with a Swahili man, converted to Islam, and changed her name from the Giriama Kadidi to the Islamic Rehema. Rehema lived with her husband on the Swahili-dominated island of Zanzibar until their divorce two years later, when she returned to Malindi and settled in Muyeye with her young child. Although she was surrounded by non-Muslim Giriama, she maintained her religious practices, covered her head, and, in a great slight to her natal community, refused to speak Kigiriama. When neighbors or I greeted her unthinkingly in that language, she behaved as though she had not been addressed at all, as if to utter one word in the language might compromise her hoped-for ethnic status. To Giriama this linguistic maneuver is an assertion of outright snobbery. One young Giriama convert to Islam, Omari, speaks Kiswahili to his customers in Malindi's market, but when he is at his parents' home, he said, "I must speak Kigiriama. If I don't, they'll think I am scorning them [*kudharau*, Kisw.]." Apparently the use of Kiswahili by Giriama in their domestic settings bears with it the disdain of an ethnic Swahili point of view.

The link between languages and ethnicities is reinforced by the fact that the languages important in Giriama and Swahili life are labeled as if discrete, despite the considerable number of bivalent terms (Woolard 1998b) between Kiswahili and Kigiriama and between Arabic and Kiswahili. Language names are derived by adding the prefix *ki-* ("language of") to the ethnic group with which they are associated: Kiswahili, Kiarabu, Kigiriama, Kiingereza (English), and so on. Language is thereby framed as a kind of patrimony, an inalienable component of ethnicity, despite the fact that in daily life in Malindi many Giriama use two, three, or even more languages to get by.

Not only are languages and ethnicities linked in the Giriama imagination, but certain languages and certain religions are more closely ideologically bound together than others. Unlike Christianity in Africa, Islam has not been linguistically democratic; its central text and prayers are tightly bound to Arabic.[22] Giriama tend to associate Arabic so closely with Islam that it is referred to not only as Kiarabu but also, sometimes, Kiislam, "the language of Islam." Giriama supplement this notion with a conceptual link between Islam and Kiswahili. There are several reasons for this, including the fact that the Swahili people, whose first language is Kiswahili, are Muslim almost by definition, while Kiswahili has many cognates in Arabic which further yokes it to Islam. Meanwhile Kigiriama is associated with the powers of Giriama Traditionalism. Giriama sometimes treat these languages not as interchangeable codes, but as potent phenomena that can invoke and even embody different metaphysical powers. The essence of a given language, in other words, is sometimes framed as if it shares and contains the metaphysically potent essence associated with a particular ethnic group.

All of these considerations inform code choice in ritual. Not surprisingly, those rituals considered quintessentially Giriama are carried out in Kigiriama, for only that language is thought to bear with it the binding forces associated with indigenous religion. These include the act of appeasing the ancestors and the divination and healing rites that invoke Mulungu, the ancestors, and the Mijikenda spirits. Rituals appealing to the Muslim side are nearly always carried out in the languages associated with Islam, and since few Giriama speak more than a tiny smattering of Arabic, the dominant language in Islamic rituals is Kiswahili. Some healers do not use Islamic symbolism at all, and others use such symbolism only in an ancillary fashion (for example, by tearing up the Quran to make talismans); still others partition their rituals to appeal by turns to the Muslim side and the Giriama side, as if to enhance the potency of the ritual by mobilizing not one but two loci of supernatural power. In such rituals, shifts in denotational content and material signs that invoke distinct loci of religious power are usually accompanied by code shifts between Kigiriama and Arabic or Kiswahili of the sort described by Hawe Baya, thereby mapping particular languages onto particular religious ontologies.

This use of code shifting to key religious ontologies has not been much explored in the linguistic anthropological literature. Most studies of code switching have understood code choice primarily in terms of social concerns, such as relationships, the presentation of self (Blom and Gumperz 1972; Myers-Scotton 1993), and what Gumperz (1982) calls a contrast between "we" and "they" codes. In the Giriama case, such boundary work is certainly in operation, but the boundaries at stake do not merely index social groups but also demarcate metaphysically different domains, for Giriama polyontologists sometimes use different languages to immerse people in different religious ontologies: different sets of assumptions about what exists and how the cosmos is organized. Shifting between languages can breathe life into the presence and potency of various ethnoreligious forces because, arguably, languages themselves are treated as the carriers of those worlds. Code shifting, in other words, can sometimes amount to ontology shifting.

In at least some cases code shifting in ritual can key a frame in which the Giriama speaker is differently situated in relation to his or her mystical interlocutors. In the cave shrine, for example, there is a subtle difference between the respectful congeniality with which the *aganga* communicate with their ancestors in their mother tongue and their apparent defensiveness when communicating in Kiswahili with the Muslim spirits. This difference in tone is not uniformly adopted by all *aganga* when addressing powers from the different sides, yet it recurs often enough that I noticed a pattern, and I provide here a particularly rich and vivid example from a healing ritual orchestrated by a male Giriama *mganga* named Kahindi, who self-identifies as Christian.

Kahindi was hired by a young woman, Sidi, who had been employed to wash dishes and sweep the cement floor in a Swahili home until she began to sleep late and ultimately lost her job. Sidi couldn't find another job after that; she went to a female diviner who had identified her problem as the result of bewitchment by either a jealous Giriama neighbor or her former Muslim employer. The diviner referred Sidi to Kahindi for a restorative ritual. Sidi allowed me to accompany her and her family to this event, which took place in a single mud-and-wattle dwelling on one side of Kahindi's home compound.

Unsure whether Sidi had been bewitched by a Giriama or a Swahili, Kahindi opted to perform a two-part ritual to cover his bases.[23] He had already set the scene by the time we arrived, and I recognized the distinctive markers of Giriama ritual. On the dirt floor he had drawn the seven parallel lines in black and white powder of *mihambo mifungahe* that Sidi would scuff with her feet to "untie" the witchcraft. In the corner was a wooden vessel containing the mixture of herbs and water (*vuo*) used to purify and sanctify people and places. Kahindi began the ritual by telling

Sidi to stand at the edge of the *mihambo mifungahe* facing him. He began to slap his hand rhythmically on a calabash filled with magical herbs while speaking in loud, rapid Kigiriama in a high-pitched monotone.

Kahindi: *Ptu salama salmini. Haha mimi ni pala na pala riri ni ra? . . . ndiwe Sidi.*[Ptu salama salimini. Here I'm in the shrine of healing and this healing place is for? . . . It's for Sidi.]

Onlookers (largely in unison): Sidi.

Kahindi: *Pala riri ni Sidi. Sidiana thabu; Sidinyotaya kwakwe yagwa, koma ya kwake yangizwa hatuhai, nyota ya kwake yangizwa gizani, nyota ya kwake yaingizwa kisimani, nyota ya kwake yangizwa maka-burini—vivi ndo fudzire haha. Pala niri ni ra Sidi. Sidi wangizwanon-gombii, nongo mbii ya fungu, nongo mbii ya kanyegere, nongo mbii ya nyoka, nongo mbii ya lufu, nongo mbii ya mavi, nongo mbii ya nguluwe, nongo mbii ya kuro, nongo mbii zosini zirizo haha duniani— ndo kwa sababu mamboge khagakala kabisa khaga nyoka; vivi-rero phu salama salimini ambavyo nidzapanga mihaso ii haha ndani hangu na akizhoga kuthalala mihambo ii nongo mbii kumala kum-bola nazambole nidzaamba phu salama salimini nyota ya kwake kumala kuuya, naiuye. Ao maromkodolera matso hebu kumloga, utsai wa kimajini utsai wa madua, utsai wa mitishamba ya kikwehu utsai wa kimidzichenda,matsai gosini garigo haha duniani arigo gomezwa nago nidzaamba kumala kusafishika nagasafishike [etc.].* [This heal-ing place is for Sidi. Sidi has a problem; Sidi's fate (literally, "star") has fallen, her spirit (ancestor) has been cast into a bad place, her fate has been cast into the darkness, her fate has been cast into the well, her fate has been cast into the grave—now why have we come here? This healing place is for Sidi. Sidi has been struck with bad omens; a bad omen of (an obscure animal), a bad omen of the bush baby, a bad omen of the snake, a bad omen of the dead man, a bad omen of excrement, a bad omen of the pig, a bad omen of the dog, all the bad omens in the world—that's why her affairs aren't working; they don't go straight. Now today *phu salama salimini* I have arranged this medicine here in my place and if she crosses and steps on these lines/traps the bad omens will want to come out, let them come out, I have said *phu salama salimini* her fate will return, let it return. Those who have opened their eyes wide or bewitched her, (with the) witchcraft of jini, the witchcraft of Quranic prayers, the witchcraft of herbs of our origin, witchcraft of Mijikenda, all the witchery which is here in the world they are trapped with I have said I want them to be purged; let them be purged (etc.).]

Onlookers: *Naiere.* [Let it be cleansed.]

Kahindi: *Nongo mbii ya mavi nayagesa kumala kuera naiere.* [The bad omen of excrement, I clean it, it needs to be (literally, "to want to be") cleaned; let it be cleansed.]

Onlookers: *Naiere.* [Let it be cleansed.]

Kahindi: *Nongo mbii ya nyoka, nyoka akionewa ni kwalagwa kare kumala kuera naiere.* [The bad omen of the snake, if the snake is seen let it be killed instantly; it needs to be cleansed.]

After incanting in this vein for several minutes, Kahindi oversaw several performative procedures. He instructed Sidi to remove her outer layer of clothing, then picked up the wooden bucket containing the *vuo* mixture and dipped a leafy branch into the liquid, swiping Sidi's arms and legs with it three times each. Next Sidi scuffed away the powdered lines on the ground at Kahindi's command. Kahindi concluded this portion of the ritual with several more minutes of Kigiriama incantation.

Finally, instructing the onlookers to be patient, he performed a rapid change of scene, sweeping the ground and spreading out a white cloth to represent Muslim purity and a brass incense burner polished to perfection. He produced a battered-looking Quran, placing scraps of paper on the ground, some with drawings of Muslim *jini* spirits and others with photocopies of Arabic script. The paper had been torn across the grain of the text, making the words themselves illegible; this is a common use of Arabic in Giriama ritual, striking for its disregard of the semantic content of the words, thereby foregrounding the talismanic power of the linguistic medium itself. Kahindi took a deep breath as if to begin anew, launched a brief invocation in Arabic, "Bismillahi Rahman Rahimu [In the name of Allah, the most Compassionate, the most Merciful]," then settled into formal Kiswahili laced with Arabized words of praise:

Ewe Mwenyezi Mungu, subhan wataala, wewe ndiwe muumba mbingu na vyote vinavyoonekana hata nchi na jua. Tumekubali ya kwamba sisi ni watu wachafu, ni watu ambao hatufai kuelekeza sura zetu mbele zake. Subhan wataala. Lakini tukifatia vitabu vyote vine furkani . . .

iliandikwa hivi: "Yeyote mwenye kumueleze mambo yake." Mwenyezi Mungu ambaye hana ubaguzi wa kabila hana ubaguzi yakwamba wewe ni tajiri au—Mwenyezi Mungu ameumba binadamu wote sawa. Mbele ya Mwenyezi Mungu hakuna aliyepita mwenzake hata inchi moja. Hapo ndiyo tumekubali tuko chini miguuni mwako ewe Mola wetu, muumba wetu, wakati huu, jioni ya leo madua yetu, ewe Mwenyezi Mungu uyapokee na uyatimize na yote uyatimize kwa ufalme wako. Naomba kwa jina lako.

In the name of God, Oh God praise be upon him, you are the creator of heaven and all that is visible, even the land and the sun. We have admitted that we are unclean people, we're people who are not worthy to face your direction. Praise be to God. But if we follow [the teachings of] all the Quranic books . . . it is written: "Anyone can appeal [to God]." God who has no segregation of tribe, who does not segregate between people because you are rich or—God has created all human beings equally. Before God there is no one who passes another, even by an inch. That's why we accept that we are under your feet, oh our Lord, our creator, at this moment, this evening, our prayer, oh God receive and fulfill, and fulfill all for your kingdom. I pray in your name.

Kahindi began to wave the Quran in circles around Sidi's head as he continued to speak in Kiswahili:

Huyu Sidi nyota yake imeanguka nyota yake haina kazi. Nyota yake imetiwa ndani ya maji, nyota yake imeingizwa kwenye mapango . . . nyota yake imepeperushwa ikafungwa juu ya miti inaning'inia haina kazi. Leo hii basi tunamzungua na kitabu hiki ambacho kina madua. Madua haya nikiamini ya kwamba kitabu hiki madua haya yameshinda kafara la ng'ombe, kafara la mbuzi, yameshinda kafara la kondoo, yameshinda kafara la aina yoyote hapa duniani kwa sababu hii ni kauli ya Mwenyezi Mungu. Kwa sababu hii ni nguvu ya Mwenyezi Mungu. Hii madua sio kwamba mimi ndiye mwenye kuandika. La. Mimi nikama naomba kwa Mwenyezi Muungu subhan Allah wataala. [Naomba] Mwenyezi Mungu amrudishie power *zake zile ambazo Mwenyezi Mungu alizomuandikia wakati alipokuwa anamuumba katika tumbo la mamake. Nikiamini ya kwamba duniani hakuna chochote ambacho kinamshinda* Mwenyezi

Mungu na nikiamini ya kwamba nikilia chini ya miguu ya Mwenyezi
Mungu, kumsaidia huyu Sidi na amini yakwamba madua yangu kauli
yangu Mwenyezi Mungu atakubali.

This one, Sidi, her fate has fallen down; it has no work. Her fate has
been drawn into the water, her fate has been put into the caves . . . her
fate has been blown into the tree tops where it dangles without work.
Today we are curing her [encircling her] through this book, it has
these prayers. These prayers: if I believe that this book, these prayers,
surpass the sacrifice of a cow, the sacrifice of a goat, they surpass the
sacrifice of a sheep, they surpass any kind of sacrifice at all in the world
because this is the word of God. Because this is God's power. These
prayers—I am not the one who wrote them. No. I am praying to
almighty God, praise be upon him. [I pray to] God to return her
power, those that God wrote for her at the time that he created her
in her mother's womb. If I believe there is nothing at all on earth that
is beyond God's ability and if I believe that if I cry at the feet of
God to assist Sidi and believe that God will agree to my prayers,
my words.

The verbal portion of the ritual concluded with further praise and supplication to God. Sidi stepped over the scraps of Arabic on the ground
and prayed to the Quran before she was considered purged of witchcraft.

The semantic and material semiotic shifts from one portion of Kahindi's ritual to the next suggest not syncretism in the standard sense of a
hybridization of religions, but polyontologism: two separate appeals to
two altogether different sources of supernatural power. The first of these
is rooted in Kahindi's "healing place": in the ancestors and Mulungu, in
the powers of *mihambo mifungahe* to trap witchcraft, in the purifying
power of *vuo* herbalism, and in the onlookers' collaborative efforts to ver-
bally expel the "bad omens" so often adduced by Giriama *aganga*. All of
these devices would be considered unmistakably Giriama to any Giriama
onlooker. The other source of power resides in an intimidating and
literate creator-God, author of the Quran and scribe of all human fate,
who demands that his followers treat him as the sole potentate. Kahindi
never overtly identifies this portion of the ritual as Islamic, but he does
not have to; the cues are clear to all.

The partitioning across two religious ontologies in Kahindi's ritual is mapped onto a juxtaposition of languages that encourages an interpretation of each language as aligned with different supernatural powers. The Giriama powers are adduced in the Giriama language, while in the Islamic half of the ritual Arabic is placed in a position of primacy, used to open his invocation, and set on the ground in a talismanic fashion as the embodiment of Islamic powers. As for Kiswahili, Giriama in Malindi use it on a daily basis for practical communication between ethnic groups, but here, as in many Giriama rituals, it is the language of Islam. The bivalent terms that recur in each language, furthermore (such as *nyoka* [snake], *nyota* [star], *kazi* [work], and *duniani* [on earth]), do not appear to encourage consciousness of the many shared lexical and syntactic elements of these languages, nor does the borrowed English word *power* attract evident attention, for those present at the ritual clearly stated their impression that half of the ritual was "done in Kigiriama" and the other "in Kiswahili."

When Kahindi juxtaposes Kigiriama and Kiswahili and Arabic in the two halves of his ritual, he draws upon and further reifies the idea that each language is naturally linked to its associated religion. But in rituals like Kahindi's, languages are not only treated as naturally linked to religions; they are also used to immerse ritual participants in utterly different and potentially incompatible religious ontologies, while situating Kahindi differently in relation to each. In the Giriama portion of the ritual, mystical powers seem to be dispersed across the ancestors and Mulungu, the *mihambo mifungahe*, the *vuo*, the incantations of the onlookers, and Kahindi himself, with his repeated use of the agentic *I* ("I have arranged this medicine here in my place and if she crosses and steps on these lines/traps the bad omens will want to come out. . . . I have said . . . her fate will return"). Yet in the Islamic portion, Kahindi portrays himself as crying at the feet of an omnipotent God, wretched and practically devoid of agency, for only God can decree what will happen: "These prayers—I am not the one who wrote them. No. . . . [I pray to] God to return her powers, those that God wrote for her at the time that he created her in her mother's womb." Indeed, Kahindi strives to avoid *ushirikina* when speaking Kiswahili ("This book, these prayers, surpass the sacrifice of a cow, the sacrifice of a goat, they surpass the sacrifice of a sheep, they surpass any kind of sacrifice at all in the world because this is the word of God"), without acknowledging the extent to which he has plunged into it while speaking Kigiriama by exercising his own agency to expunge Sidi's bad omens.

This apparent contradiction stems from a linguistically invoked poly-ontologism, in which different languages invoke a different state of affairs or a different set of forces in the external world and a different relationship between Kahindi and his supernatural interlocutors, without attention to the possible contradictions between these. Furthermore, Kahindi's own power and projected confidence shift from one portion of the ritual to the next in a way that reaffirms ethnoreligious hegemony. In Kigiriama Kahindi himself embodies direct performative power as the ritual specialist who knows how to sacralize and arrange the potent medicines of the Giriama side and who can command that the forces of witchery be purged. But when Kahindi speaks Kiswahili he is invoking a frame in which he is subject to more daunting forces. Kahindi has to remind the Muslim God not to discriminate on grounds of ethnicity or class; this in combination with his obsequious pleas ("We are under your feet"; "I cry at the feet of God") suggests his anxiety that he may not receive the favor of this distant and potentially judgmental God. To be sure, Islam demands supplication of all its followers, but when supplication so vividly evokes ethnic hierarchy while being juxtaposed against mastery of Traditionalist powers, it seems to reinforce the alien quality of the Islamic godhead. The fact that this half of the ritual is carried out in Kiswahili suggests another layer of disadvantage: this God may "[have] no segregation of tribe," but apparently he is more inclined to listen to Kiswahili than to Kigiriama.

Giriama attitudes toward Islam might sometimes be described as a kind of appropriating-while-distancing; the forces of Islam are sought out and invoked, even as they are held at arm's length, while various signals, from code choice itself to semantic indicators, suggest a distance between the supplicant and the powers in question. Hence while Giriama appropriations of Islam constitute an effort at gaining ground and partaking of some of the advantages of their Swahili and Arab neighbors, the ways *aganga* sometimes frame Islam can reinscribe a hegemonic model of ethnoreligious essentialism. Islam is linguistically marked as distant in some of these rituals, mirroring the narratives suggesting that Giriama cannot get their hands on money-gathering *jini* or even (to paraphrase Hawe Baya) be fully "with" the Quran. Appropriation of Islam is thus sometimes accompanied by subtle indicators of the very difficulty or strain of such appropriation.

The Ideology of Mono-ontologism:
Anxiety on the Margins of Swahili Islam

How do Swahili in Malindi apprehend polyontologist practices of the sort I have just described? The answer is complex, in part because Swahili ritual practice and spiritual life has historically overlapped considerably with Mijikenda. In fact, one of the best-known chroniclers of Swahili culture, John Middleton (1992: 163), sees the interpenetration of Islam and local spirit beliefs in Swahili religious life as harmonious and syncretistic: "Most Swahili accept both beliefs of the Koran and those in spiritual forces that appear to be peculiar to the East African coast, [seeing the latter as] complementary to and part of 'official' Islam, not in opposition to it." Certainly religious blending has been part of Swahili life in some areas, though Swahili everywhere are ideologically inclined toward mono-ontologism (notice that even in Middleton's formulation these syncretistic ideas are gathered under the singular umbrella of Islam) rather than toward the polyontologist, fragmented appeals to markedly discrete religious traditions seen among Malindi's Giriama. However, Swahili lifeways are diverse and shifting, and not all scholars of Swahili culture would likely agree with Middleton's generalization about harmonious religious and ritual incorporation (cf. Kresse 2003; Parkin 1985b; Pouwels 1987: 132). While many Swahili would acknowledge that spirit belief, divination, and ritual healing are part of Swahili custom (*mila*), in some areas there is great uneasiness about whether and when they are acceptable (*halali*) or forbidden (*haramu*), even pagan, in the eyes of Islam (cf. Parkin 1985b: 235). In fact, in contemporary Malindi the dominant Swahili ideology is currently shifting toward Islamic purity and away from cultural overlap with Giriama religiosity, in an anti-syncretistic direction, in other words. And it is precisely where Swahili practices resemble Giriama practices that Swahili concerned about their religious status feel the most in need of refining their piety and asserting the universality of Islam.

The mono-ontologist notion that one religious ontology is exclusive of all others and the antisyncretistic position that Islam's forms should be pure may be taken for granted by many Muslims the world over, but Asad (1993: 37, 43) has warned that religion's "general (cosmic) ideas of order" and its related "[affirmations] about the fundamental nature of reality" may not be inherent in religiosity. Instead, he suggests that we look to a given religion's "authorizing discourses" to uncover how it shores up its universalizing claims. As noted in chapter 3, a prominent authorizing discourse in Swahili Islam involves the notion of *ushirikina* (Kisw.), a term that derives from the Arabic *shirk* and refers to unacceptable polytheistic or other beliefs or practices that detract from the total authority and coherence of Allah. *Ushirikina* is often leveled by Swahili in Malindi as an accusation that someone has failed to approach Allah directly, focusing instead on diviners, healers, spirits, talismans, and so forth, and as a means of stigmatizing the "mixing of faiths." For the sake of clarity, it is worth stressing that social injunctions against *ushirikina* emerge from a mono-ontologist ideology, but are more precise than this; hence practices deemed *ushirikina* are only sometimes polyontological. When *ushirikina* involves going to Christian or Giriama Traditionalist sources for supernatural assistance, for instance, it has an obvious polyontologist flavor because such religious pluralism draws upon mystical sources from utterly different traditions. However, the set of practices deemed *ushirikina* by some Swahili religious leaders also includes interactions with and attitudes toward forces that have precedents (both emically and etically) within Islamic traditions and contexts, such as the *jini* spirits mentioned in the Quran, spirit possession itself, and Arabic divinatory texts such as Falak. Spirit possession and Arabic-style divination are thus not clear instances of polyontologism, but they tend to be considered *ushirikina* because they are potential distractions from the supremacy of God.

At the same time, as noted in the preceding chapters, Swahili traditions of spirit belief and ritual have a family resemblance to Giriama traditions, and this resemblance to the cultural practices of their subordinate, indigenous African neighbors apparently unnerves quite a few Swahili religious authorities. Like Mijikenda, Swahili go to diviners and healers, and spirit beliefs among Swahili and Giriama along the coast have historically mirrored each other (Giles 1989b, 1999; Parkin 1991a: 203). Spirits are common topics of discussion in both groups, under many appellations, including *pepo, jini, sheitani,* and *rohani.* Among both

Mijikenda and Swahili many of these spirits are associated with liminal or dangerous areas, such as the sea, empty coral rock caves in isolated areas, large baobab trees, and the streets of town after dark, and many can possess unwitting human victims or be called upon deliberately, as in Giriama divination and in the Swahili possession cult practices described by Giles (see chapter 3).[24] In Malindi such Swahili cults may no longer be operational, but possession of unwitting individuals and a few willing ritual practitioners certainly is.

Among pious Swahili in Malindi the primary danger posed by spirits is that of distracting individuals from God himself and risking *ushirikina* in the process. All Swahili are aware of this risk, though some fear it more than others. The Ahlul Sunna movement in particular has encouraged rationalist forms of worship that eschew interaction with spirits (Kresse 2003). As Beckerleg (1994a: 299) notes, within the Ahlul Sunna movement in Watamu, about twelve miles south of Malindi, "the possibility of invasion of a person by . . . a spirit is rejected, and the self is reconstituted as a bounded individual who is inviolable." Another reason so many men (in Malindi and elsewhere) reject spirit beliefs and possession is that antagonism to *ushirikina* is bound up with both strict Islamic education and ideal masculinity (cf. P. Caplan 1982, 1989: 203). Some of my male informants scrupulously reminded me that although the Quran acknowledges the ontological reality of spirits with allusions to *jini* and *sheitani*, it also asserts that spirits, like humans, are subordinate to God: "And I created not the Jinns and mankind except they should worship Me [alone]" (Sura 51:56). Human attention, the argument goes, should be focused vertically, on God, rather than laterally, on the spirit world. For other men, demonstrative claims that they don't believe in spirits at all seem a means of performatively protecting themselves from vulnerability to possession (McIntosh 1996) while distancing themselves from the emotional volatility and impressionability associated with women (cf. Swartz 1982).[25] Men who do acknowledge the existence of spirits sometimes assert that even to expend mental and physical energy contemplating, fearing, or propitiating them is dangerous: "One's thoughts should be on God," as one informant put it, describing a single-mindedness that he felt would protect him from both accusations of *ushirikina* and spirit possession itself. Such denials of not only behavioral but also cognitive and emotional involvement with spirits resonate with the Swahili emphasis on *nia;* not only should one's acts be pious, but the direction of one's thoughts and intentions should be appropriately directed at the one and only God.

Spirits are not the only contested phenomena in Swahili Islam; divination and healing rituals are equally vexed by intimations of *ushirikina* and polyontologism. Ritual techniques range widely across Swahili communities, inflected by many cultural and historical factors.[26] Swahili diviners and healers are sometimes referred to as *waganga,* particularly those who use nonliterate techniques (spirit possession, cowrie shell tossing, herbalism, talismans containing mystical ingredients from the sea, and so on) in their rituals. But in Malindi there are relatively few nonliterate Swahili diviners and healers, and most of these are women. Far more common, and more respectfully named, are the *walimu wa kitabu,* literally "teachers of the book"; these are diviners and healers, most of them literate men, who rely upon Arabic texts such as the Quran and the Arabic geomancy text called Falak. Their uses of the Quran are disputed by some clerics, but it is widely agreed that using the Quran for divination or healing, even by dissolving Quranic prayers in rosewater and drinking them as a kind of elixir (called *kombe*), is less susceptible to accusations of *ushirikina* than certain other practices, such as possession. Yet many *walimu wa kitabu* use more than just the Quran in their practices, as can be seen in the treatment received by my Swahili friend Fatma when she experienced a false pregnancy by a spirit. As her belly grew, she said, "I started to feel heavy all the time, as if someone was sitting on me, and I began to have bad dreams about a *sheitani* coming and playing around with me at night. . . . The [medical] doctors told me nothing was wrong. Finally I went to a *mwalimu wa kitabu* who wrote something in Arabic while he diagnosed me. He gave me some herbs to take daily at six p.m. Soon all my suffering began to subside."

The use of herbalism and the preparation of protective talismans (*hirizi* or *talasimu*) are often suspect; talismans, for instance, may contain occult ingredients, such as dirt from a gravesite, that can be considered *haramu.*[27] The use of non-Quranic Arabic texts such as Falak falls into a gray area, but the Ahlul Sunna movement has objected to its use in divination, in part because some of the most prominent practitioners have been the Lamu Sharifs whose mystification has, they feel, detracted from a proper focus on a single godhead (Beckerleg 1994a: 301). One pious young man, Fadili Ali, expressed his general aversion to divination and healing practices: "It's not okay to do *uganga*. If you do it, it's like saying there is more than one God. Or it's like putting the *mganga* side by side with God when they appeal to their roots and their spirits. But God is only one. He was not born, nor did he procreate [Hakuzaa, hakuzaliwa]."

There is enough ambivalence about divination and healing practices among Malindi's Swahili population that laypeople who frequent *waganga* or *walimu wa kitabu* sometimes find themselves wringing their hands over their legitimacy, while wondering what alternative they have to combat the dangerous occult forces that inflict evil on their lives. As Fatma said, "True Muslims aren't supposed to use talismans around their babies to protect them from jealousy and evil spirits; instead they should simply recite Quranic prayers. But sometimes you have no alternative but to deal with the spirits head on. Those who are very well educated will tell you they don't believe in spirits. But I have seen them for myself." Added one Swahili *mwalimu wa kitabu* with an apologetic shrug, "We know these practices are *haramu*, but what can we do? The patient is in distress, and this is the only way they can find relief."

Diviners and healers risk dabbling in *ushirikina*, but laypeople very occasionally engage in the most stigmatized and polyontologist practice of all: engaging the service of a Giriama *mganga*. Typically Swahili do this only when they are too ashamed of their problem to seek assistance within their community or when Swahili remedies have failed and they are simply desperate for help. Giriama *aganga* who have Swahili clients, such as Malindi's Kaviha, take great pride in the fact that Swahili seek them out. Kaviha practices in an outdoor shrine in the no man's land between Muyeye and Malindi's town center. Hidden by a tangle of creepers, the shrine is within walking distance of the Swahili-dominated divisions of Shella and Barani but far enough away from the dirt paths of central Muyeye that Swahili clients can come and go without mingling much with Giriama. On one occasion when I went to visit him at his workplace, two young Swahili women in elegant black *bui buis* sat on a makeshift bench made of a smooth log stripped of its bark. Amina, whose coffee-colored skin prompted Kaviha to refer to her as an Arab after she left, had recently separated from her husband, who suffered from a problem increasingly common among Swahili: addiction to heroin, or "brown sugar" (Beckerleg 1995). Fed up with his abusive and irresponsible behavior, Amina reported him to the authorities, who incarcerated him. Now she feared that her husband had fallen out of love with her, and she was anxious to regain his affection. She had visited Kaviha numerous times, each time receiving a new prescription of magical ash to sprinkle under her husband's bed or a talisman to sew into his shirt hem. Amina had come that day to report that her husband was feeling better disposed to her and was at last providing her with funds from his bank account so that she could start work on a house they would live in together. During their consultation the women seemed unsettled by my presence, stealing glances in my direction, and when they concluded they hastened out of the shrine without introducing themselves, drawing their veils across their lower faces. Kaviha speculated that they had come to him instead of a Swahili *mwalimu wa kitabu* because the case had already brought such shame upon Amina that the use of a love potion to regain the affection of a known drug user might bring further disrepute upon her. "And," he said in a satisfied tone, "she knows my powers will work."

Perhaps so, but the fact remains that in mainstream Swahili society giving credence to non-Muslim, Giriama mystical potency is anathema. Some of the occult practices I have discussed, such as spirit possession and the use of Falak, are accused of being *ushirikina*, but, as I have indicated, such practices are not clearly polyontologist because Swahili do not obviously see them as emergent from a distinctly different ontology or religious tradition. After all, Falak comes from Arabia, and spirits are mentioned in the Quran. But going to a Giriama diviner healer, particularly if he or she appeals to the god Mulungu, Giriama ancestors, and Giriama spirits (perhaps even while using Kigiriama), suggests that there may be supernatural validity to an Other tradition of modeling the cosmos—a wholly different, yet also powerful supernatural ontology, in other words, and one linked to a stigmatized ethnic group.

Elite Swahili reactions to polyontologist practice can be summed up by the words of the Swahili intellectual I mentioned in chapter 3. Abdul attended my talk on Giriama *aganga* who alternate between appeals to Giriama powers and appeals to Islam, and expressed his dismay afterward. "To me," he said gravely, "it sounds as though these *waganga* are doing trickery—playing psychological games with their clients. Because to me, I would say this chap has no faith. You can't move between one religion and another. In my culture, we would call what he is doing *ushirikina.*" Several white Kenyans in attendance nodded. "I'm inclined to agree with Abdul," remarked one woman of British descent. "It sounds like they can't possibly believe in what they're doing. How can one person believe in both Islam and Traditionalism? It doesn't make sense." I was struck by the fact that audience members coming from such different cultural backgrounds nonetheless shared a basic, Abrahamic presumption that religion is only proper or logical if it engages with a single, universal religious ontology.

In their private ritual lives some Swahili risk disobeying officially sanctioned Islamic practice, compromising not only their piety but their very grounds for allegiance with the pan-Islamic brotherhood that is currently such an important source of economic and symbolic capital for them. Despite the debates and uncertainties about Islam within Swahili communities, it is clear to many Swahili in Malindi that differentiation from all things Mijikenda is one of the more obvious ways of upholding what they consider the integrity of their religious identity. Meanwhile, even as Swahili orient themselves away from Giriama and toward an Islamic ecumene, Giriama find themselves appropriating from an Islamic locus of power that they frame as not quite their own. Their respective orientations thereby underscore the hegemonic ethnoreligious distance that currently separates these groups in Malindi.

Chapter 5 | **DIVINATION AND MADNESS**
The Powers and Dangers of Arabic

Idealized and vilified, Islam is regarded as both a source
of ritual potency and a cause of suffering among Gi-
riama in Malindi. This is in some respects a familiar pattern; in many sub-
Saharan African societies those who wield occult powers are viewed with
both awe and suspicion should they choose to use their abilities for ill,
and the same duality holds for *uganga* "from the Giriama side." But
in Malindi the extremes of hope and fear that attach to Islam seem
to outstrip the sentiments typically directed at Giriama ritual powers.
Surely, then, the ambiguities surrounding Islam are connected to the
ambivalent relationships between Giriama and their more powerful Muslim neighbors, including the stark socioeconomic hierarchy between the
two groups and Giriama's simultaneous longing for and resentment of the
status of Swahili living in the core of town.

A second expression of this ambivalence can be found in Giriama
interactions with Arabic and its associated texts, both of which Giriama
consider to be linguistic embodiments of Islam. In fact, the mysteries of
Arabic and Arabic texts are tapped by both Giriama and Swahili in their
divinatory and healing rites in ways that suggest language serves not just
as a communicative medium or as a means of projecting associations
between ethnicities and religions (as seen in chapter 4), but also as a
congealed locus of occult power. The hegemonic assumption that Arabic
is a source of exceptional mystical potency is common not only among
Swahili but also among Giriama, including non-Muslims. For members
of both ethnic groups Arabic is so tightly associated with Islam and
Muslim peoples that the language itself could be likened to the Bakh-
tinian word that "tastes of the context and contexts in which it has lived

its socially charged life" (Bakhtin 1981: 293). For many Swahili in the core of Malindi Arabic is associated with familiar contexts, including the social milieu of Arabs in town, the mosque, and the madarasa. For most Giriama living on the margins of town, however, such contexts are at a remove, and Arabic is treated as an Other locus of enunciation that offers the vague promise of apprehending and understanding the world in an extraordinary way. In a familiar dilemma, Giriama respond to this situation by ritually appropriating Islamic forces, at the same time that they reinforce the hegemonic notion that Swahili are the proprietors of Islamic power and knowledge. Swahili too sometimes reify this hegemony by rejecting Giriama ritual efforts as inadequate and primitive forms of mimicry that are less powerful, and certainly less pious, than textually based forms of Swahili divination.

As in the preceding chapters, we see that different models of person-hood among Swahili and Giriama play an important role in this hegemony by inflecting the structure of their most popular divination rituals in Malindi and indirectly feeding back into preexisting social hierarchies. The most widely accepted Swahili divination rituals in Malindi emphasize internal, individualized forms of competence such as literacy and mentation, whereas most Giriama diviners in Malindi draw on the expertise of literate possessing spirits who "read" and "write" the Arabic that their hosts do not understand. These different relationships to Arabic can thus be located along a spectrum of linguistic agency that extends from the vaunted, privately wielded mastery of Swahili *walimu wa kitabu* (diviners and healers; literally, "teachers of/by the book"), to the sharing of agency between Giriama *aganga a mburuga* (spirit-medium diviners) and the Muslim possessing spirits who speak through them. This spectrum of agency emerges from the differentially valorized models of personhood in these social groups. Ultimately, these differences play into the hegemonic dynamics I have described, for just as Swahili tend to be cynical about Giriama's spirit-forced conversions and their polyontologist rituals, so too do Swahili critics scorn Giriama divination as lacking independence and the proper intentional attitude of piety.

Although most Giriama do not share the Swahili preoccupation with intentional states and self-control, there is a limit to the amount of agency Giriama are willing to relinquish. This limit is exceeded in a particular kind of madness in which the Giriama self is unwittingly displaced by an Arabic-speaking spirit who colonizes his or her speech and actions in a grotesque and chronic simulation of Islam. I suggest that possession by these Arabic-speaking spirits may represent the erasure of Giriama personhood, the reductio ad absurdum, perhaps, of the many occult ways in which Giriama partake of Muslim powers while risking being *over*taken by them. This form of madness, furthermore, provides an acute reminder that although Giriama folk models of personhood accommodate the sharing of agency partially or temporarily with possessing spirits (particularly those who can help them in some fashion), Giriama draw the line at situations that extinguish their ability to act, whether that situation be slavery at the hands of Arabs or madness at the hands of Arabic-speaking spirits.

Arabic Mystified

A common ideology in the West treats language as a primarily referential instrument, whose role is merely to stand for things in the world. This denotational view of language is sometimes contrasted with more performative views in which linguistic signs, far from being mere signifiers, are able to effect changes upon the world in their very uttering (Austin 1962; Kang 2006). Speech acts can bring states of affairs into being by, for instance, securing a new institutional status for a bride and groom, a baptized child, or a president. Performativity in language also extends to more mystical acts, such as the recitation of magical spells or healing prayers (Keane 1997b; Tambiah 1968). As linguistic anthropologists have noted, languages and utterances can play still more expansive roles, including as objects for exchange in the marketplace (Irvine 1989) and as indices of the social order (Silverstein 2003). In the preceding chapter we saw that languages sometimes come to stand in for entire ethnic groups and to invoke the religious forces with which they are associated. Language thus has a multifunctional, socially charged life, in which the medium and its associated forces may be just as important as the message.

In this chapter my discussions of Arabic point to what might be called a *magical essentialist* function of language, for not only can speech acts be construed as magically efficacious, but entire languages themselves can also be construed as having intrinsic, underlying potencies (McIntosh 2005a, 2005b). A degree of magical essentialism seems to underlie the ritual code-shifting practices I detail in chapter 4 in which languages are selected according to the supernatural powers they invoke, but such essentialism announces itself more obviously in both Swahili and Giriama treatments of Arabic, which presume that Arabic has mystical properties that set it off from other languages. While these practices involve what Tambiah (1968) has called "the magical power of words," they also extend beyond it. Indeed, the use of Quranic verses for talismanic and healing effects is widespread across the Muslim world, but in many such contexts the medium is just as important as the semantic content of the words in question. This pattern can be found among Swahili ritual practitioners, but among Giriama the fixation on the medium is particularly obvious since so few members of their own community have achieved sufficient Arabic literacy to understand the semantics of the text (cf. Lambek 1993). Coherent locutionary statements sometimes take a backseat to individual letters, to spiritually generated simulacra of Arabic, to elixirs prepared from impressionistic visual renderings of the language, and to torn fragments of printed text whose semantic meaning cannot be discerned. The imagined essence of Arabic also confers a special part-whole relationship upon the language, such that mere linguistic fragments may contain the congealed potencies associated with the entire language. In some of its ritual uses on the Kenya coast the Arabic language isn't treated much like a language at all—not, anyway, in the Western folk sense of a semantically based medium of communication. Instead, it is treated more like an object that contains the essence of Islam's occult potency. While this mystification is enacted differently by each group, it is generally shared by Swahili and Giriama alike, with important consequences for hegemony.

The uses of Arabic in Swahili and Giriama divination in the Malindi area can be understood only with reference to the more general ideologies of Arabic that circulate through their communities and, to some degree, throughout the Muslim world. Muslims believe that Allah dictated the Quran to Mohammed in classical Arabic; since it is still read in the original, it is thought to bind the faithful to Allah as they speak his words (cf. Haeri 2003). So important is the medium of the original language that some Muslim scholars refer to attempted translations of the text as mere "interpretations." Translations of the Quran into Kiswahili (or any other language) must be flanked by the Arabic original, thus binding together text and language. But Arabic's importance extends beyond the Quran; it is regarded by most Swahili not only as the language of Allah and all the souls in heaven, but also as a connection to wealthy and sacred Arabian lands and as the pan-national language of the wider Muslim community to which Swahili aspire to belong. It is also the language of Arabs, and in the centuries leading up to European colonialism Kiswahili was written in Arabic script as if to valorize the Arab ancestry (sometimes actual, sometimes fictive) of its primary coastal speakers. Historically Arabic has had such cachet among Swahili that in his analysis of the development of Swahili civilization Khalid (1977: 55) writes, "Arabic filled for [ancient Swahili] the same function which Latin served in medieval Europe and this is, to a lesser extent, still its place today." Like Latin, Arabic serves a double function: as a sacred language that embodies the powers of a religion and a language of hierarchy and exclusion known only to citizens with specialized education. The first of these functions has by no means been historically universal to the Arab world,[1] but since the rise of Wahhabism in the 1970s many Arabs have embraced the revivified sanctity of Arabic as God's chosen language (21).

The association between Arabic and piety reverberates in the conversational habits of many of Malindi's Swahili. Romanized Zanzibari Kiswahili has been considered standard since the British colonial era, yet the Kiswahili spoken on the coast has many local variants,[2] and many Swahili who wish to sound more pious infuse their language with interjections, modifiers, greetings, phonological properties, and stress patterns of Arabic origin (Russell 1981). These include terms and phrases such as *alhamdulillahi* (praise be to Allah), *ala* (an interjection of surprise), *asalaam aleikum* (peace be with you), and *waaleikum salaam* (and with you peace), as well as an emphasis on sounds such as the rough fricative in *sheikh*. "Why do some Swahili mix Arabic into their speech?" I asked one Swahili friend. "To identify oneself [as a Muslim] [Kujitambulisha]," he replied. The association between Arabic and piety is surely strengthened by the fact that the language is often heard in overtly religious contexts: in the calls to prayer emanating from mosque loudspeakers, the chanted prayers floating out of the windows of madarasas, and the fragments of prayer woven into conversation by pious Swahili.

Swahili circulate numerous narratives about the mystical potencies and startling qualities of Arabic. At one time or another I was informed that Arabic is perfect in every way because it is the language of Allah, Mohammed, and the Quran; that it is the oldest living language, influencing all other extant languages; that it is so condensed it can express in a handful of words what might require hundreds in another language; that it has exceptional signaling power, reaching Allah "like a smoke signal," where another, more earthly language would fall short; that as a medium of prayer it invites the most favorable response from Allah; that it "feels good to pray in"; that it has the vastest vocabulary of any language; that it is so semantically rich a single term may have hundreds of meanings; that it is uniquely inscrutable and impenetrable to those who have not studied it for their entire lives; that it cannot be translated; and that it confers "weight" (*uzito*) on anything expressed in it.[3] Fluency in classical or colloquial Arabic, furthermore, is such a great source of cultural capital among Swahili that one Swahili intellectual, Sheriff Nassir, bemoaned in his Ramadan lectures of 1998 that those who study Arabic in Arabia and return to East Africa are sometimes considered authorities in Islam on the basis of their language abilities alone.[4]

Pride in knowledge of Arabic is evident in the minutiae of daily life among Swahili in Malindi. As is the case in other Muslim African societies (see, for instance, Lambek 1993), social hierarchy is at least partly established on the basis of Islamic expertise, which in turn relies heavily on textual expertise. But in Malindi's urban core basic textual knowledge of Arabic is not restricted to an elite few. Small madarasas for Quranic training can be found all over town and in some courtyards of private Swahili homes. Today girls have more opportunities than ever before to study in (single-sex) madarasa classes, while adult women sometimes speak longingly about the opportunity they missed, for most women older than thirty did not study Arabic.[5] Nowadays boys and girls alike eagerly show off their knowledge of the language. I lost count of the number of times children in a Swahili household brought me unbidden their notebooks filled with lines of Arabic or recited the prayers they had just learned. One little Swahili girl surprised me while we were on a walk by stopping at a cactus at the roadside, breaking off a spine, and proudly carving my name in Arabic letters onto one of its stiff leaves.[6] The headmaster of the ethnically and religiously mixed Malindi Secondary School reported that his Muslim pupils of both sexes perform with exceptional motivation in their Arabic classes even when their work in secular subjects is poor. And in recent decades more and more instructors in madarasas and more advanced religious schools have taken to emphasizing comprehension and content rather than rote memorization as they instruct their pupils in Quranic Arabic. This emphasis on the intellectual agency of Quranic students contrasts with pedagogic practices in some other areas of the East African coast, where students are taught to read the Quran with little understanding of its semantics and syntax (Chris Walley, personal communication, 20 May 2006; see also Lambek 1993: 141).[7]

Despite the growing emphasis in religious schools on Arabic comprehension, most students do not emerge fluent from their studies. The asymmetrical distribution of knowledge of Arabic has underpinned a decades-old debate in Malindi's Swahili community about the relationship between Arabic and sermonizing in the mosque. All Islamic authorities agree that the five daily prayers should be performed in Arabic, but some have also contended that it is *sunna* (in accordance with the practices and desires of the Prophet and his followers) to conduct the weekly Friday sermon in Arabic as well. Only a few establishments, such as the Jamii mosque, actually follow suit; others strike a compromise. In the Malindi mosque, for example, the imam first relates a translation of the sermon in Kiswahili, then climbs to the elevated *mimbar* to redeliver the sermon from a loftier vantage point in Arabic. Yet even detractors of the use of Arabic for sermonizing do not relinquish their admiration for the language. One elderly Swahili man informed me that those who insist on the use of Arabic for sermons are obstinate or bigoted (*washupavu*), that translations into Kiswahili are important for "those who have not yet had the good fortune to learn Arabic," but he added that Arabic is "the greatest language of them all [*bora kushinda lugha zote*]."

Since Swahili and Giriama live in a partially shared cultural field, the status of Arabic is not lost on Giriama. The language is so steeped in religiosity that some Swahili and Giriama alike refer to it as Kiallah, "the language of Allah." But Giriama do not see Kiallah as readily accessible to them. While some Giriama converts to Islam attend madarasa, many, such as those pressured to convert by a possessing spirit, do not have a Muslim sponsor to enroll them and feel too socially marginal and economically disadvantaged to pursue this education themselves. Several Giriama I know resisted pressures to convert to Islam on the very grounds that one *must* learn Arabic in order to do so, considering that demand beyond their reach. Said one Giriama Christian, "Islam is for those Swahili people. The Quran itself says: 'For I have sent you the Prophet who can speak your language.' Isn't that speaking to Arabs only? Jesus, on the other hand, is here for all of us." We see in this objection not only the common conflation of Swahili and Arab people in Giriama discourse, but also the notion that Swahili and Arabs, Islam, and Arabic are bound together in an ethnic, religious, and linguistic triumvirate that feels forbiddingly closed off to some Giriama.

This cynicism does not prevent Arabic from being mystified. Much of the time this mystification is so widespread it goes without saying, but I was struck when a particularly insightful Giriama friend brought this hegemony to the surface in our discussion of divinatory Arabic, saying outright, "We think their language contains their power." Some Giriama mobilize strategic counteressentialisms to uphold the forces of Kigiriama, arguing, "Our *aganga* find powers in Kigiriama they can't find in Kiswahili or English," and "If you curse God or your mother in Kigiriama it carries force" that it wouldn't in another language. Yet Arabic (or some version of it) appears again and again in Giriama divination and healing rituals, suggesting how powerfully it has captured the Giriama imagination. Its status is due no doubt to its ethnoreligious associations, but it may also be compounded by the code's sheer alterity in the eyes of most Giriama. As Helms (1993) has noted, numerous cultures impute occult qualities to foreign objects, and while language pronounced in an unfamiliar phonology and written in an unfamiliar script may not always be as object-like as some cultural artifacts, it is in a sense the ideal subject of mystification, for it hides its meaning beneath an exterior that seems wholly impenetrable to the outsider. To nearly all Giriama the obscurity of Arabic is daunting and the Otherness of its orthography vivid to any who have been schooled (to whatever grade level) only in the Roman letters of English and Kiswahili. Perhaps, then, in Giriama divination the ability to tap into such a thoroughly mystified language is treated as a synecdoche for the more general talent of discerning the unknown as a whole.

In summary, both Swahili and Giriama communities adopt a magical essentialist stance toward Arabic, imputing it with intense properties and potencies. In both groups Arabic is treated as a kind of seam that opens out from the ordinary world into a supernatural domain within which resides a wealth of special knowledge and power. In ritual the language is treated as though it contains hidden information, answers to questions, the ability to ward off danger, and healing forces. Such notions of Arabic are widespread among Muslims in Africa and elsewhere (Bloch 1968; Bravmann 1983; Lambek 1993; Whyte 1991), but in Malindi Arabic has special implications for the socioeconomic hierarchy that currently divides Swahili and Giriama, for this jointly held essentialism reproduces the hegemonic association between Islam and power, at the same time that Giriama tend to presume that such power attaches more to Swahili and Arabs than to themselves.

Textual Hegemony

As in many Muslim societies, Islam is vitally linked to literacy on the Kenya coast. When Swahili in Malindi study the Quran in madarasa, the ability to reproduce Quranic prayers with one's own pen (or chalk, as the case may be for many young students) is nearly as important as the ability to recite them. The divinatory and healing specialists in Malindi's Swahili community also rely on texts such as the Quran and the Arabic geomancy text known as Falak. In fact, Swahili in Malindi distinguish between their two types of diviner healers along lines of literacy; *waganga*, who are usually female, tend to use spirits as their primary aids, whereas *walimu wa kitabu* draw heavily on the Quran and other Arabic texts and are usually literate men (as I have noted, the growing number of girls enrolled in madarasa is a relatively recent development). In Malindi female *waganga* are a small minority, while *walimu wa kitabu*, whose work is more likely to be considered acceptable (*halali*) within the parameters of Islam, dominate in numbers and in status.

Perhaps the most popular text in Swahili divination is Falak. This Arabic book is devoted primarily to forms of astrology and numerology that allow the user to calculate propitious and unpropitious dates and times for activities such as travel, but it can also be used for more morally suspect forms of divination and spell casting. According to Pouwels (1987), Falak has its origins in *'ilm al-Falak*, astronomy and astrology practices that were brought to Africa by Omanis and other Arab groups. Apparently Omani seamen helped develop a "magical" aspect of Falak

(120), and therein lies the origin of a long-standing controversy about whether the book is forbidden by Islam (132). In the mid-nineteenth century Richard Burton (1872: 422) suggested that at least some coastal residents considered it a form of "sorcery." According to one Swahili man I spoke to, Falak was brought down to earth by two angels and wound up in the hands of the Devil (*Iblis*). Another related a lengthy tale about one Mwalimu Kisisina who used Falak so often and to such effect that his powers began to surmount those of the angels and became evil. God sent down the angel Gabriel to take the book away, but Mwalimu Kisisina used his own powers to fly up after him. Gabriel tore off the front cover of the book and tossed it to earth as a decoy to fool Mwalimu. "It worked," says my informant: "Mwalimu Kisisina chased it all the way back down and Gabriel arrived safely in heaven with the book. But Mwalimu Kisisina had written [crib] notes on the front cover, and still had them! So Falak has survived, particularly the portions that instruct a person how to destroy and kill."[8]

Many other Swahili contend that Falak has a dark side involving harmful powers forbidden by God, such as "placing a snake in someone's belly" and inflicting spirit possession. The book is said to be easily abused by witches or groups such as Somali, who are considered by some in Malindi to be bandits (*mashifta*) and inadequate in their practice of Islam. In keeping with its controversial reputation, Falak has historically been taught in some madarasas in East Africa, but it is generally avoided in those in Malindi. Less common than Falak is the short text known as *Al-Badiri*, the reading of which is widely thought to be a means of bewitching its human target.

The other main text used by Swahili *walimu wa kitabu* is the Quran. While Falak is used primarily for divination, the Quran is more often used for healing and protective purposes, since it is believed by many that, as one *mwalimu* put it to me, "there is medicine inside those prayers." Prayers may be copied by hand or (increasingly) by photo-copier, folded tight, then placed onto a door lintel, under a bed, or into a talisman worn on the body in order to facilitate various kinds of good fortune and ward off bad. Many *walimu* also concoct *kombe* cures by writing Quranic prayers (in Arabic, of course) onto a piece of paper using water-soluble ink, then inserting the paper into a bottle or glass of rosewater, whereupon the ink dissolves. The patient is instructed to drink the rosewater, ingesting the dissolved prayer in its original language.[9] The most legitimate means of mystical healing, according to most religious authorities, is the reading aloud of Quranic prayers. Several Malindi-based practitioners circulated a 1993 pamphlet in Arabic (and said to be from Arabia) by Abu Mundhir Khalid bin Ibrahim Amin titled *Lawful [Sharia] Means of Curing Witchcraft, Jealousy, and Spirit Possession*.[10] Amin instructs readers that verses of the Quran, when read aloud, contain potential cures for these ailments, and he urges them to cleave to this path so clearly sanctioned by God. He also contends that "the masses" too often turn to "witchcraft and other unlawful methods" instead of the Quranic cure (3), thus providing a Middle Eastern sanction for the lament I sometimes heard from Swahili religious authorities in Malindi as well.

Giriama are keenly aware of the close association between Arabic and textuality. "Arabic is associated with the literate side of things," said one Giriama woman, and, as mentioned in chapter 2, this "literate side" is considered relatively alien by many Giriama in Malindi. Paper is not the customary means of consolidating Giriama institutional arrangements or securing landownership; indeed, some Giriama lament the indifference of certain members of their community to the title deeds that would establish their tenure. Marriages and other institutional arrangements are traditionally documented and secured through public ceremony and orally delivered oaths (cf. Parkin 1991a). Some Giriama thus feel intimidated by Swahili's use of literate ritual technologies. "The books Swahili use—Falak, Quran, Al-Badiri—they're dangerous," said a woman who sells palm wine in Muyeye. "You can be bewitched!" Another man told me, "They can bewitch you with their pen alone," while his neighbor said he fears Swahili and Arabs "because they study." One Giriama elder articulated the common sentiment, "[Arabs and Swahili use] the original *uganga* that comes from the Quran and is more powerful than ours." Indeed, the Giriama *mganga* Hawe Baya told me, "If the Arabs know you have a good spirit [*pepo*], they'll do their *uganga* to steal the spirit. They'll lull you and then they'll take it away. They'll know you have it by reading their Quran and burning some incense, then all is revealed to them. Their own spirit [*rohani*; Hawe Baya may have intended an Islamic connotation] will come and explain that so-and-so has such-and-such a spirit [*pepo*]—then they'll just take it from you."

Giriama attribute Arab and Swahili power not only to the Quran but also to Falak, a text that everyone seems to talk about but almost no Giriama have seen. Giriama discourse about Falak is complicated by the fact that the 113th sura in the Quran is titled "Falaq," or "The Dawn." Sura Al-Falaq is a call to God for deliverance from "the mischief of those who practice secret arts . . . [and] the evil of those who blow on knots." Despite its wholly defensive content, the sura seems tainted by the magic and witchcraft it mentions, being associated, in the minds of many Giriama and a few Swahili, with malevolent powers. Furthermore, for those who are not well trained in Arabic the terms Falak and Falaq create phonemic confusion since their final consonants (the *kaaf* of Falak and the *qaaf* of Falaq) are allomorphs to any ear unaccustomed to the Arabic alphabet, and hence the two names are indistinguishable. As a result qualities that Giriama credit to the book Falak are sometimes imputed to Sura Al-Falaq, and vice versa. Regardless, all Giriama know that Falak (or Falaq) is an Arabic text with special potency used by Arabs and Swahili, though that potency is interpreted in numerous ways. "It's used by Arabs to bewitch others in the neighborhood," said one Giriama boy. "They use the book to change themselves into cats, dogs, and birds," said another. A young Giriama woman claimed, "They just read the book and speak their wish." Another saw it as mainly divinatory and an index of expertise: "It's like [Giriama-style] divination [*mburuga*], but it's more work. You have to have the special Falak knowledge to work with it." Quite a few Giriama claimed that Falak has the power to win court cases, which Giriama *uganga* does not, suggesting that Swahili and Arab *uganga* is considered an effective way to intervene in state bureaucracy through a kind of sympathetic magic in which texts combat texts.[11] The late Giriama healer Kahindi wa Ruwa told me, "Falak has more power than Giriama herbalism [*mitishamba*]; it can help you win court cases and give you the power to fly." Thus he summed up two domains associated with Swahili and Arab expertise: bureaucracy and the forms of speed, velocity, and flight attributed to the money-gathering *jini* spirits associated with Swahili. The gap between Giriama and Falak-style expertise is magnified by the fact that Giriama say one must inherit a copy of the book from Swahili or Arab kin to own or use it, something very unlikely to happen for most Giriama.

Although many Giriama fear the potency associated with Arabic and

Arabic texts, some are angered by the hegemonic assumption of Swahili textual power. Said one *mganga* cynically, "The Giriama-style ritual language hasn't been written in books so it's not considered holy; it's considered evil. Yet the Muslim style is considered holy because it's in the books!" Another *mganga* defiantly asserted the superiority of Giriama powers on grounds that the Arabs and Swahili "get their *uganga* from books, and if the books are taken away they won't have *uganga*, but the Giriama aren't book-dependent." Yet these currents of resentment are not sufficient to prevent Giriama from engaging in widespread mimetic uses of Arabic and Arabic texts in ritual. Falak may be considered inaccessible because it must be inherited or gifted, but the Quran is a widely used device by Giriama *aganga* in Malindi. Many purchase copies at book stores and printers in town; however, most unwittingly wind up with an abridged version of the full text because the owners of the store, often Swahili, sell them a children's text comprising Arabic exercises for the untutored hand and a few select chapters (*juzuu*) of the holy book.[12]

These texts are used by Giriama to divine as well as to heal and protect. Healing rituals sometimes involve tearing the original text or photocopies of it against the grain of the words and scattering the pieces on the ground for clients to step over in a repetitive fashion that resembles the classically Giriama-style *mihambo mifungahe* ritual mentioned in chapter 4. Giriama *aganga* may also wave the Quran around the head of the afflicted or tap it on the body in a kind of consecration, sometimes just below the armpits. And Giriama manufacture their own versions of *kombe*, in which the writing of the Arabic prayers is sometimes achieved by a possessing Muslim spirit who uses a scallopine hand to create a rough simulacrum of Arabic, often with paint on a white ceramic plate. In these brief examples we see that most Giriama uses of Arabic texts focus not on the semantic meaning of the words, but on the potency thought to be condensed in the language or the text itself, potency that can be transferred through simulation and contact. In divination the language becomes a source not only of potency but of specialized knowledge.

Literacy, Epistemology, and Personhood in Divination

To divine is to know through extraordinary means, and the means usually involve objects—seeds, cowrie shells, goat intestines, tarot cards, or stars, for example—that are read for the privileged information they embody. If Peek (1991: 2) is accurate in deeming divination "the primary institutional means of articulating the epistemology of a people," then we can seek broad cultural significance in the similarities and differences between the epistemological strategies of Giriama and Swahili diviners.

Both Giriama and Swahili appear to reify Arabic and its associated texts and to project powers onto them. Members of both communities hope that by using Arabic as a divinatory tool they can better grasp the forces at work in their world and bring prosperity and health to themselves and their communities. But the deep socioeconomic division between Giriama and Swahili is reflected in the fact that in Malindi most Giriama diviners are illiterate women, while most Swahili diviners are literate men.[13] These differences, in combination with the different prevailing models of personhood in their communities, beget contrasting epistemological strategies that are emblematic of the imbalance between their social groups. In many Giriama divination rituals women are possessed by Arab spirits who tell fortunes by appearing to read the Quran. In much Swahili divination men use written Arabic (including Arabic texts such as the Quran and Falak) in extraordinary ways that flout conventional relationships between linguistic sign and meaning, while requiring elaborate interpretive skills accessible only to a literate specialist.

These different epistemologies beg the question of just what is entailed in and meant by "reading" in these mystical contexts and how different forms of reading articulate with different models of personhood. Since the advent of the so-called new literacy studies (Barton 1991; Street 1984) many anthropologists have embraced the idea that literacy, a term that connotes the ability to communicate by means of visual signs, typically in the form of the written word, has no predictable social meaning or cognitive outcome. Instead, reading and writing are embedded in historical, sociocultural, and economic practices and only make sense with respect to those (see also Ahearn 2001; Besnier 1995; Messick 1993). Not only does literacy have different social valences across cultural contexts, but different ways of interacting with the written word can subtend the ordinary scope of writing and reading. During the Mau Mau revolt in upcountry Kenya in the 1950s, for instance, Kikuyu freedom fighters sometimes ingested paper with writing on it as a means of assimilating the powers associated with the colonial bureaucracy, a mode of interaction that tapped into a preexisting Kikuyu idiom in which persons are partially composed of material transactions and eating is a primary means of internalizing the social world (Smith 1998). Similarly Swahili and Giriama interactions with written Arabic in divination are inflected by their respective understandings of personhood.

Giriama divination and other ritual practices have not always been and are not everywhere so centered on Other languages. Missionary accounts in the nineteenth century indicate that Giriama divination may have relied largely on manipulating objects. Some *aganga* used a stick, putting one end on the earth, holding the other end upright with a finger, then releasing it and reading significance into how or where it fell. Others counted seeds in a bag four separate times, prognosticating evil if each counting did not turn up the same number (Sperling 1995: 93). Another device involved a gourd threaded onto a vertical string called *malumulo*; yes-no questions were asked of it, and its reply was based on where it stopped in its course up and down the string. While Islam and Arabic in the nineteenth century were regarded as powerful devices, Sperling suggests that they tended to be used by *aganga* primarily during healing rituals (*after* divination, that is), and the relationship between healer and Arabic was quite indirect. When a Giriama *mganga* wanted an Islamic healing talisman, he or she solicited the help of a literate Swahili Muslim to write Arabic prayers or incantations on scraps of paper and make talismans. The *mganga* then would purchase the talismans, the paper already closed up within them, and distribute them to clients.

It is hard to know how much regional variation there was in these practices, for historical sources such as missionaries did not always attend to internal cultural heterogeneity. However, there may have been important differences between urban and rural Giriama society due to such matters as proximity to urban Swahili and Arab life. In Udvardy's (1989) extensive account of Giriama protective charms in hinterland Kaloleni in the 1980s, for instance, Islam does not appear to factor in at all (see chapter 4, note 10 for further details on such charms), whereas Malindi's *aganga* of today very frequently include Islamic symbolism in their talismans. As for divination, mechanical devices such as those mentioned earlier were in use among hinterland Giriama in Magarini in the 1980s (S. G. Thompson 1990), as they are among Giriama in Malindi today (in fact, they are sometimes used by male healers to complement their practices). But in Malindi such devices are not used nearly as commonly as divination through spirit possession. While high-status Islamic spirits were certainly in evidence among the diviners studied by Thompson in Magarini, they seem to be still more prevalent among urban and semiurban Giriama in the Malindi area.

Another important difference in divinatory practice involves language use. In her work in hinterland Magarini in the 1980s S. G. Thompson (1990: 186) found that during dialogue with their helping spirits, diviners used a spirit language termed Kipepo (literally, "the language of the *pepos*"), which "cannot be understood at all by humans unless they are possessed diviners." Still, Thompson does not suggest that this language was thought to be Arabic or ethnically identified in any way. After a dialogue with their spirits, diviners would shift into a register of cryptic Kigiriama, described as well by Parkin (1991b), that was common among diviners in the hinterland area of Kaloleni. This register involves special lexical, indexical, and metaphorical devices. A woman is referred to as *figa* (cooking stone), for instance, and a man as *tsano* (literally, "five," which may refer to the five days of funereal ritual accorded a deceased male, or to the presence of five limbs, including the penis, of the male body). Pronominal reference tends to slip around; diviners might refer to the client as both "you" and "she" in the same narrative. Elaborate metaphors (likening the diviner to the moon, for instance) may be used. S. G. Thompson (1990: 186) argues that this register "demands a client's attention and direct participation," thus compelling the client to help clarify the nature of his or her own complaint. Similarly, Parkin (1991b: 185) found that Giriama diviners sometimes opened a divination session using what he calls "jumbled speech" that becomes progressively clearer as the diviner's language iconically tracks the client's healing path from confusion to wholeness. While Islamic spirits certainly circulated in the Magarini and Kaloleni communities, neither Thompson's nor Parkin's descriptions of divination suggest that Islamic spirits or their language were as central as they are in contemporary Malindi, where Swahili and Arab power is so close at hand.

Hence there are important differences between prevailing patterns of divination in Malindi and those described in these other sources. Sperling contends that (at least in some places) early Giriama uses of Arabic relied on Muslim intermediaries, yet in today's Malindi the appropriation of Arab powers is more direct. Diviners commonly channel the language itself through their bodies via spirit possession, using it as a window into the unknown, perhaps suggesting the rise of Giriama's mimesis of Islam even as their assimilation into Swahili communities has dwindled. Furthermore, the rise of possession language in Giriama divination in Malindi appears to have accompanied a drop in the special divination register recorded by Parkin (1991b) and S. G. Thompson (1990). That elite register, obscure and poetic, has surely been important in making clients feel they were in the presence of an expert with ties to a mystical world. But in today's Malindi the use of opaque metaphors and "jumbled speech" is somewhat less common. Giriama say (to paraphrase a claim I heard often), "Those diviners in the hinterland speak the PURE Kigiriama, the ORIGINAL Kigiriama, and you won't understand a word of it." But such claims are made precisely to distinguish the putatively uncorrupt Giriamaness of hinterland diviners from the reliance on Other languages that is now the most popular linguistic means for Malindi's *aganga a mburuga* to establish their authority. Perhaps the intense multi-ethnic context of Malindi has made the very idea of ethnoreligious difference so salient that it has become the dominant idiom for divination. In a typical divination session in contemporary Malindi the diviner summons a foreign spirit who arrives speaking a language which the spirit then translates into Kigiriama to communicate the client's problem and a suitable remedy. While some of these helping spirits come from ethnic groups with whom Giriama have interacted historically, such as Kamba, Maasai, and Somali, the most popular helping spirits are Arabs, whose language seems to be a repository of mystery and promise.

To convey a fairly representative example of Giriama divination in Malindi, I describe the routine followed by a middle-aged woman named Kadzo, who lives on the outskirts of Muyeye. Like most Giriama women of her generation, Kadzo was not sent to school as a child and cannot read or write in any language. After making her living for two decades as a subsistence agriculturalist, she developed heart trouble in her forties. A *mganga* informed Kadzo that she was being tormented by Muslim spirits who demanded that she convert to Islam and begin to practice as a diviner, working with them as her assistants. She complied and her health improved. Some time later her husband also converted to Islam of his own volition and began to practice as a healer, taking on the clients that his wife referred to him.

Kadzo's homestead consists of a small courtyard and two mud-and-thatch huts, one with a dividing wall that separates a kitchen area from an empty room where she sees clients. In this room Kadzo sits on a short, three-legged stool, holding a beaded calabash rattle (*kititi*) in one hand and a ragged Quran in the other, for she plans to call upon an Arab spirit. She bought the Quran at a printer's in Malindi and appears unaware that it is a children's version containing only a selection of prayers, preceded by instructional exercises written in enlarged Arabic script. Kadzo closes her eyes and rattles hard directly into her ear while whistling a high-pitched, meandering tune intended to invoke the spirit. She addresses the spirit in Kiswahili, following the pattern described in chapter 4 in which Giriama *aganga* use Kiswahili when invoking the powers associated with Islam. She explained her client's grievance: "I want to know quickly. His heart is saddened [Anasikitika kwa roho yake]. Nothing is working out for him, not even a little. So I want to know why things are ruined for him. What kind of thing is ruining his financial situation? His wealth? They [the client and his employer] aren't speaking well to each other. They aren't understanding each other. He [the employer] doesn't want to pay him [the client] well. [To client] Is it so, or not [Ndivyo, sivyo]?" The client agrees. Kadzo proceeds to rattle and whistle. When the spirit arrives, it announces itself not through dramatic physical symptoms, but through intermittent gasps, rapid exhalations, and twitching toes. Holding the Quran at an angle, sometimes upside down, and tilting the pages this way and that, the spirit then reads the Arabic text in a loud monotone (I use the apostrophe to indicate glottal stops in the spirit's utterance):[14]

Dakumini dhabha kharanaduni kibhando khoronodini kavi na kordhani kavano ujiri naa siki [inaudible] *varanadini ndivo kazi ya kueleza. Nii ii durini kifato komiri kazi komari ujiri kavi na rudeni kiza ai. Mm-mmh. Nadu 'iri nataka ware najiri nasoko mawaridini yazo khoromidima khavina dure nukusika 'aguri na kazi ya kueleza. Mmm-mmh. Dukubiri nazokonga 'amirijiri kavi haya kuuza ha-ah-ha-ah-ha-ah-ha-ha-ha kumira kavani kivirenadeni kiva kazi hayu kuza kaya ndiyo kazi ndiyo. Mm hmmh?*

When the spirit has exhausted its prophecy, Kadzo shifts into Kigiriama, translating for the client with a didactic air: "The spirit says you are suffering at work; your boss does not pay you enough. You feel ill at ease with worry. You may have walked through a place where the spirits attacked you to bring you problems." As she speaks to the client, she asks repeatedly whether he agrees (a form of collusion common in Giriama divination but less typical in the Swahili divination sessions I witnessed), thus co-constructing a narrative to the client's satisfaction. Her voice is somewhat louder than usual, as if to establish a professional or authoritative mien; otherwise, the only extraordinary linguistic element, that which confers on her authority as a diviner, is her use of a language she does not herself know, use that extends to reading the Quran. Interestingly, what is read from the sacred book has no obvious connection to the fixed verses within it, but instead is translated as a prophecy tailored to the contingent personal situation of the client.

The Arabic of Kadzo's spirit has little resemblance to Arabic dialects and does not make sense to local Arabic speakers (to whom I played back this and other, related samples). While Kadzo's spirit does use a few Arabic sounds, particularly the glottal stop and the guttural uvular fricative *kh* sound popular among Swahili who wish to sound more Islamized, the resemblance stops there. Instead, Kadzo's spirit uses quite a few morphemes and words from Kiswahili, including *kumi* (ten), *dini* (religion), *kazi ya kueleza* (the work to be explained), *soko* (the marketplace), and *kuuza* (to sell). None of these appears in any meaningful, propositional sequence. The Arabic of other Giriama diviners' spirits is similarly patterned. One *mganga* named Haluwa, for instance, called upon her Arab spirit in the same fashion as Kadzo to offer a client an oracle about his prospect of finding a job and produced a stream of sounds:

> *Sahadi salahari ayasadesadah. Saradahe saraya saraha hasali sadajira. Deka sahadi chera sareha sashade sadah saharadi. Dakuresarahahasrade elariya sadajira. Hatira sahadi esi areahas aya sade sadah sahidi saahnala. Isihali yakide saraya saraha hasali tirasirajia sahad.*[15]

Haluwa's spirit does not speak recognizable Arabic or Kiswahili words, but it draws repeatedly on sound groupings that may be inspired by Arabic words known to many Giriama in Malindi, such as *salama* (a popular greeting, literally "peace"), *sura* (a Quranic prayer), and *sha-*

hada (the verbal confession of faith in Islam that performatively signals conversion).[16]

But the issue at hand is not whether these spirit languages are real. To focus on proving or disproving the authenticity of divinatory techniques and other occult forms is to fail to do justice to the question of what such techniques mean to those on the ground (see Lambek 1993: 287–95 for a related, and more fully elaborated, statement). These utterances remain deeply meaningful, for clients persistently believe that Arab spirits speak Arabic. Even clients with a rudimentary understanding of Arabic tend to let spirit versions pass without question. In part this is because the firm belief that spirits speak Arabic through diviners is overdetermined in Giriama culture, and so can override evidence to the contrary. But the acceptance of spirit versions of Arabic also suggests that the most important thing about Arabic is not its formal, perceptible qualities (the way a given rendering of Arabic looks or sounds). Rather, the crux of the language, that which gives it its identity and its power, appears to be some imperceptible essence that carries the stamp of the Arab Muslim world (cf. McIntosh 2005b).[17] Interestingly, informants repeatedly stressed that spirit versions of Arabic are "original," "pure," "authentic," "ancient," or "exact." Such claims may constitute a version of language ideology in which properties imputed to languages are iconically mapped onto the speakers associated with the language (Irvine and Gal 2000); perhaps when the Arabic is "pure" or "authentic," so too are the Arab spirits who speak it, suggesting the depth of their occult potency.

These extraordinary claims about the spirits' language also underscore the achievement of the diviners themselves, who lack validation from Islamic authorities but who in the context of possession are indirectly able to lay claim to a standard they would never ordinarily attain. Indeed, despite the potentially oppressive significance of possession, it remains the case that possession can open social possibilities for diviners (cf. Lewis 1971), as they gain access to invisible worlds of knowledge. In Kadzo's case, whatever advantages she accrues come not only from the financial rewards of being a diviner (very meager for most, significant for a few who are exceptionally well known and respected), but from her ability to wield a prized epistemological tool in a social context that emphasizes Islamization and education as routes to upward mobility. With one strategy diviners lacking in Arabic literacy are able to deliver an oracle and to confer upon themselves a modicum of reflected glory as they traffic in an intrinsically potent medium.

The literate male Swahili diviners called *walimu wa kitabu* living in the heart of Malindi interact with Arabic texts in quite a different way. To be sure, not all Swahili diviners and healers use the techniques I describe. Some diviners favor the scrutiny of objects that evoke technology, education, and mastery, such as clocks or watches; others may hold stethoscopes to the client's heart to determine, in the words of one, "[whether] the person has many worries that have led to illness, and whether the source of the illness is someone else's jealousy." A few Swahili women divine in Malindi; although some are literate in Arabic and can use the techniques associated with Falak, most use other means, including mechanical means such as throwing and interpreting cowrie shells. As discussed in chapter 4, furthermore, spirit possession has a historical precedent in many Swahili societies (Giles 1987), and while possession is not endorsed as acceptable or desirable by most Swahili in Malindi it is nevertheless used by some Swahili diviners. Like Giriama, for instance, a handful of female Swahili *waganga* use the assistance of spirits to write scallopine Arabic and read the Quran, while a small minority of male Swahili diviners also use possession to augment their textual practices. Yet the technique of possession is increasingly marginalized by self-consciously modern forms of personhood and by the link between piety and rational persons encouraged by the reformist Ahlul Sunna movement in Malindi's urban core. The most prestigious Swahili diviners tend to eschew possession and to base their practice on the Quran and Falak, which they read and interpret using elaborate exegetical skills learned through apprenticeship or extensive scholarship in settings as far away as Lamu, Tanzania, or Arabia itself.

One *mwalimu wa kitabu*, Mwalimu Mzee, lives in the heart of Barani and receives clients at a desk in a one-room stone dwelling built especially for his work. The inner walls are whitewashed and covered from floor to ceiling with Arabic script. Verses from the Quran spill from one wall onto the next; a Muslim invocation (*yaa Allah*) is written large in outline and filled with Quranic prayers in smaller script, physically layering meaning within meaning. Mwalimu Mzee has inscribed small grids onto the back of the door, filling each cell with an Arabic numeral, reflecting a focus on numerology and geometric patterns associated with

Islam in many other areas of Muslim Africa and beyond (Bravmann 1983; Lambek 1993).

To prognosticate for clients Mwalimu Mzee uses several techniques widely shared by other *walimu* in the area. In Swahili belief, as for many Muslims, letters of the Quranic alphabet also correspond to individual numbers, which themselves can be interpreted as reflecting archaic meanings. In one such system (sometimes referred to as *abjad*, Ar.), the numeric values in an Arabic word are added and the sum treated as shorthand for the word itself. The number 786, for instance, means *bismillahi*, "in the name of God" (Salvadori 1983: 195). According to one *mwalimu* living in Malindi but trained in Lamu, particular numbers also correspond to one of four personality types (water, wind, fire, and earth), of which there may be harmonious and dissonant combinations that can influence a person's fate. A *mwalimu* can further manipulate letters and numbers by, for example, taking the letters of a client's name and of some other relevant name (say, that of his or her mother or a potential lover), translating each into numbers, performing sums on these, and then scrutinizing the numerical result for significance. During one session conducted for a young man who dropped by to request a divination session (*ramli*) without any introduction of himself or his problems, Mwalimu Mzee wrote three names in a row—his own name, the name of the client, and that of the client's mother—in Arabic lettering. He drew a star under each, a figurative allusion to the distinctive fate of every person. Under each Arabic letter he wrote a corresponding number, then consulted the Falak text at his side to translate that row of numbers into a second row of numbers. He added the two rows together into a third row, scrutinized the Falak again, then delivered the oracle, an open-ended diagnosis that may have allowed the client to detect his concerns in it, while bringing him back to the Quran as the remedy: "Here is the problem—sometimes your fortune [*bahati*] is good, sometimes it's bad. Many people are jealous of you. This isn't your first divination; you've done it before because you've been having problems. You sometimes get sick with a fever, sometimes feeling the cold and sometimes the heat. Sometimes you get enough sleep, sometimes you lack it. But there are jealous people. You feel worries and this brings illness. The cure for you is to have the Quran read to you."

Mwalimu Mzee also uses grids (copied out from books such as Falak or obtained from other *walimu*) with individual Arabic terms in each cell standing for "soul," "money," and other important and fateful concepts. To choose a term, a diviner may close his eyes and mutter a prayer from the Quran (in Arabic, of course) while moving his hand in a circle over the grid, then let his hand fall, apparently randomly, on a word.[18] Mwalimu Mzee prefers to place the day of the week on one axis of the grid and the time of day on another axis, so that the combination of any given date and time corresponds to one term. He then decodes the significance of the term, depending on the client's needs. One client anxious about a court case is informed that she will prevail; another is told that her wayward husband is losing interest and needs occult intervention, mediated by Mwalimu Mzee himself, to bring him home.

Falak also contains elaborate instructions for numerically generating sixteen quadrigrams that encode a client's fate, a system of prognostication that a select few *walimu* are able to study in Arabia itself but others learn through local apprenticeship.[19] When Mwalimu Mzee uses the Falak technique, he begins by writing the invocations *yaa Allah*, and *yaa Mohammed* on either side of several stars and quadrigrams (others prefer to write out a brief prayer from the Quran in Arabic). Then, placing his left hand and the client's hand atop these, he takes a pen in his right hand and rapidly draws a row of short vertical lines from right to left, starting a new row of lines when he runs out of room on the page, until he has inscribed eight rows. The physical contact with the invocation or prayer at the top of the page apparently focuses the process, influencing the diviner's hand so that the number of lines reflects the client's fortune. Then Mwalimu Mzee counts off the lines in each row, indicating to the right of the row whether it contains an odd or even number of lines. Odd rows are designated *i*; even rows are designated N. The *i*s and Ns are then ordered and recombined through an elaborate procedure dictated by Falak, until Mwalimu Mzee has sixteen quadrigrams called *koo* (pl. *makoo*), each composed of four *i*s and Ns. Falak assigns an Arabic name to each *koo*; iNNN, for instance, is termed "Mushtara Dhahika" and suggests the involvement of the client's soul, while NiNi is "Daghala" and suggests money is at stake. Yet, says Mwalimu Mzee, the significance of each *koo* can be fully understood only according to its location relative to the other *makoo*, in combination with the client's situation. The significance of a *koo* thus requires deep interpretation that goes far beyond its simple semantic meaning.

Many Swahili diviners thus rely on an exegetical approach to Arabic that presumes that individual words, letters, or numbers bear magical essentialist meanings in ways not predicted by ordinary semantics (or mathematics). As in the recursive writing on Mwalimu Mzee's wall, meanings are layered within meanings to the point that accessing an oracular message requires a quasi-algorithmic technique. This condensed notion of signs applies too in Swahili healing practices. The talismans used to effect spiritual and physical cures often consist of writings sewn into a cloth or leather pouch; these may include prayers from the Quran, individual letters from the alphabet (such as *miim* and *waaw*) repeated in rows, and mysterious symbols such as numbers, curlicues bisected by a line, pentacles, and cross-hatches, some of which may be intended to represent the *khawatim*, the "excellent names" of God (cf. Bravmann 1983: 50). The interspersion of Arabic letters amid unfamiliar symbols has a suggestive effect, as if to imply that Arabic letters themselves contain as much mysterious, condensed power as an archaic, obscure symbol. In all of these examples, the meaning of a small unit of Arabic (a letter, number, or word) is treated as so densely embedded that it requires elaborate procedures of extraction.[20]

The contrast between Swahili and Giriama styles of interaction with Arabic in Malindi emerges in part from their different models of ideal personhood. I do not mean to erase the overlap in divinatory practices between these groups, particularly the presence of spirit possession among Swahili diviners; it is nevertheless the case that the most prestigious and most popular form of divination among Swahili involves the textual interactions I have described. The contrast between private, individualized agency valorized by Swahili and the patterns of shared agency evident in Giriama possession is played out in very particular relationships between people and utterances or texts.

What kinds of agency do Giriama imagine are present among their female diviners, who nearly always receive their oracles through spirit possession? Because the diviner becomes host to a possessing spirit, the most basic task of animating the prophecy seems divided between the diviner (whose body is the channel for the animated talk) and the spirit (whose voice emanates from that body). As for the intellectual experience of understanding Arabic, this capacity seems ambiguously divided between spirit and diviner. On the one hand, in our conversations *aganga* frequently impressed upon me the sudden linguistic proficiency conferred upon them by the spirit: "When I'm possessed, I can speak [some said 'read,' some said 'write'] Arabic, and I never even studied it!" Such locutions clearly announce the spirit's role in the feat but appear to share in the glory of it, and they suggest the difficulty in teasing apart host and spirit in Giriama folk models of the possessed person. Giriama diviners also have the skill of translating the spirits' oracles into Kigiriama for the benefit and understanding of their listeners; although the *aganga* do not themselves speak or understand Arabic when not possessed, they can nevertheless translate it after the spirit has receded, a potential contradiction that never seems to attract attention, presumably because of the blurring of lines between spirit and diviner. On the other hand, the capacity to produce Arabic vanishes altogether when the spirit departs or is angered, and many Giriama, diviners included, speak with envy of the textual mastery of Swahili who have studied Arabic intensively. All in all, the literacy of Giriama diviners is contingent on their shared agency with their helping spirits, and while it is celebrated by Giriama, it is not considered a match for the competence of those who understand how to use the Falak text or those who have (to invoke Hawe Baya's words again) their "own" Quran.

Among Swahili *walimu wa kitabu* like Mwalimu Mzee agency is differently distributed, involving a kind of self-possession rather than possession by spirits. Allah, of course, is seen by the pious as the ultimate cause of successful divination, but the diviner's skill is the proximate cause. Those *walimu* who do not use spirit possession not only understand the semantic meaning of the Arabic they use as they read and write from the Quran and Falak, but through a process of ratiocination, manipulation, and interpretation they also locate deeper significance in the language. This practice goes beyond standard notions of textual exegesis. Notice that Mwalimu Mzee does not merely access obscure information lurking within Arabic; he has mastered the obscure *procedures* required to crack the language's codes. Ideally, a *mwalimu wa kitabu* will have studied his craft under the tutelage of numerous other diviners in different geographic areas, such as Oman, Yemen, Saudi Arabia, Lamu,

Zanzibar, and Tanzania. He will know how to generate the Falak quadri-grams, how to translate a single Arabic word in a grid into a proposition about a client's life, and how to decompose a client's name into numeri-cal form, intermingle it with other numbers, and translate the results back into semantic form. He will know obscure meanings of the prayers within the Quran, meanings that are treated as inherently medicinal. Such expertise amounts to a kind of epistemological one-upmanship, for its dissection of the forms of Arabic supersedes even the capacities of native Arabic speakers.

These valorized forms of agency among Swahili are linked to themes I discussed in chapter 3, in which I explained the ideological importance of rationality, faith or belief, and intention (*nia*) to Islamic piety among many Swahili in Malindi today. While directing one's deeds through pious *nia* or applying one's reasoning to religious questions are explic-itly moral acts in a way that the diviner's decipherment is not (in-deed, Swahili diviners run the risk of accusations of imperfect piety), these efforts nevertheless have something in common. All of these forms of agency—the capacity for comprehension and decipherment on the part of the diviner; the rationality, faith, and good intentions of the good Muslim—require the cultivation of a kind of inward-looking effort and private prowess, the control and mastery of one's inner states and abilities.

These themes come together in some Swahili valorizations of textual divination and critiques of spirit-based forms of divination. One *mwa-limu*, Abubakari, explained:

> There is one kind of *uganga* a person can be proud of: that of educa-tion [*elimu*], where a person uses his intelligence [*akili*] and he is not possessed. He's not possessed, and he shows that he can divine and heal without the help of spirits. If a *mganga* depends on the help of spirits alone, he'll bring problems upon himself. The kind of *uganga* where you use the help of spirits is harmful, especially when the spirit refuses to possess. That *mganga* won't be able to work at all. I use the *uganga* of reading, not the kind that requires me to be possessed.

Abubakari derides spirit-based divination on grounds that it is unreliable and overly dependent; it is better, he implies, to be in command of one's faculties and divinatory powers by drawing on one's education. Some elite Swahili laypeople also disdain diviners and healers who use possession. One cosmopolitan Swahili man told me he had tried to "research" the matter of possession among Swahili diviners in his original home, Lamu, saying (in English), "Only the poorly educated in matters of Islam engage in possession. They'll speak maybe four words of Arabic and the rest is gibberish. I've been arguing with these guys for years about whether there's such a thing as spirit language. Of course there isn't." Not surprisingly, such critiques are often leveled by Swahili not only at lower-status (sometimes female) Swahili diviners but also at Giriama *aganga*. One Swahili woman in Malindi named Fatima weighed in on the inadequacy of Giriama uses of the Quran while possessed: "When you pray in Arabic you must mean the prayer with all of your heart and your *nia*. The Giriama diviners don't even know what they are praying; they can't see what is on the page." One Swahili *mwalimu* claimed that the Falak text he uses affords "direct power," whereas the Giriama divination strategy using spirit possession is "indirect," drawing on powers that attenuate rapidly, "like a kerosene lamp running out of oil." In such critiques we see the implication that those engaging in possession to divine or heal are trafficking in a kind of weak mimicry of real skill since they lack the educated or self-possessed agency that ideally ought to underlie a person's use of texts and words.

Walimu wa kitabu may defend the superiority of their methods, but their skills at decipherment are nevertheless controversial. While reading the Quran for healing purposes is widely considered acceptable—"The Quran is medicine [*shifaa*, Ar.]," as one *mwalimu* put it—there is anxiety about whether other divinatory and healing practices might be considered *ushirikina* (Kisw.) or *shirk* (Ar.), "disrespectful of God's omnipotence." The techniques of divinatory probing used in Falak divination are so profound that some regard it as excessive; as one pious Muslim put it, Falak requires a kind of "calculation, like modern technology," the use of which requires "research . . . into matters that have been hidden and forbidden by God himself." The agency wielded by *walimu*, in other words, threatens to exceed that allowed by God. If this threat is triggered by the exceptional knowledge of these practitioners, the defense against it also involves an inner capacity, for *walimu* sometimes defend their use of Falak by way of the notions of belief and *nia*. Said one *mwalimu*, "If you still believe that God is omnipotent and you are just using Falak to help improve your knowledge of God's will, it is acceptable [*halali*]." In other words, the mere fact of inward humility, a private playing down of one's power in relation to God, can salvage the moral viability of divination. Another echoed this sentiment, underscoring as well that one must accept the epistemological limitations of Falak: "Falak should be for forecasting only. If you believe that that book is the only truth then it's unacceptable [*haramu*]. But in fact it's just a few details about causes and effects, and things that may or may not happen. If you believe that God is omnipotent and you just use your knowledge to get a little help from Falak, it's okay. Your *nia* is the key. You see, this one thing may be *haramu* but with a little turning of the point, it may become *halali*."

Among these Swahili the cultivation of skills and knowledge offers the key to successful divination but poses a potential danger to their status as good Muslims. To mitigate this agency and salvage his or her piety, the good Muslim must attend to inner states such as belief and *nia*. Hence, whether Swahili are trafficking in potentially illicit "calculations" over Arabic words, letters, and numbers or reminding themselves of their devout intentions as they use mystical texts, their discourse surrounding these actions returns again and again to a model of personhood in which internal qualities are cultivated, measured, and monitored. Yet Giriama interactions with Arabic tend to rely on an ambiguous sharing of agency in which the inner states of the diviner are not generally spoken of, and the Giriama person is reliant upon a possessing spirit in order to interact with the text.

In sum, Giriama and Swahili in Malindi appear to have jointly reified the mystical potency and epistemological potential of the Arabic language, which therefore enjoys a symbolic power that perpetuates the hegemonic notion that Islam is a supernatural force to be reckoned with, and one that attaches more to those who have studied Arabic than to those who have not. Giriama are also in awe of and fear what they perceive as Swahili diviners' and healers' mastery of Arabic texts. Giriama diviners use Arabic and the Quran in hopes of attaining mystical knowledge. While they may gain a modicum of status among other Giriama, their epistemological methods lack authority among Swahili, for the Giriama models of personhood played out in their interactions with Arabic texts allow for the sharing of agency with spirits and pay little attention to an individual's distinctive knowledge or controlled inner

states. Some Swahili diviners also use spirit possession, but their methods are regarded by many as religiously forbidden or as demonstrations
of weakness. Once again we see that the prevailing understandings of
personhood among Swahili and Giriama play a role in the sociocultural
hierarchies between (and even within) these groups.

The Language of Madness and the
Obliteration of the Giriama Person

Arabic is also interwoven with Giriama personhood in another, much
darker fashion, one that speaks eloquently to the tensions in Giriama
attitudes toward Islam. I first became aware of this phenomenon when I
encountered a peculiar man walking down the road running between
Malindi and its tiny airport. His hair hung from his head in brown
clumps, his genitalia dangled from a flimsy cloth, and as he approached
he spoke loudly and gesticulated to an invisible interlocutor. I strained
to understand him but did not recognize the sounds he produced as
Kiswahili or a Mijikenda dialect. When I described him to my Giriama
friends, they told me he was a well-known mad (*wazimu*, Kisw., Kigir.)
person,[21] who "has spoken in other languages since he went mad. Now
he speaks Arabic and the Somali language."

Madness everywhere is diagnosed by a catastrophic breakdown in the
social self. The mad may become violent, paranoid, wildly sexually inappropriate, or obsessive-compulsive. They may hallucinate, suffer from
extreme mood swings, and neglect their hygiene and clothing. Language
is often deeply compromised in this equation, for as Wilce (2004: 416)
reminds us, sane speech involves "pragmatic or indexical competence"
that is devastated by these social failures. Among schizophrenics, for
instance, the shattering of the self is often accompanied by incoherent
speech. The subtle metacommunicative signs that indicate what is going
on, how messages should be framed, and how turns ought to be structured are sometimes ignored or misperceived by schizophrenic (as well
as autistic and otherwise impaired) listeners (Ochs et al. 2004; Ribeiro
1994). These pragmatic infelicities extend to language play, babbling to
invisible interlocutors, and, in some cases, to rapid, socially inappropriate
code switching (Wilce 2004: 424).

The behavior of the mad may be chaotic, but it is not without meaning. Indeed, some have argued that madness has an intelligible poetics,

offering an imaginative intensification of the anxieties of ordinary cultural life (Comaroff and Comaroff 1987; Friedrich 1979). Among Giriama in Malindi any interpretation of the poetics of madness must attend closely to language, for one of the most recurrent symptoms of madness in this community is said to be the sudden onset of the use of Other languages, most prominently Arabic. This form of mimetic behavior begs for interpretation since its disastrous implications for the Giriama person preclude its evaluation as an appropriation of mystical power. As part of the context for interpreting this type of madness, it is worth exploring how its symptoms speak to themes addressed in chapters 2 and 3, in which I discussed the bloodthirsty *jini* spirits that gather money for their Swahili masters and the often unwanted possession of Giriama individuals by Muslim spirits who demand their conversion to Islam. Several examples will help to demonstrate how these themes play out.

Kadenge was the hardworking twenty-something son of impoverished parents who had managed to secure a well-paying job in town. He owned two cows and had begun to build himself a large mud-and-thatch house in Muyeye when he spontaneously began to babble in a tongue his family and neighbors term Arabic. There is some collective puzzlement about the cause of his condition, but a common account is that Kadenge's own grandmother was jealous of his fortune and hired someone to bewitch him. The professional who did the job, say his neighbors, enlisted Muslim spirits and "threw" them at Kadenge. "Most of the witchery involved in madness," explained Kadenge's neighbor Thuva, "originates with the Arabs." Today Kadenge wanders around the streets of Malindi eating from trash heaps, refusing to bathe, and producing a stream of largely unintelligible speech that Thuva deems "the best Arabic," most volubly on Fridays. When he requests something of another person he sometimes says "Bismillahi!" before pantomiming his desires, and at prayer time he cries out like a *muzzein.* "I don't know how he keeps time to know when [the prayers] happen," said Thuva, "but he always gets it perfectly."

Another young man, Kaluwa, began to show signs of acute madness during the Muslim calls for prayer, growing panicky and trying to hide. Eventually he began speaking what his friend Masha calls "something like Arabic," while his social behavior deteriorated into unpredictability, vacillating between violence and aloofness as he took to collecting garbage on the streets. Masha has a theory as to what happened. Kaluwa was working in a Swahili house as a cook at the time of the onset of this illness, and Masha suspects he brought pork into the house. As punishment, "the *majini* slapped him and his brain has been misbehaving ever since." Masha added, "Kaluwa's family is from Kakuyuni, close to Ganda, where there was a Swahili slave market." This allusion seems at first like a non sequitur, until I realize that it encodes the association between Swahili and ownership of Mijikenda slaves. The reference seems ominous, perhaps drawing a rhetorical link between the history of Swahili slavery, Kaluwa's employment by a Swahili, and his current subjugation at the hands of possessing Muslim spirits.

Kiponda was working for a Swahili in Shella when a *jini* pounced on him. His friends speculate he may have "picked up some money that dropped on the floor," precisely the sort of act that the money-gathering *jini* will swiftly avenge to preserve the fortunes of their Arab and Swahili masters. Said Kiponda's friend Kitsao, "[Now] he responds to the call for prayers—in fact, when the time comes, you can hear him calling on his own." Kitsao continued, "[Today Kiponda] speaks the language we don't understand; he speaks Arabic, the pure Arabic . . . especially at noon prayers and on Friday. He never spoke a word of it before he went mad." It's ironic, Kitsao added, because Kiponda never liked Swahili people, and even today, despite his state of dementia, "he likes mocking the *bui bui* women when they pass by him." Kiponda's sister Kadii asserts (independently of Kitsao) that he now speaks "the original Arabic [Kiarabu asili, Kisw., Kigir.]," prays following the calls from the *muzzein*, and fasts during Ramadan. As in a number of other cases, Kiponda also began to speak other languages with the onset of his madness, such as Kikamba and Kisomali, but his friends and relations mentioned those only in passing before their narratives focused on Arabic and on the Muslim spirits that underlie it.

I return to the matter of language below, but first it is important to discuss some of the other themes raised in these vignettes, for they shed light on the prevalence of Muslim spirits as the cause of madness. A number of cases of madness, not just Kiponda's, involve a striking association between money and the Muslim spirits that drive a person mad. Some Giriama regard madness as a common result of jealousy within their community, a sentiment that has been on the rise over the generations as opportunities for accumulation have risen and threatened to displace traditions of redistribution (cf. Parkin 1972). An elderly denizen of Muyeye, Yaah Baya, said, "Most people become mad when someone casts a spirit upon them; it can be a jealous person. . . . Our people won't let you grow rich. Once you start, they bewitch you. It's often a Swahili *jini*—you see, we don't have *jini* in our witchcraft." In this formulation jealous Giriama eager to level the playing field enlist the help of Swahili witches to send possessing *jini* to their victim. This is what Kadenge's neighbors assume happened to him. Other Giriama I spoke to pin madness directly on the cruel whimsy of the Muslim spirits Giriama encounter in their interactions with Swahili, spirits especially likely to be provoked by those who steal from Muslim employers, as Kiponda may have done. In both scenarios Muslim spirits, which are already considered brokers of Swahili and Arab wealth (see chapter 2), become punitive devices against Giriama attempting to rise above their economic station. Granted, there are cases of madness caused by Muslim spirits that don't involve economics; sometimes Muslim spirits are said to cause madness in individuals who have insulted them (for example, through cursing or drunkenness), and in other instances, "they just want to torment you," as one person put it.[22] Still, the link between madness, money, and Muslim spirits is striking and may help to account for the fact that most cases of madness I encountered involved men, who are somewhat more likely than women to serve as laborers under Muslim employers.

There are also interesting comparisons to be drawn between these cases of madness and the common pattern in which Giriama are pressured to convert to Islam by a possessing Muslim spirit. Both involve the domination of Giriama by Islamic forces and the partial or total loss of Giriama agency at the hands of a Muslim spirit. The cases of madness represent the most extreme version of Muslim spiritual coercion, for the Giriama person is completely divested of both control and consciousness. There are also, however, some intriguing patterns of difference between spirit-forced conversion and spirit-induced madness. The first difference provokes questions about just what the mimetic behaviors in madness could mean, while the second difference invites speculation about the semiotic weight of language itself to Giriama identity.

The first difference has to do with purity and pollution. In spirit-forced conversion the Muslim spirits demand and emphasize new forms of purity of their Giriama hosts, through the bodily rejection of *haramu* food and drink, fasting during Ramadan, the donning of pristine white robes, and ablutions. In stark contrast, the hygiene of the mad utterly collapses. Giriama explanations for the filthiness of the mad sometimes link the condition to the perverse wishes of the spirits, who seem to want to humiliate their victims as much as possible. It is worth exploring, then, whether the mimetic behaviors of the mad as they go through the motions of Islam have an ironic or cautionary semiotic value, the result of a lifetime of feeling beleaguered or even traumatized by Muslim hegemony. Ferguson (2002) has noted a tension in the scholarly literature between interpretations of mimesis as earnest pragmatism and interpretations of mimesis as a kind of resistant parody or mockery of the powerful. Certainly some Giriama appropriations of Islam are entirely earnest and strategic, such as their use of the Quran for divination and healing. But might their madness mark another, darker face of mimesis? For instance, perhaps the distorted condition of the mad, calling to prayer while wearing filthy rags, provides a kind of monstrous parody of Islam. Perhaps, more subtly, the behaviors of the mad parody or warn against Giriama *aspirations* to become Muslim, suggesting that once a Giriama crosses over to "the Muslim side" he or she becomes a mere shell of a person, an automaton without dignity. Perhaps the behavior of the mad could even be read as a kind of rejoinder to Muslim hegemony, a thumb in its eye, a defiant grotesquerie of its terms. A final interpretation of this phenomenon eludes, for the mad hardly know what they are doing, nor do their interpreters offer a wholly coherent account of the meaning of their deeds. At the very least, however, the mimesis involved in madness reveals what *preoccupies* Giriama in Malindi, for there is little more vexing to them than the dilemma of living on the edge of Islam.

The second contrast between spirit-forced conversion and madness foregrounds the relationship between language, ethnicity, and personhood in Giriama life. Giriama narratives about conversion tend to focus on the bodily demands the spirit makes of its host (rejection of Giriama foods, etc.), but narratives about spirit-induced madness place particular emphasis upon the linguistic domain, most often the use of Arabic. Just as many accounts of divination focus on the Arabic language used by the diviner, so too are discussions of madness often dominated by a focus on the language itself as the source of awe. Young men and women working for Muslim employers are possessed by the *jini* that live at their employers' homes and said to babble in Arabic. The curses of drunken men walking past a baobab tree offend the Arab spirits, who descend, say the narrators of such events, and take over their tongues. In fact, even some of the beach boys whose madness is thought to have been caused by smoking too much *banghi* weed are said to speak Arabic, despite the fact that their condition is not caused by spirit possession.

The association of madness with Arabic even in the absence of a Muslim spirit is revealing. It suggests that language, like spirits, can get into people in a way that can strip them of their appropriate social orientation. To be colonized not only by an Arab spirit, but by the Arabic language itself, is to have utterly lost one's bearings, a contention borne out in the words of one Giriama speculating about why the mad speak Arabic: "I think they speak it because they live in a totally different world. . . . They feel they're in their other world when they speak that other language." Arguably, in fact, the same logic that informs the use of Arabic in Giriama divination seems to be magnified in the role language plays in madness. Arabic, a wholly Other language, can offer the diviner a window into a wholly different perspective, but taken to an extreme these alternative ways of knowing can lead to the loss of self, for madness is a kind of epistemology gone haywire, an intrusive parallel universe that detaches subjectivity from the here and now.

But this parallel universe is not simply detached; it is also ethnoreligiously marked by the language associated precisely with the lives that many Giriama envy and resent. If madness and its associated linguistic failures represent what Wilce (2004: 422) calls a breakdown in "essential humanity," then Giriama madness is a breakdown of essentially *Giriama* humanity. It is precisely because personhood is ethnoreligiously marked for Giriama in today's Malindi ("Personhood is culture," as Phillip, the community advocate, insists) that the primary symptom of their madness is similarly marked. And because madness involves Arabic and Islam, it indexes with precision the kinds of aborted longing and frustration experienced by so many Giriama.

Finally, Giriama madness bears with it a lesson about the parameters of Giriama personhood and the limits of its permeability. We have seen that Giriama tend to valorize a sociocentric model of the person, in which reciprocal obligations are morally upheld, agency may be distributed between persons and other agents such as spirits, and introspective tendencies are not given much play. Yet, as Jacobson-Widding (1990: 34) observed in the Lower Congo, some African societies entertain both sociocentric and egocentric views of personhood simultaneously, with the former assuming the status of "official ideology" and the latter making itself known more implicitly, as an element of the person "to be reckoned with." Among Giriama, we are reminded of the egocentric person perhaps most palpably when personhood has been wholly destroyed.

All Giriama see madness as a terrifying and tragic prospect, for while they are not as a whole particularly invested in internalist or individualistic models of personhood, they nevertheless prize certain forms of autonomy. Sufficient agency to sustain one's social competence and sanity is clearly the sine qua non of a viable life, and this, it seems, is utterly stripped away by Arabic-speaking spirits who come and never leave. In ordinary divination, temporary, voluntary spirit possession can benefit the host, who ultimately returns to awareness to interpret the spirit's message. In madness, though, there is no such return to self-command and no such process of interpretation. The spirit is free to meddle with the possessed, who functions merely as the addled co-animator of unintelligible speech and calls to prayer. In those calls to prayer, in fact, the possessed go through the motions of advertising Islam; having been ensnared by its potencies, they proceed, zombie-like, to solicit others, even though, like Kiponda, some of them when sane reportedly despised the ethnic groups associated with Islam. (Once again, the possibility arises that such mimetic behaviors have a parodic or critical dimension; the mad individual attempts to lure others to the same fate, but what a dreadful fate it plainly is.) This untenable situation clarifies the importance for Giriama of the self-control of the sane.

All in all, the Arabic-speaking mad represent the ultimate loss of Giriama identity and autonomy in a social force field they find greatly oppressive. Giriama seem caught in a double bind, for the very devices they sometimes use to recoup power appear to reinscribe elements of this same social dynamic, one made up of ethnoreligious boundaries, essentialized social categories, and the repeated valorization of the power of other religious and ethnic groups. Recent events in Kenya at large have done much to reinforce, tragically, ethnoreligious boundaries and ethnoterritorial dynamics.

EPILOGUE

As I write this, Kenya is on fire with politically motivated violence, expressed through an ethnic idiom. It
has been several weeks since the elections of December 2007, in which
the incumbent president, Mwai Kibaki, a Kikuyu, is widely seen as having rigged himself back into power and stolen the election from the
opposition candidate, Raila Odinga, a Luo. The result has been an explosion of conflict in Nairobi and the Rift Valley and Western Provinces, in
which Luo, Kalenjin, and other groups aligned with Odinga have been
pitted against Kikuyu, Kisii, and others in a cycle of killings and expul-
sions governed by a *majimbo*ist logic in which members of each group
want the others to return to their putative ancestral homelands.

For many Westerners it has been something of a shock to hear articulate, English-speaking Kenyans, people who might once have sold them
curios or helped guide their safari in East Africa's "beacon of stability,"
tell BBC radio journalists of their zealous engagement in ethnic purges.
Indeed, the conflict appears to have boggled the Western mind, confounding explanation and reducing some major media outlets (initially,
anyway) to describe the crisis as the result of "atavistic tribal hatred."[1]
Such mystifications not only overlook Kenyan history but also reveal a
widespread assumption that cosmopolitanism ought to lead Africans to
identify primarily with larger units, such as the nation, while shucking off
the particularism of so-called tribal identities. Many scholars too once
anticipated that globalization would lead to an increase in cultural homogeneity; as Meyer and Geschiere (1999: 1) explain, the presumption
was that "through the impact of new technologies of communication and
transport, and the intensified circulation of goods and people on a global

scale, cultural difference was supposed to disappear." At the same time, political liberalization in Africa in the 1980s was supposed to lead Africans to behave like good (Western) nationalists. And yet it would seem that many communities have reacted to such changes by underscoring their cultural and ethnic particularity.

Behind this paradox are political histories of inequality across sub-Saharan Africa. Within Kenya ethnic groups have stood in especially uneasy competition since British colonials reified ethnic categories and doled out advantages and disadvantages along those lines. Subsequent Kenyan leaders have allocated land and other resources in ways that exacerbate ethnic asymmetries, and since the advent of multipartyism politicians have cultivated allegiances and coalitions on largely ethnic grounds. In such a context, free market capitalism has begotten class strata that are frequently divided along ethnic lines, while the free flow of migrants (both external and internal) seeking new opportunities in various corners of Kenya's already overpopulated landscape has led, not to an integrated sense of nationalism, but to an ethnoterritorial backlash. If the apparent primacy of ethnic identities such as Luo and Kikuyu is a by-product of twentieth-century political, institutional, and economic history (Carotenuto 2006; Lonsdale 1994), ethnic identity was further reified in the months leading up to December's election as both Kibaki and Odinga fanned the flames of ethnic resentment to garner votes. Some political observers say that both politicians cultivated nefarious plans for reprisal and destabilization in case they failed to successfully manipulate the ballots in their favor. Human Rights Watch (2008) recently reported that Odinga's Orange Democratic Movement (ODM) officials planned and organized the Rift Valley violence that broke out immediately upon the announcement of the election results; Kibaki, in turn, is suspected of playing his own sponsoring role in the retaliatory clashes.

Ethnic boundaries in the current moment have been further reified by the social logic of civil war. If ethnicity in peacetime Kenya is sometimes blurred through social intermingling and intermarriage, in this moment of crisis frustration and disenfranchisement are being shunted through the purifying discourses of ethnic hostility and the brutal certainty that comes from attaching ethnic labels unambiguously to individual bodies (cf. Appadurai 1998). As bodies become "the site of violent closure"

(913), people are erased; one person comes to stand in for any other member of his or her tribe, past, present, or even future, and the deeds of one (such as Kibaki) can be avenged upon the body of another (any other Kikuyu). Such essentialist dynamics are all the more perverse given that, in some areas of Kenya, voters' choices apparently did not break down quite so tidily along tribal lines.

The tragic events of recent weeks have been far more explosive than the subtler dramas I have described on the coast, but they share with them a common dynamic in which political forces, economic anxiety, and competition over land all reify the importance of supposedly autochthonous and essentialized ethnic identity. While the discourses of those in conflict tend to presume that tribal affiliation is an intrinsic and natural quality, this is also a prime historical moment for the ostentatious *performance* of ethnoreligious identity. The most widely known example of this dynamic comes from Mungiki, an ethnoreligious Kikuyu militia group with complex and shifting ethnoterritorial, political, economic, and cultural aims too elaborate to fully discuss here. At various historical moments (and in various ways) Mungiki members have emphasized a return to a version of Kikuyu spiritualism, including praying to the deity Ngai on Mount Kenya, administering oaths with precedents in Kikuyu political history, and attempting to enforce puritanical and supposedly traditional morals—an ironic accompaniment to their often violent and extortionist actions. Mungiki have been heavily implicated in the post-election violence, at the same time that they have accelerated their performance of ethnospiritual identity by, for instance, persecuting and stripping women wearing trousers instead of skirts, administering loyalty ceremonies for sometimes unwilling Kikuyu, and reportedly even forcing circumcision on women and girls in a perverse invocation of customary Kikuyu life. Meanwhile the young Kalenjin warriors who frame themselves as antagonists to Mungiki dramatize their own ethnicity by donning customary leopard skins and other animal hides, covering their heads with leafy headdresses, and smearing their faces with war paint, all while (like those on all sides) coordinating their efforts via mobile phones. But such indices of globalization and homogenization are relegated to the semiotic background as those in conflict play up markers of ethnic distinction presumed to predate the arrival of outside influences. It is as though the performance of a presumed authentic tradition reaching back through time might consolidate the authenticity of one's claim upon a particular territorial space.

Far away from the primary scenes of bloodshed the election results have had complex ramifications among coastal Swahili and Giriama, whose political anxieties are also being expressed in ethnic terms. On the one hand, Odinga's overtly pro-*majimbo*ist stance won many votes from Mijikenda and Swahili alike, both groups hoping that an Odinga win might mean that more proceeds from the coastal economy would remain in the hands of ethnic groups indigenous to the coast. At the same time, the prospect of an Odinga ascendancy made some Mijikenda wary, given that he was widely rumored to have promised several Muslim organizations that Najib Balala, a coastal member of Parliament and a descendant of immigrants from the Hadhramaut (a region of the south Arabian Peninsula), would become governor of the coast upon Odinga's election. This prospect fomented anxiety among Mijikenda, who feared that under Balala's leadership Islamic hegemony on the coast would tighten. Since the results came in Balala has spearheaded numerous pro-ODM demonstrations in Mombasa. While Giriama in Malindi report feeling aligned with Swahili in their disgust at a rigged election and their efforts to end coastal disenfranchisement vis-à-vis upcountry groups, they also describe a degree of political ambivalence, for they do not want to be ruled by either Luo or Kikuyu at the national level or by Arabs at the local level.

Anxiety about Balala's political ambition and its implications for Mijikenda autonomy also came to the fore in early 2006, after Balala announced that he would be making a bid for Kenya's presidency. Since Kenya's independence, Mijikenda Kaya elders have periodically conferred blessings and even honorary eldership upon various politicians, most of them Mijikenda, but a few of them, controversially, not (McIntosh, forthcoming). Framing himself as a *majimbo*ist candidate who would bring economic benefits to all ethnic groups indigenous to the coast, Balala won (and very likely paid for) the favor of a Mijikenda elder from the Rabai subgroup named Pekeshe Ndeje, who formally blessed Balala near Kaya Fungo, which Giriama consider central to their identity. Balala sat in customary Mijikenda regalia while Ndeje officiated; photographs of the event were published in national newspapers soon after.

The national media and rumors on the ground averred that Balala had been anointed as a tribal elder, a controversial claim that tapped into long-standing antagonisms of the sort I have described in this volume. Many Mijikenda were offended, even horrified, by the apparent symbolic assimilation of an Arab politician into the elite ranks of Mijikenda elders. The event was seen as having contaminated an essential Mijikenda identity with higher level political allegiances, while compromising the symbolic morality of Mijikenda elders by incorporating this representative of Arabo-Islamic hegemony. Some complained that the Kaya itself had been besmirched by this act; others worried that in conferring these political blessings elders were selling secrets to ethnic outsiders, thus weakening the exclusivity that is one of the few bastions of Mijikenda ethnic pride. In the end Pekeshe Ndeje was branded a fraud by many Mijikenda organizations, including the Kaya Advisory Council, which asked Balala to apologize for his installation as an elder.[2] It would seem that far from encouraging a blurring of cultural boundaries, Kenya's multiethnic political playing field fosters anxiety among Giriama and Mijikenda about ethnic identity loss and a backlash of Mijikenda efforts to assert their particularity.

Yet as we have seen repeatedly in this volume, this sense of particularity stands in an ambivalent relationship to Islam, both resenting and capitulating to its supposedly superior powers. Ironically, in fact, Islamic hegemony has in one small way helped to keep the peace on the coast. During the weeks immediately following the election, widespread looting accompanied the chaos in some of Kenya's major cities, including Mombasa. This dynamic, however, was rapidly brought to a halt on the coast just as it peaked in other parts of the country, and international observers were stunned to learn that dozens of coastal looters were marching back to the stores to return the merchandise they had stolen. Rumor had it that a Swahili religious authority had read the powerful Arabic text *Al-Badiri* to bewitch the looters, who then risked being struck by a range of symptoms and misfortunes. Some were said to be unable to urinate, others to be in peril of madness. Giriama in Malindi say that one Giriama who stole a television set in Mombasa was mysteriously crushed by the appliance. The television could not be lifted from him until after he had drawn his last breath. In a parallel to the *jini* narratives described in chapter 2, we see again that in Giriama discourse wealth is protected by Islamic forces determined to prevent the poor from overstepping their station by robbing the rich.

But such supernatural injunctions are hardly enough to quell Giriama and Mijikenda aspirations to change their lot. In recent weeks select groups of elders and youth have retreated to Kaya Fungo and Kaya Bombo to consult the ancestral forces and discuss their options. The current of violence that has swept the western areas of Kenya has opened a space for discussion. Is this at last the moment for Mijikenda to fight for the land and economic possibilities they say have been taken from them? Some Giriama are harboring weapons in anticipation of possible violence, saying, "To be careful isn't cowardly; it's to be ready [Kuriaria si woga; ni kudzikat'o]." A few of my Giriama contacts say they want to "chase the Kikuyu and Luo out of the coast" in a massive reprisal of the 1997 clashes. In the Likoni area of Mombasa (site of the 1997 clashes) and elsewhere, history has repeated itself as some upcountry folk have received leaflets under their doors threatening that they will be driven out if United Nations Secretary-General Kofi Annan does not lead the politicians to a satisfactory solution. A few Giriama also express hopes for a resurgence of sub-*majimbo*ism in which Mijikenda might also target and drive out Arabs, punishing this elite group by sending them "back to Arabia." Yet as I have noted the category of Arabs is nebulous in coastal discourse, often expanding to include Swahili with centuries-old roots on the coast. One hopes the impossible lines between indigenous and foreign will not have to be drawn in the violent terms of contemporary *majimbo*ism, for plenty of Mijikenda do not want a war. Even Mijikenda agitators are vexed by their limited resources, grumbling that although politicians are happy to sponsor violence in the western areas of the country, neither Kibaki nor Odinga would be willing to commit resources to clashes that would work against *both* Kikuyu and Luo. Furthermore, the Mijikenda Community Council of Elders has taken the high ground, recently presenting Kofi Annan with a list of grievances about coastal land issues and their constitutional rights. In time we shall see whether their voices are heard and whether subsequent events in Kenya will soften the stark ethnic asymmetries that spark so much bitterness and the ethnoterritorial lines that have been so brutally redrawn.

NOTES

Introduction

1. Islam-inflected divination is common in many regions on the Islamic periphery in sub-Saharan Africa, but its dynamics and meanings inevitably take shape in local terms, as I will show in the Giriama case.

2. I capitalize the term Traditionalism to honor it as a system of supernatural beliefs and practices, though I am mindful that using such a term risks invoking some connotations I don't necessarily intend (see Shaw 1990). I do not, for instance, mean to suggest a strict definition of this system as if it were frozen in time, for, as will be seen, it is flexible and improvisational. Nevertheless, there is a family resemblance within those beliefs, attitudes, and practices that are recognizably Traditionalist; indeed, Giriama themselves mark certain practices as distinctly indigenous religion, or *dini ya kienyeji*. I discuss these in greater detail in chapter 4. I also do not intend to suggest that Giriama Traditionalism is structurally similar to Abrahamic religions; in fact, as I argue at length in this book, most Giriama practitioners of Traditionalism do not prioritize belief over practice in the manner of Abrahamic faiths, and while most Swahili and Westerners tend to see Traditionalism as incompatible with Christianity and Islam, many Giriama find ways to draw on Traditionalism alongside Abrahamic practices (see chapters 3 and 4).

3. The presence of ideological and political in-groups and out-groups need not be attributed solely to Western and colonial influence or to a backlash against globalization, democratization, and liberalization. While certain political and economic orders have *encouraged* divisiveness, human beings in many cultural and political contexts seem to be capable of thinking in terms of intrinsic differences and absolute boundaries between social categories (Gelman 2003; Gil-White 2001; Hirschfeld 1996; Zerubavel 1991).

4. To keep this introduction concise, I have refrained from describing in detail

the explosion of academic propositions emerging from cultural, postcolonial, global, and literary studies that focus on such concepts as cosmopolitanism, diaspora, boundary crossing, and hybridity.

5. Essentialist reasoning appears to be common across cultures, emerging in reasoning about biology (Mayr 1988), folk systematics (Atran 1990), and social categories (Hirschfeld 1996; Rothbart and Taylor 1992; Stoler 1997). A number of cognitive psychologists and cognitive anthropologists, in fact, contend that essentialist thinking is a universal cognitive predisposition that is most typically deployed in our understanding of the natural world (Gelman 2003) but that in certain political contexts can be activated in thinking about human kinds (Hirschfeld 1996). The present study, which takes place in a circumscribed cultural context, cannot resolve the question of whether essentialism is a universal habit of the human mind, but my inclination is to think of essentialism as an interaction between cognitive tendencies and the social surround, with certain social orders facilitating and encouraging essentialism and determining the particular ways it is deployed to think about social categories (cf. Hirschfeld 1996; McIntosh 1998).

6. There are parallels between this dynamic and the colonial-era racial essentialisms described by Stoler (1997: 104), in which the illusion of fixed racial categories cloaked what she calls the "dynamic motility" of the shifting characteristics associated with these categories. In discourse about ethnicity on the Kenya coast, Swahili and Giriama distinguish the "real root" of ethnic groups along highly variable lines; sometimes the vital quality is described as blood, sometimes as innate intellectual capacity, sometimes in terms of a language presumed to be intrinsic to that group, sometimes in terms of an intrinsic character conferred by God at the beginning of time. In other cases, ethnic identity claims seem utterly tautological: a Giriama is a Giriama because she's a Giriama. What unites claims like these is the durable fact that they all adduce or seem to implicitly presume deep-seated and natural properties in explaining ethnic category membership. People within a society need not concur about what is essential to a particular category in order to traffic in the idea that such categories have essences (cf. Medin and Ortony 1989: 184).

7. See Gelman (2003: 3). The disregard of contradictory evidence is apparently a common property of essentialist ideation.

8. The terms *personhood* and *selfhood* are often used more or less interchangeably in anthropological scholarship. I elect to use the term *personhood* here because in some readings the term *selfhood* might be interpreted as referring directly to private consciousness, whereas personhood seems more amenable to thinking about how ideologies of the person situate people in

broader social contexts and moral expectations. Many of the elements of personhood I discuss, furthermore, do not refer directly to private states of consciousness, but consist of local (emic) ideological notions about the way people are or should be. These prevailing ideological differences influence consciousness but do not wholly determine it (cf. M. Jackson and Karp 1990).

9. It is worth noting some parallels, recognized by the Comaroffs themselves, between hegemony as just defined and two concepts elaborated by Bourdieu: "symbolic domination" and "habitus." According to Bourdieu (1991), symbolic domination is a social condition in which certain social groups exercise control over others by establishing their own cultural and linguistic values and standards as the norm, while others regard these standards as valid even though they may be unable to produce them. Those in subordinate groups, indeed, may intensely dislike the normative standards but remain beholden to them and position themselves relative to them. In some cases, however, those with less power wholly accept and take for granted the terms of the system of power that keeps them down, a condition with similarities to the Comaroffs' "hegemony." Bourdieu's notion of habitus, meanwhile, refers to culturally specific dispositions that govern ways of doing, speaking, seeing, thinking, and categorizing. In Bourdieu's rendering and that of his many interpreters, habitus tends to be naturalized, embodied, and taken for granted. However, the term does not overtly speak to power relations between classes or social groups in the way that the Comaroffs' definition of hegemony does.

10. Some historians, such as Martin (1973: 59), claim that Malindi had a "notorious reputation for brutal treatment of slaves," sometimes horrifying the missionaries who arrived in the late nineteenth century. However, many of these slaves were not Mijikenda but came from groups deeper in the hinterland. Mijikenda usually entered slavery not by violence but through arrangements such as the exchange of a family member for food in times of famine, and such individuals were sometimes assimilated as kin (Willis 1993). See chapter 1 for a more extensive discussion of the conditions of such slavery.

11. It is widely believed that the incumbent president Mwai Kibaki rigged the close election of 2007 in his favor. Both Kibaki, a Kikuyu, and the opposition leader Raila Odingo, a Luo, directly and indirectly encouraged political allegiance and tension along ethnic lines in the years leading up to the election. The announcement of Kibaki's victory in late December 2007 triggered a storm of politically motivated ethnic violence. By the time Kibaki and the opposition party established a power-sharing agreement in

spring 2008, at least a thousand people had perished and more than 250,000 individuals had been displaced.

12. Religious life in Malindi is still more diverse than suggested by this brief summary. Malindi is home not only to Mijikenda Traditionalism, Christianity, and the Sunni Islam of the Arabs and Swahili, but also to the Shi'a Islam of Bohra Muslims (most of whom are ethnically Indian), Hinduism, Sikhism, and Rastafarianism. The representatives of these religions, however, are few, and none of these religions enters significantly into the complex religious dialogue between Swahili-style Sunni Islam and Giriama Traditionalism that I detail.

Chapter 1. Origin Stories

1. Oathing is an idiom familiar to Mijikenda, used, for instance, in secret societies of elders (Brantley 1978), but the oathing ceremonies in the late 1990s deliberately echoed those used by Mau Mau rebels in the famous 1950s upcountry revolt that precipitated Kenya's independence. In so doing, the Mijikenda leaders of this small revolt drew upon the fact that Mau Mau had become an emblem of indigenous defiance in Kenya.

2. The meaning of this gender symbolism is tantalizing, if inchoate. Is the feminization of the Mijikenda in this origin story perhaps a reflection of the history of intermarriage between Arab men and African women? Might it set up an analogy—Arab is to Mijikenda as male is to female—reflecting any number of analogous hierarchies in domains such as social potency, wealth, or religion?

3. The sultan of Oman installed the Mazrui as governors of the coast in the eighteenth century, but the Mazrui lineage achieved independence from Oman when the Yuaarabi dynasty in Oman was replaced by the Busaidi. In 1837 the Busaidi took control of Mombasa from the Mazrui and established a seat in Zanzibar.

4. The term *Shirazi* evokes ancient Persian origins, but historians consider many claims to such ancestry to be mythical (Chittick 1965; Cooper 1980).

5. Morton (1990) has criticized Cooper and Glassman, deeming them apologists for coastal slavery. Yet in my reading the aim of these historians has not been to downplay the oppressive qualities of slavery, but to avoid oversimplification of its structures by acknowledging the complex forms of dependency it involved, as well as the ways slaves were able to subvert their masters.

6. These newcomers came from varied circumstances; some, for instance, were fleeing poverty and drought; others were offered by their kin as security for loans; still others were captives of war; and "a few—but probably

quite a few, in the early nineteenth century—were bought from coastal or other traders in return for commodities" (Willis and Miers 1997: 482).

7. For people of the hinterland, the refusal to engage in long-term wage labor was not simply a rational economic decision, but also a form of symbolic resistance against the tyranny of the clock (Cooper 1992).

8. The Swahili Twelve Tribes of Mombasa are organized into two confederations: the Three Tribes (Kilindini, Changamwe, and Tanganga) and the Nine Tribes (Mvita, Kilifi, Mtwapa, Jomvu, Pate, Faza, Shaka, Bajun, and Katwa or Somali). The Mazrui clan mediated between the Three and the Nine until their overthrow in 1837. In Mombasa the Three and the Nine Tribes sometimes face off in *lelemama*, a dance form of freeborn Swahili women that encourages expression and celebration while sometimes reproducing factions (Mirza and Strobel 1989: 12).

9. Clearly Africans played an active role in redefining their ethnic identities in the colonial era (see Glassman 2000). According to Cooper (1980: 159), many of those who claimed to be Swahili by the time of the 1924 census were "probably ex-slaves." In 1967 Prins drew on coastal censuses to demonstrate that the previous half-century showed an enormous rise in Arabs and a corresponding decline in Swahilis-Shirazis, a trend that can be accounted for only by a pattern of self-reclassification (xvii, 20–24; see also Fair 1998). Yet in mid-twentieth-century Kenya, when it became clear that the coastal strip would be integrated into the postindependence state, some Arabs began referring to themselves as Swahili to emphasize their putative African-ness and entitlement to belong (Parkin 1989: 161–62). While such jockeying indicates that a degree of ethnic fluidity perdured despite European colonial models of ethnic fixity, it seems that essentialist models of ethnicity were nevertheless on the rise. See, for instance, Glassman (2000) on the genesis of an essentialist "racial nationalism" in mid-twentieth-century Zanzibar among its African intellectuals.

10. Mboya's argument gained much of its credibility from the presumption that multiparty politics can slip easily into ethnic conflict and ethnically based civil war. Single-party elections, jealously guarded by Presidents Kenyatta and Moi, dominated until Kenya reverted to a multiparty state in December 1991. Nevertheless, even under the single-party system, antagonisms that arose were frequently couched in ethnic terms. The electorate appealed to political leaders whom Adar (1998) terms "ethnic kings," figures such as Kenyatta (a Kikuyu leader and Kenya's first president after independence), Moi (Kenya's next president, from the relatively small Kalenjin group), and Ronald Ngala (a Mijikenda minister), each of whom was often treated as the mouthpiece of an entire ethnic group.

11. According to A. M. Mazrui (1998: 9), a coastal attack against the Luo, the prominent upcountry ethnic group whose members supported the opposition, could help KANU drive opposition voters out of the district and thus engineer another parliamentary seat for KANU in the upcoming elections. The central government may also have been hoping to orchestrate a more general state of emergency so that the national elections, which threatened to tilt against KANU, could be postponed until its political position was more secure (51–52).

12. A. M. Mazrui points out the irony of the fact that almost all victims of the ensuing violence were members of the upcountry poor rather than wealthy upcountry businessmen or owners of tourist hotels. But, he notes wryly, "this is the tragedy and irony of any form of nationalism, where the enemy, 'the other,' is so inclusively defined that the super-exploiters escape unscathed, and the main victims become precisely those common folk with whom we have the greatest social and geographical proximity" (1997: 54).

13. Digo enthusiasm for the newly formed National Democratic Union (NADU), which they hoped might liberate them from "internal colonialism" (A. M. Mazrui 1997: 18), was crushed when NADU was denied registration in the early 1990s. The Islamic Party of Kenya was also denied registration on grounds that it violated the nation's secular principle, while its leader, Sheikh Balala, was forced to live in exile from 1995 to 1997.

14. The general idea of *majimbo* is that state power would be devolved horizontally into multiple substate sovereigns, each governed, more or less, by particular ethnic groups. But in the coastal territories, exactly who would be entitled to what? Will *majimbo* lead to "enough employment, greater freedom for us and a better life for our children," in the hopeful words of one Giriama man? Would "outsiders" need clearance to cross the coastal border and be required to pay a toll, as some coastal players hope? Would upcountry people be paid for their buildings and other developments on coastal land, then forced out by law, as some councilors on the coast have claimed? Models of *majimbo* thus range from the abstract and idealistic to the sometimes terrifyingly specific, as some provocateurs stipulate exactly how much each ethnic group should stand to gain or lose in the new order of things.

15. The Coastal Hinterland Scheme of 1947, for instance, was designed to develop water resources and increase productivity, but Giriama were forced to labor for this scheme under threat of arrest. Their employment conditions were appalling; workers were given five or six shillings for three months of labor. This was not enough to cover taxes, but food was in such short supply that selling crops was not a ready option. Many farmers had to

turn to trading and to nonfarm labor to supplement their meager incomes (S. G. Thompson 1990).

16. This speech was recorded by a research assistant in December 2002. The identity of the speaker will remain confidential.

17. Such a day was not soon to arrive; in the legislative elections of December 2002 the Shirikisho Party won 1 out of 212 elected seats, while KANU, although it was deposed from its position as the ruling party by the National Rainbow Coalition (NARC), won 64. In 2007 Shirikisho (which had recently joined with Kibaki's Party of National Unity) failed to clinch a single parliamentary seat.

18. Like the Shungwaya narratives, Kaya narratives are shaped and fortified by sociopolitical exigencies. Willis (1993: 38, 40) suggests that the Kaya could not have actually housed entire group populations, and that Kaya narratives today appear to justify and support the power of male elders during this era of continuing disputes over the "nature and extent" of their powers.

19. Several Kaya were named national monuments by the Kenyan government in the early 1990s, after Western ecologists pointed out how many unusual flora and fauna they sustain. This move has protected the forests' biodiversity while limiting human interaction with Kaya spaces.

20. Ironically, decades ago Swahili in Zanzibar sometimes demonstrated their social importance at weddings precisely by inviting their slaves and clients to attend (Chris Walley, personal communication, 28 January 2007). The decline of this kind of practice in Malindi (inviting ethnic underlings to weddings to index one's status) points to the rigidification of social boundaries between Swahili and Giriama.

21. The answer to the question, among scholars and Swahili themselves, of whether Swahili are essentially Arab or African has tended to vacillate depending on state actions, internal coastal dynamics, and economic exigencies (Askew 1999). On the one hand, colonial policies fetishized Arab blood; on the other hand, growing strains of nationalism have led many Swahili to argue that colonials, state officials, and scholars have dispossessed them of their Africanness for too long (Abdulaziz 1979; A. M. Mazrui and Shariff 1994). In Malindi many Swahili tout their Arab heritage as a badge of entitlement to Middle Eastern connections and a symbol of their proximity to Islam, yet when national or local politics threaten Swahili entitlement to belong in Kenya, their Africanness comes once again to the fore (cf. McIntosh 2001a; Parkin 1989). Some of my interlocutors deem themselves *both* Swahili and Arab, a formulation that allows them to maintain their socioeconomic ties with the Arab world and their entitlement to political

power and land in Africa. Significantly, when Giriama in Malindi use the term Arab as a stand-in for Swahili, it tends to have the rhetorical effect of underscoring the foreign roots of their more privileged neighbors.

These tensions between Arabness and Africanness extend to the domains of religiosity and language. In Malindi today many Swahili are leery of ritual practices such as spirit possession, which seem to them uncomfortably close to the pagan practices of their neighbors, a phenomenon I discuss in greater depth in chapters 3, 4, and 5. Meanwhile laypeople and scholars alike debate whether Kiswahili is essentially Arab or African, a politically constructed concern transposed upon the linguistic domain. Swahili nationalists sometimes claim that the language is so closely related to Kigiriama and its structure and vocabulary are so profoundly Bantu that, as Khalid (1977: 44) puts it, "no one would dream of associating it with Arabic." Yet many Swahili in Malindi and elsewhere tend to Arabize their Kiswahili, and play up the Arabic pronunciation of imported vocabulary words, as they index their piety and their alignment with the Arab world, a phenomenon I discuss in greater detail in chapter 5.

In Mombasa, the so-called Twelve Tribes have subdivided urban Swahili along the lines of their different origins. Swahili in other areas too sometimes self-identify in terms of ethnoregionalisms, such as Wabajuni (Bajuni, from the north), Waamu (those of Lamu extraction), Wamvita (those from Mombasa), or Shirazi (those with Shirazi roots). Many Swahili societies are striated along class lines, distinguishing between those with slave ancestry and those putatively without (the *waungwana*, who have historically tended to consider themselves more civilized), and between people's relative position along a spectrum from more Arab to more African. The Hadrami Sharif families, said to be descended from the Prophet, have in some communities been treated with an almost mystical respect, though, as will be seen in chapter 3, this status is challenged by some. Urban and rural distinctions are important as well; elite Swahili in Mombasa and Zanzibar town, for instance, cherish their kin ties and economic connections to the Middle East, while tending to consider impoverished Swahili in rural areas to be dirty, Africanized country folk rather than peers (see also Middleton 1992 on hierarchical distinctions between denizens of "stone" and "country" towns). However, as I note below, the distinctions made within Swahili society are rarely discussed by Giriama in Malindi, whose discourse about Swahili, being bound up with Giriama concerns about their own low status on the coast, often represents the group as a homogeneous urban elite.

22. See Glassman (2000) for examples of similar behavior among Zanzibari

intellectuals during the late colonial era, marking the rise of what he calls "racial nationalism."

23. I do not offer absolute numbers because these conversations were carried out not as part of a well-controlled study, but through varied social interactions over the span of many months. Many of these exchanges were striking enough that I wrote them up in my field notes; others simply reaffirmed the impression I already had. For that reason I cannot reconstruct exactly how many informants contributed to my clear understanding that Swahili opinions are divided, but the number of my Swahili interlocutors is at least seventy-five, and the number of Giriama I spoke to at least one hundred.

24. Swahili occasionally refer to would-be Giriama assimilates as Hajji, from the term *hajj*, the pilgrimage to Mecca. While morally benign, the classification also marks them as having come from the outside.

25. While Giriama frequently use terms for skin color ("black" and "white," typically), Kigiriama itself does not have an overarching word for "race"; the closest term is probably *ukabila*, which can mean "tribe" or "language group." Some Giriama, however, borrow the English words "race" and "racism."

26. Swahili and Arabs are sensitive about slavery in their ancestral past, and several informed me that Christian missionaries had largely invented this history to discredit Islam in the eyes of other Africans (certainly missionaries made much of it). One Swahili man in Mombasa was so incensed by what he considered the anti-Muslim slavery rhetoric among Mijikenda that he challenged me: "Those Mijikenda say we enslaved all their ancestors. I'll give you a million shillings if you can find just one whose ancestor was enslaved by ours, just one!"

27. Even those Giriama who are more or less assimilated into the life of the mosque or into Swahili households may be perceived by other Giriama as victims of the legacy of slavery. My research assistant Maxwell told me of a female friend of his who worked in a Swahili household and was told after she converted to Islam that she would no longer receive wages because she had become "part of the family." "This woman needs to be paid!" exclaimed Maxwell. "Her situation is like slavery all over again!"

Chapter 2. Blood Money in Motion

1. One concerned Swahili retiree in Shella gave me a lengthy written screed about a mysterious tenant of his, a blue-jeans-wearing Muslim woman whose louche and reckless behavior culminated in her young daughter's fatal overdose on intravenous drugs. In one passage the author complains about the

recently introduced "freedom of choice and self-determination" in urban Swahili society that allows "our girls [to] walk the streets scantily dressed or half naked while dazed with hard drugs" (Yusuf 2004: 3–4). While choice and free will are central to Swahili ideologies of conversion to Islam, as I discuss in chapter 3, religiously inflected ethical discourse precludes Swahili from idealizing freedom of choice in all domains of comportment.

2. Similarly, Masquelier (2001) describes folk perceptions of compatibility between Islam and a market economy among Mawri of Niger.

3. It is worth reflecting, of course, on why this non-Muslim ethnographer was freely allowed inside Swahili homes. In fact, the Giriama man's formulation was only partly true. From the perspective of many Swahili it is preferable that a Giriama be a Muslim to be comfortably allowed access into the interior of a Swahili home, in part because of the stigma associated with Giriama culture and Giriama poverty. But guests who have social capital, such as Western students, wealthy visitors, or those with otherwise re-spected status are likely to be shown hospitality irrespective of their re-ligious affiliation.

4. Bicycles are quintessentially masculine objects in Malindi; almost no women ride them, perhaps because of their potentially empowering quality of speed and their association with modernity. As in many cultures, Giriama women tend to be conceptualized and treated as embodiments of Giriama custom, if not Giriama backwardness, particularly because urban wage labor is male-dominated and families who can pay only for limited school fees tend to educate their boys first.

5. See Weiss (2002) for a detailed discussion of transnational fantasies among Tanzanian youth.

6. Brantley (1979: 117) claims that by the end of the nineteenth century "witchcraft-sorcery" was "considered the most prominent form of misfor-tune" among Giriama.

7. Because they are found in the Quran *jini* are widely known across the Muslim world. Their interpretation and significance, however, vary from place to place; hence I do not offer a survey of the cross-cultural literature on these spirits.

8. Some *jini* narratives make overt links between *jini* and the creative ways that Swahili ostensibly find to obtain Giriama land. One middle-aged Giriama man told me what happens if a *jini* possesses a Giriama individual: "The *jini* will demand a *kanzu* [white Muslim robe] and a *kofia* [white Muslim cap] which are not available in Giriama homes. So you'll be forced to go to a Swahili for such clothes. Once you reach them, they tell you those items are very expensive, and what you need to do is sell them a piece of land in order

to get the *kofia* and *kanzu*. If you fail to do that, you'll die. So they use the *jini* system to get our land."

9. Parkin too has described a spirit associated with accumulation among Miji-kenda in areas of the coastal strip south of Malindi. The spirit, called *katunusi*, desires a man or woman and may kill its victim by drinking his or her blood, in what Parkin (1991a: 202) suggests is "a manifestation . . . of loving and desiring to excess."

10. Smith (2001) has analyzed *jini* narratives among Wataita near the Kenyan coast. He reads *jini* as emblems of commodities from Mombasa, where some Wataita have both found work and been exposed to the *jini* as a signifier. Among Wataita *jini* are associated with women since recent politi-cal and economic developments have increasingly left the creation of con-sumer goods in female hands. Women are portrayed as sacrificing children to *jini* to garner commodities, the opposite of what they are supposed to do as women (namely, convert the commodities of [bride] wealth into chil-dren). For men, Smith suggests, anxieties about *jini* evidence their concern that women are seizing control of households and the local economy.

11. These portrayals are inflected by a distinctly coastal sexual politics. While male homosexuality is not a category indigenous to Giriama culture or language, effeminate gay males are deemed *shoga* among Swahili, and that category is widely known by Giriama living near Malindi. Swahili *shoga* sometimes walk in a limp-wristed fashion that young Giriama men in Ma-lindi enjoy poking fun of, both for its effeminacy and its connotations of ineffectualness.

12. Some Swahili express dismay that Giriama yoke *jini* so closely to Islam, as one madarasa teacher explained it to me: "It's the [Christian] missionaries who have spread a negative attitude about Muslims, telling Giriama that Islam is about *jini* rather than about religion."

Chapter 3. Toxic Bodies and Intentional Minds

1. In keeping with this value, nearly all the mosques in Malindi have (after years of debate) decided that Friday sermons delivered in Arabic, the lan-guage considered essentially linked to Islam, must also be translated into Kiswahili so that laypeople can understand their contents rather than being mystified by them. This populist argument is favored by Ahlul Sunna ad-herents and has apparently won out even in those mosques that do not officially align themselves with reformism.

2. Wahhabist movements across the Muslim world have been in existence for at least two hundred years, but they have meant many things to many people and must be understood with respect to local contexts and local

Islamic scholars' interpretations (Delong-bas 2004). Prominent proponents of reform on the Kenya coast include the scholars Sheikh al-Amin Mazrui (1891–1947), Sheikh Abdallah Saleh Farsy (1912–1982), and Sheikh Muhammed Kasim Mazrui (1912–1982).

3. I heard many Ahlul Sunna adherents, as well as those who do not overtly adhere to the movement but who pride themselves on their more modern, enlightened ways, complain about other Swahili appealing to Sharifs for supernatural assistance in anything from obtaining a lover to finding a lost key.

4. Sheikh al-Amin Mazrui, an early reformist, was the first to disseminate his critique of Swahili Muslim practices through printed pamphlets and newspapers; these, say the scholar Ahmed Idha Salim, were written to equip the layperson to make Islamic decisions "for himself" (1987: 167, quoted in Kresse 2003: 288).

5. It is not easy to tabulate what percentage of the population of various Swahili communities consider themselves reformist, though according to some Swahili I spoke to the numbers may approach nearly half of the Swahili population in Mombasa and are considerably lower in Lamu, which is the locus of the Sharif clans and the more ecstatic versions of Maulidi ritual. My informants estimate that Ahlul Sunna adherents in Malindi may number around 15 to 20 percent of the Swahili population and include members of activist groups such as the Tabligh, who attempt to enforce a more puritanical version of Islam in reaction to the cultural threats posed by tourism and drug use.

6. Some Muslim youth groups in Malindi (with no formal allegiance to Ahlul Sunna) distribute copies of several brochures that explain this ideology. One brochure, titled *Iman and Character*, explains the importance of keeping the link between beliefs and acts foremost in one's mind: "The *shahadah* is something that covers all of our lives; whether it is our prayers, our behavior in general, our sustenance, whatever the case might be, there is some relationship between that act and our belief in Islam. This fact must be ever present in our minds."

7. *Pace* Rosen, Mahmood (2001: 844) finds that for her informants, bodily actions are not so much a direct index of inner states as they are a "tool or developable means through which certain kinds of ethical and moral capacities are attained."

8. Tabligh Youth Group, "Concept of Worship in Islam" (n.d., in author's possession).

9. These certificates can prove particularly important when a convert wishes to be dealt with under Muslim law or to be buried in the Muslim graveyard.

Those who have lost their original certificate of confession and require it for legal purposes may complete an affidavit to secure their rights. (See Hirsch 1998 for a detailed discussion of the operation of sharia law in Malindi.)

10. Many Islamic texts in this didactic genre use quasi-scientific arguments that conspicuously discuss the "evidence" and the "facts" of the New Testament in order to discredit the idea that Jesus died on the cross and was resurrected. This move is typically made as part of a broader argument that Jesus was not actually divine (Bhutta 1987; Hassan 1975/1989). Another common mode of argumentation is to attack the Bible for being an unreliable and inconsistent source of data, in contrast to the Quran, which was conveyed directly to Mohammed from God and has been passed from generation to generation for over fourteen hundred years in the unblemished, original Arabic (Baagil 1984: 5). Other texts contend that the multiple translations and revisions of the Bible, combined with the authors' vagaries of memory and pagan leanings, have given rise to logical inconsistencies, such as the doctrine of the Trinity; says Joommal (1965/1992: 7), "To a rational mind, Trinity is an insult to God." Other claims in these texts include the following: that Jesus denied he was God in Luke 18:19–19 (Mohamed Ali and Matata n.d.: 6); that he never claimed in the Bible to be God (Baagil 1984: 23), or that if he did, "he meant he was God's son in the same sense as all human beings are His children" (Joommal 1965/1992: 15–16); that the miracles Jesus performed were also performed by Elisha, Elijah, Moses, and "false prophets" (Baagil 1984: 21–23); and that the New Testament and Jesus himself prophesied the arrival of the Prophet Mohammed, albeit without always mentioning him by name (Deedat n.d.). The texts also purport to find evidence in the Bible for the pillars and practices of Islam, including ablution, fasting, prostration in prayer, the *shahada*, and the demand for the pilgrimage to Mecca (Fundi and Mohamed Ali 1987). The controversial Gospel of Barnabas also circulates around the Kenya coast; this is touted as a lost or censored gospel that renounces Jesus's claim to be an heir of God, while heralding the birth of Mohammed (see O'Brien 1995).

11. In some Swahili villages, and in towns from time to time, more elaborate purifying rituals may be performed, such as *kafara*, the use of a food or a gift to absorb pollution in a house (the food or gift is then thrown into the sea or the bush). Another such ritual is *sadaka*, the use of an animal sacrifice to remove sickness sent by spirits. Such rituals vary from place to place and are not always accepted as part of Islam (see Middleton 1992: 180–81).

12. The further implications of his statement are also telling; the allusion to the telephone subtly aligns Giriama ritual with other technologies widely accepted as mysterious yet effective. At the same time, Phillip insinuates that

Swahili may gravitate toward technology such as the telephone not only because of its intrinsic utility, but also because it is associated with an ideologically fashionable wider world of development orchestrated by ethnic groups in faraway places.

13. Giles (1987: 240), whose work concentrated on Swahili communities, also found no strict consensus about the distinctions between these terms as they are used by either Giriama or Swahili. I did find, however, that in Malindi the term *pepo*, which is the only term with Bantu roots (all the others derive from Arabic), is associated more with Mijikenda terminology than Swahili, despite the fact that Giles found the term popular among Swahili in Mombasa, Zanzibar, and Pemba. This distinction may reflect the intensification of ethnic distance between Swahili and Giriama in Malindi. Another general pattern is that the term *sheitani* tends to have negative connotations and *rohani*, positive ones. *Rohani* is occasionally used by Giriama to designate a specifically Muslim spirit. And while Swahili in Malindi treat *jini* as a generic term for spirits, good or evil, Giriama in Malindi usually use it to refer to Muslim spirits or to the specific class of malevolent, money-gathering Muslim spirits.

14. Other ethnic groups who make appearances in Giriama spirit pantheons are Maasai, Luo, Somali, Kikuyu, and European. However, Arab and Muslim spirits feature more prominently than spirits from these other groups in Malindi and in the communities documented by Giles, S. G. Thompson, and Udvardy.

15. There is no noun in Giriama discourse that translates neatly to the English term "devil" except perhaps for the Quranic term for "the Devil," *Iblis*, which Swahili use only rarely. Sometimes Giriama narratives about *jini* spirits imply that they are deeply nefarious. The semantic field is clouded by the fact that Christians have tended to deem all indigenous and Muslim spirit beliefs "devil worship," so that Christians and individuals greatly influenced by Christianity sometimes use the generic Kigiriama and Kiswahili terms for "spirits" as synonymous with "devils."

16. Giles (1989a, 1989b) also documents Swahili uses of Mijikenda spirits, as I describe later in this chapter. In her conclusions she contends that alongside a hegemonic component there is a less obvious counterhegemonic element in these spirit complexes. As evidence she claims that Swahili symbolically recognize the "important contribution" Mijikenda have made to coastal history by including those spirits in their pantheon; that among Giriama the Swahili spirits operate "in conjunction" with indigenous spirits rather than sweeping them aside; and that "the representation of the Islamic spirits [among Giriama] remains rooted in Giriama spirit practice, including much

of the performance style" (1989b: 261). As my arguments in this chapter and the next suggest, however, I am not sure that the copresence of Islamic and Giriama spirits in Malindi should be considered a counterhegemony; indeed, I suggest that Giriama styles of interaction with Islamic spirits in Malindi reinforce hegemonic notions of Islam's superior potency and Giriama pollution to the forces of Islam. Furthermore I am not convinced that the Swahili recognition of Mijikenda spirits is counterhegemonic, given that Mijikenda spirits are recurrently denigrated as pagan (*kaffir*) and barbarous (*shenzi*) in the Swahili discourse Giles reports.

17. The image of "things rushing through my body" evokes the tropes of speed and flight that Giriama in Malindi so often associate with Muslims and Muslim spirits (see chapter 2).

18. It should be noted, however, that Giles (1989b: 255) reports having found "a few" Giriama diviners possessed by Muslim spirits who report praying five times a day.

19. See Parkin (1991a) for further discussion of the social geographical contrasts between zones inhabited by Giriama.

20. In fact, like me, Giles argues against the grain of Lewis's (1971) reading of spirit possession as a kind of therapeutic redress or protest against social marginality, though for very different reasons. I suggest that Lewis's approach does not neatly apply to Giriama forced converts because such individuals, while they may be socially subordinate, do not often exact redress or gain status in the way he predicts. Giles argues that Swahili possession cult activities do not constitute protests against exclusion because cult members cannot be typified as distressed or socially marginal to begin with.

21. As explained in note 15, Swahili generally describe Mijikenda spirits as pagan and barbaric. The spirits' requests of palm wine, and their hosts rebuffing of such requests, thus symbolically reaffirm Swahili disgust toward the cultural habits of this subordinate ethnic Other.

Chapter 4. Rethinking Syncretism

1. Numerous Giriama shrines dot the coastal landscape. Shrines are usually established in and around naturally occurring landmarks, such as coral rock caves or large baobab trees, both considered attractors of spirits. Occasionally some other unusual object or geographic marker will be turned into a shrine; a wooden shell of a boat, for instance, deserted decades ago on the shore south of Malindi, has been turned into a shrine for Muslim spirits in what seems to be an invocation of the historic link between Islamic culture and oceanic journeys. Shrines may harbor powers from the Giriama or the

Muslim side. It is noteworthy that the shrine I describe, the site of separation and hierarchy between forces said to be from the Giriama side and from the Muslim side, is several kilometers away from the town of Malindi, where ethnoreligious antagonisms are of daily salience to Giriama who circulate amid Swahili. Evidently the sense of ethnoreligious separation is present in at least some rural areas as well as in the urban site of Malindi. However, as we saw in the preceding chapter, one must not presume the dynamics of Giriama appropriations of Islam to be identical across all Giriama communities. I draw upon the example of this shrine because it provides an especially vivid example of the kind of ritual segregation of ethnoreligious forces that I saw in Malindi as well. Perhaps it is relevant that at least one of the three diviners who tends the shrine has several male relatives who work in Malindi and periodically return to their natal home in the hinterland, presumably bringing with them both wages and narratives about town life and Swahili.

2. *Hodi* is a Kiswahili greeting, used by those approaching a house or homestead to enquire if anyone is within, while announcing one's presence and hope of entry; it is typically greeted with the response *karibu*, "welcome." The Kigiriama equivalent of *hodi* is *enye*.

3. *Ptu* or *phu* is a spitting sound that sometimes opens and punctuates *aganga*'s ritual invocations. It indexically connects them to the earth, the site of the ancestors, while consecrating the space in which the ritual takes place as a site of healing or propitiation. *Salama salimini* is a typical invocation used to punctuate Giriama ritual. It might be translated literally as "Peace, peacefully." Ironically, the phrase has roots in the Arabic *salama* and is sometimes used in Swahili ritual, yet most of the Giriama *aganga* to whom I spoke disagreed that the invocation has anything to do with Arabic or Islam; indeed, some vociferously denied it. The invocation thus has its origins in the appropriation of the semiotic markers of Muslim peoples but has apparently become so stylized in Giriama ritual that it has lost its Islamic connotation.

4. Mbodze and Matseze are a mythic Giriama ancestral couple.

5. Baird suggests that such inconsistency and conflict is generally irrelevant to practitioners of such religious arrangements; it is, in other words, typically an etic (outsider's) rather than an emic (insider's) characterization. In the Giriama cases I describe, it is hard to say whether Giriama would themselves diagnose their rituals as conflictual. While they certainly regard the Giriama side and the Muslim side as disparate and (to some extent) representative of social tensions and hierarchy between Giriama and Swahili, and while their ontological commitments in the Muslim and Traditionalist portions of rituals (such as the one I describe below) sometimes appear to

contradict each other, Giriama themselves do not remark upon this apparent contradiction, presumably because they are not customarily preoccupied with an imperative notion of consistent and singular Truth in religion. In other words, although Giriama do not frame their ritual practice as whole, they do not seem perturbed by the possibility of ontological contradictions between the plural symbols they use. Whether Baird would see this as emic recognition of inconsistency, I am not sure.

6. One designation that has had some play in the academic literature is that of "dual religious systems" (see, for instance, Swain and Rose 1988), typically describing situations in which converts to Christianity continue to follow the practices of a second religious system while keeping the systems discrete. Yet this phrase is not an ideal alternative to the syncretism/antisyncretism dyad, both because of its history of use by Christian theologians to denigrate what are seen as "failures" of local theology (Schreiter 2004) and because it restricts the possibility of plural religiosity to binary practice (dual systems) when we can imagine the possibility of multiple religious systems in play. Spicer's (1954) term "compartmentalization" is better, but the term I favor, polyontologism, focuses attention on the radical challenge these systems pose to fundamental Abrahamic assumptions about unified ontologies and cosmologies in religion.

7. The position I call polyontologism has some similarities to henotheism, but is not identical to it. Henotheism generally refers to a condition within polytheism in which one god is treated as supreme and is worshipped, even though the existence of other gods is acknowledged. In some historical contexts of henotheism, ideological contradictions are rife. In Versnel's (1990) studies of henotheism in ancient Greek and Rome he usefully explores the fact that not all religious dissonances require resolution. Nevertheless, the concept of henotheism does not capture the religious dynamic among Giriama, for according to standard definitions of henotheism only one god is worshipped. Henotheism thus describes a kind of ontological tolerance, an admission of the possibility that other gods exist, but not the possibility of a pluralistic practice of propitiation or interaction.

The concept of polyontologism also has some similarities to the pluralistic phenomenon Herzfeld (1982) has termed "disemia": the coexistence of (and sometimes competition between) two different cultural and semiotic systems within the same society. Herzfeld's term is intended to encompass a breadth of social practices extending to such diverse corners as economic practice, linguistic diglossia, musical and architectural creativity, and social values. Polyontologism, of course, concerns the religious sphere and does not imply restriction to only two ontological systems.

8. In my view the pluralistic pattern of worship among Kaloleni Giriama that Parkin (1970) terms "syncretism" would be more aptly termed "poly-ontologism."

9. The *mwanza* societies include Mkulu, Habasi, Kinyeze, Fisi (individual members of the latter being known as Vaya), and Gohu, whose deceased members' graves are marked with the carved wooden memorial markers known as *vigango*.

10. Udvardy (1989) describes the intricacies of the *viraho* (sing., *kiraho*) charms as used by both male and female members of secret societies in the hinter-land area of Kaloleni in the mid-1980s. At least twelve objects, most of them shells or gourds, can be consecrated by ritual specialists and used for pur-poses such as the protection of land and crops from theft. The *viraho* are symbolically classified according to the kinds of illness they inflict upon their victims and according to both the gender of the ritual specialists who wield them and the gender of the charm itself.

11. The most well known of these societies is the Kifudu society, still spoken of in today's Malindi; it is associated with powers of fertility and largely responsible for the bawdy songs women sing during funerals (McIntosh 2005c; Parkin 1991a). Udvardy (1990: 223) contends that the Kifudu society played a legitimizing role in the juropolitical affairs of Giriama in the pre-colonial era but has lost its centrality as women's solidarity and power have been fragmented. S. G. Thompson (1990) also describes an earlier society known as Forudahe used by women to heal and purify the land and its people.

12. In recent decades *vigango* have been under siege of thievery sponsored by art dealers who have realized there is an international market for their exotic qualities. This is part of a broader illicit trade in cultural property (Udvardy, Giles, and Mitsanze 2003). The anthropologists Linda Giles and Monica Udvardy have been actively involved in the repatriation of *vigango*, which have turned up in the collections of several American universities.

13. Brantley (1981: 41) has argued that as the Mijikenda population dispersed from the Kaya, the rituals to induct senior males grew harder to coordinate and membership in the councils of elders has grown increasingly ambiguous.

14. One Anglo-Kenyan told me of supervising two Giriama teenagers as they dug a ditch on his property, and of his shock when he realized the wooden plank they were supporting themselves on was a *kigango* grave marker. He pointed it out to them and was equally surprised when they expressed relative indifference to this object that has customarily been an emblem of Giriama ethnic identity and continuity.

15. Social order among Giriama is customarily upheld through structured sexual behavior. Ritual sexual intercourse known as *mathumia*, for instance, is used to demarcate the life course, to stabilize the social order, to symbolically purify a homestead, to honor the ancestors, and so forth (Udvardy 1990). Sexual conduct within families is policed by mystical consequences as well. A mother who commits adultery, for instance, may bring the deadly *kirwa* illness upon her baby, while men who sleep with the wives of their male kin or otherwise symbolically defy sociosexual expectations can inadvertently cause their relatives to be struck down with the diarrheal illnesses *vithiyo* and *mavingane*. However, discourse and practice surrounding these beliefs and rites are inconsistent among young Giriama living in Malindi, particularly since the social structure that once enforced ritual sexual intercourse has been fractured so close to town.

16. The most popular *aganga* in Malindi today are spirit-medium diviners (*aganga a mburuga*) and healers (*aganga a kumbo* or *aganga a kuhundula*). *Mganga wa kumbo* is a general term for healer in Malindi; those specializing in *kuhundula* are experts in "untieing" or reversing witchcraft. There are, however, more fine-grained taxonomies to be found, as some *aganga* carry out highly specialized functions. *Aganga a kuvoyera* are diving and healing experts in witch finding, particularly important among many Giriama communities as economic development and new forms of competition bring with them accusations of witchcraft (*utsai*; cf. Ciekawy 1997, 1998). Udvardy (1990: 119) found that in the 1980s in Kaloleni healers were sometimes referred to as *aganga a kupiga madzi* (water-splashing healers). A *mganga wa kupiga madzi cha kiraho* (water-splashing medicinal medium) heals those who have fallen ill because of *viraho* charms. *Aganga a kupiga madzi cha kiraho cha kiche* are lesser herbal specialists, usually older women, who know how to reverse the spread of symptoms of those blighted by the magical *vifudu* pots, which contain a symbolically female force that can sicken humans unless the pots are ritually attended to (see, for instance, 150–52). *Aganga a pini* specialize in burying charms under a path to capture the witches passing over it (Parkin 1991a: 166). The list goes on, with specializations varying from one area to the next. The gendered division of labor varies as well, especially historically. While diviners in the Kaya era were reportedly mostly male, those in Magarini were by the 1980s almost entirely female (S. G. Thompson 1990: 97). In Malindi and at least some other areas these days, most diviners are women, while men dominate the profession of healing, which is a higher status vocation (it is said, for instance, that only men can withstand the potent black medicinal powder

used in many rites). Healing, furthermore, does not usually require possession, whereas divination in the Malindi area often does, and women are
thought particularly vulnerable to being taken over by spirits.

17. Other Giriama-style rituals involve drumming and dancing to appease spirits; mechanical traps devised by *aganga a kuhundula* that, when sprung by
the client, may release him or her from a curse; clay effigies (sometimes
called *jangamizi*) that, when they house an offending spirit, can be destroyed or thrown into the forest so as to eliminate the threat; head shaving
for purification; mock burial and rebirth to reverse witchcraft; and making
tiny razor cuts on the skin that are rubbed with ashy medicine to inoculate a
person against occult threats.

18. To my surprise, some of my interlocutors included within the Giriama side
the non-Muslim spirits from non-Giriama ethnic groups, such as the Maasai
spirit (Pepo Maasai) and the Kamba spirit (Pepo Mkamba). This conflation
suggests that for some, the category "the Giriama side" is an unmarked,
default category for entities that aren't Muslim, perhaps highlighting Islam
as both salient and metaphysically distant from Giriamaness.

19. I use the phrase *code shifting* to designate a shift from one language to
another, followed by a prolonged stretch of talk in the second, and the
phrase *code switching* to indicate rapid alternation between codes (Myers-
Scotton 1993: 46). The phrase *code choice* is an umbrella for both code
shifting and code switching. *Code choice* should not be taken to imply that
such choices are always conscious; often they are not.

20. As part of this project, some scholars have explored how the meanings of
code choices can emerge from the sequential development of codes in
particular conversational interactions (see, for instance, Auer 1984, 1998).
Relatedly, Johannes Fabian (1982) has attempted to resist "orderly" interpretations of code switching, noting the many improvisational, ironic, expressive, and other stylistic and poetic uses that emerge from the con-
textually grounded use of loan words. Other scholars have asserted that in
certain contexts the notion that code switching draws upon two or more
distinct codes is not viable because the overall code-switched speech is better modeled as "one code in its own right," in which switches are unmarked
and do not require a functional explanation, rather than as a "split object"
(Meeuwis and Blommaert 1998: 76; see also Alvarez-Cáccamo 1990).

21. In previous publications about Giriama code choice that I direct largely at a
linguistic anthropological audience, I use the popular phrase *language ideology* without attending to the Comaroffian hegemony-ideology distinction
(McIntosh 2005a, 2005b).

22. Christianity's universalism, unlike Islam's, extends to its treatment of lin-

guistic codes as transparent, interchangeable means of describing and performatively accessing True metaphysical power. Indeed, Christianity's very success across colonial contexts is partially owed to the countless translations of the Old and New Testament into numerous dialects. In Kenya church services led by Africans often take place in the local mother tongue. One American missionary explained why such practice is encouraged: "We think it is easier to reach their hearts through their own tongues." This linguistic practice has the additional effect of decoupling Christianity from one of the most obvious markers of ethnicity, giving it an ecumenical slant that has great appeal in Kenya and elsewhere.

23. A number of *aganga* I encountered subscribe to some degree to the notion that "like treats like," attempting thus to match the ethnoreligious source of a curse to an ethnoreligiously appropriate cure. Still, this mapping of cause onto treatment is rarely carried out in a wholly consistent fashion; even Kahindi attempts to counter the "witchcraft of *jini*" and the "witchcraft of Quranic prayers" in the Giriama portion of his ritual.

24. In fact, in some coastal areas where ethnic division is not such a sensitive issue, self-designated Swahili communities with closer ties to their Bantu roots propitiate ancestors and use the term "Mulungu" instead of "Mungu" (or the more respectful "Mwenyezi Mungu") for God. In Malindi, however, Swahili virtually never speak publically of ancestor propitiation, and "Mulungu" is more typically a term used by Giriama and other Mijikenda.

25. In Malindi and elsewhere one means of marginalizing spirit beliefs among Swahili has been to rhetorically feminize spirit possession. This move is facilitated by the fact that in most Swahili communities possessing spirits overwhelmingly favor women over men (McIntosh 1996; P. Caplan 1982, 1989), gravitating toward sweet perfumed smells and feminine beauty and preying on enticing women who walk alone or go out at night. Swahili women and girls describe frightening spirit encounters of their own; several schoolgirls told me of spirits that flit distractingly through their peripheral vision during class and physically harass them in their dormitory beds at night, sometimes by lying on top of them. This may be an extended metaphor for the sexual vulnerability they feel living away from home for the first time. The notion of spirits as sexual predators and seducers occasionally culminates in a woman's symbolic marriage with a spirit to placate it (Middleton 1992: 175).

26. See, for example, Alpers (1984), P. Caplan (1997), Giles (1987, 1995), Middleton (1992), Pouwels (1987), and Sperling (1995), as well as Lambek (1981, 1993) for comparison with Comoros Islands culture.

27. It is noteworthy that herbs used by Swahili *waganga* and *walimu wa kitabu*

tend to be imported from Arabia or India and purchased from stores in town, while Giriama herbalists collect theirs from the forest, a distinction that helps to distance Swahili from matters of the bush while reinscribing their alignment with commerce and faraway locales like Arabia.

Chapter 5. Divination and Madness

1. Although Swahili generally consider Arabic inherently yoked to Islam, this association has not always been paramount in Arab countries. According to Suleiman (1994: 3), Arab nations have long treated Arabic as "the core ingredient and the most prominent manifestation of nationalism" and an "eloquent symbol of group identity." Yet the conceptual link between language and nationalism was not always predicated on a link to Islam. In fact, the influential twentieth-century theorist of Arab nationalism Sati 'al-Husri rejected the notion that religion (along with geography, ethnic or racial purity, and a shared economic life) is a crucial element of nation. Rather, influenced by the German Romantics Herder and Fichte (and in an echo of other thinkers such as Renan), 'al-Husri contended that a common language and (in the words of Suleiman) a "common history, whose interaction in the life of the people creates a commonality of objectives and a vast store of shared feelings, hopes, and sentiments" are the crucial ingredients in Arab identity (11). Of these, language is central, for it creates and constitutes a reservoir of cultural and sentimental heritage. In 'al-Husri's formulation, any Arabic-speaking people are Arabs, regardless of their religion. The notion that Arabism could have primacy over the ties of Islam in an Arab nationalist movement held particular sway in the 1950s and 1960s, though it was increasingly displaced with the rise of Islamic movements in the 1970s.

2. These include Kimvita spoken in Mombasa, Kiamu spoken in Lamu, Chifundi spoken on the coast south of Mombasa, and several other dialects spread along the coast.

3. Some informants addressed these remarks specifically toward classical Quranic Arabic, but others alluded to Arabic more generally, including its spoken dialects.

4. Kai Kresse, personal communication, 17 March 1999.

5. The widespread gender divide in literacy that until very recently has held sway among Swahili has historically been reflected in many domains, including narrative genres in Kiswahili. Russell (1981) found that among Mombasa Swahili, Swahili men were more likely to relate *visa* (stories with a didactic function) and *hadithi* (stories or sayings transmitted by Mohammed), both of which arise in madarasa. Swahili women, on the other hand, were more

likely to relate *ngano*, short folk tales involving fanciful characters and spirits, without the pious edge of *visa* or *hadithi*.

6. Knowledge of the language may even figure into a woman's marital desirability among some Swahili these days. One Swahili owner of a hardware store greeted me upon my entrance and asked whether I spoke Kiswahili. When I answered in the affirmative, he asked whether I spoke Arabic. "Not really," I said, whereupon he turned to his clerk and remarked lightheartedly, "Pity she doesn't. If she had, I would have married her!" While this anecdote is surely not representative of typical Swahili flirting, it certainly points to the social desirability of facility in Arabic.

7. This emphasis on full literacy in Arabic may be influenced by both Western models of literacy and strains of Wahhabism (cf. Launay 1992: 92).

8. Lambek (1993: 3) discusses a related origin story in Muslim Mayotte, but that story is applied to *all* the books used by the *fundi* (Islamic experts) in that area.

9. Versions of this treatment can be found throughout the Muslim world; see, for instance, Bravmann (1983).

10. Pamphlet in author's possession.

11. The association between Swahili and the court system in Giriama imagination may be enhanced by the fact that Swahili in Malindi use separate Muslim kadhis' courts to adjudicate domestic matters such as divorce and inheritance (see Hirsch 1998).

12. This gesture could be interpreted as didactic, patronizing, obstructive, or all of the above. Certainly some Swahili wish to educate Giriama about Islam, while others feel deeply cynical about their essential ability (or lack thereof) to become good Muslims.

13. The predominance of female diviners among Giriama may be a relatively recent development, for sources suggest that in the Kaya era divination may have been numerically male dominated. The shift to female-dominated divination was imminent in Kaloleni (southwest of Malindi, inland of Mombasa) when Parkin (1970: 224) conducted fieldwork in the 1960s, and thoroughly in place in the Magarini area by the time of S. G. Thompson's (1990) research in the 1980s. At the time of my arrival in Malindi, only about one of every fifteen Giriama diviners there was male. I am not certain of the reason for this distribution, and it may be rationalized differently in different areas. Thompson found that in Magarini the possessing spirits themselves were often construed as feminine, sharing the supposedly "capricious emotional nature" of women (73). But in Malindi many possession spirits are Muslim and believed to be male. Furthermore, says Thompson, in Magarini spirit divination is "the most accessible means for women to gain power and

status in the customary sphere" (9), though, as she makes clear, their status and capacity to transform society is nevertheless limited. In Malindi informants explain the gender difference by saying that women are more vulnerable to the spirit possession that is currently a crucial component of Giriama divination. Healing or protective rituals, such as Kahindi's two-part ritual for Sidi described in the preceding chapter, remain male dominated, in part because women are believed to be too constitutionally weak to wield the potent black healing powders used in many of these rituals (a belief Thompson located in Magarini as well).

14. I have grouped these syllables into sound units based on their intonation and my intuition, based on my knowledge of languages spoken in the area. However, the units are not semantically meaningful.

15. Haluwa translates the spirit's words through collusion with her client, starting with general allusions to the client's frustrations and then, after the client ratifies these, formulating a more specific suggestion that the client has been bewitched by a jealous kinsman.

16. One Swahili man I played this for also remarked that certain sounds, such as *sadah* and *sahadi*, sounded "Somali-like" to him.

17. This conceptual weighting is characteristic of essentialist thinking in general (Gelman 1999; Hirschfeld 1996; Medin 1989). To essentialize is often to see past the obvious to the nonobvious, deeper qualities of an object, qualities that supposedly make the object what it is.

18. The procedure appears random, yet the results are treated as fateful; this is an instance of what DuBois (1993) terms "meaning without intention," a phenomenon that appears frequently in divinatory practices across cultures.

19. Malagasy diviners too use a quadrigram system brought from Arabia centuries ago (Verin and Rajaonarimanana 1991), but its resemblance to the Falak system is by now distant.

20. Swahili language use in divination draws on a more general epistemological architecture that reflects Swahili privacy and patriarchy. Men more than women pride themselves on their ability to memorize arcane sayings known as *jina* and to "speak indirectly" through riddles and circumlocutions, patterns sometimes known as Kiswahili *ndani* (literally, "inner Kiswahili"). Other domains of Swahili life too are characterized by a recurrent habitus—a spatial, linguistic, cognitive, and action-oriented pattern—that distinguishes between a public, outwardly accessible façade and a private, hidden inner life. The traditional Swahili home, for example, erects a plain exterior for the world's eyes, but contains a private courtyard where women are secluded and family life takes place. While these boundaries are increasingly contravened in contemporary life, they remain a kind of ideal type to some

Swahili, particularly elders. Female dress requires covering ankles, wrists, and the top of the head, while much Swahili poetry is about the mysteries and delights that women hide and men seek under their veils and within their hearts. We see here an ideological pattern in which women tend to be framed as ignorant of hidden secrets (or themselves constitute the secret) and men are couched as the agents who deftly access the obscure core of all matters. Swahili divination draws on and reinforces this division of epistemological labor, restricting deep access to Arabic's secrets primarily to men.

21. Like Wilce (2004: 414), I favor the term *madness* to *mental illness* because, as he puts it, "the latter term comes culturally shrink-wrapped in the perspective of biomedical psychiatry."

22. I also heard accounts of madness that had nothing to do with Muslim spirits. There is, for instance, the watchman who urinated at a Giriama shrine when he was drunk and was pounced on by unidentified powers that made him begin "running around," hallucinating that he was being chased by people wielding machetes. His cousin said, "[He was] talking in a funny language; I couldn't tell which." There is Wasii, a church-going Christian whose madness also began with paranoid delusions about being chased. She now sings Christian songs, in Kiswahili and Kigiriama, in a delirious fervor, entirely out of context. Nevertheless, many accounts of madness among Giriama in today's Malindi return to the theme of Islam or Arabic.

Epilogue

1. The *New York Times* journalist Jeffrey Gettleman wrote, "The election seems to have tapped into an atavistic vein of tribal tension that always lay beneath the surface in Kenya but until now had not provoked widespread mayhem" ("Disputed Vote Plunges Kenya into Bloodshed," *New York Times*, 31 December 2007).

2. "Third Name Fuels Kaya Leadership Row," *Daily Nation* (Nairobi), 5 April 2006, http://www.nation.co.ke/.

BIBLIOGRAPHY

Abdulaziz, Mohamed H. 1979. *Muyaka: 19th-century Swahili popular poetry.* Nairobi: Kenya Literature Bureau.

Adar, Korwa G. 1998. Ethnicity and ethnic kings: The enduring dual constraint in Kenya's multiethnic democratic electoral experiment. *Journal of the Third World Spectrum* 5: 71–96.

Ahearn, Laura M. 2001. *Invitations to love: Literacy, love letters, and social change in Nepal.* Ann Arbor: University of Michigan Press.

Al-Azmeh, Aziz. 1993. *Islams and modernities.* London: Verso.

Allen, James de Vere. 1993. *Swahili origins.* London: James Currey.

Alpers, Edward. 1984. "Ordinary household chores": Ritual and power in a nineteenth century Swahili women's spirit possession cult. *International Journal of African Historical Studies* 17: 677–702.

Althusser, Louis. 1971. *Lenin and philosophy and other essays.* London: New Left Books.

Alvarez-Cáccamo, Celso. 1990. Rethinking conversational code-switching: Codes, speech varieties, and contextualization. *Proceedings of the sixteenth annual meeting of the Berkeley Linguistics Society. General session and parasession on the legacy of Grice,* 3–16. Berkeley: Berkeley Linguistics Society.

Amory, Deborah. 1994. The politics of identity on Zanzibar. PhD diss., Stanford University.

Appadurai, Arjun. 1991. Global ethnoscapes: Notes and queries for a transnational anthropology. *Interventions: Anthropologies of the present,* ed. R. G. Fox, 191–210. Santa Fe, N.M.: School of American Research.

———. 1998. Dead certainty: Ethnic violence in the era of globalization. *Development and Change* 29: 905–25.

Apter, Andrew. 1991. Herskovits's heritage: Rethinking syncretism in the African diaspora. *Diaspora: A Journal of Transnational Studies* 1: 235–60.

Asad, Talal. 1986. The idea of an anthropology of Islam. *Occasional paper series.*

Washington: Georgetown University Center for Contemporary Arab Studies.

——. 1993. *Genealogies of religion: Discipline and reasons of power in Christianity and Islam.* Baltimore: Johns Hopkins University Press.

Askew, Kelly M. 1997. Performing the nation: Swahili musical performance and the production of Tanzanian national culture. PhD diss., Harvard University.

——. 1999. Female circles and male lines: Gender dynamics along the Swahili coast. *Africa Today* 46: 66–102.

——. 2002. *Performing the nation: Swahili music and cultural politics in Tanzania.* Chicago: University of Chicago Press.

Atran, Scott. 1990. *Cognitive foundations of natural history: Towards an anthropology of science.* New York: Cambridge University Press.

Auer, Peter. 1984. *Bilingual conversation.* Philadelphia: John Benjamin.

——. 1998. Introduction: Bilingual conversation revisited. *Code-switching in conversation: Language, interaction, and identity,* ed. Peter Auer, 1–24. New York: Routledge.

Auslander, Mark. 1993. "Open the wombs!" The symbolic politics of modern Ngoni witchfinding. *Modernity and its malcontents: Ritual and power in postcolonial Africa,* ed. Jean Comaroff and John Comaroff, 167–92. Chicago: University of Chicago Press.

Austin, John L. 1962. *How to do things with words.* Cambridge, Mass.: Harvard University Press.

Baagil, Hasan M. 1984. *Christian-Muslim dialogue.* Zanzibar: Al-Khayria Press.

Bähre, Erik. 2002. Witchcraft and the exchange of sex, blood, and money among Africans in Cape Town, South Africa. *Journal of Religion in Africa* 32: 300–334.

Baird, Robert. 1991. Syncretism and the history of religions. *Essays in the history of religions,* ed. Robert Baird, 59–71. New York: Peter Lang.

Bakari, Mohamed. 1995. The new 'Ulamaa in Kenya. *Islam in Kenya,* ed. Mohamed Bakari and Saad S. Yahya, 168–93. Nairobi: Mewa Publications.

Bakhtin, Mikhail M. 1981. *The dialogic imagination: Four essays.* Ed. Michael Holquist. Trans. Caryl Emerson and Michael Holquist. Austin: University of Texas Press.

Barth, Frederick. 1969. Introduction to *Ethnic groups and boundaries: The social organization of culture difference,* ed. Frederick Barth, 9–38. Boston: Little Brown.

Barton, David. 1991. The social nature of writing. *Writing in the community,* ed. David Barton and Roz Ivanic, 1–13. London: Sage.

Bastian, Misty. 1998. Fires, tricksters, and poisoned medicines: Popular culture of rumor in Onitsha, Nigeria and its markets. *Etnofoor* 11: 111–32.

Bastide, Roger. [1960] 1978. Problems of religious syncretism. *The African religions of Brazil: Toward a sociology of the interpenetration of civilizations*, trans. Helen Sebba, 260–84. London: Johns Hopkins University Press.

Battaglia, Deborah. 1990. *On the bones of the serpent: Person, memory, and mortality in Sabari Island society*. Chicago: University of Chicago Press.

Beckerleg, Susan. 1994a. Medical pluralism and Islam in Swahili communities in Kenya. *Medical Anthropology Quarterly* 8: 299–313.

———. 1994b. Watamu: Lost land but a new Swahili town. *Continuity and autonomy in Swahili communities: Inland influences and strategies of self-determination*, ed. David Parkin, 99–109. London: School of Oriental and African Studies.

———. 1995. Brown sugar or Friday prayers: Youth choices and community building in coastal Kenya. *African Affairs* 94: 23–38.

———. 2004. Modernity has been Swahilised: The case of Malindi. In *Swahili modernities: Culture, politics, and identity on the east coast of Africa*, ed. Pat Caplan and Farouk Topan, 19–35. Trenton, N.J.: African World Press.

Bell, David, and Gill Valentine. 1997. *Consuming geographies: We are where we eat*. London: Routledge.

Ben-Amos, Paula Girshick. 1994. The promise of greatness: Women and power in an Edo spirit possession cult. *Religion in Africa: Experience and expression*, ed. Thomas D. Blakley, Walter E. A. van Beek, and Dennis L. Thomson, 118–34. London: James Currey.

Benavides, Gustavo. 2004. Syncretism and legitimacy in Latin American religion. *Syncretism in religion: A reader*, ed. Anita Maria Leopold and Jeppe Sinding Jensen, 194–216. New York: Routledge.

Bennett, Norman. 1968. The Arab impact. *Zamani: A survey of east African history*, ed. Bethwell A. Ogot and J. A. Kieran, 216–37. Nairobi: East African Publishing House.

Besnier, Niko. 1995. *Literacy, emotion, and authority: Reading and writing on a Polynesian atoll*. New York: Cambridge University Press.

Bhabha, Homi K. 1994. *The location of culture*. London: Routledge.

Bhutta, A. R. 1987. *Was Jesus buried?* Nairobi: E. A. Ahmadiyya Muslim Mission.

Bloch, Maurice. 1968. Astrology and writing in Madagascar. *Literacy in traditional societies*, ed. Jack Goody, 277–97. Cambridge: Cambridge University Press.

Blom, Jan-Petter, and John J. Gumperz. 1972. Social meaning in structure: Code-switching in Norway. *Directions in sociolinguistics: An ethnography of communication*, ed. John J. Gumperz and Dell H. Hymes, 409–34. New York: Holt, Rinehart, Winston.

Boddy, Janice. 1989. *Wombs and alien spirits: Women, men, and the Zâr cult in northern Sudan.* Madison: University of Wisconsin Press.

——. 1994. Spirit possession revisited: Beyond instrumentality. *Annual Review of Anthropology* 23: 407–34.

Bohannan, Paul. 1959. The impact of money on an African subsistence economy. *Journal of Economic History* 19: 491–503.

——. 1995. Some principles of exchange and investment among the Tiv. *American Anthropologist* 57: 60–70.

Bourdieu, Pierre. 1977. *Outline of a theory of practice.* Trans. Richard Nice. Cambridge: Cambridge University Press.

——. 1984. *Distinction: A social critique of the judgment of taste.* Trans. Richard Nice. London: Routledge and Kegan Paul.

——. 1991. *Language and symbolic power.* Ed. John B. Thompson. Trans. Gino Raymond and Mathew Adamson. Cambridge, Mass.: Harvard University Press.

Brantley, Cynthia. 1978. Gerontocratic government age-sets in precolonial Giriama. *Africa: Journal of the International African Institute* 48: 248–64.

——. 1979. An historical perspective of the Giriama and witchcraft control. *Africa: Journal of the International African Institute* 49: 112–33.

——. 1981. *The Giriama and colonial resistance in Kenya, 1800–1920.* Berkeley: University of California Press.

Bravmann, René A. 1983. *African Islam.* Washington: Smithsonian Institution Press.

Brenner, Louis, ed. 1993a. *Muslim identity and social change in sub-Saharan Africa.* Bloomington: Indiana University Press.

——. 1993b. Constructing Muslim identities in Mali. *Muslim identity and social change in sub-Saharan Africa,* ed. Louis Brenner, 59–78. Bloomington: Indiana University Press.

Briggs, Charles. 1998. "You're a liar—you're just like a woman!" Constructing dominant ideologies of language in Warao men's gossip. *Language ideologies: Practice and theory,* ed. Bambi B. Schieffelin, Kathryn A. Woolard, and Paul V. Kroskrity, 229–55. New York: Oxford University Press.

Brown, Karen M. 1991. *Mama Lola: A Vodou priestess in Brooklyn.* Berkeley: University of California Press.

Brown, Linda K., and Kay Mussell, eds. 1984. *Ethnic and regional foodways in the United States: The performance of group identity.* Knoxville: University of Tennessee Press.

Burton, Richard. 1872. *Zanzibar: City, island, and coast.* Vol. 1. London: Tinsley Brothers.

Caplan, Lionel. 1995. Creole world, purist rhetoric. *Journal of the Royal Anthropological Institute* 1: 743–62.

Caplan, Pat. 1982. Gender, ideology, and modes of production on the east African coast. *From Zinj to Zanzibar*, ed. James de Vere Allen, 29–44. Wiesbaden: Franz Steiner Verlag.

———. 1989. Perceptions of gender stratification. *Africa: Journal of the International African Institute* 59: 196–208.

———. 1997. *African voices, African lives: Personal narratives from a Swahili village.* London: Routledge.

Caplan, Pat, and Farouk Topan, eds. 2004. *Swahili modernities: Culture, politics, and identity on the east coast of Africa.* Trenton, N.J.: African World Press.

Carotenuto, Matthew. 2006. *Riwruok E Teko*: Cultivating identity in colonial and postcolonial Kenya. *Africa Today* 53: 53–73.

Chabal, Patrick. 1996. The African crisis: Context and interpretation. *Postcolonial identities in Africa*, ed. Richard Werbner and Terence Ranger, 30–54. London: Zed Books.

Chittick, Neville. 1965. The "Shirazi" colonization of east Africa. *Journal of African History* 6: 275–94.

Chua, Amy. 2003. *World on fire: How exporting free market democracy breeds ethnic hatred and global instability.* New York: Random House.

Ciekawy, Diane M. 1997. Policing religious practice in contemporary coastal Kenya. *Political and Legal Anthropology Review* 20: 62–72.

———. 1998. Witchcraft and statecraft: Five technologies of power in colonial and postcolonial Kenya. *African Studies Review* 41: 119–41.

———. 2001. *Utsai* as ethical discourse: A critique of power from Mijikenda in coastal Kenya. *Witchcraft dialogues: Anthropological and philosophical exchanges*, ed. George C. Bond and Diane M. Ciekawy, 158–89. Athens: Ohio University Press.

Cohen, David William. 1994. *The combing of history.* Chicago: University of Chicago Press.

Comaroff, Jean. 1985. *Body of power, spirit of resistance: The culture and history of a South African people.* Chicago: University of Chicago Press.

Comaroff, Jean, and John L. Comaroff. 1987. The madman and the migrant: Work and labor in the historical consciousness of a South African people. *American Ethnologist* 14: 191–209.

———. 1991. *Of revelation and revolution: Christianity, colonialism, and consciousness in South Africa.* Vol. 1. Chicago: University of Chicago Press.

———. 1993. Introduction. *Modernity and its malcontents: Ritual and power in postcolonial Africa*, ed. Jean Comaroff and John Comaroff, xi–xxxvii. Chicago: University of Chicago Press.

Comaroff, John L., and Jean Comaroff. [1989] 1992. The colonization of consciousness. *Ethnography and the historical imagination,* ed. John L. Comaroff and Jean Comaroff, 235–63. Boulder, Colo.: Westview Press.

Constantin, Francois. 1989. Social stratification on the Kenya coast: From race to class? *Africa: Journal of the International African Institute* 59: 145–60.

Cooper, Frederick. 1977. *Plantation slavery on the east coast of Africa.* New Haven, Conn.: Yale University Press.

———. 1980. *From slaves to squatters: Plantation labor and agriculture in Zanzibar and coastal Kenya, 1890–1925.* New Haven, Conn.: Yale University Press.

———. 1981. Islam and cultural hegemony. *The ideology of slavery in Africa,* ed. Paul Lovejoy, 271–307. Beverly Hills, Calif.: Sage.

———. 1992. Colonizing time: Work rhythms and labor conflict in colonial Mombasa. *Colonialism and culture,* ed. Nicholas B. Dirks, 209–45. Ann Arbor: University of Michigan Press.

Coulmas, Florian. 1988. What is a national language good for? *Forked tongues: What are national languages good for?* ed. Florian Coulmas, 1–25. Singapore: Karoma.

Daniel, E. Valentine. 1984. *Fluid signs: Being a person the Tamil way.* Berkeley: University of California Press.

Deedat, Ahmed. n.d. *What the Bible says about Muhammed.* Nairobi: Jamia Mosque Committee.

Delong-bas, Natana. 2004. *Wahhabi Islam: From revival and reform to global Jihad.* Oxford: Oxford University Press.

Donley-Reid, Linda W. 1990. A structuring structure: The Swahili house. *Domestic architecture and the use of space: An interdisciplinary cross-cultural study,* ed. Susan Kent, 114–26. Cambridge: Cambridge University Press.

Douglas, Mary. 1966. *Purity and danger: An analysis of concepts of pollution and taboo.* New York: Praeger.

———. 1975. *Implicit meanings.* London: Routledge.

Dozier, Edward P. 1960. Differing reactions to religious contacts among North American Indian societies. Reprinted from *Akten des 34 Internationalen Americanisten Kongresses,* 161–71. Vienna: Verlag Ferdinand Berger.

DuBois, John W. 1993. Meaning without intention: Lessons from divination. *Responsibility and evidence in oral discourse,* ed. Jane H. Hill and Judith T. Irvine, 48–71. Cambridge: Cambridge University Press.

Dumont, Louis. 1985. A modified view of our origins: The Christian beginnings of modern individualism. *The category of the person,* ed. Michael Carrithers, Steven Collins, and Steven Lukes, 93–122. Cambridge: Cambridge University Press.

Eagleton, Terry, ed. 1994. *Ideology.* London: Longman.

Eastman, Carol M. 1971. Who are the Swahili? *Africa* 41: 228–36.

———. 1994. Swahili ethnicity: A myth becomes reality in Kenya. *Continuity and autonomy in Swahili communities: Inland influences and strategies of self-determination*, ed. David Parkin, 83–97. London: School of Oriental and African Studies.

El-Zein, Abdul Hamid M. 1977. Beyond ideology and theology: The search for the anthropology of Islam. *Annual Review of Anthropology* 6: 227–54.

Fabian, Johannes. 1982. Scratching the surface: Observations on the poetics of lexical borrowing in Shaba Swahili. *Anthropological Linguistics* 24: 14–15.

———. 1985. Religious pluralism: An ethnographic approach. *Theoretical explanations in African religion*, ed. Wim van Binsburgen and Matthew Schoeffeleers, 138–63. London: Routledge and Kegan Paul.

Fair, Laura. 1996. Identity, difference, and dance: Female initiation in Zanzibar, 1890–1930. *Frontiers* 17: 147–72.

———. 1998. Dressing up: Clothing, class, and gender in post-abolition Zanzibar. *Journal of African History* 39: 63–94.

Fanon, Franz. 1967. *Black skin, white masks*. New York: Grove Press.

Fardon, Richard, and Graham Furniss, eds. 1994. *African languages, development, and the state*. New York: Routledge.

Ferguson, James G. 2002. Of mimicry and membership: Africans and the "new world society." *Cultural Anthropology* 17: 551–69.

Foucault, Michel. 1995. *Discipline and punish: The birth of the prison*. Trans. Alan M. Sheridan. New York: Vintage Books.

Fried, Morton H. 1966. On the concepts of "tribe" and "tribal society." *Transactions of the New York Academy of Sciences* 28: 527–40.

Friedrich, Paul. 1979. *Language, context, and the imagination: Essays*. Ed. Anwar S. Dil. Stanford, Calif.: Stanford University Press.

Fundi, Ngariba Mussa, and Kawemba Mohamed Ali. 1987. *Islam in the Bible*. Zanzibar: Al-Khayria Press.

Gal, Susan. 1987. Codeswitching and consciousness in the European periphery. *American Ethnologist* 14: 637–53.

Geertz, Clifford. 1973a. Person, time, and conduct in Bali. *The interpretation of cultures*, ed. Clifford Geertz, 360–411. New York: Basic Books.

———. 1973b. Religion as a cultural system. *The interpretation of cultures*, ed. Clifford Geertz, 87–125. New York: Basic Books.

Gellner, Ernst. 1974. *Legitimation of belief*. Cambridge: Cambridge University Press.

Gelman, Susan A. 1999. Essentialism. *The MIT encyclopedia of the cognitive sciences*, ed. Robert A. Wilson and Frank C. Keil, 281–83. Cambridge, Mass.: MIT Press.

——. 2003. *The essential child: Origins of essentialism in everyday thought.* Oxford: Oxford University Press.

Geschiere, Peter. 1997. *The modernity of witchcraft: Politics and the occult in post-colonial Africa.* Charlottesville: University of Virginia Press.

Geschiere, Peter, and Francis Nyamnjoh. 2001. Capitalism and autochthony: The seesaw of mobility and belonging. *Millennial capitalism and the culture of neoliberalism,* ed. Jean Comaroff and John L. Comaroff, 159–90. Durham, N.C.: Duke University Press.

Giddens, Anthony. 1991. *Modernity and self-identity: Self and society in the late modern age.* Stanford, Calif.: Stanford University Press.

——. 1997. *Sociology.* London: Polity Press.

Giles, Linda L. 1987. Possession cults on the Swahili coast: A re-examination of theories of marginality. *Africa* 57: 234–58.

——. 1989a. Spirit possession on the Swahili Coast: Peripheral cults or primary texts? PhD diss., University of Texas at Austin.

——. 1989b. The dialectic of spirit production: A cross-cultural dialogue. *Mankind Quarterly* 39: 243–65.

——. 1995. Sociocultural change and spirit possession on the Swahili coast of east Africa. *Anthropological Quarterly* 68: 89–106.

——. 1999. Spirit possession and the symbolic construction of Swahili society. *Spirit possession, modernity and power in Africa,* ed. Heike Behrend and Ute Luig, 142–64. Madison: University of Wisconsin Press.

Gil-White, Francisco J. 2001. Are ethnic groups biological "species" to the human brain?: Essentialism in our cognition of some social categories. *Current Anthropology* 42: 515–54.

Glassman, Jonathon. 1995. *Feasts and riot: Revelry, rebellion, and popular consciousness on the Swahili coast, 1856–1888.* Portsmouth, N.H.: Heinemann.

——. 2000. Sorting out the tribes: The creation of racial identities in colonial Zanzibar's newspaper wars. *Journal of African History* 41: 395–428.

Goffman, Erving. 1974. *Frame analysis.* Cambridge, Mass.: Harvard University Press.

——. 1981. Footing. *Forms of talk,* ed. Erving Goffman, 124–59. Philadelphia: University of Pennsylvania Press.

Gramsci, Antonio. 1971. *Selections from the prison notebooks of Antonio Gramsci.* Ed. Quintin Hoare and Geoffrey N. Smith. New York: International Publishers.

Gumperz, John J. 1982. *Discourse strategies.* Cambridge: Cambridge University Press.

Gupta, Akhil, and James Ferguson. 1997a. Beyond "culture": Space, identity, and the politics of difference. *Culture, power, place: Explorations in critical anthropology,* ed. Akhil Gupta and James Ferguson, 33–51. Durham, N.C.: Duke University Press.

Gupta, Akhil, and James Ferguson, eds. 1997b. *Culture, power, place: Explorations in critical anthropology.* Durham, N.C.: Duke University Press.

Haeri, Niloofar. 2003. *Sacred language, ordinary people: Dilemmas of culture and politics in Egypt.* New York: Palgrave Macmillan.

Hall, Stuart, and Tony Jefferson. 1976. *Resistance through rituals: Youth subcultures in post-war Britain.* London: Hutchinson.

Harries, Patrick. 1988. The roots of ethnicity: Discourse and the politics of language construction in south-east Africa. *African Affairs* 87: 25–52.

———. 1989. Exclusion, classification and internal colonialism: The emergence of ethnicity among the Tsonga-speakers of South Africa. *The creation of tribalism in southern Africa,* ed. Leroy Vail, 82–117. London: James Currey.

Hashim, Abdulkadir. 2005. Muslim-state relations in Kenya after the referendum on the constitution. *African Association for the Study of Religions Bulletin* 24: 21–27.

Hassan, Mir Abulfath. [1975] 1989. *Jesus Christ was not crucified.* Trans. Mir Mahmood Haji. Arusha, Tanzania: Muslim Alert Network.

Heller, Monica. 1988. Introduction to *Codeswitching: Anthropological and sociolinguistic perspectives,* ed. Monica Heller, 1–24. New York: Mouton de Gruyter.

Helms, Mary. 1993. *Craft and the kingly ideal: Art, trade, and power.* Austin: University of Texas Press.

Herzfeld, Michael. 1982. Disemia. *Semiotics 1980,* ed. Michael Herzfeld and Margot Lenhart, 205–15. New York: Plenum Press.

Hirsch, Susan. 1998. *Pronouncing and persevering: Gender and the discourses of disputing in an African Islamic court.* Chicago: University of Chicago Press.

Hirschfeld, Lawrence A. 1996. *Race in the making: Cognition, culture, and the child's construction of human kinds.* Cambridge, Mass.: MIT Press.

Hirschkind, Charles. 2001. The ethics of listening: Cassette sermon audition in contemporary Cairo. *American Ethnologist* 28: 623–49.

Hocking, William E. 1956. *The coming world civilization.* New York: Harper and Brothers.

Holy, Ladislav. 1991. *Religion and custom in a Muslim society: The Berti of Sudan.* Cambridge: Cambridge University Press.

Human Rights Watch. 2002. *Playing with fire: Weapons proliferation, political violence, and human rights in Kenya.* New York: Human Rights Watch.

———. 2008. *Ballots to bullets: Organized political violence and Kenya's crisis of governance.* Report. http://www.hrw.org/.

Hutchinson, Sharon E. 1996. *Nuer dilemmas: Coping with money, war, and the state*. Berkeley: University of California Press.

Hymes, Dell. 1984. Linguistic problems in defining the concept of "tribe." *Language in use*, ed. John Baugh and Joel Sherzer, 23–48. Englewood Cliffs, N.J.: Prentice Hall.

Iliffe, John. 1979. *A modern history of Tanganyika*. Cambridge: Cambridge University Press.

Irvine, Judith T. 1982. The creation of identity in spirit mediumship and possession. *Semantic anthropology*, ed. David Parkin, 241–60. London: Academic Press.

———. 1989. When talk isn't cheap: Language and political economy. *American Ethnologist* 16: 248–67.

———. 1996. Shadow conversations: The indeterminacy of participant roles. *Natural histories of discourse*, ed. Michael Silverstein and Greg Urban, 131–59. Chicago: University of Chicago Press.

Irvine, Judith T., and Susan Gal. 2000. Language ideology and linguistic differentiation. *Regimes of language: Ideologies, polities, and identities*, ed. Paul Kroskrity, 35–83. Santa Fe, N.M.: School of American Research Press.

Jackson, Jean. 1974. Language identity of the Colombian Vaupes Indians. *Explorations in the ethnography of speaking*, ed. Richard Bauman and Joel Sherzer, 50–64. Cambridge: Cambridge University Press.

Jackson, Michael, and Ivan Karp, eds. 1990. *Personhood and agency: The experience of self and other in African cultures*. Washington: Smithsonian Institution Press.

Jacobson-Widding, Anita. 1990. The shadow as an expression of individuality in Congolese conceptions of personhood. *Personhood and agency: The experience of self and other in African cultures*, ed. Michael Jackson and Ivan Karp, 31–58. Washington: Smithsonian Institution Press.

Jaffe, Alexandra. 1999. *Ideologies in action: Language policies on Corsica*. New York: Mouton de Gruyter.

Joommal, A. S. K. [1965] 1992. *The riddle of Trinity and the sonship of Christ*. Mombasa: Bilal Muslim Mission of Kenya.

Kane, Ousmane. 2003. *Muslim modernity in postcolonial Nigeria: A study of the Society for the Removal of Innovation and Reinstatement of Tradition*. Leiden: Brill.

Kang, Yoonhee. 2006. "Staged" rituals and "veiled" spells: Multiple language ideologies and transformations in Petalangan verbal magic. *Journal of Linguistic Anthropology* 16: 1–22.

Kanyinga, Karuti. 1998. *Struggles of access to land: The "squatter question" in coastal Kenya*. Centre for Development Research Working Paper. Copenhagen: Centre for Development Research.

Keane, Webb. 1997a. From fetishism to sincerity: On agency, the speaking subject, and their historicity in the context of religious conversion. *Comparative Studies in Society and History* 39: 674–93.

———. 1997b. Religious language. *Annual Review of Anthropology* 26: 47–71.

———. 2007. *Christian moderns: Freedom and fetish in the mission encounter.* Berkeley: University of California Press.

Khalid, Abdallah. 1977. *A handbook for African nation-building.* Vol. 1, *The liberation of Swahili from European appropriation.* Nairobi: East African Literature Bureau.

Kirsch, Thomas G. 2004. Restaging the will to believe: Religious pluralism, anti-syncretism, and the problem of belief. *American Anthropologist* 106: 699–709.

Knappert, Jan. 1970. Social and moral concepts in Swahili Islamic literature. *Africa* 40 (2): 125–36.

———. 1971. Swahili religious terms. *Journal of Religion in Africa* 3: 67–80.

Kraemer, Hendrik. [1938] 2004. Syncretism. *The Christian message in a non-Christian world,* ed. Hendrik Kramer, 200–211. New York: Harper and Brothers.

Kresse, Kai. 2003. "Swahili enlightenment?" East African reformist discourse at the turning point: The example of Sheikh Muhammed Kasim Mazrui. *Journal of Religion in Africa* 33: 279–309.

Kritzeck, James, and William H. Lewis. 1969. Introduction to *Islam in Africa,* ed. James Kritzeck and William H. Lewis, 1–9. Toronto: Van Nostrand-Reinhold.

Kusimba, Chapurukha M. 1999. *The rise and fall of the Swahili states.* Thousand Oaks, Calif.: Alta Mira Press.

Lakoff, George, and Mark Johnson. 1980. *Metaphors we live by.* Chicago: University of Chicago Press.

Lamb, Sarah. 1997. The making and unmaking of persons: Notes on aging and gender in north India. *Ethos* 25: 279–302.

Lambek, Michael. 1981. *Human spirits: A cultural account of trance in Mayotte.* Cambridge: Cambridge University Press.

———. 1993. *Knowledge and practice in Mayotte: Local discourses of Islam, sorcery, and spirit possession.* Toronto: University of Toronto Press.

Lambek, Michael, and Andrew Strathern, eds. 1998. *Bodies and persons: Comparative perspectives from Africa and Melanesia.* Cambridge: Cambridge University Press.

Lan, David. 1985. *Guns and rain: Guerrillas and spirit mediums in Zimbabwe.* London: James Currey.

Launay, Robert. 1992. *Beyond the stream: Islam and society in a west African town.* Berkeley: University of California Press.

Leinhardt, Godfrey. 1985. African representations of self. *The category of the person: Anthropology, philosophy, history,* ed. Michael Carrithers, Steven Collins, and Steven Lukes, 141–55. Cambridge: Cambridge University Press.

Lienhardt, Peter. [1966] 1980. A controversy over Islamic custom in Kilwa Kivinge, Tanzania. *Islam in tropical Africa,* ed. I. M. Lewis, 289–300. 2nd ed. Bloomington: Indiana University Press.

Leopold, Anita M., and Jeppe S. Jensen. 2004. General introduction to *Syncretism in religion: A reader,* ed. Anita M. Leopold and Jeppe S. Jensen, 2–12. New York: Routledge.

LePage, Robert B., and Andrée Tabouret-Keller. 1985. *Acts of identity: Creole-based approaches to language and ethnicity.* Cambridge: Cambridge University Press.

Lewis, I. M. [1966] 1980. Islam and traditional belief and ritual. *Islam in tropical Africa,* ed. I. M. Lewis, 58–75. 2nd ed. Bloomington: Indiana University Press.

——. 1971. *Ecstatic religion: An anthropological study of spirit possession and shamanism.* Harmondsworth, England: Penguin Books.

Lonsdale, John. 1994. Moral ethnicity and political tribalism. *Inventions and boundaries: Historical and anthropological approaches to the study of ethnicity and nationalism,* ed. Preben Kaarsholm and Jan Hultin, 131–50. Roskilde, Denmark: International Development Studies.

Luhrmann, Tanya. 1989. *Persuasions of the witch's craft: Ritual magic in contemporary England.* Cambridge, Mass.: Harvard University Press.

MacGaffey, Wyatt. 1970. *Custom and government in the lower Congo.* Berkeley: University of California Press.

——. 1994. Kibanguism and the question of syncretism in Zaire. *Religion in Africa: Experience and expression,* ed. Thomas D. Blakely, Walter E. A. van Beek, and Dennis L. Thomson, 240–56. London: James Currey.

Mafeje, Archie. 1971. The ideology of tribalism. *Journal of Modern African Studies* 9: 253–61.

Mahmood, Saba. 2001. Rehearsed spontaneity and the conventionality of ritual: Disciplines of salât. *American Ethnologist* 28: 827–53.

Markus, Hazel R., and Shinobu Kitayama. 1991. Culture and the self: Implications for cognition, emotion, and motivation. *Psychological Review* 98: 224–53.

Martin, Esmond Bradley. 1973. *The history of Malindi: A geographical analysis of an east African coastal town from the Portuguese period to the present.* Nairobi: East African Literature Bureau.

Marx, Karl. [1867] 1967. *Capital.* Vol. 1. New York: International Publishers.

Masquelier, Adeline. 1999. "Money and serpents, their remedy is killing": The pathology of consumption in southern Niger. *Research in economic anthropology*, vol. 20, ed. Barry L. Isaac, 97–115. Stamford, Conn.: JAI Press.

———. 2001. *Prayer has spoiled everything: Possession, power, and identity in an Islamic town of Niger.* Durham, N.C.: Duke University Press.

———. 2002. Road mythographies: Space, mobility, and the historical imagination in postcolonial Niger. *American Ethnologist* 29: 829–56.

Mauss, Marcel. [1938] 1985. A category of the human mind: The notion of person; the notion of self. Trans. W. D. Halls. *The category of the person: Anthropology, philosophy, history*, ed. Michael Carrithers, Steven Collins, and Steven Lukes, 1–45. Cambridge: Cambridge University Press.

Mayr, Ernst. 1988. *Toward a new philosophy of biology: Observations of an evolutionist.* Cambridge, Mass.: Harvard University Press.

Mazrui, Alamin M. 1997. *Kayas of deprivation, kayas of blood: Violence, ethnicity, and the state in coastal Kenya.* Nairobi: Kenya Human Rights Commission.

———. 1998. *Kayas revisited: A post-election balance sheet.* Nairobi: Kenya Human Rights Commission.

Mazrui, Alamin M., and Ibrahim Noor Shariff. 1994. *The Swahili: Idiom and identity of an African people.* Trenton, N.J.: Africa World Press.

Mazrui, Ali A., and Alamin M. Mazrui. 1995. *Swahili state and society: The political economy of an African language.* Nairobi: East African Educational Publishers.

McIntosh, Janet. 1996. Professed disbelief and gender identity on the Kenya coast. *Gender and belief systems: Proceedings of the fourth Berkeley Women and Language Conference, April 19, 20, and 21, 1996*, ed. Natasha Warner, Jocelyn Ahlers, Leela Bilmes, Monica Oliver, Suzanne Wertheim, and Melinda Chen, 481–90. Berkeley: Berkeley Women and Language Group, University of California.

———. 1998. Symbolism, cognition, and political orders. *Science and Society* 62: 557–68.

———. 2001a. Strategic amnesia: Versions of Vasco da Gama on the Kenya coast. *Images of Africa: Stereotypes and realities*, ed. Daniel Mengara, 85–104. Lawrenceville, N.J.: Africa World Press.

———. 2001b. "Tradition" and threat: Women's obscenity in Giriama funerary rituals. *Gender in cross-cultural perspective*, ed. Caroline B. Brettell and Carolyn F. Sargent, 409–22. 3rd ed. Upper Saddle River, N.J.: Prentice-Hall.

———. 2002. Cracking codes and speaking in tongues: Language, gender, and power in two Kenyan divination rituals. *Gendered practices in language*, ed. Sarah Benor, Mary Rose, Devyani Sharma, Julie Sweetland, and Qing Zhang, 151–73. Stanford, Calif.: Center for the Study of Language and Information Publications.

——. 2004a. Maxwell's demons: Disenchantment in the field. *Anthropology and Humanism* 29: 63–77.

——. 2004b. Reluctant Muslims: Embodied hegemony and moral resistance in a Giriama spirit possession complex. *Journal of the Royal Anthropological Institute* 10: 91–112.

——. 2005a. Baptismal essentialisms: Giriama code choice and the reification of ethnoreligious boundaries. *Journal of Linguistic Anthropology* 15: 151–70.

——. 2005b. Language essentialism and social hierarchies among Giriama and Swahili. *Journal of Pragmatics* 37: 1919–44.

——. 2005c. Liminal desire: Sexually charged Giriama funerary ritual and unsettled participant frameworks. *Language and Communication* 25: 39–60.

——. Forthcoming. Elders and "frauds": Commodified expertise and politicized authenticity among Mijikenda. *Africa: The Journal of the International African Institute*.

Medin, Douglas L. 1989. Concepts and conceptual structure. *American Psychologist* 45: 1469–81.

Medin, Douglas L., and Andrew Ortony. 1989. Psychological essentialism. *Similarity and analogical reasoning*, ed. Stella Vosniadou and Andrew Ortony, 179–95. New York: Cambridge University Press.

Meeuwis, Michael, and Jan Blommaert. 1998. A monolectal view of code-switching: Layered code-switching among Zairians in Belgium. *Code-switching in conversation: Language, interaction, and identity*, ed. Peter Auer, 76–98. New York: Routledge.

Mehta, Uday Singh. 1999. *Liberalism and empire: A study in nineteenth-century British liberal thought*. Chicago: University of Chicago Press.

Messick, Brinkley. 1993. *The calligraphic state: Textual domination and history in a Muslim society*. Berkeley: University of California Press.

——. 2001. Indexing the self: Intent and expression in Islamic legal acts. *Islamic Law and Society* 8: 151–78.

Meyer, Birgit. 1992. "If you are a devil, you are a witch, and if you are a witch, you are a devil": The integration of "pagan" ideas into the conceptual universe of the Ewe Christians in Southeastern Ghana. *Journal of Religion in Africa* 22: 98–132.

——. 1995. "Delivered from the powers of darkness": Confessions of satanic riches in Christian Ghana. *Africa* 65: 228–56.

Meyer, Birgit, and Peter Geschiere. 1999. Introduction to *Globalization and identity: Dialectics of flow and closure*, ed. Birgit Meyer and Peter Geschiere, 1–15. Oxford: Blackwell.

Middleton, John. 1992. *The world of the Swahili: An African mercantile civilization*. New Haven, Conn.: Yale University Press.

Miers, Suzanne, and Igor Kopytoff, eds. 1977. *Slavery in Africa*. Madison: University of Wisconsin Press.

Mignolo, Walter. 2000. *Local histories/global designs: Coloniality, subaltern knowledges, and border thinking*. Princeton, N.J.: Princeton University Press.

Mills, Mary Beth. 1995. Attack of the widow ghosts: Gender, death and modernity in northeast Thailand. *Bewitching women, pious men: Gender and body politics in Southeast Asia*, ed. Aihwa Ong and Michael G. Peletz, 244–73. Berkeley: University of California Press.

Milroy, Lesley, and Pieter Muysken. 1995. Introduction: Code-switching and bilingualism research. *One speaker, two languages: Cross-disciplinary perspectives on code-switching*, ed. Lesley Milroy and Pieter Muysken, 1–14. Cambridge: Cambridge University Press.

Mirza, Sarah, and Margaret Strobel, eds. 1989. *Three Swahili women: Life histories from Mombasa, Kenya*. Bloomington: Indiana University Press.

Mkangi, Katama. 1995. The perception of Islam by the Mijikenda of Kenya coast. *Islam in Kenya: Proceedings of the National Seminar on Contemporary Islam in Kenya*, ed. Mohamed Bakari and Saad S. Yahya, 109–15. Nairobi: Mewa.

Mohamed Ali, Kawemba, and Othman Matata. n.d. *The Message of Jesus and Muhammed (P.B.U.H.) in the Bible*. Manuscript. Zanzibar: Al-Khayria Press.

Morton, Fred. 1990. *Children of Ham: Freed slaves and fugitive slaves on the Kenya coast, 1873–1907*. Boulder, Colo.: Westview Press.

Myers-Scotton, Carol. 1993. *Social motivations for codeswitching: Evidence from Africa*. Oxford: Clarendon Press.

Needham, Rodney. 1972. *Belief, language, and experience*. Chicago: University of Chicago Press.

Nemeroff, Carol, and Paul Rozin. 1994. The contagion concept in adult thinking in the United States: Transmission of germs and of interpersonal influence. *Ethos* 22: 158–86.

Niehaus, Isak. 2001. *Witchcraft, power, and politics: Exploring the occult in the South African Lowveld*. London: Pluto Press.

Noble, D. S. 1961. Demoniacal possession among the Giryama. *Man* 61: 50–62.

Obeyesekere, Gananath. 1977. Psychocultural exegesis of a case of spirit possession in Sri Lanka. *Case studies in spirit possession*, ed. Vincent Crapanzano and Vivian Garrison, 235–94. New York: Wiley.

O'Brien, Donal B. Cruise. 1995. Coping with the Christians: The Muslim predicament in Kenya. In *Religion and politics in east Africa: The period since independence,* ed. Holger Bernt Hansen and Michael Twaddle, 200–219. London: James Currey.

Ochs, Elinor, Tamar Kremer-Sadlik, Karen Gainer Sirota, and Olga Solomon. 2004. Autism and the social world: An anthropological perspective. *Discourse Studies* 6: 147–83.

Oded, Arye. 2000. *Islam and politics in Kenya.* Boulder, Colo.: Lynne Rienner.

Okondo, Peter H. 1995. *A commentary on the constitution of Kenya.* Nairobi: Phoenix.

Ong, Aihwa. 1987. *Spirits of resistance and capitalist discipline: Factory women in Malaysia.* Albany: State University of New York Press.

Parkin, David J. 1970. Politics of ritual syncretism: Islam among the non-Muslim Giriama of Kenya. *Africa: Journal of the International African Institute* 40: 217–33.

——. 1972. *Palms, wine, and witnesses: Public spirit and private gain in an African farming community.* San Francisco: Chandler.

——. 1985a. Being and selfhood among intermediary Swahili. *Swahili language and society,* ed. Joan Maw and David Parkin, 247–60. Vienna: Beitrage zur Afrikanistik.

——. 1985b. Entitling evil: Muslims and non-Muslims in coastal Kenya. *The anthropology of evil,* ed. David Parkin, 224–43. Oxford: Blackwell.

——. 1989. Swahili Mijikenda: Facing both ways in Kenya. *Africa* 59: 161–75.

——. 1991a. *Sacred void: Spatial images of work and ritual among the Giriama of Kenya.* Cambridge: Cambridge University Press.

——. 1991b. Simultaneity and sequencing in the oracular speech of Kenyan diviners. *African divination systems: Ways of knowing,* ed. Philip Peek, 173–89. Bloomington: Indiana University Press.

——. 1992. Ritual as spatial direction and bodily division. *Understanding rituals,* ed. Daniel de Coppet, 11–25. New York: Routledge.

——, ed. 1994a. *Continuity and autonomy in Swahili communities: Inland influences and strategies of self-determination.* London: School of Oriental and African Studies.

——. 1994b. Introduction to *Continuity and autonomy in Swahili communities: Inland influences and strategies of self-determination,* ed. David Parkin, 1–12. London: School of Oriental and African Studies.

——. 1994c. Language, government, and the play on purity and impurity: Arabic, Swahili, and the vernaculars in Kenya. *African languages, development, and the state,* ed. Richard Fardon and Graham Furniss, 227–45. New York: Routledge.

Parmentier, Richard. 1994. *Signs in society: Studies in semiotic anthropology*. Bloomington: Indiana University Press.

Parry, Jonathan, and Maurice Bloch, eds. 1989. *Money and the morality of exchange*. Cambridge: Cambridge University Press.

Peek, Philip. 1991. Introduction: The study of divination, present and past. *African divination systems: Ways of knowing*, ed. Philip Peek, 1–22. Bloomington: Indiana University Press.

Piot, Charles. 1999. *Remotely global: Village modernity in west Africa*. Chicago: University of Chicago Press.

Pouwels, Randall L. 1987. *Horn and crescent: Cultural change and traditional Islam on the east African coast, 800–1900*. Cambridge: Cambridge University Press.

Prins, Adriaan H. J. 1967. *The Swahili speaking peoples of Zanzibar and the east African coast*. London: International African Institute.

Pye, Michael. 2004. Syncretism and ambiguity. *Syncretism in religion: A reader*, ed. Anita M. Leopold and Jeppe S. Jensen, 59–67. New York: Routledge.

Ranger, Terence. 1989. Missionaries, migrants and the Manyika: The invention of ethnicity in Zimbabwe. *The creation of tribalism in southern Africa*, ed. Leroy Vail, 118–50. London: James Currey.

Rasmussen, Susan J. 1995. *Spirit possession and personhood among the Kel Ewey Tuareg*. Cambridge: Cambridge University Press.

Ribeiro, Branca Telles. 1994. *Coherence in psychotic discourse*. New York: Oxford University Press.

Rosaldo, Renato. 1989. *Culture and truth: The remaking of social analysis*. Boston: Beacon Press.

Rosander, Eva Evers, and David Westerlund, eds. 1997. *African Islam and Islam in Africa: Encounters between Sufis and Islamists*. Athens: Ohio University Press.

Rosen, Lawrence. 2002. *The culture of Islam: Changing aspects of contemporary Muslim life*. Chicago: University of Chicago Press.

Rosenthal, Judy. 1998. *Possession, ecstasy, and law in Ewe Voodoo*. Charlottesville: University of Virginia Press.

Rothbart, Myron, and Marjorie Taylor. 1992. Category labels and social reality: Do we view social categories as natural kinds? *Language, interaction, and social cognition*, ed. Gün R. Semin and Klaus Fiedler, 11–36. Newbury Park, Calif.: Sage.

Ruel, Malcolm. 1982. Christians as believers. *Religious organization and religious experience*, ed. John Davis, 9–31. London: Academic Press.

Rumsey, Alan. 1990. Wording, meaning, and linguistic ideology. *American Anthropologist* 92: 346–61.

Russell, Joan. 1981. *Communicative competence in a minority group: A sociolinguistic study of the Swahili-speaking community in the Old Town, Mombasa.* Leiden: E. J. Brill.

Ryan, Patrick J. 2000. African Muslim spirituality: The symbiotic tradition in west Africa. *African spirituality: Forms, meanings and expressions,* ed. Jacob K. Olupona, 284–304. New York: Crossroad Press.

Saleh, Mohamed Ahmed. 2004. "Going with the times": Conflicting Swahili norms and values today. *Swahili modernities: Culture, politics, and identity on the east coast of Africa,* ed. Pat Caplan and Farouk Topan, 145–55. Trenton, N.J.: African World Press.

Salim, Ahmed Idha. 1973. *The Swahili-speaking peoples of Kenya's coast, 1895– 1965.* Nairobi: East African Publishing House.

——. 1985. The elusive "Mswahili": Some reflections on his identity and culture. *Swahili language and society,* ed. Joan Maw and David J. Parkin, 215–27. Vienna: Beitrage zur Afrikanistik.

——. 1987. Sheikh al-Amin bin Ali Mazrui: Un reformiste moderne au Kenya. *Les voies de l'Islam en Afrique orientale,* ed. Francois Constantin, 59–71. Paris: Éditions Karthala.

Salvadori, Cynthia. 1983. *Through open doors: A view of Asian cultures in Kenya.* Nairobi: Kenway.

Scheper-Hughes, Nancy, and Margaret M. Lock. 1987. The mindful body: A prolegomenon to future work in medical anthropology. *Medical Anthropological Quarterly* 1: 6–41.

Schreiter, Robert J. 2004. *Constructing local theologies.* New York: Orbis Books.

Scollon, Suzanne. 2002. Political and somatic alignment: Habitus, ideology and social practice. *Critical discourse analysis: Theory and interdisciplinarity,* ed. Gilbert Weiss and Ruth Wodak, 167–98. New York: Palgrave Macmillan.

Scott, James. 1976. *The moral economy of the peasant: Rebellion and subsistence in Southeast Asia.* New Haven, Conn.: Yale University Press.

——. 1998. *Seeing like a state: How certain schemes to improve the human condition have failed.* New Haven, Conn.: Yale University Press.

Sharp, Lesley Alexandra. 1993. *The possessed and the dispossessed: Spirits, identity, and power in a Madagascar migrant town.* Berkeley: University of California Press.

Shaw, Rosalind. 1990. The invention of "African traditional religion." *Religion* 20: 339–53.

Shaw, Rosalind, and Charles Stewart. 1994. Introduction: Problematizing syncretism. *Syncretism/Anti-syncretism: The politics of religious synthesis,* ed. Charles Stewart and Rosalind Shaw, 1–26. London: Routledge.

Shipton, Parker. 1989. *Bitter money: Cultural economy and some African meanings of forbidden commodities*. Washington: American Anthropological Association.

Shweder, Richard, and Edmund Bourne. 1991. Does the concept of the person vary cross culturally? *Thinking through cultures: Expeditions in cultural psychology*, ed. Richard A. Shweder, 113–55. Cambridge, Mass.: Harvard University Press.

Silverstein, Michael. 1979. Language structure and linguistic ideology. *The elements: A parasession on linguistic units and levels*, ed. Paul R. Clyne, William F. Hanks, and Carol L. Hofbauer, 193–247. Chicago: Chicago Linguistic Society.

———. 2003. Indexical order and the dialectics of sociolinguistic life. *Language and Communication* 23 (3–4): 193–229.

Simmel, Georg. [1900] 1978. *The philosophy of money*. Trans. Tom Bottomore and David Frisby. London: Routledge and Kegan Paul.

Smith, James H. 1998. Njama's supper: The consumption and use of literary potency by Mau Mau insurgents in colonial Kenya. *Comparative Studies in Society and History* 40: 524–48.

———. 2001. Of spirit possession and structural adjustment programs: Government downsizing, education and their enchantments in neo-liberal Kenya. *Journal of Religion in Africa* 31: 427–56.

Southall, Aiden W. 1997. The illusion of tribe. *Perspectives on Africa: A reader in culture, history, and representation*, ed. Roy Richard Grinker and Christopher B. Steiner, 38–51. Oxford: Blackwell.

Spear, Thomas. 1978. *The Kaya complex: A history of the Mijikenda peoples of the Kenya coast to 1900*. Nairobi: Kenya Literature Bureau.

Sperling, David C. 1985. Islamization in the coastal region of Kenya to the end of the nineteenth century. *Hadith 8: Kenya in the nineteenth century*, ed. Bethwell A. Ogot, 33–82. Nairobi: Bookwise Limited and Anyange Press.

———. 1993. Rural madrasas of the southern Kenya coast, 1971–1992. *Muslim identity and social change in sub-Saharan Africa*, ed. Louis Brenner, 198–209. London: Hurst.

———. 1995. The frontiers of prophecy: Healing, the cosmos, and Islam on the east African coast in the nineteenth century. *Revealing prophets*, ed. David M. Anderson and Douglas H. Johnson, 83–101. London: James Currey.

Spicer, Edward H. 1954. Spanish-Indian acculturation in the Southwest. *American Anthropologist* 56: 663–78.

Spiro, Melford. 1993. Is the Western conception of the self "peculiar" within the context of world cultures? *Ethos* 21: 107–53.

Spivak, Gayatri C. 1990. *The post-colonial critic: Interviews, strategies, dialogues.* New York: Routledge.

Stewart, Charles. 1999. Syncretism and its synonyms: Reflections on cultural mixture. *Diacritics* 29: 40–62.

Stoler, Ann L. 1997. On political and psychological essentialisms. *Ethos* 25: 101–6.

Stoller, Paul. 1984. Horrific comedy: Cultural resistance and the Hauka movement in Niger. *Ethos* 12: 165–88.

——. 1994. Embodying colonial memories. *American Anthropologist* 96: 634–48.

Strandes, Justus. [1899] 1961. *The Portuguese period in East Africa.* Trans. J. F. Wallwork. Nairobi: East African Literature Bureau.

Strathern, Andrew. 1996. *Body thoughts.* Ann Arbor: University of Michigan Press.

Strathern, Marilyn. 1988. *The gender of the gift: The problems with women and the problems with society in Melanesia.* Berkeley: University of California Press.

——. 1992. *After nature: English kinship in the late twentieth century.* Cambridge: Cambridge University Press.

——. 1999. *Property, substance, and effect: Anthropological essays on persons and things.* London: Athlone Press.

Street, Brian. 1984. *Literacy in theory and practice.* Cambridge: Cambridge University Press.

Suleiman, Yasir. 1994. Nationalism and the Arabic language: A historical overview. *Arabic sociolinguistics: Issues and perspectives,* ed. Yasir Suleiman, 3–23. Richmond, Surrey, England: Curzon Press.

Sundkler, Bengt. 1948. *Bantu prophets in South Africa.* London: Oxford University Press.

Swain, Tony, and Deborah Bird Rose, eds. 1988. *Aboriginal Australians and Christian missions: Ethnographic and historical studies.* Bedford Park: Australian Association for the Study of Religions at the South Australian College of Advanced Education, Sturt Campus.

Swartz, Marc J. 1982. The isolation of men and the happiness of women: Sources and use of power in Swahili marital relationships. *Journal of Anthropological Research* 38: 26–44.

——. 1991. *The way the world is: Cultural processes and social relations among the Mombasa Swahili.* Berkeley: University of California Press.

Tambiah, Stanley J. 1968. The magical power of words. *Man* 3: 175–208.

Taussig, Michael. 1980. *The devil and commodity fetishism in South America.* Chapel Hill: University of North Carolina Press.

———. 1993. *Mimesis and alterity: A particular history of the senses*. New York: Routledge.

Taylor, Charles. 1989. *Sources of the self: The making of the modern identity*. Cambridge, Mass.: Harvard University Press.

Thompson, E. P. 1971. The moral economy of the English crowd in the eighteenth century. *Past and Present* 50: 76–136.

Thompson, Sally Gaye. 1990. *Speaking "truth" to power: Divination as a paradigm of facilitating change among Giriama in the Kenyan hinterland*. PhD diss., School of Oriental and African Studies, University of London.

Thornton, Michael C. 1996. Hidden agendas, identity theories, and multiracial people. *The multicultural experience: Racial borders as the new frontier*, ed. M. P. P. Root, 101–20. Thousand Oaks, Calif.: Sage.

Tooker, Deborah. 1992. Identity systems of Highland Burma: "Belief," Akha Zan, and a critique of interiorized notions of ethno-religious identity. *Man* 27: 799–819.

Udvardy, Monica L. 1989. The gender of magical medicines and malaise: The symbolism of protective charms among the Giriama of Kenya. *Culture, experience and pluralism: Essays on African ideas of illness and healing*, ed. Anita Jacobson-Widding and David Westerlund, 45–57. Uppsala, Sweden: University of Uppsala.

———. 1990. *Gender and the culture of fertility among the Giriama of Kenya*. PhD diss., University of Uppsala, Sweden.

———. 1995. The lifecourse of property and personhood: Provisional women and enduring men among the Giriama of Kenya. *Research in Economic Anthropology* 16: 325–48.

Udvardy, Monica L., Linda L. Giles, and John B. Mitsanze. 2003. The transatlantic trade in African ancestors: Mijikenda memorial statues (vigango) and the ethics of collecting and curating non-Western cultural property. *American Anthropologist* 105: 566–80.

Vail, Leroy. 1989. Introduction: Ethnicity in southern African history. *The creation of tribalism in southern Africa*, ed. Leroy Vail, 1–19. London: James Currey.

Van Binsbergen, Wim. 1994. Minority language, ethnicity and the state in two African situations: The Nkoya of Zambia and the Kalanga of Botswana. *African languages, development, and the state*, ed. Richard Fardon and Graham Furniss, 142–88. New York: Routledge.

Van den Berghe, Pierre L. 1984. Ethnic cuisine: Culture in nature. *Ethnic and Racial Studies* 7: 387–97.

Van Hoven, Eduard. 1996. Local tradition or Islamic precept? The notion of zakât in Wuli (Eastern Senegal). *Cahiers D'études Africaines* 144: 703–22.

Varisco, Daniel. 2005. *Islam obscured: The rhetoric of anthropological representation.* New York: Palgrave.

Verin, Pierre, and Narivelo Rajaonarimanana. 1991. Divination in Madagascar: The Antemoro case and the diffusion of divination. *African divination systems: Ways of knowing,* ed. Philip Peek, 53–68. Bloomington: Indiana University Press.

Versnel, Henk S. 1990. *Inconsistencies in Greek and Roman religion.* Vol. 1, *Ter Unus: Isis, Dionysis, Hermes: Three studies in Henotheism.* Leiden: Brill.

Vroom, Hendrik M. 1989. Syncretism and dialogue: A philosophical analysis. *Dialogue and syncretism: An interdisciplinary approach,* ed. Jerald D. Gort, Hendrik M. Vroom, Rein Fernhout, and Anton Wessels, 26–35. Grand Rapids, Mich.: Eerdmans.

Walley, Christine J. 2004. *Rough waters: Nature and development in an African marine park.* Princeton, N.J.: Princeton University Press.

Weismantel, Mary. 2001. *Cholas and pishtacos: Stories of race and sex in the Andes.* Chicago: University of Chicago Press.

Weiss, Brad. 1993. "Buying her grave": Money, movement, and AIDS in northwest Tanzania. *Africa* 63: 19–35.

———. 2002. Thug realism: Inhabiting fantasy in rural Tanzania. *Cultural Anthropology* 17: 93–128.

White, Luise. 2000. *Speaking with vampires: Rumor and history in colonial Africa.* Berkeley: University of California Press.

Whyte, Susan Reynolds. 1991. Knowledge and power in Nyole divination. *African divination systems: Ways of knowing,* ed. Philip Peek, 153–72. Bloomington: Indiana University Press.

Wilce, James M. 2004. Language in madness. *A companion to linguistic anthropology,* ed. Alessandro Duranti, 414–30. Oxford: Blackwell.

Williams, Raymond. 1977. *Marxism and literature.* Oxford: Oxford University Press.

Willis, Justin. 1993. *Mombasa, the Swahili, and the making of the Mijikenda.* Oxford: Clarendon Press.

———. 1998. Soured wine: The development and suppression of the palm wine economy, c. 1850–1960. *Kenya Past and Present* 30: 35–39.

———. 2002. *Potent brews: A social history of alcohol in east Africa, 1850–1999.* Kampala: Fountain.

Willis, Justin, and Suzanne Miers. 1997. Becoming a child of the house: Incorporation, authority and resistance in Giryama society. *Journal of African History* 38: 479–95.

Woolard, Kathryn A. 1998a. Introduction: Language ideology as a field of inquiry. *Language ideologies: Practice and theory*, ed. Bambi B. Schieffelin, Kathryn A. Woolard, and Paul V. Kroskrity, 3–47. New York: Oxford University Press.

———. 1998b. Simultaneity and bivalency as strategies in bilingualism. *Journal of Linguistic Anthropology* 8: 3–29.

Woolard, Kathryn A., and Bambi B. Scheiffelin. 1994. Language ideology. *Annual Review of Anthropology* 23: 55–82.

Yelvington, Kevin A. 1991. Ethnicity as practice? A comment on Bentley. *Comparative Studies in Society and History* 33: 158–68.

Yusuf, Yusuf Abubakar. 2004. "The smile death could not rob." Malindi, Kenya: Unpublished manuscript.

Zehner, Edwin. 2005. Orthodox hybridities: Anti-syncretism and localization in the evangelical Christianity of Thailand. *Anthropological Quarterly* 78: 585–617.

Zerubavel, Eviatar. 1991. *The fine line: Making distinctions in everyday life.* Chicago: University of Chicago Press.

Baird, Robert, 278n5

Bakhson family, 112–15, 199

Bakhtin, Mikhail, 221–22

Balala, Najib, 260–61

Balkanization, 47

Bantu, 269n21

baobab trees, 107, 216, 277n1

baraka, 182

Baya, Hawe, 2–3, 4, 206

Beckerleg, Susan, 175, 216

Benavides, Gustavo, 187–88

Bhabha, Homi, 26–27, 175

Bible, the, 275n10

bicycle taxis, 101, 272n4

bivalent terminology, xiii, 205–6, 212

Bloch, Maurice, 118

boda bodas, 101, 272n4

Boddy, Janice, 12, 164–66

Bohannan, Paul, 119

bori possession, 14

boundaries: ethnoreligious obstacles in, 9–16, 46–49, 264n6; fluid crossings of, 5–11, 15–16, 263nn3–4. *See also* ethnic essentialism; ethnoreligious essentialism; ethnoterritoriality

Bourdieu, Pierre, 21, 265n9

Brantley, Cynthia, 51, 280n13

Britain. *See* colonial control

British East African Company, 55. *See also* colonial control

bui bui, 150, 151

Burton, Richard, 230

Busaidi clan, 50, 266n2

bush Swahili, 74

charitable activities, 19, 95–96, 108, 170

Christians/Christianity: affective associations with, 194; domination of government by, 29–30, 60, 61; Giriama practices of, 3, 11–12, 32, 191–93, 207; Malindi's churches, 35–36; missionaries, 6, 36, 140; models of native culture of, 6; Muslim didactic texts on, 140–41, 275n10; on spirit (devil) worship, 275n14; syncretic practice of, 182, 194, 279n6; vernacular language use in, 228, 282n22

Ciekawy, Diane M., 110

civil war. *See* ethnic violence

clothing, 35; of madness, 253; as markers of Islam, 90, 97–98, 144, 150–52, 160–61; Western dress, 93, 150

Coastal Hinterland Scheme of 1947, 268n15

Coast Development Authority, 96–97

code choice, 282nn19–22, 283n23; indicating relationships with spirits, 207–13; indicating religious ontologies, 5, 7, 202–7; magical essentialism of language in, 223–29; "we" and "they" boundaries in, 206–7. *See also* language use

colonial control, 27–32; of African labor, 27–29, 55–56, 267n7; British protectorate, 50–51, 55–58; ethnic partitioning and stereotyping under, 9–10, 49, 55–58, 258, 267n9; of Giriama economic activities, 98–99; of Indian Ocean trade, 112; of land ownership, 62, 103, 107; rebellion of 1913–1914, 103

Comaroff, Jean, and John L.: on chain of consciousness, 24, 168–69; on essentialist models of ethnicity, 47–48; on hegemony and ideology, 21–24, 26, 122, 130, 203, 265n9, 282n21; on political community, 24; on spirit beliefs, 110; on spirit possession (Jean Comaroff), 164–65

Constantin, Francois, 51

conversion to Islam, 3–5, 127–75; agency and free will in, 142–43, 171–75; among coastal slaves, 54, 98, 148–49, 271n26; Arabic study for, 228; assimilation goals of, 70–71, 73–75, 78–79, 127–29; essentialist barriers to, 11–12, 48–49, 81–87, 130–31, 271n24; forced conversions by spirits, 90, 129–31, 154–75, 252–53, 276nn13–16, 277nn17–21; improvisational approaches to, 149–54; intention (*nia*) in, 138–42, 150, 274nn6–7; occupational conversions, 149, 151; personhood in, 129–30, 169–70; purity practices in, 143–48, 150, 275n11; signed confession (*shahada*) in, 138–39, 274nn6–7; spatial tropes of, 33–34; Swahili exclusion of Giriama converts, 151–54, 275n12; Swahili notions of religiosity, 131–48, 170–71; as therapeutic redress by marginalized communities, 164–67, 277n20; through intermarriage, 149, 150; use of didactic texts in, 139–41, 275n10. *See also* Muslim spirits

Cooper, Frederick: on coastal slavery, 29, 266n5, 267n9; on conversion, 148; on land ownership, 28–29; on permeability of coastal communities, 49, 56

coral rock caves, 216, 277n1

cosmopolitanism, 257–58

Deedat, Ahmed, 140, 275n10

diet, 15–16, 144–48, 150, 154–55, 168

Digo: ethnic clashes of 1997, 45, 59, 61, 268n13; Swahili identification of, 68, 127

dini ya kienyeji. See Traditionalism

disemia, 279n7

divinatory practitioners, 196–97, 233–49, 281n16, 282n17; agency of, 244–49; Arabic-laden possession, 222–29; forced conversions, 163–64; gender contexts of, 233–34, 284n5; impact of Arabic texts on, 229–33; socioeconomic status of, 164, 234; spirit-based literacy of, 234–45, 286nn17–20; spirit possession of, 156–57. *See also* spirit practices

DuBois, John W., 286n18

Dumont, Louis, 16–17

East Africa Company, 50, 55. *See also* colonial control

East African Muslim Welfare Society, 139

Eastman, Carol M., 9–10, 47, 68

economic contexts, 89–125, 261–62; of African labor, 27–29, 55–56, 267n7; of Giriama marginalization, 9–10, 27–34, 62, 83, 96–101, 268n15, 272nn3–4; of greedy *jini* narratives, 15, 41, 90–93, 110–20, 123, 272n8, 273n10; of individualism vs. interdependency, 19, 25–26, 98, 108, 116–17; of land ownership, 103–10; of money values in exchange, 118–19; of philanthropy, 19, 95–96; of squatting, 28–29, 55–56, 62, 89, 99, 103–4; of Swahili dominance, 90–96, 271n1; of travel

economic contexts (*continued*)
and mobility, 91–95, 101–6, 111; of
women's options, 93–94, 100
elections: of 1997, 39–40, 45–46, 59–
60, 267n10, 268nn11–13; of 2002,
269n17; of 2007, 31, 58–59, 257,
265n11, 287n1
El Niño, 30, 100
English language, 37
essentialism. *See* ethnic essentialism;
ethnoreligious essentialism
essentialization, 286n17
ethnic essentialism, 6–12, 257–62;
colonial versions of, 9–10, 31, 49,
55–58, 258, 264n6; definition of, 10,
264nn5–7; of dietary practices,
144–48, 154–55; Giriama notions
of, 75–87; in *jini* narratives, 119–22;
linguistic markers of, 72–73, 80; in
origin narratives, 46–49; racial
tropes of, 83–86, 152–53, 267n9,
271n25; social logic of civil war in,
258–59; in Swahilis' fixed identity,
67–75, 269n21, 270n22, 271nn23–
24. *See also jini* narratives
ethnic violence, 39–40, 45–46, 59–63,
257–62, 267n10, 268nn11–13
ethnoreligious essentialism, 151–54,
183; in barriers to conversion, 11–
12, 48–49, 81–87, 130–31, 271n24;
in ethnic violence of 2007–2008,
259–62; in *jini* narratives, 121–22;
linguistic markers of, 183, 201–14;
in notions of personhood, 129–30,
169–70, 177–78, 183–84, 254; in
perceptions of Islam, 3–5, 9–16, 21,
25–26, 82–87, 271n24. *See also* conversion to Islam; religious practices
ethnoterritoriality, 7–8, 43, 147–48;
colonial origins of, 9–10, 49, 267n9;

majimboism of post-independence
era, 58–67, 257, 260, 262, 267n10,
268nn11–15, 269nn16–20
Europeans. *See* whites

Fabian, Johannes, 282n20
Falak, the, 190, 217, 219, 229–33, 241–
48
Farsy, Sheikh Abdallah Saleh, 273n2
female circumcision, 260
Ferguson, James G., 253
field work, 38–40, 55–56, 271n23
fluidity of boundary crossings, 5–11,
15–16, 263nn3–4; essentialist contradictions to, 46–49; fethishiza-
tion of, 7–8; obstacles to, 8, 10–11;
through kinship ties, 10–11. *See also*
syncretic practices
folk essentialism, 10, 264n5
food, 15–16, 144–48, 150, 154–55, 168
forced conversions. *See* conversion to
Islam; Muslim spirits
Foucault, Michel, 21–22, 167–69
fractal recursivity, 33
free will. *See* agency and free will

Gal, Susan, 33
Gama, Vasco da, 27, 83, 112
Geertz, Clifford, 187
Gelman, Susan A., 10
Gescheire, Peter, 110, 257–58
Gettleman, Jeffrey, 287n1
Giddens, Anthony, 17, 22–23
Giles, Linda L.: on conversion to
Islam, 164, 177n20; on Mijikenda
spirits, 275n16; on Muslim spirits,
133, 157, 174–75, 275n13, 275n16,
277n18; on spirit helpers, 198; on
vigango posts, 280n12
Giriama communities: agency and

interiority in, 19–21, 25–26, 109–10, 129–30, 188, 244–45; ancestors and elders of, 195–97, 260–62; assimilation hopes in, 3–4, 8–10, 67, 78–79, 127–29, 271n24; burial practices in, 46, 146–47, 161, 168; consilient syncretism in, 191–94; economic marginalization of, 9–10, 27–29, 33–34, 62, 83, 96–101, 268n15, 272nn3–4; election of 2007, 260–62; entrepreneurship in, 99–100; essentialist thinking in, 46–49, 69–70, 75–87; hegemonic capitulation of, 23–24; interdependence and reciprocity in, 18, 19, 25–26, 32, 98, 108–9, 116–17; Islamic practices in, 11–12, 14–16, 129–30, 137; land rights in, 65, 103–10; language use in, xiii, 2, 5, 15, 20–21, 37–38; limited mobility of, 101–6; literacy in, 231–32; *majimbo*ism in, 43, 45–46, 60–67, 262, 266n1; origin narratives of, 46–49, 61, 64–66, 75–76, 266n2, 269nn18–19; religious self-categorization in, 194–95; ritual purity in, 143–45; shifting religious affiliations of, 3–6, 11–12, 14–16, 20, 32, 149–50; slavery experiences in, 53–55, 83–85, 100–101, 152–54, 170, 266nn5–6, 271n27; socio-sexual conduct in, 196, 281n15; squatting in, 28–29, 55–56, 62, 89, 99, 103–4; trade activities of, 52, 62, 98–99; traditional permeability of, 49–58

Glassman, Jonathan, 49, 266n5, 267n9

globalization, 257–58

Gramsci, Antonio, 21–22

Gumperz, John J., 206

habitus, 265n9

Hadith, the, 132–33, 284n5

Hadrami Sharif families, 269n21

Halali Sunna. *See* Ahlul Sunna movement

Hauka spirits, 165–66

healers. *See* divinatory practitioners; spirit practices

hegemonic understandings, 9, 21–27; chain of consciousness in, 24, 168–69; of code valences, 203–4; definitions of, 21–23, 265n9; ideology vs., 22–25; of naturalized social formations, 121–22; of personhood, 25–26, 169–70, 177–78, 222; in shared political communities, 24–25; of spirit possession, 130–31, 155, 167–70, 276n15

Helms, Mary, 228

henotheism, 279n7

Heri, Bwana, 53

heroin addiction, 218

Herzfeld, Michael, 279n7

high spirits, 8, 163, 181, 189–90, 198–99

Hirschkind, Charles, 137–38

homosexuality, 273n11

Human Rights Watch, 258

Hutchinson, Sharon E., 118, 119

hybridity. *See* fluidity of boundary crossings; syncretic practices

identity. *See* ethnic essentialism

ideological understandings: hegemonic understandings vs., 22–25; language ideology, 203–4, 282n21; of spirit possession, 130–31, 155, 167–69

Imperial British East African Company, 50, 55. *See also* colonial control

individualism, 16–20, 25–26, 108, 116–17. *See also* personhood

intermarriage, 49–50, 68–70, 74, 78, 149–50

Irvine, Judith T., 33

Islam, xiii, 12–16, 31–32, 131–48, 261–62; *baraka* in, 182; burial practices in, 274n9; charity and almsgiving in, 19, 95–96, 108, 170; dietary practices in, 144–48, 150, 154–55, 168; economic activities in, 95, 272n2; ethnic frame of, 3–5, 9–16, 21, 25–26, 82–87, 130–31, 271n24; the Falak (geomancy text), 190, 217, 219, 229–33, 241–48; free will in, 142–43, 171–75; Giriama practices of, 11–12, 14–16, 129–30, 137; the Hadith, 132–33, 284n5; the *hajj* pilgrimage, 93, 271n24; individualism in, 18, 19–20, 129; intention (*nia*) in, 136–42, 274nn6–7; language use in, 205–6, 284n1; local imaginings of, 12–13, 133; Malindi's mosques, 35–36; Maulidi celebrations, 133, 134, 274n5; proscription of syncretic practices by, 184; purity practices in, 143–48, 157–59, 275n11; Ramadan, 128, 144, 159; spirit practices in, 13, 15, 133, 172–73, 241–44, 272n7; traditional permeability of, 6–7, 12–13, 79, 98; Wahhabist reform movements in, 13, 133–35, 216–18, 273n2, 274nn3–5. *See also* Arabic language; conversion to Islam; *jini* narratives; power of Islam; the Quran; Swahili communities; syncretic practices

Islamic Party of Kenya (IPK), 29–30, 39, 63, 268n13

Jacobson-Widding, Anita, 255

jini narratives, 15; about whites, 123; of Bakhson family practices, 112–15; economic roles of, 41, 90–91, 110–20, 123, 261–62, 272n7, 273n10, 275n13; ethnoreligious boundaries in, 121–22; human victims in, 115–17, 273nn9–10; Islamic origins of, 216, 272n7, 273n12; productions of identity in, 119–22; sexual politics in, 120, 273n11; speed and mobility in, 91–93, 111–15, 117, 119, 277n17; in Swahili communities, 122–25, 273n12

jini spirits, 155, 198, 215–16

Joommal, A.S.K., 140–41, 275n10

Kalenjin, 59, 260

kanzu, 144, 150, 161

Katsumba Kazi, 181, 189–90, 198

Kaya: ancestors and elders of, 195–97, 260–62; compounds of, 65, 104–5, 260–62; origin stories of, 64–66, 75–76, 269nn18–19; spirit practices of, 195–97, 280nn9–14, 281n15, 284n5

Kaya Advisory Council, 261

Keane, Webb, 17–18

Kenya: Al Qaeda-sponsored terrorism in, 29–30, 39, 100; Christian domination of, 29–30, 32, 60, 61; elections of 1997, 39–40, 45–46, 59–60, 267n10, 268nn11–13; elections of 2002, 269n17; elections of 2007, 31, 58–59, 257–62, 265n11, 287n1; ethnic violence in, 39–40, 43, 45–46, 59–63, 257–62; ethnoterritorial divisions of, 59–67; Mau Mau rebellion, 234–44, 266n1; official languages of, 37. *See also* colonial control; post-independence era

Kenya African National Union
(KANU), 29–30, 59, 268n11, 269n17
Kenyatta, Jomo, 105–6, 113, 267n10
Khalid, Abdallah, 269n21
Kibaki, Mwai, 59, 257–58, 262, 265n11
Kifudu society, 280n11
kigango posts, 195–96, 280n12, 280n14
Kigiriama, xiii; as marker of ethnic
    identity, 38, 204–5, 269n21; ritual
    uses of, 202
Kikuyu: ethnic violence among, 58–
    59, 257–62, 265n11; *majimbo*ism of,
    65; managerial roles of, 30; Mau
    Mau rebellion and, 234–44
kin ties, 10–11
Kipepo, 236
Kiswahili, xiii, 5, 37, 204–5; Arabic cog-
    nates in, 205–6; daily use of, 212;
    Giriami ritual use of, 8, 15, 178–84,
    202, 206; local variants of, 68, 72; as
    marker of ethnic identity, 72–73,
    269n21; mixing of Arabic with, 225–
    26; multivalence of, 193; in Muslim
    worship and study, 132–33, 227,
    273n1; private forms of, 73, 286n20
Kiswahili *ndani,* 73
kofia, 97–98, 150, 152, 161
Kraemer, Hendrik, 186, 191
Kresse, Kai, 133–34

Lamu, 133, 217
Lan, David, 164–65
land: Giriama property rights, 65,
    103–10; grabbing, 103–4, 112–14;
    Kaya compounds, 65, 104–5; real
    estate values, 104; squatting, 28–
    29, 55–56, 62, 89, 99, 103–4, 107;
    white ownership of, 106–7. *See also*
    ethnoterritoriality; spa-
    tiality/spatial relations

language ideology, 203–4, 282n21
language use, xiii, 37–38; bivalent
    terms in, xiii, 205–6, 212; in Chris-
    tianity, 228, 282n22; code choice, 5,
    7, 202–14, 282nn19–22, 283n23;
    code valences, 203–4; in everyday
    usage, 212; in field work, xiii, 40;
    Kipepo, 236; as locus of power, 3–
    4, 21, 209–11, 221–22; in madness,
    249–55, 287n22; magical essential-
    ist function of, 223–29; as marker
    of ethnic identity, 72–73, 80; as
    marker of ontological systems, 190,
    201–14; by Muslim spirits, 156; in
    Muslim worship and study, 132–33,
    226–27, 273n1; spirit-based literacy,
    236–45, 286nn17–20; in spirit prac-
    tices, 2–8, 15, 20–21, 178–84, 192–
    93, 263n1, 278nn2–3. *See also* Ara-
    bic language
*Lawful Means of Curing Witchcraft,
    Jealousy, and Spirit Possession*
    (Amin), 231
Leinhardt, Godfrey, 18
lelemama dance, 267n8
Lewis, I. M., 164–67
Likoni, 59
low spirits, 8, 198–99
Luo: on bitter money, 118; ethnic vio-
    lence among, 58–59, 257–62,
    265n11, 268n11; *majimbo*ism of, 65;
    managerial roles of, 30
Luyah, 65

madness, 15, 249–55, 287nn21–22
magic. *See* spirit practices
Mahmood, Saba, 137, 274n7
majimbo movement, 45–46, 58–67,
    257; federalist goals of, 31, 260,
    268n14; Giriama aspirations in, 43,

262; oathing practices of, 45–46, 60–61, 266n1

Malindi, 1–9; access to resources in, 9–10; communication technology in, 102; court system of, 284n5; ethnic tension in, 39–40, 45–46; everyday encounters in, 66–67; historical overview of, 27–32, 265n10; language use in, xiii, 37–38, 204–5; layout of, 34–37, 266n12; Swahili's identity in, 68–75; transportation businesses in, 94–95, 101, 272n4; Vasco da Gama pillar of, 112

Malindi Council of Imams, 93, 95

Malindi Education and Development Association (MEDA), 93–94, 96

Malindi Islamic Centre of Orphans, 96

Mambrui, 135

marginalization, 27–34; economic, 27–29; of Kigiriama users, 38; political, 29–30, 31; spatial tropes of, 33–34; by tourism, 30, 32

Martin, Esmond Bradley, 265n10

Marx, Karl: on delusional beliefs, 22–23; on labor theory of value, 116; on the "money–commodity–money" cycle, 99; on power relationships, 21–22

Masquelier, Adeline: on ambivalence of *bori* practitioners, 14; on mediums of exchange, 119; on spirit narratives, 111; on spirit possession, 164, 167

mathumia (ritual sexual intercourse), 281n15

Maulidi celebrations, 133, 134

Mauss, Marcel, 16–17

Maxwell (research assistant), 1, 39, 66–67, 117, 271n27

Mazrui, A. M.: on ethnic violence, 59–61, 268nn11–13; on Kaya narrative, 65; on Swahili identity, 68

Mazrui, Sheikh Al-Amin bin Ali, 139, 273n2, 274n4

Mazrui, Sheikh Muhammed Quasim, 139, 273n2

Mazrui clan, 50, 148, 266n2, 267n8

Mboya, Tom, 59, 267n10

Meyer, Birgit, 110, 257–58

Middleton, John, 49, 214

Mijikenda Community Council of Elders, 262

Mijikenda groups, 3, 27–30, 265n10; agricultural production of, 52; election of 2007, 260; oathing practices of, 45–46, 60–61, 266n1; origin stories of, 46, 64–66, 75–77, 266n2; slavery experiences of, 53–55, 83, 266nn5–6; spirit practices of, 184, 275n16; squatting of, 55–56; traditional permeability of, 49–58, 98, 112–13, 148. *See also* Giriama communities; Kaya

Mills, Mary Beth, 110

Mipoho (prophetess), 106

mobility. *See* travel and mobility

Moi, Daniel arap, 59, 107, 267n10

Mombasa, 27

money, 118–19

mono-ontologism, 190, 214–20

Morton, Fred, 266n5

Mswahili *sana*, 73

Mulungu, 64, 107, 189, 196, 201, 283n24

Mungiki, 259–60

Muslims. *See* Islam

Muslim spirits, 2, 90, 129–31, 154–70, 261–62, 275n13; embodied symptoms of possession by, 157–61, 168–70, 173–74; in the Falak, 230,

241–48; in Giriama polyontology, 197–202; hegemonic readings of, 167–70; host resistance to, 161–64, 166–69; language use of, 156, 222–23; in madness, 251–54; perceived power of, 158–59, 190–91, 198–200, 207–13, 282n18; prestige-enhancing requests of, 158. *See also* conversion to Islam

Muslim Task Force on Constitutional Review, 29

Muyeye, 2–3

Mwambao movement, 29–30

Mwambao United Front, 58

mwanza societies, 195, 280n9, 280n11

Nassir, Sheriff, 226

National Democratic Union (NADU), 268n13

National Rainbow Coalition (NARC), 269n17

Ndeje, Pekeshe, 260–61

Ngala, Ronald, 267n10

ngano, 284n5

nia (*niyya*), 136–42

Niehaus, Isak, 110

Niger *bori* practices, 14

Nine Tribes of Mombasa, 267n8

Noble, D. S., 156, 198

Nyika (perjorative term), 49–50, 74, 81–82

Odingo, Raila, 59, 257–58, 260, 262, 265n11

Okondo, Peter, 59

Ong, Aihwa, 164–65

Orange Democratic Movement (ODM), 258, 260

origin stories, 45–87; essentialist versions of, 46–49; of Giriama/

Mijikenda groups, 46, 64–66, 75–76, 195–97, 266n2, 269nn18–19; in post-independence ethnoterritorialism, 58–67; traditional permeability of coastal communities and, 49–58

palm wine: ceremonial uses of, 107, 108, 159, 181, 196; entrepreneur producers of, 163; as iconic of Giriama culture, 144–45, 174, 277n21; legality of, 98–99

Parkin, David J.: on divination practices, 236–37; on Giriama conversion to Islam, 128–29, 149, 158, 161, 163; on Giriama personhood, 109; on Giriama spirit practices, 156; on *katunusi*, 273n9; on Kaya origin story, 75–77; on land ownership, 106–7; on new essentialisms of coastal Kenya, 47; on permeability of coastal communities, 49, 68; on purity rituals, 144; on Shungwaya narrative, 64–65; on spirit helpers, 198; on syncretism, 184–85, 280n8

Parry, Jonathan, 118–19

Pepo Simba, 198

pepo spirits, 155, 156, 215–16, 236, 275n13

personhood, 4–5, 9, 16–21, 264n8; agency and interiority in, 17–21, 109–10, 129–30, 169–70, 188; of divinatory practitioners, 244–49; ethnoreligious markers of, 254–55; hegemonic notions of, 25–26, 169–70, 178, 222; individualist forms of, 16–20, 25–26, 108, 116–17; interdependent forms of, 17, 19, 98, 108–10, 116–17; in polyontologist contexts, 189; in religious practices,

personhood (*continued*)
129–30, 169–70, 177–78, 183–84,
187–88
philanthropy, 19, 95–96, 108, 170
pluralism. *See* polyontologism; syncretic practices
political contexts, 7–12, 29–32,
264nn5–7. *See also* colonial control; Kenya; post-independence era
"Politics of Rural Syncretism" (Parkin), 184–85
polyontologism, 42, 189–202, 279n7;
aganga practitioners of, 196–97,
281n16, 282n17; consilient syncretism vs., 191–94; linguistic markers
of, 190, 201–14; loci of distinct
powers in, 158–59, 190–91, 198–201,
207–13, 277n1, 282n18; personhood
in, 189; self-categorization in, 194–
95; subaltern nature of, 191; Swahili
practices of, 214–20, 283nn24–27;
taxonomy of spirits in, 197–202.
See also syncretic practices;
Traditionalism
possession. *See* divinatory practitioners; madness; Muslim spirits;
spirit practices
post-independence era: ethnic clashes
of 1997, 39–40, 45–46, 59–60, 262,
267n10, 268nn11–13; ethnoterritorial *majimbo*ism of, 45–46, 58–
67, 257, 260, 262, 267n10, 268nn11–
15, 269nn16–20; federalist experiment of, 58–59; Giriama economic
activities in, 98–99; Giriama identities in, 75–87; land grabbing in,
103–4; Swahili identities in, 67–75
Pouwels, Randall L., 139
power of Islam, 2–4, 25–26, 177–78,
261–62; in Arabic language, 3–4,

21, 209–11, 221–22, 228–29, 284n1;
in the Falak, 229–33, 241–48; in
Giriama polyontologist contexts,
158–59, 190–91, 193–94, 207–13; in
Muslim spirits, 158–59, 198–99,
207–13, 282n18; in the Quran, 2–3,
4, 217, 224, 229–33. *See also* hegemonic understandings; *jini*
narratives
Prins, Adriaan H. J., 267n9
property. *See* land
Pye, Michael, 186

Quran, the, 224–25; in Giriama divination, 1–3, 8, 197, 206, 211, 224,
232–33, 238–39; local interpretations of, 12–13; origins of, 275n10;
perceived power of, 2–3, 4, 217,
224, 229–33; spirits mentioned in,
216, 230–33, 241–43, 272n7; study
of, 132–33, 172, 226–27, 229–33; in
Swahili divination, 2, 217; Wahabbist understanding of, 134–36. *See
also* Islam

race: in ethnic essentialist narratives,
84–86, 267n9, 271n25; in religious
essentialism, 152–53
religious practices, 35–36, 266n12;
agency and interiority in, 19–21,
129–30, 188; of antisyncretism, 186–
89, 214–15, 220; of burials, 46, 146–
47, 161, 168, 236, 274n9; of consilient syncretism, 191–94; custom
vs., 135–36; essentialist aspects of,
130–31, 151–54, 183; of monoontologism, 190, 214–20; of personhood, 129–30, 169–70, 177, 183–84,
187–88; pluralist approaches to, 11–
12, 25–26, 149–50, 177–84; of poly-

ontologism, 189–95, 197–202, 279n7; role of belief in, 142–43; self-categorization of, 194–95; Swahili notions of religiosity, 131–48, 170–71; of universality, 187–88. *See also* Christians/Christianity; ethnoreligious essentialism; Islam; spirit practices; syncretic practices; Traditionalism

ritual practices. *See* spirit practices

rohani spirits, 215–16, 275n13

Rosen, Lawrence, 136–37

Rosenthal, Judy, 156, 164

rosewater, 178–79, 181, 231

Ruel, Malcolm, 142

Salim, Ahmed Idha, 274n4

secessionist movements, 58–59

self-consciousness, 16–17

selfhood, 264n8. *See also* personhood

sexuality, 120, 196, 273n11, 281n15

shahada, 138–39, 274nn6–7, 274n9

Sharif clans, 134–36, 217, 274n3, 274n5

Shariff, Ibrahim Noor, 68

Shaw, Rosalind, 186–87

sheitani spirits, 155, 215–16, 275n13

Shipton, Parker, 118

Shirikisho Party, 63, 269n17

shoga males, 120, 273n11

Shungwaya origin story, 64, 269n18

Shutu, Charo, 39, 77, 112–13, 199–200

Simmel, Georg, 118

slaves/slavery, 27–28, 45, 51–56, 265n10; abolition of, 27–29, 55–56, 267n7; autonomy of, 54–55, 266nn5–6; conversion to Islam among, 98, 148–49, 271n26; modern tropes of, 83–86, 100–101, 152–54, 271n27; self-identity as Swahili

by, 53–54, 267n9, 269n21; Swahili embarrassment about, 170

Smith, James H., 110, 273n10

spatiality/spatial relations, 8, 28–29, 32–38; fractal recursivity in, 33; in Giriama origin stories, 64–66; in Giriama spirit practices, 33–34; in language use, 37–38; in Malindi's physical layout, 34–37; in polyontological practices, 201, 277n1

Spear, Thomas, 64

Sperling, David C., 148, 235, 236

spirit practices, 1–5, 13, 269n21; code choice in, 5, 7, 202–14, 282nn19–22, 283n23; ethnoreligious essentialism in, 130–31, 154–55; in Giriama communities, 8, 11, 33–34, 40, 89–90, 109–10, 156–57, 263n1, 272n6, 275n14; hegemonic readings of, 167–70; in Islam, 13, 15, 133, 172–73, 241–44, 272n7; in *jini* narratives, 15, 41, 90–93, 110–25; of the Kaya era, 195–97, 280nn9–14, 281n15, 285n13; in land transfers, 107; of magical travel, 102–3; mimesis of human society in, 155–56, 164–67, 253; in polyontological systems, 197–202; practitioners of (diviners), 156–57, 163–64, 196–97, 233–49, 281n16, 282n17, 286nn17–20; as resistance by marginalized communities, 164–67, 277n20; in Swahili communities, 2–3, 13, 32, 40, 109, 133, 172–75, 184, 214–20, 275n16, 283nn24–27; Zar rituals, 165–66. *See also* Muslim spirits; power of Islam; Traditionalism

spirits: Hauka spirits, 165–66; high spirits, 8, 163, 181, 189–90, 198–99; *jini* spirits, 155, 198, 215–16; low

spirits (*continued*)
spirits, 8, 198–99; *pepo* spirits, 155, 156, 215–16, 236, 275n13; *rohani* spirits, 215–16, 275n13; *sheitani* spirits, 155, 215–16, 275n13. *See also* Muslim spirits

squatters, 28–29, 55–56, 62, 89, 99, 103–4, 107

Star of Hope, 95

Stewart, Charles, 7–8; on antisyncretism, 186–88; on perceptions of syncretism, 181, 184–86; on religious juxtaposition, 188–89

Stoler, Ann L., 264n6

Stoller, Paul, 164–66

Strathern, Marilyn, 17

Sufi Islam, 133

Sunna Islam, 132–33. *See also* Islam

Sura Al-Falaq, 232

Swahili communities: Arabic study in, 226–27; assimilation into, 3–4, 9–10, 67, 78–79, 151–54, 271n24; economic privileges of, 90–96, 110–20, 271n1; election of 2007 in, 260–62; enclosed private spaces in, 33, 97, 272n3, 286n20; female modesty in, 286n20; fixed identities in, 46–49, 67–75, 269n21, 270n22, 271nn23–24; heroin use in, 218; historical overview of, 27–32, 265n10; individual agency in, 19–21, 25–26, 108, 116–17, 129–30, 188, 245–47; *majimbo*ism in, 60–61; marriage customs in, 93; mono-ontologism in, 214–20; origin narratives of, 46–49; personhood in, 17–21, 25–26, 31–32, 109–10, 129–30, 169–70; political marginalization of, 29–30; as possessors of Islam, 2–5, 9–16, 21, 25–26, 82, 130–31; privileging of Arabness in, 51–52, 269n21; property-ownership in, 62; religiosity in, 131–48, 170–71; secessionist movements in, 58–59; *shoga* males in, 120, 273n11; slavery experiences in, 53–54, 170, 267n9, 269n21, 271n26; spirit practices in, 2, 13, 32, 40, 109, 133, 172–75, 184, 214–20, 275n16, 283nn24–27; traditional permeability of, 6–7, 15, 47, 49–58, 79, 98, 112–13, 148; transnational connections of, 91–95, 114–15, 117; Twelve Tribes of, 57, 267n8, 269n21. *See also* Islam

Swartz, Marc J., 57

syncretic practices, 5, 177–220; antisyncretism, 186–89, 214–15, 220; boundaries of juxtaposed religions in, 181–82, 184–89; consilient approaches to, 191–94; in Giriama pluralism, 11–12, 25–26, 149–50, 177–84, 278n5; linguistic shifts in, 178–79, 182–84, 192–93, 278nn2–3; Parkin on, 184–85; permeability of Islam and, 12–13; polyontologism vs., 189–95, 279n7; scholarly understandings of, 185–89, 278n5, 279n6; in Swahili spirit practices, 214–20, 283nn24–27. *See also* ethno-religious essentialism

Tambiah, Stanley J., 224

Tanganyika, 53

Taussig, Michael, 110

Tawfiq Muslim Youth, 95–96

Tawheed Muslim Association, 96

telephones, 102

text-messaging, 102

Thompson, S. G.: on conversion to Islam, 157–58, 164; on the Forudahe society, 280n11; on spirit practices, 161, 198, 236–37, 285n13

Three Tribes of Mombasa, 267n8

Tinga, Kimati, 113–15

tourism industry, 30; employment in, 32, 100; local investment from, 60; real estate values in, 104; white ownership in, 94

Traditionalism, 4, 11–12, 263n2; agency and interiority in, 19–21, 129–30, 244–45; ancestor roles in, 195–96; divination and healing in, 196–97; public presence of, 36, 277n1; spiritual agents in, 189–90, 196. *See also* polyontologism; spirit practices; syncretic practices

transcriptions, xiii

travel and mobility: of Giriamas, 101–6; in *jini* narratives, 91–93, 111–15, 119, 277n17; mobile telephones, 102; of Swahilis, 91–95, 114–15, 117

tribalism, 59. *See also* ethnic essentialism; ethnoterritoriality

tuk tuks, 94–95, 101

Twelve Tribes of Mombasa, 57, 267n8, 269n21

Udvardy, Monica L., 198, 235, 280nn10–12

uganga practices, 196–97

ushirikina practices, 215–20

Varisco, Daniel, 12

Vasco da Gama pillar, 112

Versnel, Henk S., 279n7

vigango posts, 195–96, 280n12, 280n14

viraho (charms), 195, 280n10

visa, 284n5

wabara tribes, 45

Wahhabism, 13, 133–34, 216–18, 273n2, 274nn3–5

Weismantel, Mary, 110

whites: as expatriate residents, 94; in Giriama essentialist frameworks, 84–86; *jini* narratives about, 123; land ownership and, 65, 106; Mipoho's prophecy of, 106; tourism industry and, 30, 32, 94

Wilce, James M., 249, 254

Williams, Raymond, 21–22

Willis, Justin: on colonial administration, 50; on conversion, 148; on ethnic permeability, 49, 52–53

World Assembly of Muslim Youth, 95–96

Zanzibar, 58, 267n9, 269nn20–21, 270n22

Zar possession, 165–66

Zehner, Edwin, 187

Zikiri Maiti, 198

Janet McIntosh is an assistant professor of anthropology at Brandeis University.

Library of Congress Cataloging-in-Publication Data
McIntosh, Janet, 1969–
The edge of Islam : power, personhood, and ethnoreligious boundaries
on the Kenya Coast / Janet McIntosh.
p. cm.
Includes bibliographical references and index.
ISBN 978-0-8223-4496-4 (cloth : alk. paper)
ISBN 978-0-8223-4509-1 (pbk. : alk. paper)
1. Ethnic conflict—Kenya—Malindi—Religious aspects. 2. Swahili-speaking
peoples—Kenya—Malindi—Social life and customs. 3. Giryama (African
people)—Kenya—Malindi—Religion. 4. Giryama (African people)—Kenya—
Malindi—Social life and customs. 5. Giryama (African people)—Kenya—
Malindi—Religion. 6. Muslims—Kenya—Malindi. 7. Malindi (Kenya)—
Ethnic relations. 8. Malindi (Kenya)—Social life and customs. I. Title.
GN659.K4M35 2009
305.80096762—dc22   2009005182